JANE WELSH CARLYLE

THE MACMILLAN COMPANY
NEW YORK · BOSTON · CHICAGO · DALLAS
ATLANTA · SAN FRANCISCO

MACMILLAN AND CO., Limited
LONDON · BOMBAY · CALCUTTA · MADRAS
MELBOURNE

THE MACMILLAN COMPANY
OF CANADA, Limited
TORONTO

JANE WELSH IN THE YEAR
OF HER MARRIAGE

By courtesy of the Scottish National Gallery

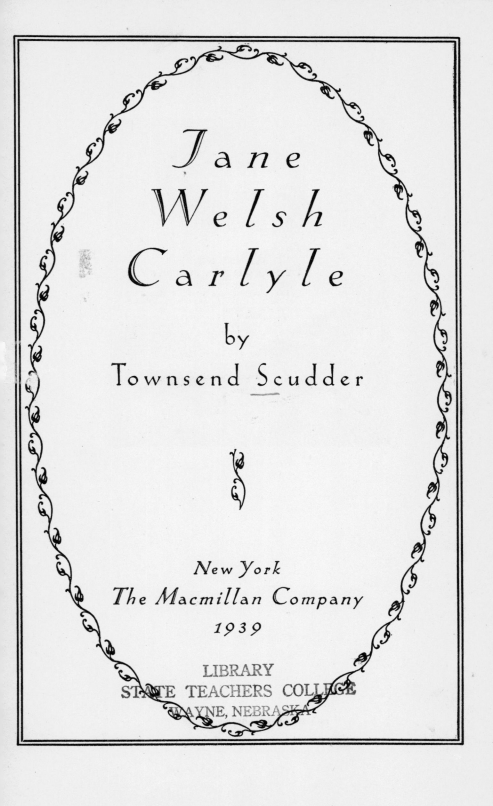

Jane Welsh Carlyle

by

Townsend Scudder

New York
The Macmillan Company
1939

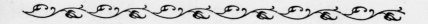

Contents

CHAPTER   PAGE

I. A DANCING, FLEETING, LIGHT-HEARTED CREATURE, QUITE READY FOR ANY ADVENTURE.   1

II. NOT THE MARRYING KIND.   12

III. AND WHAT GREATER CHANGE EXISTS THAN MARRIAGE?   16

IV. SHE HAD BEEN DISTINGUISHED AS A FLIRT.   23

V. WHAT WOULDN'T ONE GIVE TO HAVE DE QUINCEY IN A BOX, AND TAKE HIM OUT TO TALK!   34

VI. FAREWELL TO EDINBURGH.   39

VII. CRAIGENPUTTOCK NO SUCH FRIGHTFUL SPOT AFTER ALL.   49

VIII. THE OUTWARD FIGURE OF ONE'S ABODE.   64

IX. IT IS A WORK OF GENIUS, DEAR!   79

X. SHE WAS LIKE A FEUDAL DAME WHOSE LORD WAS GONE TO THE WARS.   91

XI. IN LONDON, HER OWN LIGHT COULD SHINE TO GREATER PURPOSE.   103

XII. WHO WOULD NOT BE PROVOKED TO SEE TITANIA IN LOVE WITH BOTTOM?   122

XIII. A HOUSE IN UNFASHIONABLE CHELSEA.   136

XIV. SHE COULD HAVE MARRIED EITHER MAN; SHE HAD NOT CHOSEN IRVING.   154

XV. ORDEAL BY FIRE—THE *French Revolution*.   159

XVI. LONDON'S INFINITE VARIETY.   171

CHAPTER   PAGE

XVII.   TRY ALL THAT EVER YOU CAN TO BE PATIENT
          AND GOOD-NATURED WITH YOUR *povera pic-*
          cola Gooda, AND THEN SHE LOVES YOU AND
          IS READY TO DO ANYTHING ON EARTH THAT
          YOU WISH.   183

XVIII.   LET NO WOMAN WHO VALUES PEACE OF SOUL
          EVER DREAM OF MARRYING AN AUTHOR!   199

XIX.   VARIOUS MOUNTAINS WERE NOW COMING TO
          MAHOMET.   210

XX.   A CLEVER DEVIL, CERTAINLY, THIS LADY
          HARRIET, *belle laide,* BUT FULL OF WIT.   222

XXI.   HE WAS GETTING UP STEAM FOR A NEW BOOK,
          A PROCESS ALWAYS FULL OF HISS AND SPUT-
          TER.   232

XXII.   "YOUR MOTHER IS DEAD!" THEY TOLD HER.   239

XXIII.   OLD STAND-BYS AND NEW, THEY THUMPED
          THE BRASS KNOCKER AT NO. 5 CHEYNE ROW.   253

XXIV.   JANE WAS HAVING HER PORTRAIT PAINTED.   265

XXV.   EARTHQUAKES AND CONFLAGRATION.   273

XXVI.   THE CONSPIRATOR MAZZINI—WITH THE
          FACE OF A HIGHLY INTELLECTUAL, HIGHLY
          SPIRITUAL, HIGHLY IDEALISTIC PRIEST.   284

XXVII.   TENNYSON—A BEAUTIFUL FIGURE OF A POET.   292

XXVIII. IS YOUR HUSBAND AS MUCH INFATUATED AS
          EVER WITH LADY HARRIET?   299

XXIX.   THAT'S JEANNIE WELSH! NO OTHER WOMAN
          WOULD CLIMB THE WALL INSTEAD OF
          GOING IN AT THE GATE.   313

XXX.   THE DECADE AFTER THE YEAR OF REVOLU-
          TIONS.   323

XXXI.   CHRISTMAS—AND PEACE ON EARTH?   332

XXXII.   THE CHIEF INTEREST OF TODAY EXPRESSED
          IN BLUE MARKS ON MY WRISTS.   339

Contents

CHAPTER   PAGE

XXXIII. JANE'S HUSBAND AN OLD LION NOW, BUT VERY
         MUCH KING OF THE LONDON JUNGLE.   349

XXXIV.   TEN YEARS IN THE VALLEY OF THE SHADOW
         OF *Frederick*.   360

XXXV.   A PERFECT TRIUMPH!   372

XXXVI.   IN THE WARM SUMMER DUSK; IN THE QUIET
         OF THE HOURS.   383

         BIBLIOGRAPHICAL NOTE.   385

         INDEX.   397

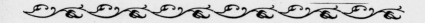

Illustrations

Jane Welsh in the year of her marriage	Frontispiece
	FACING
Jane Carlyle in her fifty-sixth year	342
"An Interior at Chelsea"	356
Thomas Carlyle	374

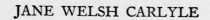

JANE WELSH CARLYLE

Chapter One

*T*HEY were veterans of many walks together, these two young men tramping for their pleasure from Edinburgh towards Haddington, seventeen miles southeast of the city. The finest spirit of their friendship, its deepest intimacy, had grown from just such excursions as this. In earlier days they had visited the lakes and glens of Perth. They had crossed the Trossachs side by side, starting the long excursion, rather insanely, late one evening with a twenty-two mile reach from Kirkcaldy along the Forth to Torryburn, Irving striding on the way as though he owned the sands and sea.

Notwithstanding their youth—Edward Irving was on the threshold of his twenty-ninth birthday, Thomas Carlyle half-way between his twenty-fifth and sixth—they were veterans, too, of the warfare that ambitious boys, with no advantages other than their wits, must fight if they refuse to accept the clinging obscurity to which they were born. For neither of them was the battle over, though Irving, at least, had some cause to believe that his hardest struggles lay in the past.

Both came from humble enough lineage, from many genera-tions of Scottish peasant stock, enriched now and then by an infiltration of the blood of the proprietors of small landhold-ings in the neighborhood. Yet this peasant origin carried a richer heritage than that which was brought by occasional unions with the local lairds—it drew strength from the unfailing grit, stubbornness, and independence of a long line of sharp, tough-minded, tough-handed men who kept Scotland the home of a free race although fate prevented its retaining national liberty. The family of each young man had sacrificed to send the fittest among the children through school and college—Tom, the son of an Annandale stonemason and farmer; Irving, the son of a tanner in the burgh town of Annan.

When a poor Scotsman, at the turn of the nineteenth century, had ambitions for his boys, the direction suggested by his hopes led generally towards the Kirk. Irving had followed the orthodox way, with marked success, through Edinburgh University and its Divinity School. A growing vein of skepticism, a tendency towards independent thinking, forced Carlyle to quit the beaten path three years after finishing the regular bachelor's course.

For the accommodation of scholars as impecunious as these, the University had devised a scheme whereby candidates for ordination could fulfill requirements through six terms of absentee enrollment, necessitating only occasional brief appearances at Divinity Hall. This arrangement permitted students, while completing courses, to teach school for a living.

Always a step behind Irving because of the difference in their ages, Carlyle had been a domine first at Annan then Kirkcaldy on the Firth of Forth near Edinburgh. At Kirkcaldy the two were thrown together as masters of competing schools. Before this close association, latent rivalry between the young men had a way of bursting at times into active flame. Irving's ingenuous ways, however, his openness and friendliness, soon cooled Tom's animosity. The two became boon companions.

On holidays, and in the long vacations, they had roamed the hills together. Often the pair, on their trips, were joined by two or three of their former college mates. Irving, when they set afield, was physically the natural king of the group. He was a leader by instinct and by character. His honest-heartedness, his readiness for laughter, kept everyone in good spirits even when the cold rains of the Highlands drenched their skins. Nothing subtle about his sense of the ludicrous—a simple, lovable fellow, a man of utter transparency.

Only when he preached his sermons—Carlyle heard him on several occasions—did Thomas find Irving something of a puzzle. He watched Edward's fervor in the pulpit—his apostolic earnestness—with keen interest and some wonder, speculating as to the ultimate result of such intenseness. Some thought the manner affected; Carlyle loyally refused to believe the charge.

On their walks, certainly, Irving was naturalness itself. It was easy to perceive his kinship with these rugged districts. Ned possessed a Herculean frame (Carlyle himself almost as tall) and a wedge-shaped, energetic face with broad forehead and powerful chin. His coal-black hair set off his swarthy, clear skin. A personable fellow, with a jovial look. The one fault was a curious, pronounced squint in his deep-set, small dark eyes—a blemish caused by some defective muscular adjustment. Yet Irving carried this flaw with unconcern, and if anything it contributed to his distinctive appearance.

Though less tall than Irving, Carlyle possessed height enough; five feet eleven inches of gaunt, thin frame. His thick, shaggy, dark brown hair, confused and leonine, gave an illusion of greater stature, while the coarse homespun Scotch twill he liked to wear somewhat filled out his leanness. A noticeable young man, with piercing, blue-violet eyes under curling lashes and broad massive forehead, a straight nose, and determined, tight-lipped mouth. A handsome face in certain lights—strong, with high cheek bones, farm-boy complexion, and powerful teeth slightly discolored from smoking. A face of surprising mobility of expression, responsive to every slightest mood: one instant disarming and childlike, the next grim, the next relaxed and defenseless in a mighty, chest-filling laugh. His long arms ended in an extraordinary bunch of fingers—attenuated, bony, highly sensitive.

Wherever Carlyle and Irving appeared, separately or together, they won attention.

Irving's strength matched his size. No interlopers on those hills dared dispute his sway. Once when the friends had established themselves at a little mountain inn, arranged for their meal, then gone for a brief stroll before eating, a party of tourists had taken possession. Even after polite remonstrance, they refused to surrender the dinner which they had not ordered. Irving—tall, squint-eyed, swift gesturing—marshaled his forces. Standing in readiness, he called to one of the group, "Will you toss out or knock down?"

The opposition melted away.

In the days right after college, Irving's first school was at Haddington, where he added to his modest pay by tutoring the seven-year-old daughter of Dr. John Welsh, a leading citizen of the town. When Irving moved away, young James Brown, fellow graduate of Edinburgh, had taken the post. Brown was later one of the company on a jaunt to Loch Katrine. When he and Irving talked together, they naturally spoke of Dr. Welsh and his little girl. She was quite a young lady now. Her tomboy nature was blending with a sensitive highly feminine provocativeness. Irving readily agreed. He had discovered as much himself. Jeannie Welsh had grown into a lass fit to turn the head of any man.

To these details Carlyle had listened with interest, wondering about the girl. He had often heard his friend Irving speak enthusiastically of Dr. Welsh.

When Irving, after finishing his Divinity course, left Kirkcaldy in order to await a call to some church, his friend Thomas soon gave up his post and followed Ned to Edinburgh. Though he taught well, Carlyle loathed school-teaching; loathed the task of drumming knowledge into pudding-brained twelve-year-olds. To be a writer, an editor, or a University professor—that might do. But to remain a school teacher in a small town was the life of a mill-horse. It could be lived with about as much respect and consideration from employers and other human witnesses as that poor beast customarily received.

Irving, with his usual good fortune, was presently summoned to Glasgow to become the assistant of no less a person than Dr. Thomas Chalmers, as celebrated a preacher as could be found in all Scotland. Advancement to an excellent church of his own seemed a sure step in the near future. But Tom, left alone in Edinburgh, was a man without profession—a man with only his excellent mind to depend on. The sole thing he could do, while looking for a better chance to use his brain, was to gather a few guineas here and there by private tutoring.

The first quarter of the nineteenth century, after Napoleon had ravaged and impoverished the world, was no easy time in which to be young. For the son of a Scottish mason and farmer to raise himself from the soil which encumbered him needed something of a miracle. Bankruptcy had broken the rich, and the poor were starving. Englishmen whispered speculatively concerning the dread possibilities of revolt and anarchy even in their own nation. How rise in such a world of discouragement? Few editors or publishers dared to print articles or books by writers not firmly established; all gates to advancement seemed barred.

Young Carlyle would not relinquish hope, but the difficulties weighed on his spirit. He became capable of grim vituperation at the folly of the human beings who had brought the world to such a pass, and of an irony that ripped and lacerated.

Irving, on his visits from Glasgow, laughed at his friend's picturesque eloquence and rallied him from the depths he sometimes plunged to. When Carlyle was himself, Edward believed there was no one more fitted to swell the enjoyment of convivial hours. It was a shame to let him mar himself by black moods and cheat others of the pleasure which they might take in him. He had no right, Irving would declare, to cultivate misanthropy or shut himself off from man. He might think himself a recluse, but that belief, said Edward, was the unhappy result of the stagnation his present life had sunk him into. He should mingle again with men and give his best qualities fuller opportunity to be seen. Why, Irving delighted to exclaim in his big, hearty voice, the time would come when like giants they two would clasp hands in triumphant greeting, Irving as top man in British divinity, Carlyle as head of British literature, and admirers would remark, "Both these fellows are from Annandale," then ask, in wonder, "Where is Annandale?" never having heard of it before.

Haddington, of late years, was once more accustoming itself to the eye-filling spectacle of its former schoolmaster energetically striding down the High Street. For susceptible Edward Irving had further pursued his discoveries there. Amazing how this child, Jane Baillie Welsh, had developed since the time when he was her tutor! He found himself entertaining for her a more than preceptorial, more than brotherly feeling—though the old supervisory relationship, especially now that he was a minister of the church—insured him a kindly, unsuspicious greeting from Mrs. Welsh. Jane's suitors were beginning to flock about her like Penelope's of old, and Mrs. Welsh was sometimes her daughter's too vigorous ally in standing them off. Mrs. Welsh was now a widow, and felt her responsibilities. Her daughter was becoming more than a local attraction; outside of Haddington, Irving had listened to men who were enthusiastic in her praises. From the first day of his rediscovery of Jeannie, he had moments when he deeply regretted his engagement to Isabella Martin, daughter of the minister at Kirkcaldy.

Irving's susceptibility was extreme, making him flighty and uncertain. He was capable of fancying himself in love with any attractive girl he saw. Women and the church were his emotional outlets: he treated both alike as mistresses. After a sight of Jane, he was quite ready to begin a new campaign, this time at Haddington, and to negotiate for release at Kirkcaldy. And he wrote a sonnet on Jeannie's black hair which might have been a mere exercise in verse writing—and then again, might not. Poor Irving, life could become so complex, and he was really a most honorable, simple man, wishful to follow his conscience. The Martin family were insisting that he stick to his bargain.

In May, 1821, the General Assembly of the Church of Scotland brought Irving to Edinburgh from Glasgow. As usual, he lodged with Carlyle. Why not seize the opportunity for a call at Haddington? And yes, he might as well take Carlyle with him. The trip would give his friend the diversion he obviously needed. Surely that society would revive him!

Thus the present walk had come about.

Irving was positive that his Haddington friends would like Carlyle. It was a pleasure to show him off. The time must inevitably arrive when he would be snatched by the world from the minute circle of his present admirers.

Neither friend was aware of it, but Jane had already learned of Thomas Carlyle. An acquaintance of the Welshes, meeting Carlyle once in Edward's company, and sharing Irving's sanguine views for his friend's destinies, had spoken most favorably of him in Jane's presence: "Talent plenty; fine vein of satire in him!" Even clever young men were no novelty in Jane's life. They swarmed about her. Before Jeannie lost her father, she had been gay and frivolous enough—a dancing, fleeting, light-hearted creature, quite ready for any adventure. After Dr. Welsh's passing, these days, and their more trivial gayeties, were over. The stupider young men—and too earnest, mooncalf suitors are apt to be stupid—bored her.

Irving was a kind good fellow, thought Carlyle gratefully,

as the two companions strode toward Haddington that lovely afternoon near the end of May—a friend indeed. It was like the old, less troubled times: the vigorous days of their life at Kirkcaldy. The countryside through which they passed was a glorious escape from the grind at Edinburgh. They were like boys again, tramping along the road or easing their feet on the lush fresh grass along its borders. Behind them the sun was gradually sinking towards the heights of the city. On their left, at elevations in the highway, they saw the dazzling expanse of the waters of the Firth of Forth, dark blue under the spring day. A hazy barrier to the southeast, sprawled the great mass of the Lammermuir Hills bounding the fertile plains of East Lothian where lay, in its opulence of farming country, the ancient burgh town that was their destination.

Haddington was situated far enough from the capital to follow its own independent career. On Friday market days it stirred with healthy bustle and activity. The social life was carried on with a nice regard for the proprieties of birth and position—the Welshes were indisputably of the elect—and the townsmen derived a mild excitement from the presence of many soldiers in the neighboring barracks. At the time when fear of a Napoleonic invasion troubled sleep in the British Isles, Haddington, as a strategic point for concentration of armed forces to resist a possible landing on the Forth, had witnessed the construction of capacious barracks outside the town, and these were only now being emptied, six years after Napoleon's exile at Saint Helena. The scarlet coats of officers lent vivid color to the teas and dances attended by Jeannie Welsh and other young girls of the royal burgh.

Dusk, the mild, lingering, beneficent northern twilight of earliest summer, was hovering over the town, over the substantial two- and three-story houses of the High Street, when the two companions entered Haddington: Dr. Welsh's dwelling, with its dignified façade, easily one of the most impressive in the row. Irving and his companion turned down a little passageway between the house and its neighbor, an alley which led to the walled garden in the rear and to the living-quarters of the family. As Carlyle glanced up at the large, triple-spaced second-story window which opened on the courtyard and its flower beds, he noticed, in the gloom within, two bright eyes fixed on him with questioning interest. The next moment he was face to face with Jeannie Welsh.

Guests were drifting in and out of the house—chatting in the garden and in the living room. Jane had on a little bonnet, and the picture of her, in that first instant of meeting, never faded from Tom's memory. He knew her to be the loveliest creature he had ever seen. Here in this choice group of young people, she appeared to him like a star glowing among rushlights. So painful was his first embarrassment, his bashfulness in the presence of this radiance, that he scarcely dared look at her. Yet neither she, nor the others, were allowed to be aware of his confusion—he quickly entered the stream of talk, and in conversation no one could excel him.

"From Wallace and from Knox," said Irving in his half-laughing, grandiose way, with a sweep of his arm toward Jeannie, "there's a Scottish pedigree for you!" Carlyle was aware, too, of the hearsay that she had gypsy blood in her veins and was a reputed descendant of a notorious Matthew Baillie, robber and chieftain. Did that explain her jet-black hair and her dark, large eyes? Strangers often thought her to be of French extraction. Jane herself, however, cared little about these doubtful fireside legends.

The group drifted into the garden, into the placid summer evening, among the rich foliage and the clusters of roses and the scent of many flowers. Carlyle had learned of her nickname, the sentimental phrase used by these East Lothians—for the rugged Scotch have an unexpected vein of sentiment blended with their toughness. "Flower of Haddington" they sometimes called her, and here, in her garden, it was not a misnomer. Yet save for her winsome grace and litheness and her modesty of bearing, there was little about her to suggest a harmless wayside blossom. Her dark, expressive eyes, though they could be tender and sympathetic, more often flashed with the animation of her thoughts and with her rapid changes of mood. They were mirrors to reflect the energy of spirit preserved in that little body; an energy, in its consuming force, almost dangerous to her survival.

Carlyle had listened to high praises of her, but he had been warned as much about her caprices, her gift of mockery, the extraordinary keenness of her mind and sharpness of her words.

That was as it should be. He had scant interest in tepid inanities whose prettiness was their only claim for attention. One moment Jane would be all gayety, and quick, arch humor. Then if a stupid or provoking thing were said, her expression would shift to contemptuous indifference or wrath. But not for long: soon a naïve, affectionate glance would come to her face, and even the victim of her scorn would feel compensated. Such looks tempted one to fall down in abject worship. Yet woe to him who tried so humble a pose! He was sure to be laughed at for his pains. Was there ever before, thought Carlyle, such a wicked, beautiful, cruel, adorable, capricious little gypsy sent into the world for the delight and vexation of mortal man!

By their entrance, he and Irving had interrupted a learned disquisition, a veritable lecture—for no man there knew how to check it—by one young scholar of the company, on the subject of the human mind. Serious age, this speculative opening of the nineteenth century, and serious youth—superficially wise in its new wisdom! Tom listened with some amazement to this overconfident laying down of the law by this sophistical young man. Then, by an adroit question or two which could not be answered and led the unfortunate declaimer into manifest contradiction, Carlyle checked the torrent of wind. It faltered and died away. Thomas noticed Jeannie's glance resting for a moment on him, a look of relief and congratulation in her eyes. An irrepressible grin seemed to tug at the corners of her mouth, threatening every moment to burst into a laugh at the discomfiting of the Philistine, who presently withdrew into the night.

For some brief moments the conversation dealt with books. A soldier in a red coat—a gallant Captain in that civilian company —was advising Jane against too much study and reading. The craze to become a bluestocking ruined many an attractive girl; he had a horror of bluestockings. Jane should not court the risk of becoming one. Yes, agreed Carlyle, study, if it imperiled health, was a menace—but *that* was the sole valid stricture against learning. He did not speak in an argumentative spirit. But he held a high opinion of women—perhaps too idealized. He had been reading Madame de Staël's brilliant writings, and this young girl with whom he was conversing seemed to him a Madame de Staël of the future. He spoke of his own interests, and of his enthusiasm for new foreign literature. Miss Welsh must become better acquainted with German. He quickly found she could read the language. He would send her books, and lists for her study. Irving, hearing these plans, was somewhat troubled. Was not this admiration of Carlyle, this Goethe, a pagan, licentious writer? And Schiller too? Edward could readily persuade himself, at need, that his chief interest in Jeannie lay in her immortal soul. Should not these rubbishy volumes of Byron, which he noticed on her table, be swept out of the house? But for the present he held his tongue, and Carlyle drew up his plans to lay a groundwork for Jeannie's future literary career.

One of Jane's remarkable gifts, developed to an even greater extent with the passage of time, was her ability to talk to any man on his own subject, so that he would forget he was speaking with a woman, though with Jane before him—for she was feminine to her fingertips—that was a marvel in itself. As Carlyle chatted with her now, in this congenial gathering, in the benediction of that lovely evening, no such phenomenon threatened. Spring and twilight and his own starved being were all against it. The words from her lips came over him like dew on thirsty grass. It was *good*, his thankful spirit told him, to be there with her. He was like a man awaking from a haggard dream. His old hopefulness returned; his past bitterness was sweetened. Once before he had thought himself in love. Thomas possessed a faculty for interesting attractive girls, though his poverty and lack of a profession stood in the way of serious thoughts of marriage. Few men exorcise completely the ghosts of an old passion. But Carlyle held to the conviction that a man can have but a single genuine first love, and as soon as he saw Jane Welsh, he knew that she was the one. He could perceive clearly the hazards of the course he was determined to follow. These women of genius, if you took them on the wrong tack, were the very devil, and no mistake! His own temperament, he readily admitted, was not the easiest to get along with. Should he win Jane, he might find life with her a most turbulent, incongruous mixture. Yet better risk the whirlwinds, the frost and sleet and thunder and lightning, to gain the hours of clearest sunshiny weather that were bound to be interspersed with the storms. If only he could gain her love, he did not doubt the warmth of Jeannie's heart.

As he and Irving bade good-night, in the dusk of the garden, with the kind stars above, Tom, young cynic though he pretended to be, recognized the fact of his utter captivity. In spite of his efforts to be reasonable, he was forced to admit that love had many points in common with insanity, though perhaps not altogether a delirium.

Before going to their room at the George Inn, Irving, with his friend, stopped for a moment at the house of the Rev. Mr. Sibbald, minister of the Kirk where he was to preach that Sunday. Irving had a fatality for knowing ministers with marriageable daughters. Augusta Sibbald stood there to greet them—a tall and shapely girl, Carlyle noticed, but airy and prone to giggles. "What a consummate fool!" was his uncharitable thought, perhaps forgivable because of the contrast he was making.

As the two young men were stripping for bed in their room at the George, Irving shot a mischievous glance at Carlyle. "What would you take to marry Miss Augusta, now?" he asked.

Carlyle was horrified. A bribe of the most precious jewel in the universe would not lure him to such a sacrifice.

"What would you take to marry Miss Jeannie?" inquired Irving, watching his friend narrowly.

"I should not be so hard to deal with there I would imagine!"

Ned gave a bit of a laugh. The two friends slept.

Chapter Two

*F*IVE and a half years of intermittent courtship lay between Carlyle's first visit to Haddington and his marriage, in 1826, to Jane Baillie Welsh. Jeannie was not the marrying kind. Perhaps multiplicity of suitors had something to do with the delay. Difficult indeed for a girl of many lovers to know her own heart. Besides, with a mind as active as hers, she found other interests to draw her thoughts away from the grooves that held most young women. She had social genius, but other gifts as well.

Jane was a great reader. She liked to scribble, and her creative vein, though she drew on it by fits and starts, had produced acceptable verse—far better poetry than that addressed to her by her admirers, including Thomas Carlyle. She had also started a novel or two.

Early in his daughter's life Dr. Welsh had discovered her brilliancy of mind. That was why he retained Irving as her tutor, and gave her the sort of education usually reserved for boys. Her father's death—she was eighteen years old at the time—spurred her to even greater effort. She worshiped him, and his loss almost shattered her high strung nature. She accused herself of frivolity and too great love of pleasure. Then, at the very time when she was casting about for means to go on with her studies (Mrs. Welsh was no encourager of her daughter's aims) Irving had brought to Haddington his friend, Thomas Carlyle. She gladly accepted Carlyle's offer to be her volunteer director.

This arrangement gave him the opening he needed to enter into an active correspondence. The very first communications she received from him, though they begged for her tolerant attention by suggesting a course of reading, were love letters. Amazing letters—filled with the extraordinary personality of their sender, and often vivid as the flash of a sword. Even before she could judge by the books he began to publish—a *Life of Schiller*, a translation of Goethe's *Wilhelm Meister*—she was convinced by his letters that her new admirer was a man of genius. Yet in the beginning, as soon as she saw the drift beneath its surface, she tried to bring the correspondence to an end. She was not looking for another lover. But Carlyle always found the means to keep the way open, and Jane herself could hardly regret his doing so.

In the first months of Tom's courtship, and earlier, Jane's emotions were taken up with George Rennie, son of a wealthy family who lived on a large estate near Haddington—*Phantasee*, once the property of the Countess of Aberdeen. She and Rennie often quarreled, but Jane found it difficult to forget him. His departure for Italy to study art—he would be away several years—gave Carlyle a better chance, though George was only one among the many that hovered round Miss Welsh.

Jane harbored a keen, incisive, realistic mind and a tough sense of practicality. Had these alone made up her traits, men might have found her easier to understand, but nowhere near so fascinating. As though in direct opposition to this side of her character, a powerfully romantic, poetic spirit dominated her. Byron was an early idol whom she did not outgrow for years. Irving, with what she thought a rather bigoted, sanctimonious motive, kept warning her against these writers; against Carlyle's favorites, Goethe and Schiller, as well. She continued nevertheless to read them. She also discovered Rousseau's *La Nouvelle Héloïse*, and went eagerly through the novel in its original French text. The book came as a fascinating revelation. It seemed written to guide her own complicated problems in life, and even to parallel, here and there, her own position. Its story was that of a patrician girl whose tutor, of lowly birth but in person manly and honorable in the extreme, fell in love with her, though the differences of birth, and presently the marriage of Julie to an aristocrat of her family's choosing, stood in the way of any realization of the hopes of St. Preux, her young teacher.

Most intriguing! She—Irving—Carlyle: the first man, her one-time tutor, the second, her volunteer guide. Not only did she test Carlyle by the standard of Rousseau's hero; she applied the same measure to her other lovers. Admittedly, Thomas

Carlyle had talents that were equal to those of St. Preux: he had *his* vast and cultivated mind, *his* vivid imagination, *his* independence of soul, and *his* unbending principles of honor. But then—ah! these *buts*—! Want of elegance! Want of elegance, Rousseau said, was a defect no woman could overlook. Could *she* be an exception? Carlyle's arms and legs, in their actions, were fantastically awkward. Not long after his first visit, he came a second time to read German with her. They had got on famously with the language. She delighted to hear Carlyle talk. But only his tongue should be left at liberty. His boots had ruinously scratched the fender. Should he come again, she told herself, she would have handcuffs and a pair of carpet shoes ready. St. Preux, Jane was sure, never marred the furniture with his shoes or made puddings in his teacup.

Irving fell more and more to the rear. True, during a brief time, Jane had passionately returned his love. But she became disgusted by his involvements at Kirkcaldy—she had refused to encourage him as long as he was engaged. And the changes of character which she thought crept over him with his advancement in his ecclesiastical career further alienated her. He had been called to London as minister of the Caledonian Chapel. His success as preacher there had been phenomenal; he had become the rage of the town—battalions of fashionable carriages, on Sundays, clogged the streets that led to his church. But his triumphs, Jane insisted, had gone to his brain and stuffed it with affectations. Even Carlyle's loyal pleas that she be tolerant with Ned were unavailing. The studied piety of his manner, his abuse of his great powers through melodramatic appeals (so Jane analyzed his conduct), presently brought down her scornful wrath on Edward's bewildered head. So Irving vanished from the foreground of the picture.

Carlyle was a far more brilliant St. Preux.

For years, though her emotional nature was deeply troubled, Jane could not be sure of her feelings. She put off as long as possible the necessity for ultimate decision.

The accidents of Carlyle's life kept him much of the time at a distance from Haddington. Even when he was free to visit, Jane frequently would not let him come for fear of intensifying her mother's disapprobation. Mrs. Welsh was suspicious and resentful enough as it was, and even insisted on reading Carlyle's letters, though Jane was careful to hide special ones away.

In *La Nouvelle Héloïse,* the action of the entire story is carried out by means of letters between the principals. Impossible for Jane not to recognize the similarities. She could not escape doing so. And there was a strong temptation to take a cue from the inflated idealism preached by Rousseau—the creed that friendship and sisterhood are greater than love. Through much of the courtship, Jane insisted that Carlyle follow that formula. Rousseau, of course, gave license for the broadest possible interpretation of friendship. He allowed it to include stronger words as well. So she bade Carlyle address her as a friend. Part of the time he complied, but sometimes he rebelled at her injunction. "I must exhibit the true state of my feelings when I write, or else write like a shallow fool: and I never felt *friendship* of this sort towards anyone!"

Because of her uncertainties, because of the urge to follow her own star, she tried to make herself believe in Rousseau's pseudo idealism. Yet save for the fiction of sisterhood, many of her letters to Carlyle were as fervent as a lover could wish. When at last she dropped the barriers, Rousseau's philosophies burned away in the warm intenseness of her love.

Thomas had won over a host of rivals. He had won even over himself. It took courage to accept Carlyle in the face of her mother's opposition and that of most of her family. But courage was a quality of which Jane had no lack.

"I am yours," she wrote, "Oh, that you knew how wholly yours!"

Chapter Three

*I*T *WAS* nothing short of amazing, reflected Jane, poking round in her sewing box, how inexorably a man's buttons could fly away from his clothes! Somehow she had not quite thought of marriage in terms of restoring buttons to a husband's coat, or of mending his trousers. And men's stockings (she was far too recent a wife to know the correct appellation), why, they acquired holes by geometrical progression! Her training in mathematics, as a child, or even in Latin, had not equipped her to cope with anything like this.

But it was all part of the day's work, she assured herself, and the husband she had got was worth the pains.

She had married him on Thursday, the seventeenth of October, 1826, at her grandfather's place in Dumfriesshire—Templand, where her mother had now established a home. Her mother should be comfortable at Templand Farm, a pleasant old dwelling on a broad knoll above the river Nith.

On the move from Haddington, a month or two before the marriage, some of Mrs. Welsh's furniture had been sent to equip the house leased in Edinburgh for Jane and Thomas, the rest had followed Mrs. Welsh to Nithsdale. The need for economy, and her father's increasing ill-health at Templand, had made it advisable for Mrs. Welsh to sell her own house. Dr. Welsh's death had put an end to the small family's chief source of revenue—the income from his excellent practice. An ancestral farm at Craigenputtock, Dumfriesshire, eighteen miles from Templand, still paid a modest rental. Because Dr. Welsh had died intestate, this farm had passed to Jane. But prior to her marriage, though she herself could readily use the money, she had saved her mother embarrassment by deeding the rentals to her for life. Carlyle's sense of pride justified this action, and the gift made Jane easy in mind concerning her mother's future welfare.

Some of Jane's relatives, some of her friends, had chosen to look askance at her husband's poverty and to sniff at his humble origins. Those among them whose positions were very little better had been especially critical. But Jane tossed her head and mustered her pride. What did she care about these strictures? Was not Thomas one of the cleverest men of his day? She had no doubt of that nor of his other qualifications. They included all she deemed essential in a husband—a warm true heart to love her, an intellect and spirit to be her guiding stars. In time all would acknowledge him for what she knew him to be: a poet, a wise and noble man, a philosopher, and a scholar.

Her mother, in a tirade against him, had warned Jeannie once of Carlyle's irritability. A most unjust, an untrue accusation! The curse, the plagued curse of his dyspepsia, which brought him so much suffering, was his sole demon. When he was well and happy, no man could be better-humored than he. And she would help him conquer even illness. She loved him. What was love if it could not smooth the roughest places? When he praised her, when she read devotion in his face, she soared away right to the seventh heaven.

His adjustments to marriage had at first been a little painful, she was forced to admit, especially when he spoke of her as "a new circumstance in his lot" and flew to the consolation of a pipe in the garden instead of to her own caresses. Right after their marriage she had tried the experiment of forbidding his smoking. The proprieties of the social life to which she was accustomed ruled against men using tobacco in the presence of women. Besides, such furious smoking, surely, could not be good for his health. Thomas had acquired a technique for combating his ills: he poured large drafts of castor oil down his gullet in the conviction that only by vigorous attacks could he defeat his ailments. Without the solace of his pipe, he resorted with such determination to the castor oil bottle that it was awful to behold, and Jane was glad to give him back his tobacco.

Though restless in temperament, Carlyle was easily upset by shifts in his routine. And what greater change exists than marriage? Unaccustomed ways of living confused him and preyed on his nerves. When he was ill, Jeannie speedily found out he could be despondent enough. But she was prepared to make the best of that. She was ready cheerfully to lend him her hopes for his success till he could recapture his own. She was content to let her heart rule her, unfettered by mental analysis. Her emotions did little business with her precocious mind. She adored her husband, and these mishaps would pass. So she was tolerant, and kind, and gay, and Thomas rallied to her love with affectionate gratitude. He was getting used to marriage. The bewilderment of it was clarifying daily. Soon he was ready to acknowledge that he had not had such cause to rejoice, nor experienced such true happiness, in years. What if his dyspepsia should refuse to be routed? Other men had put up with similar burdens.

After the interruption of marriage, he was once more at his writing. Just what was coming this time from his pen he was not yet prepared to say. It would be some kind of novel—spun from his own experiences, and from his work with Goethe, Schiller, and his other favorite modern writers.

They had married on next to no money at all. But cash enough for a year was due from four volumes of translations from German romance which Carlyle was about to publish. After that sum was gone, perhaps the novel would be finished. Or Tom would gain a post as editor of some Edinburgh periodical. Even a professorship, there or in London, might fall to his lot, for he had influential backers—at the University and elsewhere. The times, Jane knew, were desperately bad for young writers. The bookselling tribe were a timid lot, her husband told her; loath to run the slightest risk. But as long as he refused to lose courage, she herself was satisfied. His quill would not grow idle, he assured her. So she faced her life with resolute, cheerful equanimity, proud to be mistress of her home.

The house in which they were now living pleased her well. A lucky compromise of town and country, it stood among green fields, one of a single terrace row of urban houses, each in the pattern of the other, wall to wall in close formation, ranked like an advance platoon outside the city's army of buildings. Something a bit incongruous about it: this stone-built oblong of trim two-story dwellings neighbored by farms and wooded hills. But made to suit their requirements, for her husband could enjoy vigorous walks in such a region, while for her the center of Edinburgh lay but twenty minutes away.

Behind the house lay the Firth. In front rose the eminences
and towers of the city, to be gazed at from their very windows,
through the branches of their private forest—a single tree that
stood within the little enclosure of their courtyard. Jane loved
this wee garden: a patch of their own ground no bigger than
two quilts laid side by side. A little wall and the iron fence common to the entire row bounded it from the street, and a flagged
walk led to the doorstep. China roses grew in it, and other
flowers and shrubs. It amused her to watch Tom cultivating
these ample acres, clipping and pruning as if at his father's
farm. She had not yet surrendered to the extent of letting him
smoke within doors. But he could puff his pipe in great contentment in the garden. Jeannie herself was developing a curiosity about this habit of his; had even ventured to draw a gagging puff or two. Tom's mother loved a pipe, and Jean, on her
first visit to his family, had watched old Mrs. Carlyle sit
placidly among the wreathing clouds she was creating.

To spare her husband as much as possible the woes of indigestion, Jane had learned to plan his meals with care. Not that
her maid, Alison Greave, lacked reasonable skill in cooking.
But Tom liked to think of his wife as practical mistress of her
house and the commanding officer of its kitchen. He had fixed
habits in eating, and possessed definite ideas of his own. He
had no taste for food. Instead, he had a keen, shrewd power
of detection for poor cooking, and when this sense warned
him of culinary errors, he could be instant and loud in his
lamentations.

Jeannie, busy with pencil and paper, set to work to place
her household accounts in order. When she finally emerged
from her deliberations, she had evolved a budget so moderate
that Thomas, who was to be banker and weekly paymaster, was
incredulous and delighted, though life with his thrifty mother
had made him used to economies.

Marketing was no great task. Milk and butter could be had
from nearby Corstorphine farm. With shops at Stockbridge, a
suburb of Edinburgh, only a brief walk from her door, there
was no need for Jane to go to the city to make her household
purchases. Tom's family, to help out, sent provisions now and
then by the carrier from their Annandale farm. It was a miracle
how eggs, even, could survive that journey! The packing of the

box for Tom's new wife was a sacred rite with Mrs. Carlyle and her handy, sure-fingered daughters. Rarely did an egg come smashed to Comely Bank, and if a few were cracked on the way, through the mischances of the journey, Jeannie thriftily ordered her cook to fry them and they were eaten on the spot. Now and then a fine, beautifully cured ham arrived with the other produce, and Jane would proudly hang it up in her pantry, she and Tom declaring that it positively ornamented the house.

There was a great plenty to occupy the young wife's attention. Winter was coming on, and in Edinburgh that meant preparing for a state of siege. Carlyle was somewhat horrified at the invasions of needlewomen Jane led into his castle. Such clipping and stitching—pelisses and petticoats and other attire —till at last Jeannie had gained dominion over frost, and marched her seamstresses out. Jane drove her slight body with relentless force—she reveled in bursts of action. But too often there was a penalty exacted. Her excesses of vigor would be followed by blinding, bursting headaches or weeks of influenza and racking coughs. When these catastrophes happened, Tom, though helpless almost to the point of ludicrousness, nursed his wife with clumsy tenderness. He was so good to her, she wrote his mother, that she almost cried at thought of it.

Because of her frequent excursions to town when she was a girl in nearby Haddington, she was quite familiar with the city. But in those early days a vigilant mother had put her through the restricted paces of a marriageable daughter attending the correct, genteel entertainments, balls, and ceremonies. Now she was tasting the heady wine of freedom, and she found it good. She had no craving for expensive, complicated pleasures—her instincts did not lead her in that direction. But an afternoon's stroll down Princes Street, surely one of the handsomest thoroughfares in the world, she thought it, where she could watch the tide of busy, idle people, was like a password leading to adventure. The fine shops, the exclusive clubs, the dignified old buildings on one side; on the other, gardens, and then, beyond, Edinburgh's miraculous, ancient castle, thrusting upward betwixt sky and earth. It rose, a giant crown, so solidly above the rock that bore it. Yet when the mists were round its base, it seemed like the unbodied dream of some long-dead

Scottish chieftain asleep in Paradise, fated to vanish in its unreality on the moment of his celestial awaking.

Yes, Jeannie loved the city. She perceived that it meant far more to her than to her husband. As an unknown, hard-pressed young scholar at its University, and, later, during the confused years when he was attempting to gain even the scantiest foothold from which to climb aloft as man of letters, his life there had been far too grim a struggle, spoiling the pleasures he might otherwise have taken from the many offerings of the city. The troubles, misgivings, and doubts of those years, she could see, still haunted him. As he stood in their little courtyard, looking across green fields toward the smoke of the town rising between them and Salisbury Crags, he would thank his stars for their isolation from it all.

Jeannie could not accompany him on the tremendous walks he enjoyed taking. But she found sufficient exploring of her own to occupy her. Even the monastic doors of Edinburgh University did not keep her out, though traditionally barred to women, and she listened undaunted to lectures there on such subjects as chemistry and geology. Jane had a most innocent, guileless, quite unconscious way of becoming a sharer in the world of men and of men's thoughts.

When Tom came back from his excursions, Jane would be waiting to receive him with a kiss, the tea things set out, the kettle whispering and steaming by the fire. Tea was her special pride, a drink far too ambrosial for brewing in the kitchen. It was her finest offering to her household gods, a pagan act of prayer for delight and solace. Tom's numerous cupfuls gave proof of his satisfaction with her conduct of the rite. They were home indeed, safe and secure within their own four walls. Discouragement enough might lurk in the outer world—articles unpaid for; disappointed hopes. From the moaning sea, the white mists—bitter cold—rolled like pestilence landward from the east. They were snug inside; in these immediate moments, they could neglect the past and future and sip their tea.

Evenings, too, were all their own for sharing. Jeannie sitting at her piano, laughing and joking at her husband's ignorance of music, would play for him the Scottish songs he liked, or please herself, and him too, with Mozart and Beethoven. Enough to see her seated there, her black curls framing her forehead and dark against the whiteness of her neck. Some nights they read aloud, or Tom, in the mood, would unloose his picturesque eloquence of description till Jeannie could almost see standing before her the persons he was characterizing with such mirth and gusto—punctuating with his roars of laughter the quaint and telling words which he employed. At some pause for breath, at some sudden silence, when his rich, husky, expressive voice was stilled, he would notice her eyes fixed worshipfully on him, her mute, rapt attention. Here! He had again been doing all the talking! She should answer him, he jokingly commanded. He could not guess how much she loved just to sit there gazing at him, listening to his words, admiring this eloquent, talented man who was her husband. It was all so new to her still, and so delightful. There was plenty of time, yet, to learn her answers. He must content himself, instead, with the little kiss she gave him.

Then night, and sleep in the gigantic bed she had brought with her from Haddington—the big red bed with its wide spreading canopy—now hers alone no longer, but theirs.

Chapter Four

*T*HOUGH Jane Welsh and Thomas Carlyle had stepped so quietly into married life in Edinburgh, here and there people were finding them out and coming to their door. When they could hear talk like Thomas Carlyle's, when they could meet a bright and dazzling girl like Jeannie, few men, once having sampled these excitements, would willingly forego so choice a dual attraction. Not that women did not enjoy a call at Comely Bank. But in general the early hospitality of the Carlyles made its greatest appeal to men. As these began to gather in increasing numbers, Jeannie fell with easy grace into her rôle as hostess. She did not need to stuff her guests with food. They did not come to eat, but for the fun of talking, and rarely did they leave unsatisfied. Tea was enough to suit them, and a few trimmings, or coffee poured steaming from a brown jug. Jane sparkled on her company, and they sat long past the hour for going home. When Tom was present he carried all before him and they were willing to be listeners. But sometimes he was loath to quit his work and left the callers to his wife. He could rest assured that they would be well cared for. If, as occasionally happens, the conversation threatened to break from thinness, like a brittle vine that had grown too rapidly for its supply of nourishment, and guests were dull, Jeannie knew how to cultivate and nourish it until it throve again. Hard work for a young hostess, but imperative for the practice of her art.

Carlyle had some right, in these early months, to take exception to the mental qualities of many of the visitors, and to look for ways of escape. Too large a number were poor drifters in the backwash of the city's intellectual life, anemic minds barred from the company of the recognized wise men of the city— Scott, Jeffrey, Sir William Hamilton, John Wilson and the rest. Thomas, with the genius of these great ones, had no such

23

armor of justifiable exclusiveness to frighten away little men who came to waste their time and his. The house at Comely Bank was to them an oasis—these young divines who could command no churches, these poor young teachers lacking pupils and authors who would never write a book. When their numbers became really threatening, Carlyle and his wife hit upon the scheme of appointing a single day a week—Wednesday— for receiving chosen guests. Jane loved her day at home, and even though her husband might pretend, now and then, still to deplore time lost, he enjoyed the little ceremony too and was hearty and cheerful to all comers. As a man of surging, thronging ideas, he was in need of an audience to try them on, even if made up only of persons such as these. Yet before six months were out, he had better men to talk to, and Jane's gifts as hostess received a worthier test.

Since the day in 1802 when its first issue startled the city, the *Edinburgh Review* had become a mighty power. Indeed its dogmatic omniscience, the urbane assurance with which it gave forth *its* version of the truth, its cocksure plotting of the course for Britain and the world, had all contributed to give it a unique and commanding position. It legislated concerning taste in literature, and laid down the law on all other things besides.

Perhaps the very peculiarities of its origin helped explain the sway it gained and the arrogance with which it maintained dominion. Its founders and furtherers were no mere scribbling professionals. They were busy young gentlemen who wrote with ease—a congenial, diverse, sociable company held together by their bonds of friendship and by their political faith as Whigs. They included well-educated noblemen unwilling to accept the privilege of their class to let their brains lie idle, lawyers of acknowledged promise with great careers ahead of them, scientists too, and men of medicine. Youth was on their side, keen wit, and limitless assurance.

Though each was occupied with his own immediate interests or profession, as a group they had resolved to try the pleasures of conducting, on the side, a magazine in the anonymous pages of which they could speak their minds without let or hindrance, risking no danger to their personal careers yet experiencing the delights of unrestricted expression of opinion. Like naughty, clever little schoolboys lurking unseen in the shrubbery and shouting at the masters, they could safely bait the world. As they met to lay their plans one stormy evening in the Buccleuch Place lodgings of one member of the group, Francis Jeffrey, they had laughed and joked, while the rain and wind beat against the panes, hilarious at thought of the far worse storm they themselves were bent on raising.

Actually, they had underestimated their power. After the first few issues had come before the public, few could oppose the Juggernaut strength of the *Edinburgh Review*. It had rushed into a vacuum—for the old periodicals were moribund or dead—and filled it to the cracking point. Secure behind their shield of namelessness, the editors and their associates found themselves well-nigh invulnerable. They could sting with wasp-like delicate thrusts, or crush with the force of a battering ram. Their very urbanity was a potent weapon. Never dropping this characteristic, a pose so difficult to combat, they found amusement, and gratification, too, in varying the system of attack and instruction to suit the need—now bludgeoning to death some hapless policy or author, now wounding with light superior laughter, now withering the vitality of their opponents by sarcasm and scorn.

The *Review* made serious mistakes, of course, and gained enemies who lacked only an answering voice to become dangerous. But for a time its victims lay helpless before it. Its harsh contempt for Wordsworth and the Lake School of poets pained only the group assaulted and their few followers. The vast majority of readers, trained to accept its criticisms as infallible, were amused at this exposure of poetic madness. In questions of national policy, its opinions, perhaps, ran into more formidable opposition. The Earl of Buchan, shocked at an article condoning Napoleon's usurpations in Spain, took measures which he at least must have deemed effective. Ordering a footman to place the offending issue on the floor of the lobby, the noble Earl kicked it hard into the muddy center of the street to be trodden under foot.

The one man to whom the *Review* most owed its success was Francis Jeffrey, at the time of its founding a young advocate only twenty-nine years of age but already famous in Scotland as an expert trial lawyer. The original scheme of organization had called for cooperative direction. But as so often happens where men are busy with their own affairs, most of the group dropped away from active management, and the mantle of editorship had been assumed by Jeffrey. He it was who gathered the articles for each quarterly appearance, supplying enough himself, through his amazing industry, to fill its pages when his contributors failed to deliver promised work. As busy as the rest of them with his own career, he somehow managed to find time, by his devoted labors, to bring out once every three months an issue fit to continue the enviable reputation of the magazine.

What had become of those gallant supporters who had voted blood and treasure to hold aloft the enterprise?—he would write to some tardy colleague. Will you or will you not do your essay about Malthus for the April number? Is it fair to the *Review*, or kind to me, or well for yourself, to hold up an article of this sort for so enormous a time?

But though he chided his brilliant, procrastinating company of associates, he rarely lost his patience or his natural good humor. Sometimes of course the pressure made him rebellious, especially when his practice of the law happened to become most vigorously active just when his fellow editors were most dilatory. Sometimes, in his haste, his own writings, though their quality did not necessarily fail, would suffer from far too little restraint, and he would regretfully admit to his intimates that he had overstepped the bounds. A quickly done attack sometimes landed him in a mess of trouble, such as his criticism of Thomas Moore's *Odes* on the score of immorality, an article which led to a challenge from the offended poet, though the duel itself, through prudence or good fortune, ended harmlessly and farcically enough.

The policy he established of paying exceptionally high prices for contributions widened his range of authors and gave him command of many of the best minds available, even after the Tory *Quarterly Review*, in 1809, and, eight years later, *Blackwood's Edinburgh Magazine*, had been founded to challenge the supremacy of the pioneer.

The anonymity that perhaps might conceal with its thin cloak the identity of a mere contributor was quite unavailing to hide the name of the prime mover of the *Edinburgh Review*, and Jeffrey's renown as editor grew in friendly rivalry to his legal fame, threatening even to eclipse his legitimate career. An acquaintance with Jeffrey was a precious boon to any young writer. The articles he used almost never came from strangers. He gathered his crops among his own associates, and they rarely failed to yield him a rich harvest.

Carlyle had long known Jeffrey by sight and reputation. Even in his student days he had listened to him as he pled cases before the judges in the Inns of court, or noticed him walking on the streets of Edinburgh. But he had never met him, and his sensitive independence would hardly permit him to take steps of his own toward that objective. He was proud of his peasant stock, but pride filled him with a sense of struggle often harmful to his interests. Once, when he first began to write, he had sent an essay to the *Review*. But the ensuing silence chilled him, and he had launched no further ventures in that direction.

Only a lucky circumstance at last broke down the barrier which might otherwise have kept him from ever knowing Jeffrey. When Carlyle visited London two years before his marriage, he had become intimate with several established men of letters there, among them the poet who wrote under the name of Barry Cornwall: W. B. Procter, son-in-law of his and Irving's friend, Mrs. Basil Montagu. Tom's letters to Mrs. Montagu had kept his London well-wishers in touch with his progress. He did not ask for favors. But it was not difficult to read between the lines that he was seeking work to do. His four volume edition of translations was out of the way, having been published in January, 1827, and the novel he was attempting to write was hanging fire. Why not have Carlyle and Jeffrey meet? Such a relationship might lead to excellent results. Suiting the action to the thought, Procter sent the necessary letter of introduction.

One evening early in February, Tom put this open sesame to a new and promising realm into his pocket and strode off towards George Street where Mr. and Mrs. Jeffrey had their city house. He would see what the famous editor might be ready to do for him.

Eager to hear his account of the visit, Jeannie awaited her husband's return. He would stay only a few moments, he had

said, so as not to trespass on Jeffrey's crowded hours. But time
moved on; the minutes lengthened into hours. When Tom at
last got back, Jeannie learned that what had started as a business call ended as a social visit. Yes, Jeffrey had received him
most kindly. Jane listened as her husband described how he
had found him in his study, seated behind a large baize-cov-
ered table, a table groaning with a heavy weight of reading—
big legal volumes next to books of poetry and novels buried
among bundles of briefs and manuscripts: law and literature
mingling together as in the lawyer-editor's own brain. The
flames of two candles had cast their yellow glow over the desk,
emphasizing the keenness of Jeffrey's mobile, lean, and delicate face, and a fire had given warmth and friendliness to the
book-filled, none too tidy room. His entrance, Carlyle reported,
had been Jeffrey's signal to push aside his work (his dual
career exacted a heavy daily toll of hours) and chat in the most
cordial fashion. What had Mr. Carlyle done; what had he
published? So Tom's whole history was modestly revealed—
his *Life of Schiller* and its fair reception, his translation of
Goethe's *Wilhelm Meister*, and the four most recent volumes.
These were his works, though no title page as yet bore his
name: he was not ready in such books as these to step before
the public. "We must give you a lift!"—Carlyle repeated the
editor's final remarks, and told how Jeffrey had suggested some
articles for the *Review*. At times her husband's modesty and
caution were rather trying to Jeannie. She learned how he had
answered the offer by saying it would be well for Jeffrey first to
glance at the *German Romance* volumes to see what sort of fish
he might be hooking.

Jeffrey's kindness had not stopped with his extension of the
hospitality of the *Review*. Did Carlyle know Sir Walter Scott?—
he asked. Would he like to meet some other interesting men?
It could be easily arranged. When her husband told her of
these offers, Jeannie feared lest Tom would take no steps to
bring about their realization; he was so loath to accept help
of that sort. It had been an excellent visit, however, easy, un-
embarrassed, and filled with an abundance of good will. If only
Jeffrey were not too busy, Tom concluded, a real friendship
might be possible between them.

Carlyle underestimated Jeffrey's knack for cultivating the

wide fields of his interests. His diminutive body seemed made for rapid, easy flight from place to place wherever his will led him. Of late years he had been on the alert to find new talent. The old associates one by one were dropping away; his own time was becoming more crowded; new blood was needed to bring relief. Perhaps this young man could be trained to take a major place some day in the management of the journal. Jeffrey thought very well of him; he did not intend to let him drop. The rough edges and the radicalism he had detected were minor blemishes, easily forgiven. With careful polishing, he hardly doubted but that they could be made to vanish away.

Punctiliously, Jeffrey returned his new contributor's visit by a formal call. What he discovered at Comely Bank was something of a surprise. He thought to find a struggling, obscure young married couple. He had expected to meet an average wife. Instead, here was a radiant, gay, and lovely girl. Such an apparition as Jeannie Welsh Carlyle had not cheered his sight for many a year. He laid himself out to be ingratiating. His curiosity and interest were at once aroused. He must become better acquainted with this household.

Jeannie was delighted to pour tea for her distinguished guest. Her keen eyes took him in, contrasting what she saw with the idea that she had received from Tom's descriptions. When Jeffrey chose to do so, no man in Edinburgh could muster equal charm and gallantry. One quite forgot his years—he was fifty-four. One noticed only this amazing Ariel of a creature, with his swift, graceful, amusing ways, his unlimited fund of anecdotes, his easy compliments. His appearance itself was fitted to his talk. His short, light frame, his quick gait as he moved about the room, matched his rapid flow of words. His piercing eyes, under high arched brows, flashed with a quizzical, roving glance. His dark hair, short-cropped, stood upright from his finely modeled head, as if glad to escape from the tyranny of an advocate's wig, an article of dress which Jeffrey, except for the most solemn occasions, had the courage to discard. Jane noticed his pugnacious, slightly pointed chin, his mobile, thin-lipped mouth, his sharp aquiline nose, its bridge joining the forehead well above the eyes.

Jeffrey had come in performance of a duty; he lingered for his own pleasure. There was nothing which so intrigued him as a gay hour of social badinage and chitchat, and Mrs. Carlyle, he quickly perceived, gave fully as good as she got.

When Carlyle first met him, Jeffrey had impressed him as a person with heavy demands on his time. Now Thomas had to adjust his views to include Jeffrey at ease, a light-hearted being with apparently not a care in the world and with a superfluity of hours at his disposal. Here was something new in his experiences of men. He hoped for his wife's sake as well as his own that Jeffrey would give them much of his brilliant company.

Thomas did not need to trouble his mind; one sight of Jeannie had made continued friendship a necessary thing for Jeffrey.

Chatter from the upper realms of Edinburgh's literary society did not readily take its airy, surreptitious flight across the open spaces to remote Comely Bank. Jeffrey's fame as editor and lawyer was of course common property. What Tom and Jane could hardly be aware of was another factor in his reputation, an element subterranean and obscure, yet familiar enough to the sophisticates and gossips of the city. Clever, pretty young wives, so the story went, were Jeffrey's special weakness.

His instincts could not be called predatory; he was no deliberate wrecker of homes. But he loved feminine society, and could not get enough of it. Perhaps the circumstances, because they were so disarming, made him more dangerous than a cold-blooded confessed amorist. His demonstrative nature craved the regard of women, and under a mask of airy persiflage he eagerly sought its fulfillment. The mere fact that his favorites were wedded did not necessarily govern Jeffrey's predilections. But married women generally best fulfilled his unconscious needs—in their houses he was sure of the warm domesticity he could not get enough of, in spite of the fact that he had an agreeable home of his own. His friends' wives were at ease. They knew how to manage. They had outgrown the shy awkwardness which so many girls exhibit in the presence of urbane, clever men much older than themselves.

Who was this radiant person, this charming girl to whom his latest find was married? This new contributor was proving himself a sufficiently surprising phenomenon in himself. He became even more remarkable through the wife whom he had got to marry him. Jeffrey's brother, John, when asked if he knew anything concerning the young woman, had some rays of light to shed into the darkness. Yes, he had heard of her. Before her marriage, he said, she had been distinguished as a flirt. So that was it! When next he met her, he would tease Mistress Jeannie on her reputation. And that pleasure would not be long deferred, either.

Thus it was that Jeannie and Thomas found themselves among the select list of Francis Jeffrey's acquaintances. Within a short space he had established himself as an intimate at Comely Bank and came and went at pleasure. The preliminaries to friendship had speedily been concluded. By invitation, the young pair had called at the Jeffreys' town house and met Mrs. Jeffrey, a pleasant, forthright woman, who took at once to Carlyle. The way was open for what might follow.

Every summer, the Jeffreys moved to their delightful house, Craigcrook, on the eastern slope of Corstorphine Hill, within easy walk of Comely Bank. There Jeffrey played the country gentleman and received his friends. Only at Abbotsford, the home of Walter Scott, could the fortunate visitor hope for as cordial hospitality. The Jeffreys loved to entertain a multitude of guests, and at their table, where food was always plentiful and good wines flowed in almost too lavish variety, one could be sure of meeting celebrated and interesting company. Diners were not asked to Craigcrook because they were famous. They were invited because they were intimates, a rule that made for honest conviviality. The Carlyles' turn was not long in coming. Jane was well content with the company at table. She watched her husband and their host. Certainly Jeffrey thought well of Carlyle. This was as it should be. She was happy that they were so highly placed in Jeffrey's favor. Tom belonged among such people; not just with the lesser folk of Edinburgh. To-night he was talking his best, though somewhat extravagantly perhaps, astonishing several of his hearers with the violence of his phrases. His tumultuous ideas occasionally brought a smile even to Jeffrey's Puckish mouth.

Coleridge?—exclaimed Thomas. Coleridge was a man talking in maudlin sleep an infinite deal of nothing. And what had become of history? It was turning aside from truth to stumble over dry bones in a valley no longer of vision!

Jeffrey took a certain mischievous delight in arguing on the other side of every question, in lawyer fashion, submerging for the fun of it whatever honest convictions he might possess. But he was a skillful host, as facile in avoiding friction as in parrying thrusts. When Tom was at last ready to leave for home, the shocking lateness of the hour bore witness to the pleasures of the evening.

Before his day's work in the city began, or after its close, Jeffrey liked to seek relaxation at Comely Bank. His light rap echoed repeatedly on the door. In he would come, morning, evening, or afternoon—the hour made little difference to him—for a chat or longer visit, depending on his quick perception of the time at his disposal. If Tom were busy writing, and Jane idle, he might challenge her to a round of battledore and shuttlecock, wielding his racket with astonishing agility. Or they would bandy persiflage instead, tossing their words lightly, Jane placing her shots with a skill that rivaled the old campaigner's. She understood perfectly the game, the methods and the rules of it, and could lead her clever little gentleman through its mazes as far as she saw good—always deft and sure in her procedure. Her mastery of the arts of quizzery and teasing, and her youth, gave her a wide advantage with which to keep the upper hand.

If Tom joined them, returning flushed at tea time from his walk, he welcomed Jeffrey's presence. He trusted Jeannie; it did not trouble him that she enjoyed the older man's light gallantries. There was wrath in some hearts in Edinburgh; but not in his. They were feminine hearts, these heated ones, which burned with envy and vexation at the new favorite.

Carlyle may have underestimated the temptation that lay in his Jeannie's way. Perhaps he passed on to his wife's young shoulders a heavier responsibility than was fair or wise. Jeffrey was a great and famous man; the devoted attentions of such as he might well have turned the head of any girl. The gypsy strain which legend placed in Jeannie's veins surely would urge her to such a conquest. But mingled with it was the blood of Protestant reformers. Jane's instinct told her that she had merely to crook her little finger at Jeffrey to bring gravity enough into what could otherwise remain a light, delightful relationship. Fifty-four and twenty-six add up to a dangerous figure. It was right good fun, Jeannie discovered, to keep her slender arm held out in friendship—to listen to Jeffrey's flattering compliments, to hear him call her "cousin" and "my dearest." Those serious confidences, those serious conversations, when he discussed life as he understood it, with the authority of all his years, were a subtle tribute to her power and understanding. Yet Jane was bred to prudence. Besides, she was in love with her husband. Tempting and graceful though the act might be—a finger curved to beckon—Jane avoided the least suspicion of the gesture.

Chapter Five

*S*IR WALTER SCOTT; John Wilson, the "Christopher North" of the convivial adventures set forth so glowingly as the "*Noctes Ambrosianae*" in *Blackwood's Edinburgh Magazine;* Sir William Hamilton, the precocious, learned occupant of the Chair of History at the University of Edinburgh: these were the leaders whose names gave luster to the city's fame as an intellectual as well as a political capital. Their doings often furnished substance for Jeffrey's amusing chatter. They were an unfailing source for the anecdotes with which he delighted to entertain Jane. She had a natural curiosity about persons. She rejoiced when her husband chanced to meet a few of these greater luminaries, though his pride and independence always stood in the way of his seeking out the most famous of the group, Sir Walter Scott, in spite of the fact that there were opportunities to do so and friends willing to be of aid.

There was one elusive occasional resident of Edinburgh, however, as difficult to track down as a hare in a covert, in whom her husband showed a lively interest. This was Thomas De Quincey, known to thousands of readers as the English Opium Eater. The origin of Tom's inquisitiveness dated back several years to the time when he chanced to read, in a bookseller's littered shop in Birmingham, the Opium Eater's hostile, demolishing review of the translation of Goethe's *Wilhelm Meister.* In his article, it is true, De Quincey was bent chiefly on dragging down the German from the pinnacle where Carlyle's admiration had placed him, but Carlyle as translator came in for a share of censure. As a student of German literature, De Quincey possessed a reputation older than his own, and Thomas, in all fairness, was ready to admit some justice in the charges brought by the reviewer—blame for Scotticisms which had crept into the English and for a certain awkwardness in the prose. Yet the review had thrown a discouraging landslide into Carlyle's early pathway, an obstruction hard enough to clamber over. After his bruised shins had healed, Carlyle was determined some day to meet his critic. Though far more sensitive to disapproval than he pretended to be, Thomas did not harbor rancor. What impelled him was a vague wish to see in the flesh this man whose words had administered the first lash to his hard-pressed, struggling, creative ego.

Though one rarely met De Quincey himself, the atmosphere of the city was peopled with his legend. And all England was aware of his fame. His *Confessions*, written in the exquisite prose of which he was the master, had excited intense curiosity. Even more provocative was the author's calm assurance, when the authenticity of the experiences was brought in question, that every least detail was absolute fact. Such insistence on self-exposure was irresistible; henceforth every article signed by the Opium Eater was sure of many readers. Yet all this notoriety had brought to poor De Quincey almost no financial ease. When sums of money tumbled into his hands, he washed them away like water. His utter ignorance of the use of silver was as remarkable as his skillful management of words. If he was in funds, he became the patron saint of mendicants. When he lacked cash, the landladies of Edinburgh became his scourge. He could starve with a draft for a hundred pounds in his pocket because he did not know how to turn it into ready money.

His friend John Wilson, who in the *Noctes* had praised him as a man in a million, needed often to be his saviour. When Tom and Jeannie were living at Comely Bank, De Quincey, a hunted deer dodging before the pack of all his debts, was spending part of his time at Grasmere, near Wordsworth, part in Edinburgh.

So Tom was on the lookout for him. One could never be sure just where he might appear. They both walked the same fields and woods and heights, though one by day, the other by night. De Quincey, almost always alone, would glide past the lighted shops of Princes Street like a man clothed in an invisible garment, the home-going citizens scarcely conscious of his tiny form. He loved to stroll after dark in the immense loneliness of the waterfront, in the desolate neighborhood of the Leith docks when the day's work was over and busy life was stilled. He had no fear of thieves or footpads; he knew their world as thoroughly as they, though frequenting it as a harmless spy. In the country lanes and over the narrow bridges the little bull's-eye lantern which he carried would gleam like a fitful will-o'-the-wisp to startle the belated celebrant returning unsteadily home. At such moments, by accident, the light was apt to flicker out, making the little figure in the shadows a still more chilling apparition, though as unterrifying in reality as the piping frogs that shared the darkness with him.

It was at the home of a mutual friend, John Gordon, that Thomas finally ran to earth his former critic. De Quincey, told of Carlyle's wish to meet him, had shivered at the thought. He was uncertain of the motives—the translator of Goethe, in the Opium Eater's painful imagination, had joined the witches' brood of landladies and creditors who haunted his retreating steps. He had turned pale as ashes, poor little soul, Carlyle told Jane, when he learned who was with him in the room. But Tom, by never once referring to it, soon laid the ghost of the review and won De Quincey's confidence. He even gained his promise to call at Comely Bank.

Carlyle had a passion for observing faces. The one he studied now, in the wavering candlelight as the talk flowed on and on, seemed at first glance almost like a child's—a wise and beautiful child—blond-haired, with eyes of unfathomable blue. But only for a moment. Then a look would cross it to shatter the illusion, rousing one's sluggish perceptions like a stab of pain. A child indeed, thought Carlyle, yet behold, this child has been long years in deepest Hell.

Only a very few houses in Edinburgh shared the favor of De Quincey's visits. Soon Comely Bank was added to the number, and Jeannie's understanding, sympathetic nature found one thing more to occupy it. De Quincey's old-fashioned courtesy, the sweetness of manner lodging in that gnomelike body, could not fail to make their appeal to any woman of gracious instincts and gentle character. His sensitive mouth, his delicate weary face with its broad forehead and sharp, slightly cloven chin, his tired eyes—one could not forget these features. He was so very little—his smallness emphasized by his habit always of wearing clothes made for a larger man. His face was like a delicate etching: a network of the finest minute lines, crisscrossing and interweaving. But with every passing mood, the lines, too, would alter, endlessly rearranging their patterns.

To become intimate with De Quincey was wrecking to one's snug routine of life. When the candles were lit, gleaming late over Tom's and Jeannie's reading, he might flit to their door. He was like a moth from the dark, entering unexpectedly. His friends could never be sure of his coming when they awaited him, or safe from his entering when they least expected it. His best hours were those after midnight, for then his words and thoughts came freest.

One could not tell what absurd catastrophe might overtake him. Bending over the candles, examining some book, his large eyes glowing as a moth's would, he was like as not to set fire to his hair. When saved from disaster by a timely warning, he would gravely thank his rescuer, brushing away the flame with a mild, abstracted gesture.

"What wouldn't one give to have him in a box, and take him out to talk!" Jeannie exclaimed, recalling the amazing range of conversation which had kept her spellbound. He loved to toy with varied topics, developing each in turn, spinning them out like shining strands of colored silk into a perfect texture. First he would give himself a sharp pinch in the arm, like an organist pulling out some hidden stop, then away the music would flow. Ridiculous happenings, reports of the law courts, strange police cases, wills that showed the whimsical crotchets of dying eccentrics—these and many other things delighted his fancy. He preferred to stand while talking, fixing his eyes not on his audience but on the opposite wall of the room, as though reading printed there the remarkable prose he used with equal felicity in writing or in speech. Never at a loss, he managed the intricate array of his words with consummate ease, his musical voice rarely mounting much above a whisper. But when he was through with his whimsical jocularity, his harmless bantering humor, the mood would suddenly change. A startling intensity would enter into his voice and as the words ran on, the hearer could glimpse visions of this strange man's inner life—its sublimity and degradation, its pathos and its sorrow.

Jane and Thomas Carlyle were quite aware of De Quincey's manifold tribulations. They knew of his chronic lack of cash and of the ills he suffered from. In his *Confessions,* he had told of his victory over opium, but this was but a temporary conquest. His former habits would return, and when his manuscripts came to the offices of *Blackwood's*, they sometimes bore a telltale symbol—a purple ring discoloring the paper where he had set down the glass of laudanum which he was drinking. After dinner, when he visited, he would place two little boxes before him, one of snuff, one of opium pills, and his delicate, bird-claw hands would flicker over them from time to time while he conversed.

When Jane heard that he lay ill at one of his migratory lodgings, she brought him to her house and nursed him back to health. It was no easy battle: De Quincey later spoke of this sickness as one of the most critical he had ever experienced.

He never forgot his benefactress. It was not merely her kindness that he gratefully recalled, though he was always insistent on claiming for her what he described as her angelic goodness—a characterization which might have set Jeannie's mischievous, quick-tongued self into peals of laughter. What a clear intelligence she possessed, he would say; how swift and fine and keen a mind!

Chapter Six

*A*LL the while that Jane was becoming more firmly established as a citizen of Edinburgh, she was conscious that this present settlement might prove merely transitory. She realized from the outset that it had been an experiment. Her husband's affection for country living was well known to her, and she recognized how powerful was the impulse which drove him toward realization of his dream. When his dyspepsia did not seriously torment him, he was ready to toy even with the thought of living in London, the place which Jane believed would give his talents widest range. Had he not things to say and books to write worthy to gain the attention of that center of the Universe? But when his nerves tricked him, as they had done in the first months after marriage, aggravating his particular illness, a refuge among fields and moors distant from any city, in the regions he loved, was to his mind the one salvation.

What a delightful russet-coated idyl that stay at Hoddam Hill had been, the year before their marriage, when he was living in Dumfriesshire with his mother and his sisters to keep house for him, and Jeannie had come for a visit at harvest season! Her initiation to simple living had been a happy one, making less preposterous Carlyle's suggestion, during his courtship, that they should begin married life at Craigenputtock, the Welsh family property in the hills near Dumfries.

Jane had quickly made up her mind that her husband needed coddling. Noises were a serious menace to his productivity, and when they harassed his supersensitive ears, he would pace the room like a wild thing in a cage. Work under such circumstances, he would vehemently announce, was intolerable. Then Jane would bring to bear her diplomacy to mitigate the disturbance—silencing an old maid's house dog through a tactful letter and writing away another family's pet bantam cock.

39

If the country was necessary to her husband, she would not question his decision. Jeannie's heart told her that she was ready to follow Carlyle wherever his choice and the demands of circumstance might lead. When the possibility of a move to Craigenputtock again rose, she was willing to consider it.

Besides the search for health, there was also the question of expense. Even with Jane's rigid economies, living came high in Edinburgh. Could a man support himself there solely by writing? In the country they could get along on far lower costs. The problem of what to do caused Tom much anxiety, though Jane preferred not to occupy her thoughts too seriously with it, trusting to her husband's genius and industry to pull them through. Her part was the frugal, skillful management of the household.

Jeffrey's lift had opened the way for Tom's career as essayist and critic, but though the *Review* paid well for contributions, it published only four issues a year. An author could hardly subsist on pickings scanty as these. Moreover, essays of the type that Carlyle was now writing took work and time. They left no room for the creation of books of one's own. He had been forced to lay aside the romance at which he had been scribbling. Jane accepted the necessity with regret: poor Wotton Reinfred, the hero, he was becoming so romantic a figure! She had enjoyed her afternoons of reading about his adventures, the output of her husband's morning labors, while Tom strode forth on his walks across the countryside.

Perhaps their income was in no immediate danger of falling below Jane's stipulated £200 a year. But if uncertainty troubles the future, ease of mind is hard to gain.

Mrs. Welsh was having difficulties with her tenant farmers at Craigenputtock. They were delinquent with the rent, and were letting the property run down. When she visited her daughter and son-in-law at Comely Bank, early in 1827, Jane's mother discussed ways and means to remedy the abuse. The upshot was a scheme whereby the Carlyles themselves should live on the Welshes' land. The present tenants would be asked to vacate. Then Tom's plowman brother Alick was to lease the farm in their stead. He could begin his husbandry as soon as his stock was ready. A new small farmhouse would be built for Alick, and the old house altered and enlarged for the Carlyles.

In April, to see what could be done about the business, Carlyle set out on a brief trip to Dumfriesshire. Jeannie remained in Edinburgh with her mother for company.

How strange not to hear her husband stirring about the house! He could be so clumsy, oversetting things in the most amazing fashion. But this silence was harrowing; she felt quite morbid about it. How dreadfully she missed him! She even missed having to drop everything she was doing to hunt for some precious book or paper he had lost. Before he left, she made him promise to think of her. Was he doing so? He had assured her, with that teasing manner he occasionally assumed, that he might—*sometimes*.

Jestingly she threatened to be inconsolable and take to her bed during his absence. But her head ached so, from worry over what might be happening to him and distress at the muddle she feared he would discover at Craigenputtock, that the joke was becoming no joke at all. She tried relief through work, and busied herself with dressmaking and sewing. With a feeling of virtue she read some of the more serious books Carlyle had lately recommended to her. She even attempted a little writing of her own, though she had largely ceased to heed her girlhood ambition of becoming a famous writer. Shortly before her marriage she had kindled a bonfire with all her past scribblings, and little new had been accomplished to replace them. Yet writing served to pass the time during her husband's absence. Callers arrived, too, but with Carlyle away, she did not feel in a mood to receive them. So she wrapped a piece of flannel about her throat, as though she had a cold, then bade her mother make apologies.

How the hours dragged! She thought with a shudder of ever having to put up with a longer separation. Was not her life so closely interwoven with her husband's that it could never endure an independent existence? She would dwell no further on such unwelcome possibilities as future absences. How Carlyle would laugh at these sentimental fears, assuring her that even her mocking temper became her better!

When by chance she met the postman, Jane told herself that she could really not expect word for another twenty-four hours. Yet why not ask for letters?—no harm in that.

There *was* one for her! She was so glad and so frightened all at the same time that the tangled emotions hurt her; so eager to know the whole contents immediately that she could hardly make out, in her anxiety, any single part. A tobacconist's stall, patronized by her husband, stood near at hand. She hurried into it as a retreat in which to read, her heart beating so violently that she feared the shopman would notice its agitation.

Yes, all was well. She was an angel of a creature, he wrote, more precious to him than ever. He had found Craigenputtock an incredible mess, a chaos of filth and misuse.

Alas for poor Craig o' Putta! The thought of damaged property was distasteful to her Scottish sense of thrift. But never mind that! He had written how much he loved her. That was the great essential! Craigenputtock, he added, still remained a hope. She would learn more concerning its future in his next letter.

"Dear, Dear"—she wrote excitedly, as though she were speaking the words, not dashing them on paper; "cheep, cheep!"—like an eager, delighted bird. She was longing for his return; she could bear his continued absence, she told him, only in the faith of its being brief.

"Not unlike what the drop of water from Lazarus's finger might have been to Dives in the flame was my dearest Goody's letter to her Husband yesterday afternoon," Carlyle told his wife. The immediate troubles were over; the tenants ousted after some hours of wrangling and adjustment. "O Jeannie! How happy shall we be in this Craig o' Putta!"

She could believe it, if he declared it so. He was not entering into the scheme with eyes blind to its defects—it would be no Arcadia, he knew. But at least, he assured her, they could sit under their own hawthorn tree, with none to make them afraid. "My little wife will be there forever beside me, and I shall be well and blessed, and the latter end of that man will be better than the beginning!" Jane was his greatest treasure; he would ever learn to value her more. Shame on him, he declared, for complaining at life when sickness plagued him. "O Jeannie, O my wife, we will never part; never through Eternity itself! But I will love thee and keep thee in my heart of hearts!—That is, unless I grow a very great fool—which indeed this talk doth somewhat betoken."

Tom's brother Alick moved to Craigenputtock that spring to begin his farming. An extra story was being added to the main house, and the cottage for Alick was to be started. But the delays of building postponed any move for the Carlyles that summer. Neither of them minded. Tom's work for the *Edinburgh Review* was keeping him increasingly busy. The modest sphere that Jane had made for herself in the city was steadily pushing out its boundaries. Two articles in successive numbers of the *Review*, the summer and autumn issues, were building for Carlyle a reputation as a fearless writer with strong opinions. Nothing which the paper printed could escape notice. When a resounding voice, not at all in the tradition which Jeffrey fostered, began setting up a shout in championship of the new metaphysics from Germany, there was inevitably something of a sensation. More conservative readers began to ask themselves from what strange monster these sounds were echoing to disturb their quiescence and challenge their assumption that the world in which they lived was a well-ordered, comprehensible unity. This insistence on inexplicable higher mysteries, in articles that at first glance seemed merely innocuous discussions of a body of foreign literature, was disconcerting. As those opposing such doctrines and the small minority who discovered good in them squared off for a bout or two in the public print, Jane's mischievous spirit rallied to the fray. But her pride in her husband shone through her teasing at this fuss he was stirring up. Jeffrey, too, was amused, though he told himself he must curb his radical young friend in order to preserve his usefulness. Quite unmoved by Goethe and the rest, he often marveled at Carlyle's enthusiasms. He had warned him not to write as though he considered unconverted persons to be fools. Tom had not fully obeyed his editor's injunctions. But Jeffrey, recognizing his potentialities, took no more drastic measures than resorting to a little banter on his protégé's enviable position as founder of a Scottish clan of neo-mystics. He must be referring to just herself and husband, said Jane, amused at the solemn title, "The Master Mystic," which Jeffrey insisted on conferring on her.

Since shortly after his translation of Goethe's *Wilhelm Meister*, Carlyle had been in correspondence with its famous author. Few events brought greater pleasure or excitement to the house at Comely Bank than packages from distant Weimar. Not merely letters came; the boxes Goethe sent were full of pleasant, unexpected things: books, and little gifts.

Goethe was not just her husband's correspondent; Jane, too, was recognized. She held an ample place in his esteem, a feeling he showed through sending her presents accompanied by a sentimental verse or two spun from his fancy. First had come a dainty box, so carefully and tastefully arranged that Jane guessed some feminine member of his household must have taken charge of the packing. And so it proved. Ottelie, his daughter-in-law, had lent her German neatness to the enterprise. Out of the little chest had emerged varied gifts. For Jane there was a black, wrought-iron necklace. A shining medallion of the poet hung from it as a pendant, done in colored glass and framed in gold. A bracelet soon arrived as a companion piece. The first box had also contained a dashing pocketbook for Thomas. And there was a beautifully bound five-volume set of Goethe's poetry, inscribed to "the valued marriage-pair Carlyle." A ribbon with the Order of the Garter could not have flattered either of them more.

As these treasures from Weimar gathered, Jane proudly assembled them in her small drawing room where they could be exhibited to favored friends. The necklace, Jane vowed, should be reserved for use exclusively on state occasions: never to be worn save when great men entered her door.

"Can you tell me in confidence who wrote the article on 'The State of German Literature' in the *Edinburgh Review?*" Goethe asked by letter. "Here, people believe it was Mr. Lockhart, Sir W. Scott's son-in-law. Its earnestness and good feeling are alike admirable." He had written it himself, Carlyle modestly admitted. More flattering than conscious praise, this inquiry from Goethe!

When a new journal, the *Foreign Review*, was started in London with the express purpose of bringing to Great Britain reports of things European, its editors naturally turned to Carlyle for contributions. Soon Jane's husband was busier than ever—reading and studying with conscientious diligence for days and weeks before setting down with high-strung intensity the living words of his thirty- and forty-page articles.

Work enough to do. Yet still of the kind which yielded neither a safe living nor time for other literary effort. The immediate future looked none too promising.

Then Thomas learned that two professorships, one at newly founded London University, the other at ancient St. Andrews, were waiting to be filled. Carlyle's prominent friends rallied to his aid. John Wilson sent a testimonial. From London, Procter responded, Edward Irving—a famous man now—and others. Charles Buller, once Carlyle's pupil, now an influential young man on the threshold of a public career, was glad to assist his friend and former tutor. Even Goethe wrote, though his letter came too late to be of service.

Jane felt sure that Francis Jeffrey would be of help. But so far as concerned the London position, he did not prove to be the pillar of strength expected. As Jeffrey saw it, he had valid enough reasons for hesitancy—objections which he was ready to explain fully and frankly. Carlyle, he pointed out, was too active a rebel for the conservative new college. He was the partisan of a style of thought and writing sure to be distasteful to the patrons of the University. Nor could Thomas be expected, because of his sincerity and outspoken frankness, to cloak his enthusiasms or to modify them for the sake of expediency. Even if the authorities could be persuaded to do so, asked Jeffrey, ought they appoint such a man as their professor of literature? Jeffrey minced no words in speaking out what he believed it his duty to say. Though he had been willing, because of their manifest excellence, to publish Carlyle's articles, he saw no reason for concealing his belief that, in some particulars, Tom's preferences were dangerous to the point of viciousness.

Jeffrey liked his young protégé, and cherished the belief that such Spartan pummeling as he was now administering might be of benefit. A wise man past middle life, he had studied the world and felt himself qualified to dictate the sanest course.

Tom was nettled—it could not have been otherwise. He was proud and thin-skinned; easily disturbed by opposition. But however much he might object to the chiding, he admitted the reasonableness of Jeffrey's view. Before this, small differences had risen between them, though nothing serious. In his arguments with Jeffrey, Carlyle had sometimes answered with a frankness which the younger man realized did not quite beseem the differences in their ages or their respective places in the world.

So Jeffrey failed him in the London venture. But his hearty recommendation to St. Andrews, where a somewhat different set of factors existed, was everything that even Jane could wish to have said in favor of her husband.

The witnesses had spoken, but to little purpose. Only dull nobodies, Jane consoled herself, gained such positions. Certification from the Angel Gabriel himself could not have helped.

Her husband insisted that he had not expected success for his applications. The Devil take them. It did not matter. They could live at Craigenputtock quite independent of all persons whatsoever, with neither fear of debt nor need of asking favor. Their health would benefit by the change. Jane's headaches, he assured her, would be fewer away from the reek of the city. Ironic enough that the world should thus withhold employment, but a fact which needed bravely to be faced. Nothing to do but to trust to literature for support, and on the moors, with expenses cut in half, some more ambitious writing could once again be attempted—some book so powerful and outspoken that it would compel the attention of mankind. Jane had always wished him to win freedom as an author; never to enslave himself to mere gaining of bread.

The reluctance of their friends in Edinburgh to have them go somewhat delayed their departure. "Do not run away to Dumfriesshire" pleaded Jeffrey, "you can be as quiet here as there, when the reading or studious fit is on you, and you surely may divert yourself as well, and certainly give more pleasure, when you can condescend to be social." Perhaps his objections, he admitted, were somewhat selfish. Yet they represented his best judgment. Did not Jane agree with him?

But as their plans hung fire, they lost their lease on the house at Comely Bank. There was nothing for it save to move. Unfortunately the alterations at Craigenputtock were not yet finished. They would have to make the best of things as they were. That May, in the year 1828, they would take possession of their new dominions.

Shortly before departure, Jane and Thomas received a call

from their old friend Edward Irving, married now and with a house of his own in London.

The changes wrought in him by his career as a sensational preacher were painful to witness. Was the carefree, natural Edward lost forever? He had come from England to speak in Scotland and to be fêted by his Edinburgh admirers. The crowds that thronged to hear his fervid oratory, Jane knew, contained many earnest disciples. Yet what an emotional, vapid, perilous throng they were: inflammable as dry tinder and ready to kindle into wild conflagration! The Carlyles were not in ignorance of the fact that he had enemies as well. These fell within two classifications: unbalanced men, on the one hand, who were far more radical than he; on the other, the stern conservers of the orthodoxy of Scotland's unyielding Kirk. His championship of heresies and of startling doctrines, both Jane and Thomas felt, was in some measure a deliberate bid for notoriety, though his aim—to bring the people to God's word—could hardly be censured. When his pronounced religious mannerisms had first appeared, their staginess eclipsing his genuine piety, Jane, recalling her old feeling toward him and remembering what he once had been, had done her best to curb his pose.

As he talked with her, the troubled look in his face was proof enough of his puzzlement and inner confusion. Might it not be possible to save him from the excesses which threatened to brand him as a charlatan in the eyes of sober people who did not really know him? Yet even as he left them, he melodramatically insisted on praying over Tom and Jane, ignoring the protests which sprang from their sense of the unreality and forced sanctimoniousness of the act. He was on his way to a public dinner in his honor. Yet he spoke as though he were journeying to his crucifixion.

"Farewell! I must go, then,—and suffer persecution, as my fathers have done!"

Indeed, if he persisted in his course, it might come to that.

Late in May, six carts rolled up the street and halted at the door. The sack of Comely Bank was ready to begin. In Jane's first move, from Haddington to Edinburgh, her mother had been on hand to assist, and the drays had only seventeen miles to go. Now she must send her goods to a remote dwelling in

the moors on the other side of Scotland. She dared not count
very heavily on Carlyle's aid. Wiser not to entrust him with
details of the flitting. She would manage alone.

So Jane passed her wares once more in review, on this
journey to the next phase of her life: her fine upholstered chairs,
her tables and her spacious bureaus. The dainty little high stool
which she had used as a child was carefully nestled into place.
Carlyle felt a sentimental attachment for it which quite surprised her. Before their marriage he had noticed it tucked away
in a hidden nook, and it was largely through his wish that the
chair had gone to Comely Bank at once, rather than modestly
hiding till needed for active use. Perhaps that time would come
at Craigenputtock.

Jane's furniture was solid, heavy stuff, set in its ways and
wedded to inertia. But when young Mrs. Carlyle was bent on
action, no obstacles could check her—men scurried to do her bidding and wonders were wrought at her behest. She could both
raise and give direction to the whirlwind. Her husband, sore
pressed in the confusion, gladly resigned to Jane the high command.

Two days after the carriers' wagons had rolled westward on
the road toward Dumfries, over the height of land to Peebles
and through Moffat, Jane and Thomas followed by coach. The
flight to the wilderness was drawing toward its destination.

Chapter Seven

*M*ASONS and joiners and hewers and plasterers—they still infested Craigenputtock. They were tracking indoors and out, thumping and raising the dust, swashing and swattering wet compounds of mortar, and daubing on their paints. Little chance of any speedy abatement, Jane realized, taking stock of progress so far made. She and her husband must resign themselves to a summer of confusion in the house. But finally the work would be done. That realization made the present upheaval tolerable. Meanwhile the surprising novelty of her situation and its demands on her ingenuity helped to keep Jane amused and cheerful. The first few difficult hours were over; she told herself she could once more look hopefully on the future. From Comely Bank, with the town of Edinburgh just a short walk away, to Craigenputtock with its endless moors and stormy sea of hills—surely a most amazing change. She could survive it, she declared with a laugh. Craigenputtock was no such frightful spot after all.

Great alterations had been made since her husband first set in motion the building operations which were to fit the place for use of its Laird and Leddy. In its impressive setting on the uplands, the house had become a new accent in the landscape. Its solidly built walls of stone had doubled in height to include a second story, converting the old farm cottage into an oblong manor big enough to suit the Carlyles' modest needs. The extra cottage for the land tenant was still in process of construction. Meanwhile they could manage well enough all huddled together—she and her husband and his brother Alick, with Mary, the sister who had been keeping house there during the year of Alick's occupancy as farmer.

Before autumn set in, Alick and his sister had moved to their own house, and Jane and Thomas were left to themselves. The two establishments kept mostly to their separate routine, the only formal bond between them lay in drinking tea together every Sunday night.

Jane and Thomas had no intention of becoming active farmers. The farm was Alick's care, and they left him to direct his own battles. But Jeannie had quite enough to do without concerning herself with Alick's problems. The solitude, she discovered, was not so irksome as one might expect. She could agree with her husband that though they were for the most part cut off from good society, they were also delivered from bad. Rough pathways that led nowhere over the spongy moors or vanished among the hummocks of the craig might not furnish as pleasant strolling for a woman as the pavements of Princes Street, but Jane now had a horse and was developing into a bold and tireless equestrian. Harry was her pony's name, and Tom's mount was Larry. Since Templand lay only eighteen miles away, it was an easy ride when Jane wished to visit her mother, and Mrs. Welsh, in turn, could make the trip by carriage to Craigenputtock.

Really, it was astonishing! She had never felt more contented with life. She and her husband enjoyed such liberty and peace on these eight hundred acres of their own among the long and rolling slopes.

Her brother-in-law's farming was still a curious ritual to Jane. How many cows, exactly, did Alick keep? They persisted so in moving about when she tried to count them that she was never sure of their number. Her interest in cows, thus far, was purely academic. She had not yet discovered their potentialities to the highest degree. Poultry was somewhat different—less mysterious and not the least terrifying. Even its housing seemed to furnish no problems. When prepared to rear its broods, it took to the woods. A hen with eleven eggs was nesting in a sylvan bower, and a duck had retreated to the grove to hatch a dozen ducklings.

Since all supplies must be brought by cart or saddle-back from Dumfries, sixteen miles to the southeast, there could be no daily shopping in Jane's routine. When she did not feel like reading, she concerned herself to a greater degree than at Edinburgh with the actual management of the house. Servants, she had feared, might be difficult to lure into this wilderness. In the beginning, however, luck was with her. Her first Craigenputtock maid was Grace Macdonald, careful, tidy, and honest. Grace enjoyed the luxury of a sharp temper, but this was a characteristic which Jane's diplomacy mastered. Far worse than any fit of bad humor was the accident which had befallen Grace almost at the outset of her stay in Craigenputtock. Just when things were confused enough anyway, Grace broke her arm. During her maid's incapacity, Jane took on her own shoulders most of the work.

Country living exacted a heavy toll on clothes. There was plenty of mending to attend to. With no shops conveniently at hand, it was easier to make some of the garments her husband required. Jane attempted with fair success even the manufacture of nightshirts.

Most important, of course, once Alick had been moved into his own demesne, was the final disposition of Jane's goods and furniture. Certain materials were ordered from Glasgow. Jane wanted chintz, which also suited Carlyle's taste, but she suppressed their preferences and contented herself with moreen because of its cheapness and durability. Sanquhar, not far off in the valley of the Nith, was a town where good carpets were to be bought cheap, so Jane ordered a new one to brighten the drawing room. Here, with her fine upholstered chairs and the rest of the living-room furniture from Comely Bank, stood her piano, looking very sophisticated against the spick and span wallpaper. The drawing room was to the right of the hall which ran from front to back of the house where the curving staircase led to the new upper story with its four bedrooms. The dining room, converted from an old kitchen, stood to the left of the entrance. Behind it lay the ample kitchen. Carlyle's workroom was on the opposite side of the house to the rear of the drawing room. The space it occupied had formerly served as Alick's bedroom and sitting room, now at last released to Thomas for the manufacture of literature. Tom had rued the loss of time and lack of accomplishment which marked the period of their first moving in. A whole cartload of books, and of French, German, American, and English reviews and journals, had traveled with him from Comely Bank. These had for months been cluttering up the house. Impossible to write in such a mess. But now, with his volumes arranged about him, his tables and desks set up, and all his gear in order, he was once more prepared for steady work. Would circumstance permit the writing of a book?

Since the departure from Edinburgh, frequent letters had passed between Jeffrey and the Carlyles. Those to Jane were affectionate, unstudied, and confidential—notes coming from a busy, often weary man who wrote for the relief and pleasure which this intimate, delicately poised friendship gave him. A strange compound, some of them, for the recipient to ponder over: letters such as a father might write who had noticed that his daughter, whom he had always thought of as a child, had grown suddenly into a woman. But there was this difference, a difference which contributed its subtle accent. Jane was not Jeffrey's daughter; she was the wife of that puzzling young discovery of his, Thomas Carlyle.

The nature of his letters to Carlyle was undergoing a change. The time had come, Jeffrey had decided, when guidance was absolutely necessary if anything useful was to be made of this uncontrolled genius—direction even to the point of curbing his protégé's too wilful independence and forcing conformity to the recognized standards of literature which Jeffrey never doubted must control the pens of even the most brilliant and original writers. This article on Burns, for instance, which Carlyle had posted to him! It was not a review; it was a prodigious essay sixty pages long which no editor in his right mind would dare to publish. *Edinburgh* subscribers liked articles which were pithy and clear, or at worst harmlessly Johnsonian. But here was section after section of mystical jargon, of palpable exaggeration, and, Jeffrey was convinced, of downright wrongheadedness which sane readers could never excuse. What was the matter with the man? Was he suffering from an unlucky ambition to appear as an eccentric and original, a self-conscious rebel desperately resolved to shock the world? Jeffrey could not persuade himself that what he was criticizing came direct from the fundamental nature of his contributor. This affectation must be cured at all costs. So Jeffrey wrote a preceptorial letter which was not sparing in its criticism. He had resolved to shear away these mannerisms which, to his mind, did not really belong to Carlyle at all.

Of course his thrusts fell like a sharp sword upon the heart of the man they were supposed to cure. Jane could have told Jeffrey that he was wrong in seeking to bend her husband away from his natural self. Yet Jeffrey was a great editor and critic. He might be supposed to know what he was about. A real dilemma, which time must finally resolve. But her faith in her husband's beliefs and in the genius of his writing remained unshaken.

Jeffrey had promised to see them at Craigenputtock. Jane feared that he might arrive before her house was ready to receive him. But summer changed to autumn, and a flock of other visitors, after the social doldrums of the summer, accustomed Jane to the resources of her household. Her uncle Robert Welsh, an Edinburgh lawyer, who enjoyed the grouse shooting at Craigenputtock and found it very convenient to have the place there open again, under a niece's efficient management, stayed awhile with his dogs and guns. Friends from the group at Comely Bank came also.

In spite of all precautions, however, the long anticipated visit took Jane almost by surprise. Letters came tardily to Craigenputtock. When Jeffrey wrote that he and his family would arrive on the seventh of October, Jane received the news barely in time to order her provisions.

To watch Jeffrey's big carriage, after its long climb from the valley, roll swinging and rocking through the grove of trees which marked the approach to the house was a sight indeed. Even country wagons found the ascent difficult. Other guests had come on horseback or in light gigs. This fine coach looked like a tempest-blown Spanish galleon perilously coasting the high-cliffed, rock-encumbered shores of the Outer Hebrides. Within the very sight of port, the equipage foundered ignominiously in the sea of mud which was supposed to be the new road to the door but now, after the seepage of autumn rains, far more resembled a pond. So the passengers had to alight and make their way ashore on foot—Mrs. Jeffrey, her daughter Charlotte, the servant who traveled with them, and Jeffrey himself picking his way daintily over the sodden ground. In these uplands, October could turn a dour face to strangers.

Inside all was hospitality and warmth. The living room, the

dining room, and Carlyle's study each had its fireplace. While intermittent storms lashed the house during most of the visit, the hearths were kept blazing.

The Jeffreys knew how to adapt themselves to any setting and were soon at home—even to the lapdog, Fanny, who accompanied them on all their journeys. Francis Jeffrey needed no entertaining to keep him amused. A superlative conversationalist with a gift for talk of all dimensions—large or small—he was a one-man debating society. Jane did not believe his voice was silent during the entire visit. Even her husband, except when something Jeffrey said provoked his argumentative mood, gave way before this easy eloquence. Never had Jane assisted at such a talking, either in respect of quantity or quality. It began as soon as the carriage, under a cover of glazed sheeting, was tucked away in the back court of the house—no sheltering stable or outbuildings had as yet been finished to accommodate so resplendent a vehicle. Through tea Jeffrey rattled on, multiplying anecdote on anecdote as one suggested the next in endless, never wearisome succession. A clever man who talks to please himself rarely fails to please others. As the winds beat against the stout walls which checked for a second their mad rush over the granite ribs of Scotland, Jeffrey's tongue played busily through the mounting hours of the night till Jane, Mrs. Jeffrey, and Charlotte at last went to bed, aware that the men wished to discuss the essay on Burns which was still hanging in suspension between Jeffrey's ideas of what a review should be and Carlyle's determination to write only in accordance with his convictions.

Jeffrey had the proof sheets with him, cut and slashed with a severity that exceeded even the usual prunings which he believed himself privileged to indulge in as guardian of the *Review*. This editorial tyranny was already in Carlyle's eyes a too familiar usurpation of an author's rights. His earlier articles for Jeffrey had suffered mutilation. Even at the cost of appearing unduly willful, he was determined to save Burns. He dreaded to read the corrected proofs.

Before handing over the sheets, Jeffrey scolded him for what he insisted were his dangerously speculative whimsies and his emphasis of opinions which sensible persons could never be expected to accept. So earnest did he become, in contrast to his usual joking manner, that his eagerness to shape Carlyle into something he believed would be far more profitable betrayed Jeffrey even into a burst of irritability. The little editor regretted the strain thus put on the friendship. But perhaps the incident might persuade Carlyle how seriously he meant the advice.

When Thomas came to read the proof, prudently set aside till after the Jeffreys had departed, he was shocked by the liberties taken. This was no article at all! It resembled nothing sanely real under the sun. Jeffrey's effort to shorten it had produced fantastic results without any regard for sense.

Carlyle wrote only after the most intensive study and with a scrupulous care that made composition a weary effort. Editorial hacking and hewing, removing in a few moments what had taken hours and days to set on paper, were serious irritations. Against what appeared to him as high-handed dictatorialness he was ready to rebel, though not, he hoped, against reasonable and intelligent correction. This thing was like a man cut into bits to make him fit a doll's house—his thighs removed, his hips joined to his knees!

During their evening of talk, Carlyle luckily had not realized the full extent of Jeffrey's butchery. When the next morning brought the group together again, discussion of shop was fortunately dropped.

While the rain paused, Carlyle and his guests walked abroad to see the landscape, tumultuous but beautiful under threatening clouds. Then came dinner, a feast appreciated to its least detail by Jeffrey, who was a connoisseur in such matters as well as in the other amenities of life. Surely Jane could be proud of her cook!

The twinkle in her eye caught his notice. He looked at her incredulously. What! Had she really made these cakes herself? Was it possible that she could twirl them over in a frying pan, and catch them in the air? He gravely acknowledged his admiration of such skill, but this discovery of the efforts Jane was putting herself to for the sake of her visitors came as something of a shock. Was there not danger that she might become a drudge? That would never do! Jane, he realized, managed her house with such quiet art that one was lulled into a belief its smooth and easy ways were a mere phenomenon of nature.

A gentleman neighbor of the Carlyles', James Anderson

(most of the thin-spread populace, of course, were farmers), dropped in during one evening of the visit. Perhaps the circumstances of this gathering on the moorlands were responsible— black night and infinite silence without, and within, warmth and brightness and good company. Whatever the cause, the next few hours became electric with good fellowship. Somehow the conversation turned to the subject of oratory. In his long and active life as a public man, Jeffrey had been the victim of much speech-making. Year in and year out he had listened to the candidates—those in office and those who wished to be—make their promises and deliver their pronouncements. How badly most of them plied the art, bringing to it nothing but boredom! Jeffrey's powers of mockery lent him a devastating weapon with which to revenge himself for hours wasted by the orators. Here, in this little group of admiring friends, he was quite ready to employ his skill. To exhibit the failings of the mediocre performer, Jeffrey divided all politicians into classes and gave for each a swiftly extemporized example—the windily grandiloquent spell-weaver, the stupid, heavy-worded plodder, the airy, lightly skimming talker whose erratic flights generally ended broken-winged.

Tom and Jane had scarcely realized how extraordinary were Jeffrey's gifts as an actor. He had missed his calling; he should have gone on the stage! Never before had they seen him so entertaining. The grand climax was his imitation of a heavy orator breaking down in the midst of an impassioned speech, goggle-eyed and mute. To see Jeffrey, who never for a moment was at a loss for words, opening and closing his mouth in seeming helplessness, his bright eyes staring with a bull-like glare at the empty wall as though searching there for the one word to save him, was the essence of incongruity. Then suddenly he broke the spell, returning to the company in his own guise like Ariel after assuming strange shapes at Prospero's bidding.

Jeffrey was no great equestrian. He preferred to walk his horse sedately, whereas Carlyle's notion of enjoyment was to ride at full gallop over the roughest roads of that rough country. But they managed one excursion together to see the further reaches of the district, while Jane stayed at home with Jeffrey's wife and daughter. Carlyle took his guest for a glimpse of Loch

Urr, which lay some distance below them, not visible from the house because of the intervening mass of the craig. After the rain, the hillsides streamed in countless rills, swelling to proportions of a torrent the dark flow of Urr Water, the burn which threaded its twisting, difficult track to the Solway Firth.

The visit was over almost as soon as begun, so quickly did its three days pass. A lively, cheerful reunion; hosts and guests were loath to bid farewell. The Carlyles must visit them at Edinburgh soon, urged Jeffrey; a welcome was always ready for them.

After his return to Edinburgh, Jeffrey renewed his steady correspondence with the inmates of Craigenputtock. Winter would soon shut them in. How would they fare in their upland solitudes? The handling of Carlyle as a contributor to the *Review* was a good deal of a problem. The article on Burns had come back with most of the omissions restored. If Jeffrey could not accept it as originally conceived, wrote its author, perhaps it would be best to withdraw it entirely from publication. Jeffrey, however, did not wish that to be done. It had a brilliance he did not care to lose. So he finally admitted the essay in the form and style insisted on by its author. Few contributors could thus have defied his editorial commands. But Jeffrey's chief concern did not spring from his interest in Thomas as a writer; it rose from his solicitude for the Carlyles as human beings. Even after the visit to Craigenputtock, where most indications gave assurance of well-being, he was not at ease about his friends. He could not persuade himself that they were well placed in their remote home, sure during much of the winter to be cut off from any contacts which might even by courtesy be described as social. There was scant wisdom, as Jeffrey understood it, in this deliberate isolation. He had advised Carlyle about his articles. He felt justified, too, in admonishing him about his management of a wife. He knew better than to give counsel too openly. Experience had taught him how sensitive Jane's husband could be. His letter of advice, when it was finished, was a model of diplomacy. It began by sympathizing with Carlyle's reasons for seeking Craigenputtock. But perhaps the day would come, the writer added, when such withdrawal would no longer appear necessary. That time, he hoped, would soon arrive. Meanwhile, Carlyle was to think seriously of taking refuge in Edinburgh during the worst few months of the winter. The Jeffrey house in Moray Street stood ready to receive him and his wife whenever they might choose to avail themselves of the offer. "Take care of the fair creature who has trusted herself so entirely to you. Do not let her ride about in the wet, nor expose herself to the wintry winds that will by-and-by visit your lofty retreat." Jeffrey had counsel also for her emotional well-being: "Be gay and playful and foolish with her at least as often as you require her to be wise and heroic with you." He would give Carlyle his own philosophy of life, then let him make of it what he would. "You have no mission upon earth, whatever you may fancy, half so important as to be innocently happy—and all that is good for you of poetic feeling and sympathy with majestic nature will come of its own accord without your straining after it. This is my creed, and right or wrong I am sure it is both a simpler and a *humbler* one than yours."

Jeffrey was troubled by the thought of what extreme poverty might do to Carlyle's wife. The danger threatened as long as Carlyle forfeited advancement through his unwillingness to heed the standards of the world. Protracted isolation from men had its perils, also, and bred misanthropy and cynicism. For his wife's sake, as well as for his own, Thomas should be on his guard. Jane's great heart, warned Jeffrey, and willing martyr- dom, would in the end make the sacrifice all the more agonizing to Carlyle himself.

But Jane refused to worry about her position. When the little influx of guests that came with the autumn had ceased—among them Tom's lively sister Jean, always a favorite with her, and James, Carlyle's father, released after harvest from the sum- mer's pressure of work on his farm at Scotsbrig, near Eccle- fechan, less than twenty miles south on the coach road from Dumfries—she and her husband could enjoy the more each other's company. He was her best companion. When she had him by her side, she wished for no other happiness.

Together, in the long evenings, they deciphered the story of Don Quixote, working out the Spanish of Cervantes and learn- ing the language as if the enterprise were a game. If the day itself were gobbled up under the necessity of finishing some articles for the *Foreign Quarterly*, the early mornings before work, and the evenings as well, were for them to share. Country breakfasts, Jane found, contributed a real blessing to life—they became at Craigenputtock a major event of the day. Even with temperamental chickens that laid fitfully, there were eggs enough and to spare. Jane, wishing to build up her husband, experimented with such concoctions as tea with an egg whipped up in it. Home-baked bread far surpassed that which they used to buy in Edinburgh. And porridge was ever a staple.

Carlyle, fresh and rested in the morning—both he and Jeannie were sleeping better in the pure, fine air which streamed so invigoratingly across the ridges—thoroughly enjoyed a chat with his wife before his day began. It made little difference what the subject might be—some transcendental matter, perhaps, spun from abstruse fancy, or the equally vital question of just why hens were so secretive in laying their eggs, yet, once they had laid them, announced the deed to all the world. Jane liked to prolong as far as possible these *matin causeries*. When Tom, the breakfast over, went to the washroom to lather his face for shaving, she would follow after and perch on a chair behind his back, pressing her advantage to talk while he manipulated his long-bladed razor. He could see her eager, animated face in the glass beside his own, the dual image like a picture of Harlequin and Columbine.

The approach of winter curtailed her hours out of doors, and there were times, while her husband was preoccupied with work, when her resources, and even the many tasks to be performed, were not adequate to dispel the boredom which crept over her. In such emergencies, of course, she could always correspond with friends. One had to sow letters in order to reap them, and Jane found an increasing pleasure in their composition. She dashed them off rapidly, not stopping to correct dubious spellings. She wrote as she talked, nimbly skipping from one event of her day to the next, putting into each description so much of her own liveliness and vivacity that the whole account sparkled like sunlight shining on what might otherwise appear a dull enough ditch of water.

To get at Craigenputtock a letter from Edinburgh was an event. Jeffrey wrote delightfully. And she was always glad to find a note from Bess Stodart, since early girlhood her friend and confidante. How strange to receive at this outlandish spot letters from Weimar addressed to her husband in Goethe's fine script! Goethe was very curious too. "Which and where is the awfully cacophonous place where you have taken up your residence?" inquired Charles Buller.

There was plenty of time to get up one's expectation for letters. Once a week, once only, did the post find its way to Craigenputtock. That joyous moment came on Wednesday, the weekly market day at Dumfries. In pleasant weather, Jane often made the trip herself, riding the thirty-two miles to town and back. But in winter it was more prudent to send the man-of-all-work on this mission. In addition to the servant in the kitchen, Tom and Jane found it necessary to employ a general factotum to do the chores about the place. They were a migratory lot, these farm boys. They came and went so often (board and keep, with wages at a sovereign for every quarter year, offered slim inducement for a lengthy stay) that it was sometimes difficult to remember their names: William; Elliot; Canny Bretton, once herdsboy for Tom's father; brisk young McWhir—such was the partial roster. They blended under the leveling process of their daily functions, which varied mainly with the seasons of the year. Whatever fell outside Alick's province as farmer but needed a man's attention was for them to perform. So they trimmed the saddle horses, and carted coals, and yoked the gig when the Carlyles owned one. Indoors, they scoured knives, and on great occasions, such as that of the Jeffreys' visit, were even pressed into service to wait on table. But Wednesday, with the trip to town, was their gala day. As night drew on, a rising excitement would animate the stay-at-homes. Then from the frozen soil would echo the clip-clop of a pony's hooves. Out would stream the household, into the chill air, to greet the messenger returning from civilization. Papers and groceries, letters and supplies—down from the saddlebags on to the table would pour the strangely assorted mass, a weekly haul of trash and treasure which sometimes carried with it great surprises. Breath-taking to think what seven days might bring forth in the world outside, while on the hills each unit of four and twenty-hours looked much like that which came before.

Post day did not confine its excitement to Tom and Jeannie

alone. Sometimes Alick got a letter, or the sister who was keeping house for him. Even Grace Macdonald, the doughty, red-armed serving girl, was honored on rare occasions.

This trek to town, because of the sociabilities of market days, sometimes found McWhir, or William, or Elliot, or whoever it might be, not ready to leave till night had made the way back impossible. When that happened, the residents of the Craig were forced to bear with their impatience till Thursday morning, when daylight brought the truant home again after an interlude of relaxation in Dumfries patterned on the lively model made famous in that town by Robert Burns. On one such Thursday morning the boy returned just at breakfast, with a letter even for the kitchen. The aroma of brewing tea filled the room while Jeannie and Tom inspected their share of correspondence—a note from Henry Inglis, the friend who had been their most recent visitor, a letter from New York in distant America which seemed promising enough till a glance at its contents showed that it had been delivered to the wrong Thomas Carlyle, being intended for an advocate in Edinburgh whose identical name had caused much confusion in the city. It was exasperating to have this *alter ego* pop up even in the wilderness. While Tom, in some disappointment, was folding up the changeling and the pleasant smell of toast mingling with the scent of tea was growing stronger in the room, a sudden crash echoed from the kitchen. Jane sprang from her chair to investigate. There stood Grace, her letter open in her hand, Jane's precious brown earthenware jug in fragments on the ground, over which flowed an ocean of tea. While Jane scurried about to prepare another potful, she made vain efforts to learn the contents of the fatal missive. But Grace, though dazed, was crafty in the extreme—a sweetheart, evidently a Highland soldier, was to blame, but whether as a deserter in love, or as too bold a suitor, Jane never could find out.

Broken hearts and jugs might not be mended, but a second breakfast was soon ready, and the day slipped quietly back into the groove of its routine.

Only once, at Craigenputtock, was a breakfast truly ruined. A small mouse, in some inexplicable fashion, had found its way into the mess of porridge. As luck would have it, Carlyle's dish received the interloper, parboiled for his sins. Tom, nor could he exactly be blamed, exploded when he found the horror. Not even his wife's tearful face could at once arrest his anger.

Whether or not her troubles dated from the crash of the earthen pot, Grace Macdonald, who stood high in Jane's opinion as an excellent servant, was presently forced because of ill health to leave the Carlyles' employment. From that time on, servants became a really serious problem. Trained ones would not stay in the moorlands, and those whom Jane had to break in herself were as bad a trial during the period of their training as having no servants at all. As with the men-of-all-work, an erratic migration of them, with longer or shorter stays, took place through Jane's kitchen. Some were so manifestly inefficient that Jane had to discard them. Others would or could not adapt themselves. A few were quaint or eccentric enough to afford amusement in spite of their exasperating behavior. Two had developed a taste for literature, and Jeannie found them scrubbing the floor with one hand while in the other they held an open copy of Carlyle's translation of *Wilhelm Meister*. Tom's pious mother had found Goethe's novel somewhat distasteful to her because of what she termed the licentiousness of the women in it. Perhaps the servants had discovered that quality, too.

Then there was Nancy, a blithe, fond, coarse little stump of a body. She also took liberties with property not rightful for her use. She had found that the master's razors were most helpful in dealing with a beard of her own, and as her secret employment of them was far from skillful, she spoiled the edges, greatly to Carlyle's mystification.

During intervals between servants, Jane herself took over entire management. These crises, fortunately, were somewhat rare. When they came, Jane did her best to manage the work smoothly so as not to disturb her husband in his routine. If a sister-in-law, her favorite Jean, for instance, could be got over to help, the problem was greatly simplified. At Edinburgh, where she had started to learn the art, housework had been mere play. Here it was a grim necessity. But she tried to face these emergencies bravely. One's attitude, she told herself, made all the difference between drudgery and something that could be tolerably borne.

By the time Jane had learned her lesson, she was as expert

as the women of Carlyle's own family who had cooked and kept house all their lives. Yet she never let herself get swamped— she kept inviolate her time for leisure, so that her husband could hardly guess how busy she had been while he was at his writing.

She had tested her theory that work was art with the baking of her first loaf of bread in the formidable stone oven of ancient manufacture that had served generations bearing her name. A mysterious process, surely! No alchemist could perform a greater wonder. She faced her array of supplies and implements with something almost akin to awe. From these ingredients, if the fates did not prohibit, would emerge a mound of bread. She had watched skillful practitioners go through this rite. Now, the cook book open before her, she herself would try the miracle. Carefully she mixed the dough and left it to rise. The oven was made ready. As she slipped the pan through the door, shielding her face from the heat, she told herself that she was like a sculptor casting a statue in bronze.

It was late when Jane sat down to bide results, the house silent as the night without. In his study, Carlyle read by the fire, his candle burning lower as he turned the pages of his book. Not till after eleven o'clock was the loaf ready. First attempts are generally slow, and in making bread or molding statues there is always a sore temptation to peep into the fiery furnace. When Jeannie at last drew the loaf from the oven, she was dismayed to find one part of the crust a little scorched. But a second glance reassured her. Save for this small blemish, it was a thing of beauty—golden and bright and sweet. She ran with it in triumph to Carlyle.

"See!" she cried, holding it out. Was she not like Benvenuto Cellini? She spoke with a quizzical gaiety, but seriously, too. They had been reading *Cellini's Autobiography* together. As he watched his Perseus emerge from the cast, had he not felt as she did now? Carlyle, looking into his wife's face, could well believe so.

Chapter Eight

*T*HE first winter at Craigenputtock passed without justifying the dire predictions of Francis Jeffrey. The illnesses which he had ominously foretold did not develop. Indeed Jane's health, in spite of sleet and cold winds that rushed across the uplands, was better than at Edinburgh. Tom, because concentration on his writing tautened his nerves and made him live and think too acutely, suffered as usual from dyspepsia, but he had made up his mind to be stoical in enduring the evil and his general well-being enabled him with fair success to keep to his resolve.

Before the snows made transportation difficult, Jeannie had obtained through her friend Bess Stodart those supplies which could be had more readily from Edinburgh than from Dumfries. The broken tea pot had been replaced. Six pounds of tea, enough for many steaming gallons, were ordered. A small mountain of sugar had been bought—two mountains in fact, one of coarse, the other of refined. Jane dreaded lest rains might soak the carrier's wagon which plied between Edinburgh and Dumfries just on the particular journey when it bore her load of goods. Suppose her sweets were to be melted into a useless mess? But fortunately no such accident occurred. Rice in quantity was also purchased, and other staples. And as of equal necessity for the household, Jane sent for writing paper, a quantity of pens, and two sticks of red sealing wax.

There would be sufficient cash, this winter, to pay for all these things. Her husband had a gratifying list of articles to write for the reviews. True, improvements at Craigenputtock had raised the year's expenses and Tom was in large part financing the trip to Germany which his brother John was taking to complete his training in medicine. He had paid for much of John's earlier study as well. But in spite of these burdens, expenses fell well below the level of Edinburgh. A comforting thought to persons dependent on literature for support. Might it not be helpful to other writers, and pleasant for themselves, if a small colony of kindred-minded persons could be persuaded to come live beside them on the Craig? Jane and her husband discussed this ephemeral notion as a mere fancy with which to amuse themselves, but the more they developed it, the more plausible the idea became till they were ready to take it seriously. Wordsworth had his group in the Cumberland hills. Why not found their own in these unmolested quietudes? At Windermere and Rydal Water swarms of tourists in search of the picturesque crowded annually on the privacy of the residents. The main highway skirted Rydal Mount, bringing in traffic from outside and loosing the raucous breath of coach horns over the landscape. Here, though Dumfries was close at hand to keep them in touch with the world and coaches ran daily southward to the border or north to Edinburgh, there was solitude almost Druidical. If one needed silence, here truly it could be found. Instead of post horses, Arcturus and Orion— all the heavenly concourse of the stars—were the sole movers, pursuing their eternal way across the heavens. The place was ideal for such a project. With select company, the threat of loneliness would vanish.

As they chatted about the scheme, Tom grew so eloquent that his wife, whose enthusiasms were among her choicest pleasures, was ready to persuade herself that this plan was to become reality. Word had reached them that De Quincey was in need of rescue in Edinburgh. Poverty and opium, as ever, were hounds upon his track. Why not invite him to Craigenputtock? Jane was eager to nurse him back to health. So, under her eye, Tom composed a letter of invitation. De Quincey's pride demanded an excuse for offering help. This was achieved by turning the favor they were hoping to confer into a plea for his society. Jane and he, wrote Tom, thought often of the old association in Edinburgh. Moreover Jane, through a mutual friend, had learned that De Quincey, inquiring after her, had dropped the hint that he would accept an invitation to visit. "I am to say, therefore, that your presence at this fireside will diffuse no ordinary gladness over all the members of the household." Their warmest welcome was ready for him.

Tom mentioned his and Jane's day-dream of a colony.

"Would *you* come hither and be king over us; *then* indeed we had made a fair beginning, and the 'Bog School' might snap its fingers at the 'Lake School' itself, and hope to be one day recognized of all men." The house, he explained, was amply supplied with books and periodicals, and there could be no better place for conversation. A thousand things were in the air to talk about. What of De Quincey's doings, sufferings, and pleasures? Would he not come himself to satisfy their inquiries? "Believe it, you are well loved here, and none feels better than I what a spirit is for the present eclipsed in clouds. For the present it can only be; time and chance are for all men; that troublous season will end; and one day with more joyful, not deeper or truer regard, I shall see you 'yourself again'."

Henry Inglis, at Craigenputtock on a second visit from Edinburgh, was entrusted with the letter. But alas for the kind intentions of the Carlyles, he was not able to find De Quincey. Probably at his opium again, Thomas explained; he was rarely visible during these lapses. The bog school would have to continue as it had begun—a plaything of the imagination.

Over the holidays, while the year 1828 slipped into 1829, Jane went to Templand, alone, to spend the Christmas season with her family. Though he told her how very weary for her he would be, her husband, Jane believed, would not find the time heavy on his hands. She took comfort in the thought of how much he would accomplish while she was away. When he was steadily at work, he labored under a great impulsion, throwing his every energy into the effort.

It was pleasant to be in Templand. When her mother was in a good mood, full of affectionate kindness and not variable as a weather vane, Jane enjoyed companionship with her. Mrs. Welsh brought to bear all her persuasiveness to make her daughter prolong her stay another week. Every arrangement had been made at home for meeting her, Jane protested. Never mind, her mother answered, the plans could be countermanded. She would be absent from her husband on New Year's Day, Jane pleaded. Since marriage, no such thing had ever happened. Jane was superstitious about the beginning of the year. If the first person who came to her on that particular morning was dear to her, good luck was sure to follow. She and her husband must be each other's "first foot." But even this obsession her mother argued away. So she lingered another week.

It was the Carlyles' longest absence from each other. To be a truant from housework had its charms, no denying that. But suppose Craigenputtock were running short of provender? Suppose her husband was not getting the sort of food that was best for his health? A young wife's apprehensions have a knack for multiplication. She had ordered chicken broth for Thomas. Were there cocks enough for the purpose? And would the hens continue laying at this season to keep him supplied with eggs? Worst thought of all—was he sleeping? She dreaded to think of him alone at night, awake, his brain whirling, his lean body tossing on the bed. A memory, half pitying and tender, half heartless as a child's quick laugh at recollection of some painful absurdity which had befallen a member of the family, crossed her mind. She could see her husband in his nightshirt, with a candle to guide him in the blackness, wandering on and on through the empty rooms at Craigenputtock, smoking the cigar or pipe to which he always turned for comfort. In his other hand, ready for action, he would be carrying a stick. A mouse would rush suddenly across the floor, its tiny eyes like sparks thrown from the hearth. A quick sweep of the cane, a triumphant grunt. Many a time Jane had watched that drama during her husband's wrestlings with insomnia. "Goody, Goody, dear Goody," she wrote. "It will be so sweet to make it all up to you in kisses when I return. You will *take me* and hear all my bits of experiences, and your heart will beat when you find how I have longed to return to you." No man was his equal, she told him. "I love and admire you, like—like anything!" Appalled by her imaginative picture of his distress, she told him how much he dwelt in her thoughts. "Oh, if I was there I could put my arms so close about your neck, and hush you into the softest sleep you have had since I went away."

Yet Jane, in spite of all her tenderness, was far too vibrant a creature to brood. When company dropped in at Templand, she chatted and joked with her customary liveliness. And Tom, with his writing, his brisk walk on the dim hillside as the winter sun dipped in saffron mist behind the western ridge, his final goodnight pipe beside his brother Alick, drew assurance from the thought that he was performing daily a man's task in these solitudes. No winter had yielded fuller labor, though merely of the reviewing kind.

When Jane came back to Craigenputtock, both found that they had survived quite undamaged their little separation.

Though the Jeffreys repeated their invitations for a visit to Edinburgh, there was no time in which to make it, that winter. Tom and Jane had tested sufficiently their mode of life on the moors to know that even the worst season need not force them to leave. Carlyle was busy with the last article of the three which he had set himself to write, and interruptions were not to be thought of.

This final essay was on Voltaire. Turning from German metaphysics to the clear-headed Frenchman was like a descent from the clouds to some glacier on Mont Blanc, with nothing but solidness beneath. Yet Carlyle enjoyed the change. A shift in his thinking and his interests was taking place.

But though writing on Voltaire, he did not hold himself aloof from those who lived within the secure house of the Scottish Kirk. If they were honest men, that was all he required. He felt no urge to quarrel with personal beliefs, provided they were genuine. So, though he and Jane had stopped attending church since the early months of their married life, they were on good terms with the local minister, Dr. Bryden, and welcome at his Manse in Dunscore. No clergyman who talked with Carlyle long remained ignorant of what might vaguely and politely be referred to as his heresies. Yet few churchmen dreamed of cutting his company. Something about the man—perhaps the curious blend of mysticism with a hard-headed insistence on the dictatorship of fact—prevented an outright charge of infidelity. Furthermore, unless goaded into argument, the Christian faith was one of the few subjects Carlyle would not unguardedly talk about. Even with Edward Irving, long perhaps his closest friend, he had always been reticent, and he was sorry, when Irving, years ago, had pressed him, to be obliged to declare that he could not think as Edward did.

So it was really no incongruous experience for Jane and her husband, early in the summer that followed their initial winter at the Craig, to find themselves the only lay persons breaking bread at the Manse in Dunscore with a flock of reverends from the vicinity. The occasion of this feast was another of Irving's spectacular eruptions from London to preach his gospel in his native Scotland. His reputation as an orator who could enthrall multitudes seemed every year to grow brighter. But clouds were continuing to gather on the horizon. Those who loved the man were fearful that a storm threatened which would at last quite overwhelm him should he persist in attracting trouble by his championship of notions which could bring forth nothing but opposition from those who held rigidly to the letter of Calvin's laws. The Scottish Kirk, recognizing the power of the man, and believing in his sincerity, was not yet ready to turn from him. But here and there his enemies were making much of certain passages which they had been quick to discover in his recently published sermons. Did he not question the Godhood of Christ? Irving might insist that such views were not heretical, but how deny what stood revealed in black and white? When such attacks were leveled at him, Irving, who had scarcely the faintest notion of diplomacy, was apt to bridle in anger—opposition merely served to convince him of the essential rightness of his views. And his success with the crowds he swayed through his preaching strengthened his faith in himself and in his mission. What the world most needed, he was sure, was to win its way again to the state of religious intensity which stirred it in ancient times when the prophets foretold the coming of the Lord's judgment on mankind. Only when faith was immediate and vital—a thing of strong emotion—only then did it have significance. This conviction was so powerful in Irving as to control the entire manner of the man. He liked best to think of himself as a later brother to Isaiah and Ezekiel. This conception of his rôle was largely responsible for his archaic language, for the picturesque exaggeration of priestly clothing which he affected, for his many idiosyncracies of conduct.

Since the last, not too happy meeting with Irving, Jane and Thomas, even on their remote hillside, had been conscious of the din set up by Edward's course of action. There was no escaping it, especially in Scotland. Most of the tales that came to their ears had to do with the enormous crowds which gathered to hear him preach, whether he spoke before his own congregation in London or in towns and hamlets on either side of the border.

Every public appearance seemed one more victory on his triumphal march. In his native Annandale, especially, he had met with almost miraculous success. When he preached at Annan, thirteen thousand persons had listened to his voice. It was said, of its carrying power, that once, when he was speaking out of doors, a woman sitting in her house a quarter of a mile away had heard distinctly every word he uttered.

The day before his arrival at Dunscore, he had preached twice in Dumfries. In the morning, though he spoke for three solid hours, he held the attention of a crowd of ten thousand persons. His text, in the afternoon, had been drawn from the Book of Revelation, a source that always stimulated his powers to their highest degree. Though he preached during the span of four whole hours, the time had not seemed too long for his listeners. Seven hours of oratory in a single day, yet Irving insisted that he was not tired.

Some of his most effective sermons were extemporaneously delivered. Like many great orators, his words could sway even himself. In the grip of emotion, forsaking the written sermon, Irving would utter his most compelling, his greatest passages, though at such moments he was peculiarly exposed to the dangers of unreason and overstatement. His mighty voice—melodious, deep, and satisfying to the ear—would ring out clearly, filling earth and sky. When chance, like a divine assistance, offered its aid, he knew how to seize it. Once, in Perth, Irving was prophesying the second advent of the Lord. The church suddenly darkened under a single immense thunder-cloud. Before, the skies had been clear—no rain, no mutter of thunder. Then, in the gloom, a jagged flash leapt across the heavens. Irving's voice stopped, though powerful enough to carry even above the storm. There was a momentary silence, a tense breathing. Then, solemnly, in the shadows, the preacher spoke: "For as the lightning cometh out of the east, and shineth even into the west, so shall the coming of the Son of Man be."

Jane and Thomas were glad of the opportunity again to see Irving. Dr. Bryden had agreed to let them take him away to Craigenputtock immediately after the dinner. Among the hills, the boy in Irving once more emerged, though buried now so deep within the engrossed man who was slave to the idea that no time was his own but belonged instead to his mission and to the character in which he was determined to fulfill it. But now he forgot who he was. The Carlyles, watching him, felt that he was franker and happier than they had seen him since his first days of popularity in London, seven years before.

The mellow June weather lent its kindliest influence. Dr. John Carlyle, back from his travels on the continent, was a welcome fellow guest. Together the four sauntered in the grove near the house. Dr. John had many anecdotes to tell of Germany—its easy mode of life, its *Bierstuben,* its endless, harmless philosophizing. The exact sciences which he had gone to study at his brother's expense had made a slighter impression on him. Irving's relaxed mind, as he stretched himself out under the free sky, on the wide moorlands, was in a retrospective mood. He could not utterly resist the temptation to boast a little of the great crowds he had drawn about him on his present venture into Scotland. But mostly, he spoke of times gone by and of old scenes: Haddington, where he had brought Carlyle when they were young men seeking what fate might offer; Edinburgh of the days before Tom's marriage and his own departure for London.

They strolled over the fields, and rested, now and again, on the green knolls among the granite outcroppings, with leagues of heather-covered slopes below them, and the ridges of more distant hills bounding the wide sweep of vision. In these surroundings, in such weather, no feeling of strain could mar the immediate contentment they felt with one another. Past turbulence could not intrude.

After this visit, the Carlyles were not again to see Irving in Scotland. But they heard of him. And what they heard failed to bear out the favorable hope that had risen because of the visit. At Glasgow there had been a rude contrast to the friendly reception in Annandale and Nithsdale. The gatherings to hear his preaching were as large as ever, but hostile. During the sermon his power had checked the turbulence of the congregation. But when he left the church, the crowd, packed about the door, was ominous and threatening. Taunts were flung at Irving, and the mob refused to disperse. Glasgow was a city rigid with conservatism; it would not bend to new interpretations. "Ye're an awfu' man, Mr. Irving," shouted an objector, "they say you preach a Roman Catholic baptism and a Mohammedan heeven!"

Irving feared nothing on earth. Through his long study of the prophets he had come to live so intensely in the mood of ancient religion that the hope even of martyrdom lurked in his mind. But not before a rabble such as this! He drew himself up to his full height, removed his hat, and with a bow and a rumbled "fare ye well," he strode calmly through the very center of the crowd. As if a door had been flung wide on its hinges, the solid wall of people opened before him.

During the rest of that summer no other exciting guests dropped in on the Carlyles. Various members of Jane's family, of course, or of Tom's, found it easy to drive or ride to Craigenputtock. Sometimes they came for a brief visit, sometimes a longer stay.

Late one afternoon John and his sister Margaret had arrived. Jane liked her husband's doctor brother. He was easy-going and not ambitious, but an amusing companion and good-natured almost to a fault. His and Mag's arrival assured a lively evening for the Laird and Leddy of Craigenputtock. But when John fished out of his pocket a letter from Goethe, picked up at Dumfries, the occasion became a golden one—bright as the splendor of the sun dipping that instant below Blackcraig Hill. Tom, lounging out of doors, pipe in mouth, read the letter through, then went inside to share it with the others.

Margaret, Tom's oldest sister, was his favorite, though his love for his entire family was remarkably strong. The Carlyles were a harmonious group, knit together by natural ties and by the struggle to subsist which was a vital concern in the lives of the Scotch peasantry. Jane, through her sympathetic understanding, had made herself so completely one of their number that it was difficult to realize that she had not been brought up to their mode of living.

Margaret had been very unwell, but was better now. Jane, however, was not sure the danger was over. To her sharp eyes there were ominous signs that Mag was still a seriously ill person. Yet seldom was there a cheerfuller evening than the present one.

Goethe wrote that he had been puzzling over such maps of

Dumfriesshire as could be obtained at Weimar. He was able, he declared, to construct a fair picture of Carlyle's region. But when in fancy he visited his friends, he was loath to have his imagination roam too widely and aimlessly in space. Would not Carlyle furnish him with a sketch of his house and its surroundings?

An opportunity to gratify the wish came at last with the arrival of George Moir, an Edinburgh friend. Though an advocate by profession, he was also a fair artist. The sketch of Craigenputtock which he drew was soon on its way to Weimar.

Jane was aware that a German translation of her husband's *Life of Schiller* was soon to come from the press, under Goethe's benevolent watchfulness, at Frankfurt-am-Main. Not long after John and Mag had left, the first proof sheets had been delivered at Craigenputtock along with a box of gifts. Jane was even more pleased than Tom by these manifestations of friendship and of fame. To Carlyle, though he was gratified by Goethe's interest, his *Schiller* always brought only qualified satisfaction. What he had written so long ago now struck him as stiff and cold, like an exercise done as part of one's college training.

But when a copy of the German edition came to Craigenputtock, Jane and Thomas received a real surprise. There, prominently at the top of the title page, embellished with delicate scroll work, stood two words: "Thomas Carlyle." After the difficulties she had met with because of her husband's unwillingness to court fame, Jane rejoiced that in a foreign edition his reticence was powerless to enforce his wish to remain incognito. Below the author's name came the title of the book, and under that a brief announcement that the introduction was by Goethe. The words stood out from the page like letters painted on a looking-glass; behind, in clearest detail, lay George Moir's sketch of Craigenputtock.

Even Carlyle had to admit that this was one of the most beautiful books he had ever seen. Goethe's introduction, he told himself, would have been more fitting for a far better book, for some as yet unwritten epic. Yet the flattery of the association warmed his heart. To see himself publicly set forth as Goethe's friend was an honor he had scarcely believed possible. As for Jane, she had rarely experienced keener delight. Here and there in the banking places of the world's intellect, her husband's coinage, rightfully acknowledged, was beginning to gain currency.

To her husband's letter of thanks Jane added a postscript of her own. Along with the book for Carlyle, Goethe had sent for her an inscribed edition of his poems, and some trinkets to wear. She could almost believe that Goethe was a friend met personally. Since first his letters and gifts had come from Weimar to her husband, her own collection had been steadily growing: jewelry, sheets of German music for her to play—these and many things besides. In return, Jane had sent on request a little portrait of herself. She forwarded also a lock of her dark hair, an act which had brought from Goethe a sentimental verse and a humorous lament that though he had made search a like return was for him impossible.

"Accept my heartfelt thanks," she wrote, acknowledging the latest packet, "for this and so many other tokens of your kindness, and still think of me as your affectionate friend and faithful disciple."

A repetition of the previous year's visit from Jeffrey and his family would have been welcome to Jane, but circumstances would not permit. The summer of 1829 had been an extremely busy one for Jeffrey. Further honors, not actively sought for, were complicating his life just at the time when he was ready to think of retirement to his gardens and pleasant house at Craigcrook. Under the traditional title of Dean of the Advocates, he had been appointed head of the Scottish Bar. Additional political responsibilities were impending. It grew obvious that his continued management of the *Review* would place too heavy a burden on his shoulders. Furthermore, if he were to become a Lord Justice of Scotland, an honor which his friends agreed would be a fitting climax to his career, he must free himself of party entanglements. His connection with the *Review*, a Whig paper, should not be allowed to stand in the way. So he resigned, passing along the problems of editorship to a younger man, MacVey Napier.

Had Carlyle been more tractable, had he been able and willing to curb his radical spirit and put some check on his impulses, directing his tastes along the channels which Jeffrey felt more suitable for a potential journalist, he might just possibly have found himself in the post now occupied by the cther man. But Jeffrey, though there was something about Carlyle which still held his interest and his affection, had long ago dismissed that hope. He was loath to see Carlyle, by his willfulness and his refusal to become an opportunist, destroy the advantages which, he felt sure, lay in the path. With a certain complaisance, Jeffrey recalled that he himself had put not a few of these opportunities in the way. But Carlyle, so Jeffrey thought, had not merely stumbled over them, he had deliberately kicked them aside. How else explain his young friend's disregard of the injunctions which he had given; his sometimes flagrant rebellion? Thomas was a good deal of an enigma to Jeffrey.

Carlyle's wife was quite aware of the repulsion and attraction —the latter much stronger in Jeffrey than in her husband— which complicated the two men's relationship. She hated to see Thomas quarrel with Jeffrey, though differences were inevitable. When the waves became too vexed, Jane could at least pour oil on the waters, and this she did with a light touch and the best of humor—the only attitudes, where Jeffrey was concerned, which would quiet her husband.

Before surrendering his active direction of the *Review*, Jeffrey had undertaken one final stroke for Carlyle. He had commissioned him to write an article in summary and criticism of the day. This essay Carlyle entitled "Signs of the Times." In spite of its outspokenness, Jeffrey had accepted it as his own valedictory—an act both of courage and good will.

After bringing his editorship to a close, Jeffrey and his family left Scotland for a visit to England. Though they planned their trip to carry them through Dumfries, there would not be time for a halt at Craigenputtock. Would the Carlyles come down from the hills to be their guests there for the night? So on Saturday the eighth of August, when the Jeffreys—father, mother, daughter, and incidental baggage—piled out of their coach at seven in the evening, Jane and Thomas were waiting to receive them.

The King's Arms, in the Dumfries High Street, was a cavernous old structure, the haunt of drummers and traveling men. But Jeffrey knew how to turn the most unpromising spot into a scene for pleasant meeting. Sleep, that night, however, was not a very plentiful commodity. An overpopulation of insect life ruined all hope of rest. And the following day began somewhat unfavorably, with heavy mists and rain. The travelers had far to go. But before their departure, Jeffrey, with Jane in tow, skipped across the street for a brief chat with Mrs. Caroline Richardson, a novelist whose work and person he much admired. She had been a flame of his, indeed, some twenty-five or thirty years before.

"These old loves don't do!" remarked Mrs. Jeffrey to Carlyle with a quiet touch of sarcasm.

Presently the new Dean of the Advocates returned from his investigations. Good-byes were exchanged and promises to meet again. The Carlyles had accepted an invitation to visit that autumn in Edinburgh.

The private coach rolled off towards Annan, the border, and London. Soon the rains descended—violently. Not till six that evening were Jane and her husband able to ride back to Craigenputtock.

In October, the Carlyles took their first long vacation from Craigenputtock. Their previous stay at Craigcrook had occurred during the hectic days just before the move to Dumfriesshire a year and a half ago. Again to be near the city blended strangely a new experience with a very old one. That the house at Comely Bank should be occupied by strangers was anomalous. Roots always remain behind where one has made one's beginning. The urge to enter the familiar door is overwhelming. Within, surely, is one's accustomed life—the same routine, one's furniture still in place, one's carpets on the floor. There, in the drawing room, tea should be ready for serving; familiar knocks would echo at the portal—De Quincey's, perhaps, or John Wilson's; Jeffrey's itself.

Their host at Craigcrook, however, did not allow much time for retrospection. By day there were strolls, bouts of the outdoor games with which the grounds were amply equipped—Jane's husband would rarely be more than spectator—and talk. In the evening, more talk, always. Jeffrey and Carlyle had fallen into the habit of sitting up, arguing, far past a sane hour. When Jane and the others of the family went to bed, the two debaters would be still contending. Jeffrey as a lawyer, and Carlyle as himself, could not let differences of opinion drop. The result was a series of verbal fencing bouts. Miraculous that no damage to friendship should result. Perhaps there *was* damage—Jane did not like to think of a breach occurring. Though Mrs. Jeffrey could refer laughingly to these stormy sittings, Jane saw little wisdom in their continuance.

Her husband insisted that Jeffrey's trouble was a lack of depth, and that he failed to possess the highest kind of insight, either into literature or life. He would not believe in truth beyond words. If the merits of a proposition could not logically be expounded to a jury, it had no merit for Jeffrey. Intuition and feeling, Carlyle insisted, had deserted the lawyer-editor. His dual career had ruined his better possibilities—law giving him too great a zest for arguing, the *Review* too fixed a notion on the rules for writing.

Jeffrey, in turn, had his complaints to make, though he spoke them lightly. "You are so dreadfully in earnest!" he would say to Carlyle, his eyes twinkling, an almost inaudible light laugh following his thrust.

Fortunately these discussions which so emphasized the differences in Jeffrey and Carlyle were incidentals of the visit and did not set its tone. The conflicting ideas which produced the clashes were like angry, growling dogs, locked up during most of the day and let out at night to exercise. Really, Jane told herself, this stay at Craigcrook had been a shining affair. Perhaps they had stayed a bit too long. But Jane, in retrospect, closed her eyes to everything save the hospitable kindliness of these people. The three weeks' absence from Craigenputtock was almost over. She had been very happy in Edinburgh. November and winter lay ahead. As the coach bore her from the city, Jeannie wept.

Before they reached their house, darkness had fallen. The night was sodden and wet, with an autumn gale blustering among the spectral trees and swirling the tattered yellow leaves. Over the tumult of the wind echoed a clangor as if some earth Titan were forging his weapons. It was Alick. In one of the outbuildings, he had set up a smithy for himself with which to pass the time when farm work was over. The metallic hammering struck ominously on the senses of the home comers. Neither spoke: preoccupied, both, with their own thoughts.

The hush next day, after the noises of the city, was at first unbelievable. These wide expanses brooded in utter silence, except
for the few sounds which tended merely to accentuate it—rooks
calling, the lowing of distant cattle at pasture near Loch Urr,
the tremulous mournful cries of the curlews.

Jane's husband had been ready to return. But to Jane the first
day of solitude was actually frightening. By the second her isolation had become tolerable, and on the third, so quickly did she
readjust herself, she found life at Craigenputtock again definitely pleasant. John Milton had been right after all, though he
gave to Satan the experience which emphasized the philosophy.
The mere outward figure of one's abode was moonshine. One's
heaven or hell lay within. Jane had only one amendment to the
creed in *Paradise Lost*. Unlike Lucifer, she was not the posses-
sor of a self-dependent mind. Therefore the single quality, she
decided, that made one place the pit of Tophet, another Paradise,
was the quantity of heart in it. In Edinburgh there had been
plenty of that commodity, but here by her husband's side she
could also find it. As to the practical matter of which mode of
existence was the more fitting for them—town life with its society and its intellectual stimulation, or life here among these
empty fastnesses—she could not make up her mind. But since
her husband preferred the country, she could make herself as
content at Craigenputtock as in Edinburgh.

Soon after the return, a letter came from Jeffrey addressed
to Tom. "And so you are back again at Craigenputtock, in full
enjoyment of solitude and tobacco, unmolested by those idle sociabilities you hold in such contempt, and those audacious contradictions which wear out your spirit still more. Well, if you
are happier there, I am sure we ought not to repine. But it is
impossible not to wish that you were a little more tolerant of
this lower world, and difficult to believe that it is really good
for you to be so alone. I do not care a farthing for your opinions, and never imagine that either your speculative errors or
mine are much worth inquiring into. But the unsocial dispositions
which yours leads you to indulge are a matter of regret to me,
and I cannot but suspect a source of discomfort to yourself."

Chapter Nine

*T*HE winter of 1829–1830, more severe than the first at Craigenputtock, closed in. Tom, peering out where the barn ought to be, could find nothing but mist and snow. Within that isolating curtain and for miles beyond lay deepest silence. There were occasions—his thoughts reverting to Comely Bank—when he felt a nostalgic wish again to experience those Wednesday evenings of Jane's devising, with their tea and company. He wrote letters to intimates, begging a visit, but a trip from Edinburgh at that season of the year was a valorous, almost a foolhardy undertaking.

There was work to be done, however, and opportunity in which to do it. Carlyle had started a new project. It was to be some sort of historical view of German literature—he had not outlined it yet; was aware only that the scheme would involve an immense amount of investigation and reading. Additional books for study would be required. Exasperating to realize that in this place so ideally fitted for writing, the tools to work with, when sent for, arrived only after long delay. But at least he could make a beginning with the small number of volumes at hand. He started with a fierce energy, only to be brought time and again to a dead halt and anxious, impatient waiting. Would this, after all, be an unproductive, shabby winter?

Toward the Christmas season, Tom's sister Jean came from Scotsbrig for what was intended as a brief visit but ended as a longer stay because of deep snows blocking the return. For New Year's, Jane had planned that her storm-bound garrison should feast on a plump goose, yet when the day arrived she was not at table to enjoy it. A violent sore throat forced her to bed. She was so ill that her husband, thoroughly frightened, ordered the herd boy to be in readiness to gallop to Dumfries for the doctor. In spite of the weather, Jane's mother had been sent for at Templand. Her care presently had Jeannie out of danger. When Mrs. Welsh was obliged to return home, afraid to be longer away from her father, who was ailing, Carlyle himself took over the duties of nurse. When not at her bedside, he would study in his writing room, his ears alert for the little knock which Jane agreed to give if she needed him. She was sitting up again, with her shawl round her, looking, her husband told her, like a veritable queen of the gypsies, her large dark eyes and black hair more beautiful than ever because of her pallor. Being ill had some compensations. There was plenty of time in which to write letters, even though incidents were few and one had to spin the material out of one's own inside like a silkworm busy at its cocoon.

Jane had more to write about as soon as she was better. In quick succession, little domestic catastrophes took place, which, viewed in retrospect, had their humorous aspect. There was the death of her little pig. That pig had been the apple of her eye: such a wise, sweet little pig! Jane's raptures were not motivated entirely by dovelike affection; she was thinking what delicious bacon could be made from the creature when a few weeks more of life had plumped him out. But her eagerness to fatten her pig ruined him. He ate too heartily one evening and the next morning was dead.

Greed caused this first mishap; starvation brought about the second. Jane had provided for the day's repast a juicy beefsteak. For safe keeping she had put it in the larder. But desperation sometimes opens every door. A stranger cat, under the pangs of hunger, gained entrance to the room. Sooner than eye could wink, it snapped up the steak and darted off. The loss of a dinner was bad enough. But the cat, in its precipitous retreat, had done further mischief by smashing the dish.

Accidents to china never arrive singly. Through some quirk, Nancy, the maid, became suddenly possessed with a demon of destruction and shivered into fragments everything she laid hands on. Just after she had loaded onto a tray the full complement of dishes with which to set the table for supper—bowls, plates, crocks, everything—a sudden motion of her body gave her petticoats such a whirl that they swept to the floor the entire contents of the platter. Even Nancy's picturesque account seeking to prove the mishap an act of God could not mitigate the

gravity of the loss. Dishes were so very hard to replace at Craigenputtock, especially in winter.

Oh, for the sight of green fields, or even the black peat moss
—anything rather than this wide waste of snow! Jane was ready
for the siege to end. Well for her that the details of the visit to
Edinburgh were fading from memory. Had they remained
vivid, life in this spot, she decided, which looked like the head-
quarters of the North Wind, in this grimmest of weather, might
prove intolerable. The gaunt-armed trees, the little rills impris-
oned by the ice, furnished scant promise that the scene could
alter. Yet even to these uplands would come the magic change—
the brown, dead-looking heather would offer a hint of green. In
the dampest sheltered pockets behind the outcroppings of the
rocks, golden disks of buttercups, marigolds, and crowfoot
would gleam like tiny suns. The first cuckoos would chant in the
mists, their notes muted and soft.

Throughout the year, Jeffrey was a better correspondent than
the Carlyles. He was much of the time in doubt as to how they
were faring, and he patiently sought for news. "Tell me what
you are doing," he wrote to Jane. "What is C. working upon?
That view of German literature? Or only things for his *Foreign
Quarterly?*" Tom's hesitance to write for the *Edinburgh Review* somewhat piqued its old editor. He refused to analyze
Tom's unwillingness, preferring to regard it as mere desertion.

But in his letters, he gave proof of his wish to keep open the
channels of friendship. Perhaps more than he realized, Jeffrey
depended on Jane's understanding heart. Before his Edinburgh
contemporaries he must remain the shrewd critic, the skillful
lawyer, the witty host and raconteur. With Jeannie Welsh Carlyle he could be both more and less: the famous man; the little
boy with injured finger. "Pity me, my dear child, for I am sick
and sorry, and obliged to work through it all like an old pauper."

Carlyle's own quick response to news of his poor health
cheered Jeffrey. "I am much touched and gratified by your
kind and genuine sympathy, and feel almost that it is but selfish in me to make such call on it." What could he offer in exchange? To what practical future did Carlyle look forward in
life? What did he most wish for that could be procured by his
own efforts or those of his friends? Was this isolation really es-

sential? Why must he so despise his fellow creatures, and especially his fellow scribblers—writers whose place in the hierarchy of man was surely near the top? If only he would break the spell and come back, a cordial greeting was ready for him and Jane at Edinburgh. Did relaxation play any part in his immediate existence? "What portion of your time do you pass in talking idly, or do you ever at all indulge that gentle and fair spouse of yours with a measure of gossip?"

It was not contempt for man, Tom painstakingly explained, that kept him mewed up in the wilderness. There, and there alone, could he support himself by such hack work as he could get—distasteful though much of it was. A hundred pounds a year were essential for existence, and these he must win as best he could.

So that, really, was it? "My dear Carlyle, why should there be any ceremony or any awkwardness between people who have an affection and respect for each other? You would be more comfortable if you had more money, and I would be *much* more comfortable, and more happy, if you would take a little of mine." Jeffrey wrote as though Carlyle, in accepting an annuity large enough to meet his needs, would be conferring the greater favor. All his skill as a pleader, all his diplomacy, went into his fine letter. Carlyle's own straits, he pointed out, were the result of his past generosity to members of his family. Surely he ought not to monopolize the practice of giving aid.

Carlyle was deeply touched. Perhaps he had been too insistent in his stand-off-ishness. Perhaps he had been partly wrong concerning his cherished individualism—man should not be independent of his brother. Yet one thing he was sure of. He had within him the power to help himself. His own shoulder was sufficient to the plow. So he wrote the gentlest letter of refusal. Twice more Jeffrey tendered his offer, but Tom stood firm. He did accept a loan—repaid within the year—when his back, for the time being, was to the wall. Further he would not go.

As a farmer, Alick, though very hard-working, was apt to blunder. He was erratic in his judgments, trying first by one course then another to squeeze subsistence from the difficult land. He had attempted to grow potatoes—a barren crop in that rocky soil. He had boarded cattle to fatten though the grass was none too rich even for sheep. He had tried pigs and turnips, grain and poultry. Yet he was not entirely to blame for his failures. In much of Scotland the husbandman played a losing game. Not many tenants had farmed with any degree of profit at Craigenputtock. Alick encountered difficulty in meeting his rent, and when he had the cash, he was often so busy he could not spare the time to pay it in. More than once, so her mother would not be in need, Jane had herself gone on horseback to Templand with the farm money.

Alick believed he might do better in the dales. These uplands were strange to him; they did not suit what knowledge he had. Clearly he should move. They would miss him. Jeannie liked to hear him gee-haw-ing to his cattle, or shouting behind his plow to the straining horse.

In September, Carlyle rode to Scotsbrig for a family conference to decide what course would be best for Alick. Jeannie remained home at Craigenputtock. Fuel must be gotten in; peat heaped for winter use. She could set the man-of-all-work to these chores. The time for guests was over.

But Jane did not reckon on the Jeffreys. Taking her completely by surprise, a letter reached her announcing their coming arrival. They had found a vacant space in their schedule; they would fill it, if agreeable to the Carlyles, with a visit to Craigenputtock.

Three members of the family, and a servant! Jane's pleasure was mingled with dismay. There were almost no supplies in the larder. More desperate still, there was practically no money in the house with which to buy them. And her husband was away; she had little notion when he would return.

There was not any time to lose. After a brief consultation with her servant and a hurried appraisal of the storeroom, Jane mounted her horse and set out at a gallop for Dumfries. As she rode she made her plans. She would not trust any deputy to order supplies. That, and most other arrangements, she felt it safer to attend to herself.

Lower Craigenputtock with its cluster of poor farmhouses tucked in the valley below the rock, the tiny hamlet of Milton, then Dunscore with its gray church. It was glorious to ride in autumn weather. Galloping alone gave such a sense of freedom.

At intervals, Jane caught glimpses of Cairn Water, fed by its many rills—from the eastern slope of the Craig, down Bogrie Hill, from Brockloch, from many another ridge, they tumbled to mingle at last in the Nith, the quiet river that passed at Dumfries under the Buccleuch Street Bridge, to flow in dignity to the Solway Firth. Jane's first act, after crossing the six stone arches that connected Maxwelltown to Dumfries, the last stage of her journey, was to send a messenger to Scotsbrig for Carlyle. Next, her marketing, and then home.

She kept her house in the neatest order. It was ready at any moment to receive a visitor; fit to do honor even to a king. But Jane, like many another housewife, could not be convinced of that. She fell to work as though her dwelling were a littered tenement which had never seen a broom. When the Jeffreys' coach, for the second time since the occupation of Craigenputtock, stood before the door, everything was swept and garnished within and Jane was triumphantly prepared to welcome her guests. No sign yet of Carlyle. But soon they heard the noise of hard riding. In another moment, Tom also was greeting the Jeffreys. He had brought with him a hamper of butter and eggs from Scotsbrig, the gift of his mother. These bounties Jane bore off rejoicing to the kitchen, thankful to providence and human thoughtfulness. The Jeffreys were prepared, they said, to stay four days. With the added supplies from Scotsbrig, Jeannie was equipped to keep them under her roof for an even longer visit.

Now that Jeffrey found himself in a position to choose almost any high post he might care to fill, because of the coming rise to power of the Whig party, his horror at Carlyle's radicalism audibly increased. Radicalism, he declared, was nothing but the age-old feud against property, under a different name. As usual, he pretended not to take very seriously Carlyle's brand of it: his angry insistence on a decent chance in life for the underdog. Quite speculative, he pooh-poohed, and for the present, fairly harmless. Yet with a new revolution in France, with England restless and disturbed, how long, he asked himself, would Carlyle's intellectual ferment remain merely passive? Would it not be wiser to dampen the metaphorical flames with the cold waters of common sense? Jeffrey was always willing to talk to Carlyle as though his hearer were a jury, and could put to a vote any doubts within himself, casting the ballots with a matter-of-fact eye open to the dictates of expediency. But Jane knew how wrong was this view. A hundred times she had listened to her husband. She realized what a deep, slow-burning, inextinguishable sense of justice smouldered within him—glowing and hot as Alick's forge. Jeffrey, with his tactics, could never change him. And his half-admitted skepticism about Carlyle would always interfere with his affectionate wish—its genuineness could hardly be doubted—to be of service. Best to leave Tom alone. Jane never had a moment's doubt concerning her husband's future greatness. Of course, as to the pattern it would take, that was a thing not to be foretold. The gifts were there; that alone mattered. Deftly she turned the conversation to other matters. Safer to have Jeffrey make one of his engaging dissertations in a vacuum than in a roomful of explosive gases.

By chance the conversation turned to Jeffrey's most famous criminal case, in which, by his power over the jury, he had won acquittal for a notorious poisoner, Nell Kennedy by name. Did he really believe Nell innocent, Tom inquired? Jeffrey avoided a direct answer. At the time of the trial, he said, he would have sworn, if required, that there was reasonable doubt of guilt. Jane and Thomas, though they did not press the matter, were afraid that in this one instance, though legal morality was on his side, Jeffrey had obstructed justice. Strange trade, this of advocate, where you hung up your brains for sale, at the service of the purchaser, whether he might be the sheriff or some arch foe of society.

When Jeffrey, with the ready skill of long practice, changed the subject, his inquisitors were willing to let him go. Never had he seemed more friendly or amusing. Four days of intimate conversation, and Jeffrey allowed not a single moment to lapse into dullness. When he himself controlled the talk, he preferred to keep it effervescent and lively: dainty, full of tricks, and airy even when he fell into debate. That was the easier way. He was growing old; he wished to keep alive the bright sparkle of youth. All his life, though he seemed so worldly and kept up such a gay pretense, he had been the dupe of work. Few men in his circle labored anything like as hard as he. And now that he had dropped certain burdens, others were being thrust upon his wiry little body, though it was worn, now, and desired rest. A certain pathos in the gleaming little

Ariel of a man, as though he had been forced too long to do the bidding of a Prospero less brilliant than the one of Shakespeare's devising. Jeffrey was his own Prospero, commanding himself to perform tasks into which fate and his abilities had thrust him.

Jane, and Thomas also, noticed this weariness—weariness not quite concealed by the rapid fluttering of his wings. They warmed the more to him because of it. When Tom's compassion was aroused, it intensified his sympathies. He liked Jeffrey better on this visit. There had been less disputation. He would not deny the fact: in many ways the little man was one of the best persons alive. A shame that the prose spirit of the world had choked the poet. Why should Jeffrey regard the highest aspirations of the soul as mere ornament? Though he insisted so on logic, the truest thing within him was his kindness and his craving for friendship. A spiritual man in spite of himself, yet he thinned the essence of his spirit with persiflage, cheating himself and others. That was his tragedy, the fault which had kept him from being a truly great interpreter of literature.

As for Jane, she had gained in wisdom concerning the delicate business of human affinities since first she had grown to know Jeffrey. Her regard for him did not alter, but after the move from Edinburgh, his attraction to her caused her less of a problem. She could more readily manage him with sympathetic tact.

Jane's observations of her husband had long since led her to the point where she could tell how his work was faring. He had no gift for concealment. After finishing his recent articles for Jeffrey and for the *Foreign Quarterly*, he had been restless and ill at ease. Though the need to meet expenses kept him a contributor to journals he longed to be a writer in a loftier sense. Even periodicals, Jane had learned with dismay, were untrustworthy for steady income. Frightened by her husband's independence of thought and expression, editors were not always willing to agree to essays of his own suggesting, and topics which they ventured to name were generally not welcome to him. The *Edinburgh Review* had paid handsomely, but now that source had dwindled like Urr Water after a dry season. When John, in August, repaid some of the cash his brother had given him, the act was providential. By midwinter funds were once again at ebb tide. Tom reckoned that there was little more than five pounds in hand to front the world with—and no hope of replenishment for several months to come.

Surely an honest man, if he would live by writing, must prepare himself for an existence like that of Diogenes in his tub! But as long as he believed that he had something to tell, Carlyle refused to desert his calling. If he had two potatoes in the world, and a single true idea, he declared, he would consider it his duty to sell one potato for paper and ink, and live on the other. Jane, though she said little, was ready to join him in the diet. Complaint over poverty never crossed her lips.

But where was the idea? Its illusiveness, as he cheered himself on and bade himself be of courage, harassed Tom with uneasy dismay while he searched the chaos of the world for it and painfully examined his own mind. Was this latter source not the proper one to dip from now? Though everything that he wrote was filled with his personality, the subjects had come from outside—all except Wotton Reinfred, his futile attempt at autobiographical fiction.

His history of German literature was on the shelf. No publishers would take it; readers, they said, were weary of the subject. So was Carlyle. Most of German literature was becoming stale to his taste—only Goethe, who transcended it and towered with the great of all ages, remained worthy; Goethe and one or two others. Jeffrey had asked if he were not losing his idolatry for these muddy-headed, half crazy, half affected scribblers. Carlyle would never admit as much to Jeffrey, yet it was true. He had never regarded his history of German literature as more than a way to make money. Now that it was going to fail him in this, he was more glad than sorry that it never would be published. He would attempt no more compilations; henceforth, what he wrote would come from his own heart.

A while longer, Jane had to watch her husband groping restlessly for a subject. He was searching in the forests of his own thought like a wild thing in time of famine. Ever since she had first met him, Jane, too, had been waiting for that great, original book which she knew he would some day write. When he began Wotton in their first year at Comely Bank, Jane had told

herself that this at last was the thing she was looking for. Its
coming to a halt was her severest lesson on her husband's aims
and ideals. She saw how exacting, how high and difficult they
were. She realized how hard it was for him to be satisfied with
what he wrote.

His creative temperament functioned like a slowly gathering
storm over a parched and thirsty land. Its hour of precipitation
could never be foretold. The clouds would assemble among
the contrary winds. There would be long hours when appearances foretold no results at all—merely unsettled weather. But
at last the sky would seem full to bursting. A sudden, tropical
storm to be expected? Or a long and steady downpour? Perhaps even, in defiance of every sign, the winds might change and
blow the mass away.

The course of symptoms had run almost to the end. This
time, said Carlyle, he would scribble—nonsense.

Bit by bit Jane could watch the growth of the mosaic of her
husband's scheme. The central notion had long been in his
mind. He had tried, once, to insert it in greatly abbreviated
form into the essay on Burns. But Jeffrey, overruling Carlyle's
protest, had slashed it out. "How can you dream of restoring
that very simple and well-used joke of the clothes making the
man and the tailor being a creator?" Jeffrey, of course, had not
bothered to understand Carlyle's motive. He merely thought
that his contributor was slipping into print a rusty witticism.
He did not realize that Carlyle's use of the figure of speech
went far beyond the obvious—that its purpose was an ironic
contrast of the materialistic philosophy of the day with the
transcendental point of view.

As long as he remained primarily a mystic, Carlyle wrote
best through elaborate metaphor and symbol. He was preparing to set on paper his own mental biography. To make the
revelation, Carlyle invented a half humorous, half serious character. Jane and her husband shared many a laugh at the christening of this hero. His first name should be Diogenes—both
to honor that old philosopher and for the virtues of the word
itself: the man born of a God. Coupled to this, as surname, Tom
hit on the Rabelaisian "Teufelsdröckh." God-born devil's dung:
there was a sobriquet to mystify the innocents! As for the part

this biped was to play, Carlyle decided to model him on the
semicomic pattern of a wool-gathering professor in a small German municipality. John, back from Munich, had described the
species and the beer-guzzling atmosphere in which it throve.
Diogenes could be made a member of a select gathering which
should meet in a German *stube* or drinking parlor—an informal
club where one could hear expressed views on all subjects that
came within the bounds of the universe. Dröckh should be the
leading spirit of the group.

On this creature's shoulders, with disguises and variations,
Carlyle would place the burden of his own past history—his
childhood, his education, his thoughts on things in general, his
mental and moral proving.

The fantastic texture which he spun like a magician's garment to hide his proper person delighted him. Sardonic fool-
ing accorded with his immediate humor. He was discovering
that he could fit into this structure more of his own opinions on
life and politics, on heaven and earth and all things in them,
than had been possible in his entire previous writings. At last,
he felt almost confident. Jane, breathing the exciting atmosphere
of creative effort, could share his mood. No longer need he be
a slave to the tyranny of magazine editors. He had a book within
him that would cause ears to tingle. The utter negation of
materialism, the triumphant, divine importance of man's noblest
thoughts and emotions—these were the large objectives he was
after. And along with his insistence on these lofty principles,
he would pour a lava flow of scorn on man's greed and selfishness, his crass stupidity and blindness.

Jane had developed the perfect gift of silence. As her husband's pen moved over the sheets of paper, filling them, page
after page, with his close packed writing, she enjoyed sitting in
the room with him, on the opposite side of the hearth, quiet
as a mouse that never even nibbled. When his pen paused, she
could ask to see what had been written.

Thus, under the eye of the Flower of Haddington, was
Teufelsdröckh composed. Its author had begun it in the autumn
of 1830. During the winter he labored, and through the spring.
Hopefulness and mistrust alternated within him. Sometimes his
belief in what he was creating wavered discouragingly, and Jane
would seek to cheer him up. The thing was not right—was not

art, he would insist. But his wife, calling to mind some stirring passage, would challenge his assertion. "It is a work of genius, dear," she told him.

Jane grew to love the book, though its exposure of the follies of the world also made her sad. Who could be heedlessly cheerful after reading Dröckh? She for one found it no longer possible. As to its curative virtues, they were indeed designed as a caustic stimulant for the ailing times, like an abstract mustard plaster against a tender conscience. Jane reveled in her husband's turn for phrases. That was it: the book would prove a kind of medicinal assafoetida for the pudding stomach of England! Yet its gentler characteristics, surely, would win it friends: the portrait of the little boy growing up so innocently in Ecclefechan (it was hard to transmogrify that familiar name into the outlandish Entepful); the glowing passages that told the story of the courtship of Blumine.

Chapter Ten

*N*EARLY three years at Craigenputtock had passed when *Dröckh*, toward the end of July, 1831, was at last finished. Ever since *Dröckh* had begun to grow, the previous autumn, into a sizeable bundle of closely written leaves, Carlyle had been weighing various schemes for printing. Could he permit this child of his mind to journey unaccompanied to London, there to seek alone the backing of some publisher who would be willing kindly and honorably to introduce it to the public? Why not go himself as guardian? A father might find stimulus in the city along with his prodigal son. During the winter Jane and he had saved every penny that could be spared. Fifty pounds by way of reserves should suffice. It was time to risk another venture into active life.

In family council, the decision had been reached that Tom should go alone to London. Carlyle and Jane were both eager to get the manuscript off as speedily as possible. Because of uncertainties, plans must remain tentative. After *Teufelsdröckh's* business should be satisfactorily concluded, Tom could either return home or stay in the city to be joined by his wife as soon as she might be ready.

Before leaving, Carlyle had one duty to perform. At a large dinner in Dumfries given to honor the poet Allan Cunningham, once a stonemason in the town, he gave a public address. His topic was Robert Burns. When reports of the speech began to drift back to Craigenputtock, Jeannie was reassured by their tenor. The little stream of visitors who dropped in after the event were full of praises. Best of all, Christopher North, in Edinburgh, somehow got wind of the performance and lauded Carlyle in *Blackwood's Magazine*.

"They all know of his cleverness now, Mem," remarked Jane's servant, mingled awe and pleasure in her voice. Yes, but when *Teufelsdröckh* should begin public life as a book, the whole world would recognize her brilliant husband and award him the fame which was his due.

Jane was well along with her preparations to send Tom on his journey. No telling how long he might be gone from her. Best to have him ready for any emergencies. She packed his traveling chest, including in it all things which might prove needful at London. His mending! How would that get itself attended to? Socks to be darned; buttons to be replaced. At least she could arm him at all points. So she hunted in her closets and cupboards till she found a neat little box, once used for sweets. Into this she put the necessities for effecting repairs: worsted, needles and pins, and other objects of a similar homely nature.

Fortunately, during her husband's absence, she would not be left without a man at Craigenputtock. Tom's plowman brother Alick, newly married, was still living there. He was no longer tenant on the farm, but instead of leaving to try his luck elsewhere, he had decided to bide his time before renting new acres. He was determined to choose his next land with care lest his small reserve of capital, already dangerously shrunk, be wiped out entirely. To tide him over, Jane and her husband had been lending him the peat house. He had transformed it into a dwelling almost as comfortable as the farmer's which he had been obliged to surrender. Under the circumstances, Jane was glad that her brother-in-law had planned to remain a while longer. She liked him. His very misfortunes predisposed her in his favor, for she was quick with her sympathies to those who deserved them. Alick, with his nut-brown, rugged face, was a solid man though an improvident husbandman. His shortness of temper never offended Jane, who was never touched by it. To her, he was always obliging and thoughtful.

Carlyle's boat—Glencaple to Liverpool—sailed at a very early hour. Alick was to drive with him from Craigenputtock at two in the morning. So Jane and Tom kept vigil together that evening: he resting on the sofa in the drawing room, she sitting near him with her work while they talked.

Time to be off. Carlyle's manuscript lay safe beneath his arm. Jane herself had wrapped it up and secured the bundle with a bit of tape. She kissed her husband and wished him luck.

When he was gone, she strained to catch the last faint rattle of the iron-shod wheels, then went back to the empty house. She must try for an hour or so of sleep. How low the candles had burned!

Carlyle always grew uneasy if Jane wept. Tears bothered him. He did not object so much to the good cries she indulged in every now and then when she permitted herself to luxuriate in the emotions of a romantic novel. Of course these harmless pleasures sometimes made her husband snort contemptuously. But he had been known even to abet them by getting for her some volume highly charged with lachrymose qualities. But tears that flowed because of her own feelings, she had learned, were another matter. So she kept them back at parting. No need to restrain them now. She cried herself into a troubled sleep, a sleep which presently deserted her, leaving her to toss restlessly first to one side then the other of the big red bed. Rarely had she felt so alone. There, on the pillow, lay Tom's nightcap. Her husband could be so stubborn about his clothes! Jane's efforts to make him more presentable ended, generally, in failure. He clung to his idiosyncrasies of dress as though they were part of his own skin. That nightcap was an example. How she detested red nightcaps! But seeing this one beside her now, where her husband himself had been, she found it a strangely pathetic, strangely moving object. Horrid, yet irresistible! Leaning over, she kissed it.

She rose, tired, in the morning, and sat down to breakfast. Betty, the current servant, had attained that phase of competence, after a heroic struggle on Jane's part, where keeping house with her was something of a pleasure. Either these Craigenputtock maids proved themselves hopelessly inadequate and Jeannie had to part with them, or, like this one, the crude clay of their beings molded into a utensil fit to adorn any gentlewoman's kitchen, whereupon they would flit to take employment elsewhere at wages higher than the Carlyles were able to pay. Jane glanced at the efficiently laid table. She had not thought of meals without her husband. How solitary everything looked: one cup, one porringer, one tumbler, one everything! This was no feast over which to linger. Jane hurried off to her Cinderella work. There was butter to be made, there was polishing and dusting. And when she chose to, she could move the hands of her clock past the hours of drudging, and emerge as a fair creature waiting to receive the attentions of Prince Charming. True, he was a very old Prince Charming, the one who for the present occupied her evenings. Yet he was none the less delightful. The very day of Carlyle's departure for London had brought another well-filled packet from Weimar. In the miscellany of books and gifts and little notes she had found the newest edition of Goethe's poems. Goethe was her companion and this her reading during the first few nights after her husband's departure.

For some time yet, she could not hope to receive a letter from Carlyle with a report of *Dröckh's* fortunes. The post was so infernally slow! Her own correspondence was lively and cheerful. She prattled along as though Carlyle were beside her in the room. Her letters were like her talk. But in her salutations there were chances to express her love which the daily routine of living together, with its bustle and hustle and practical work, somehow had a tendency to block. "Bless you, bless you, my dear good Husband," she wrote, "I am ever thine!" As she finished her evening letter and prepared for bed, it was consoling to add these words, "dream of me!"

By no means all her days were passed alone. Her mother came for a short visit and so did various friends. Isabella Mac Turk, who arrived with Mrs. Welsh, was a lively, irrepressible person. In her company, Jane found herself bubbling over with an effervescence such as she had not experienced since her girlhood at Haddington before her father's death. Bella enjoyed trivial things. She liked to dance, a pastime Jane, since her marriage, had almost lost the art of. Imagine Thomas at a ball! The very thought of it was ludicrous enough to call forth shouts of laughter. What Jane and her friend were up to now also made an absurd picture. She passed it along for Carlyle's amusement. "Eleven at night.—What think you we have been doing, Bella and I, for the last hour and a half? Verily dancing quadrilles, with all the seriousness in the world, to the sound of our own singing."

It was pleasant at times to follow Jeffrey's advice. He was always bidding her to laugh and dance and drink red wine; always telling her that her chief purpose was to be gay and happy. Yet was that indeed life's true objective? Less and less was Jane ready to believe it. With so much suffering in the

world, so much injustice, could one's conscience leave one free
to be heedless as a cricket? Who that had read *Dröckh*—with
its severe arraignment of the world—could be light-hearted any
more? For all his advocacy of play, even Jeffrey himself was
obedient to his own undeclared ideal of duty.

Templand saw a good deal of Jane, during August. She loved
the ride down from the thin soil of the hills to the richness
of the valley of the Nith. Her mother and she were less apt
to have disagreements there than in Jane's own home. They
had a special reason, that summer, for trying to avoid the quar-
rels that strained the fundamental bond between them. Elizabeth, Jane's aunt, was ill. She suffered from a pain in her side,
and her eyes shone with a deceiving brightness. "I have a
cough now, too," she remarked with a smile that alarmed Jane
far more than it reassured her, "and what will come of that I
don't know; but we shall see." All the symptoms were there,
thought Jane with a rush of terror; all the signs that had
prophesied death from consumption for so many members of
her family. Her fear was mostly for her aunt; but some, too,
was for herself. She could not repress a warning voice which
kept insisting that thus, one day, might she too look. Jane had
no wish to die; her life with Carlyle was a precious thing which
she wanted desperately to prolong beyond the span allotted to
most of those in whose veins flowed the blood of the Welshes.
Out of Elizabeth's sight it was easier to banish mistrust. When
these apprehensions rose like miasmas to cloud the brightness of
her spirit, Jane longed for her husband more than ever.

It became harder and harder to control her impatience for his
letters. And writing without up-to-date knowledge of him was
like conversing with one's image in a looking-glass. It was like
calling from the portal into a dark house where surely people
were living, yet none gave answer. Never before had Jane recognized so keenly how unfortunate it was to be living sixteen
miles from a post office, where perhaps even at the moment a
message might be waiting.

When his first letter had come, Jane had pounced on it with
all the eagerness of her hens scrambling after a choice grain of
corn. Tavistock Square—that was where he was staying. Near
Regent's Park, was it not? Jane admitted to an infinite curi-

osity over London. Would she ever really see it? Her husband
was staying with George Irving, Edward's brother. George
owned a house large enough to permit the rental of lodgings.

Yet what of *Teufelsdröckh?* Jane skimmed the lines for a
reassuring word. Nothing definite as yet. On Jeffrey's advice,
the publisher Murray had the manuscript. Her husband had
asked for and been promised a speedy answer.

So Jeffrey was once more interesting himself in her husband's behalf? Jeffrey was busier than ever now. He had been
elevated to the high post of Lord Advocate of Scotland, and
sat in the British Parliament. Jane had learned to expect little
real assistance from Jeffrey. She must warn Carlyle, in the next
letter, to set no great store by Jeffrey's proffered help. Apparently this time, however, the Lord Advocate had matched words
with deeds. At least he had introduced Carlyle to Murray's
favorable attention. "Of the probable issue I can form no conjecture: only Murray seemed to know me, and I dare say is
very anxious to keep well with Ministers, so will risk what he
dares."

One little bit of news her husband let slip: Jeffrey still kept
her picture with him in London. He had seen it at Jeffrey's
house. Useless, apparently, to attempt regaining the miniature.
Jane had several times asked him for it in vain. Not only did
he have it; he told of showing it to one and another of his
London ladies of fashion. "I lent it for a week to Mrs. Montagu, and I believe they have been copying it. You do not
grudge that? She says she had fancied you would look nearly
so. I do not believe it—nobody ever anticipated that peculiar
countenance. Those very lovely, but *too thoughtful* eyes, and
that half-*obstinate*, half-capricious lip, which does not agree
very well either with them or with itself." Jeffrey was always
trying to define for her the nature of her personality. "I have
studied the enigma carefully, and think I half understand it."
He had better not be too sure; her character was her own property.

The next letter from Carlyle, and the next, though filled
with other news, brought no definite word of the book. Murray,
wrote Carlyle, had a reputation for honorableness and even for
munificence. Yet he was noted also for procrastination. Impossible to hurry his decision though he had tried repeatedly to

do so. "My prospects apart from him are not brilliant; however, loss of time is the worst of all losses; he shall not keep me dancing round him very long, go how it may."

She had counted so on this brilliant work of her husband. With every hour's delay, it was plain to see that he was fortifying his spirit to turn away disappointment and despair. If *Teufelsdröckh* met with present failure, she must also not become disheartened. Her letters remained brave and reassuring. Never for a moment must Carlyle be left in doubt as to her belief in him; her readiness to accept unshaken whatever the future might bring. She too could assume her husband's armor of seeming indifference and in addition she could lend him the sword of her own defiant spirit. Her latest news from Jeffrey gave the opportunity. "He 'will *do what he can for the Book,*'" she reported, quoting what Jeffrey had written her, " 'but fears its extravagance and what will be called its affectation.' " Never mind such hesitations! *Teufelsdröckh* remained the work of genius which she had first declared it to be. "If they will not publish him, bring him back and *I* will take care of him and read him and admire him, till we are enabled to publish him on our own account."

Tom's next letter told of the storms he and Diogenes Teufelsdröckh, the latter still a private citizen—had weathered with her help. Murray, it was plain to see, was killing the book's chances by a campaign of deliberate though not declared neglect. He had not even troubled to read the manuscript. He had offered to keep it yet another month, for decision, but this proposal Tom had spurned. With his bundle thrust under his arm, he stalked out of Murray's sanctum. There were other publishers in London.

Jane could picture her husband leaving the room in silent fury; going on his errand from one firm to the next. She had advised him to seek out some young adventurous bookseller for so new and strange a book. Carlyle admitted the wisdom of this counsel. On this basis, one could still cling to a little hope. The story all publishers were telling, however, was the same: the din of political reform at home, of revolution abroad, filled English ears and left no opening for literature. But that very excuse, her husband wrote, gave strength to his belief that *Teufelsdröckh*—with its plea for honesty in life, its attack on

sham in men's affairs—had a message which the world must
heed. The philosophy of the book, the doctrine of rebirth, of
stripping away the worn, outmoded fashions of life, was exactly
what intelligent men were seeking.

"The more the Devil pecks at me, the more vehemently do
I wring his nose!" That was the defiant spirit Jane admired.
Her husband had not lost his confidence. He could even still
joke and banter. He had taken up with no other woman, he
wrote, though daily he saw charming ones in fine satin, or
dressed like Amazons for a ride in the park. If he wanted to,
he could easily enough do so. He had won feminine admirers,
she was aware, on that London visit of seven years past. Mrs.
Buller's charming, wealthy niece, Kitty Kirkpatrick, about whom
he had teased her at the time, was in the city. He would see
her and the other women who were members of Mrs. Buller's
set. "I perceive that of all women my own Jeannie is the wife
for me; that in her true bosom (once she were a mystic) a man's
head is worthy to lie." Her husband's joking because of the
broad practical streak in Jane's many-sided nature was an old
story. "Be a mystic, dearest; that is, stand with me on this everlasting basis, and keep thy arms around me: through life I fear
nothing."

Jeffrey had looked again at the manuscript. The description
in it of night-time London had won his admiration. "Thank
him for nothing," Jane retorted. "He would have been the
dullest of mortals if he had not. My beloved *Dröckh!* My
jewel of great price! The builders despise thee; but thou wilt
yet be *brought out with shouting* and I shall live to see thee
in thy place. All these discouragements do but increase my confidence, as a candle burns brighter for being snuffed; for
Dröckh is imperishable, indestructible as the substance of the
four elements; and all Booksellerdom, all Devildom cannot
prevail against him!" Jeffrey would put in one more word,
perhaps, with Murray, Carlyle reported hopefully. Jane smiled
at the thought. "He will not, Dearest, dare not. Trust only in
yourself, and there trust *to all lengths.*"

Jane's words were a battle cry to rouse his courage. She had
been the first patroness of this book before any other eye had
seen it. Now that men had beheld and scorned it she was ready
to be its champion despite the neglect of the entire world.

In the first week of September, when Jane opened her next letter from her husband, a bit of printed paper fluttered out. One glance sufficed to tell what it was—a page of *Dröckh* himself, set up in proof! Jeffrey had conquered his scruples and worked to good purpose after all. Murray had capitulated. Her husband's volume was going through the press. True, wrote Carlyle, the bargain was a poorish one. But at least they would themselves be put to no expense. Eventually there might even be some profit. "Let us hope nothing, Goody: then we fear nothing. By one or the other means our poor little pot *will* keep boiling, and shall, though the devil himself said nay."

When joy possessed her, no skylark soaring above the house at Craigenputtock was more vibrant than Jane. Her pleasure made the day a festival. Soon Carlyle's book would be ready so that all might read it. Soon her husband would return to her. Or perhaps she might go to him for the winter in the city. The very thought of these things was an intoxication.

As to London, scarcity of cash had been the chief obstacle in Jane's path. Now the way looked clearer. She did not hide from herself the fascination which London held for her. Since earliest girlhood, her dreams of the metropolis had been like visions of a city of the Pharaohs. But the journey thither must be prudently undertaken. She would not venture to urge it, nor would she acquiesce till her husband was sure of its wisdom and ready himself to bid her come.

No harm in thinking of it though. How filled with activity London's streets must be! What interesting people, what new ways of life her husband had met there! Of course, he indulged in his usual contempt for many of these persons and adventures, yet his vivid accounts of them betrayed his interest. A few people, indeed, had won his hearty liking and approval. One such was young John Stuart Mill. Tom was sure Jane would find him a lovable being. Mill seemed in the way of becoming an active disciple, even to the extent of looking kindly on the new mysticism. A triumph indeed, since Mill's father was none other than James, the grim advocate of the logical doctrines of utilitarianism as preached by Bentham, whose very name was anathema to Carlyle—Bentham, who placed all human emotions in the scales for measurement and classified each within a feather's weight.

Tom's next letter contained a stunning blow. Because of a disagreement between author and publisher, Murray's proposal had been revoked.

The issue was clear: *Dröckh,* in these critical times, could not be disposed of in London.

How ironic now was that single leaf of printing!

But even from the wreck of present hopes, new ideas and new projects were rising. Carlyle wrote of falling back on journalism. In spite of the book's failure, might he not do well to remain longer in the city? Might not Jane still possibly join him in London?

The thought that troubled him most was his poverty. Under the circumstances, even for a single winter, they could not keep house. There could be no carriage for Jane, he whimsically added; she would have to go on foot like any washerwoman.

On that score Jane was quite prepared to reassure him. She did not care three puffs of tobacco whether she were poor or rich. "You would not have your Goody a gigwoman, and yet you would fain leave her her gig. I cannot, you think, jostle my way thro' the crowd on foot. Thou unbeliever! Do you forget the *pattens* which I boldly avowed as 'my carriage' at the very outset of our married life?"

Jane's declaration, she hoped, would settle her husband's quandary. If he bade her stay, she would be sorry indeed: sorry not for herself alone but for him as well. He had written that he longed for her. But the decision whether she should come must be his own; she would do her best not to sway his judgment. Far better, she believed, to have him settle for himself each issue in their lives.

Waiting for the post was like waiting for a reprieve from prison. Betty the maid had gone to town with McKnight, the man-of-all-work. Evening was almost come. Yet no sign of the pair. Jane, having given up her vigil, was waiting inside when Betty at last entered the room. Did she have the mail pouch? She was quite capable of losing it on the way.

McKnight, said Betty, with deliberation, had been so tardy. "He left the town, too, at the usual hour, Mem."

"For God's sake give me the letters," Jane exclaimed with some apprehension, observing that the mail pouch was nowhere to be seen. But Betty, once started on her long-winded discourse, was not easily to be checked.

"For the love of God will you produce the letters?" ordered Jane in a transport of impatience, with the fiercest look which she could muster.

From somewhere among her petticoats the maid fished out the little bag. So the mail was safe after all! The apprehensions with which she had been tormenting herself had all been quite superfluous. She snatched the bag from Betty's hands and peered inside. Not just one letter within from her husband; there were two! So intense was her pleasure that it made her for the moment almost ill. She seated herself beside her little fire and spread out both sheets of paper.

"Now you will put yourself off your sleep, Mem," said Betty, surveying her mistress's flushed face. Jane did not care. Her husband wanted her in London—sleep was an easy loss for such tidings. She felt like rushing out-of-doors to tell her news to the lonely craigs and brooks.

When her excitement had abated somewhat, Jane prepared to turn in for the night. How sad she had been, the other evening, when Betty, through some caprice or mere absence of mind, had made up the bed with four pillows, instead of the two she had been using since her husband's departure! That foolish little circumstance had produced insomnia and one of her few lapses from cheerfulness in writing to Carlyle. "I do not like to say how much I weary for you, lest I make you too impatient under these unavoidable delays, but in truth it is very lonely here for *one*."

Very different was her present sleeplessness. Toward one in the morning she climbed out of bed, lit her candle, put on her dressing gown, and whiled away two hours looking vacantly at the pages of the *Dumfries Courier*. Her mind would not tally with her eyes. Instead, her thoughts kept turning toward London and her journey thither. How she looked forward to seeing her husband; how good he was, and loving! There on the mantel, in the usual place, lay one of his cigars. Tentatively Jane picked it up. Why not take a puff or two? Not for any real liking for strong tobacco. Jane had tried cigars before, and found them overpowering. But it was fun, and somehow reassuring, to mimic Carlyle. Before she knew it, half an inch of ash marked the extent of her dissipation. She crushed the glowing tip and scrambled into bed. In the stillness her heart beat audibly. The wind, moving through the trees and round the corners of the house, made strange noises in the utter darkness before dawn. For the first time since she had been alone, Jane experienced a little shiver of nervousness at thought of her unprotected state in those moorlands, where Irish vagabonds came now and then by daylight for the morsel of food she was always willing to spare them. But what of strollers by night? Jane was vexed with herself for not having learned to fire the gun which served as armament for Craigenputtock. She had fully intended to, but had put the business off. A little late to think of it now. While Alick occupied the peat house near the manse, Jane knew that a shout would bring him. But he and Jean his wife had left for Scotsbrig. She was like a feudal dame whose lord was gone to the wars, and whose henchmen and retainers, one by one, had dropped away.

When Betty arrived with tea at seven in the morning, all was as familiar and reassuring as it had been the day before. Jane's active mind had been the only prowler to disturb her rest. It was high time to be efficient and practical.

Chapter Eleven

*J*ANE visited Templand, made her farewells at Scotsbrig, then was off on her adventure to London. Beside clothing and some household effects, she carried with her a supply of oatmeal (no telling what inferior thing she might find in England!). She had thought also of taking from Craigenputtock some butter of her own manufacture. She had salted it in warm weather, however, and was not confident enough of her skill to have faith that this churning might not spoil. So she brought, instead, a quantity made by Carlyle's mother.

She was eager to be going. The tone of Carlyle's latest messages was disturbing. He was evidently out of sorts; perhaps ill. She feared he was again quarreling with Jeffrey. An open rupture would never do. That she admired and liked Jeffrey was no matter for concealment. He was a great man now, even more famous than when he had first entered her little drawing room at Comely Bank. Yet for all his success, there was something in the sprightly, worldly little man which tugged at her sympathies. Somehow, with all his adequacy, his effrontery even, he appeared at times so careworn and helpless. There had been paragraphs in the newspapers reporting that he was ill. She hoped these rumors were unfounded. In London she would find out for herself.

But her chief concern lay with her husband. If he was still disgruntled and unhappy, as she feared, she could soon kiss him into better humor. And if that should fail, among the trials, anxieties, and disappointments which seemed for the present to be his lot, she was ready to share his troubles and bear him company even in his darker mood. She was bringing with her a group of silhouettes of his family at Scotsbrig. These, surely, would cheer him.

Jane had good luck with her coach journey. She succeeded in booking her seat right through from Liverpool to London,

and thus escaped the bother of shifting luggage. But the voyage
by boat from Glencaple to Liverpool had been a trial. She was
no sailor. Four-and-twenty hours on the Irish Sea almost in-
capacitated her for the drive south through England.

How welcome London appeared to her tired eyes; how
doubly welcome the sight of her husband's face among the hundreds of strange ones she saw as the coach jolted to a halt before the Angel Tavern, Islington. More than eight weeks had
passed since the beginning of their separation: their longest
time apart.

John, easy going, imperturbable as ever, had come with his
brother to meet the stage. With her two men, Jane entered
the Inn for a dinner of chops and rice. Refreshed, her tired-
ness forgot in the excitement, she drove with her escorts to
Tavistock Square, George Irving's house, where Tom still had
his lodgings. In the evening, Edward called to bid her welcome.

She had triumphed in her enterprises; had put everything to
rights at Craigenputtock and successfully managed her whole
journey.

But the energy that had thus far held her up vanished, and
a splitting headache kept her in bed during the next forty-
eight hours. Not till the third day could she begin her explorations of London.

Once Jane was with her husband, Carlyle's mood visibly
improved. He had obtained commissions to write several essays, and funds from these would replenish their shrinking
purse. No other publisher would touch poor *Dröckh*. "Keep
it," Jane said, "it will come of use some day." When her husband's spirits sank at thought of the idle manuscript and all his
hope for it, she did her best to keep his courage up. Several of
his clever London friends had read and praised it. Jane could
see that Tom had won a little group of followers and disciples
—far better men than those who had gathered about him in
Edinburgh. Their numbers were sure to grow. To hear Carlyle talk brilliantly among appreciative company, to watch his
expressive face respond to each mood or break into uproarious
laughter at some whimsicality: that was like Comely Bank,
only better, far, far better in this gigantic London. After too
long isolation at Craigenputtock, Thomas, Jane secretly noticed,

had grown restless and unhappy. Surely he was wasting himself there.

Jane also had grown stale. In London, Carlyle wrote to his wife prior to her arrival, her own light could shine to greater purpose before a wider audience. Here, he reported, were many gifted women—authors, actresses, and social potentates. "I long to see how the Scottish sense of my little Dame will comport itself amid the copious outpourings of a Mrs. Austin." This Mrs. Austin, he explained, wrote for publication. "Why should not Mrs. Carlyle, whose endowment I suspect is considerably greater?"

Thomas's bachelor lodgings in Tavistock Square were quickly tested by Jane and found wanting. They were intolerably noisy, she discovered, and not above suspicion as to possible infestations of bugs. So a move to better quarters followed. Their new habitation stood on quiet Ampton Street, not far from the bustle and life of Gray's Inn Road which led toward Holborn—toward the river, Fleet Street, and the Strand. They had learned of the place through Edward Irving. It was a dwelling owned by members of his congregation, a family named Miles: gentle, unobtrusive people whose standards of housekeeping were as high, even, as Jane's. Eliza, the daughter, soon developed a crush on Jane almost embarrassing in its intensity. With Eliza's help, Jane converted into snug, attractive quarters the two rooms she and her husband had rented. The drawing room was about the size of the one at Craigenputtock. The bedroom, though small, was comfortable.

In London, in another person's house, there could be no smoking within doors for her husband. Jane was stubborn in the matter, and deaf to all pleadings. She insisted on enforcing the proprieties. To the rear of their apartment, outside the staircase window, stood a large cistern for water. Let him perch on that if he must use his pipe. Gingerly her husband complied, making himself as easy as he could on this dais. Cruel to laugh at him, of course! Yet he appeared so absurd there, his long clay pipe trailing from his mouth, its little smoke rising to join the giant cloud hanging over London. He would make a perfect emblem, Jane declared, for some tobacconist's door. Even Milton could have drawn inspiration from him! Thus, surely, had Satan looked on that fatal day when he usurped God's throne in Heaven.

"How strange to be in big London here; isn't it?" Jane and Thomas were strolling together down Piccadilly toward Hyde Park corner. Though October had begun, the air was warm and soft, like a summer evening. Tom was amused and touched by Jane's delighted exclamations. Why, this was so like the descriptions of the city in his book! Upwards of one million, five hundred thousand persons, with their joys and their sorrows, gathered together under this myriad of roofs. And in the north, under that arching sky, lay her house at Craigenputtock, quite silent now, unreal and distant—almost without existence, like some imagined dwelling on the waste spaces of the moon. Here, as her husband had reported, was life in all its variety; its many phases separated only by thin walls of masonry. On one side, human beings at their evening prayers; on the other, men cursing, gaming, or dying. All these things heaped and huddled together! Near at hand, between Hyde Park and the river, within those imposing groups of public and private buildings, councillors of state would be plotting the fate of nations, while in the stews of the city, disease, poverty, and hunger played their chess game with far greater infallibility, snatching this human pawn or that forever from the board. Jane knew these sinks existed: *Dröckh* had seen and described them. Places such as these made her husband, in his hurt sensitivity and outraged compassion, declaim violently against London—these grinding millions; this monstrous wen of civilized life! But tonight he was leading her to the quiet places of the city, along the stately streets and squares and calm green recesses where nothing of this abomination was allowed to enter. There, in that grand dwelling, Apsley House, at the corner of the park, lived the aging Duke of Wellington, once, and perhaps for always, a hero of England. But iron blinds covered every window— blinds thick enough to resist bullets, as protection against any repetition of the mob's fickleness such as had marked the tumult and riot over the reform bill still in debate before Parliament.

At the corner, where the apex of the triangles of Green Park and Hyde Park meet in geometrical design, Carlyle looked round for a bench where he and Jane might rest. The town was empty now of the magnificence of society—the Grandees all away on their country estates or not yet returned from the continent. Some of the bigger mansions, which would be gay with diners and dancers when the season began, were tenanted only by caretakers and liveried footmen. No fine carriages making the rounds of Kensington and the chain of parks, or elegant riders on Rotten Row. Not till spring would Jane be able to see the show and take stock of the parade of fashionable people. But even in its quietness, this tree-girt solitude in the heart of London, under the stars, had charm. It would become memorable for her as the terminus of her first stroll. She would come there often. Perhaps, if they ever settled in London, she would some day make the circuit of Hyde Park and the Serpentine in a carriage of her own.

Her next walk with Carlyle was on a matter of business. There were saucepans to be got for light housekeeping—kettles and other homely objects of ironmongery. Jane was a sharp purchaser with a keen eye for a bargain. What a difference between the various parts of the city! Here, among the shops, all was bustle and hurry, with the rattling of wains and the clatter of butchers', bakers' and brewers' drays. From curlews uttering their ventriloquial notes above the Scottish moorlands to this unresting hum of carriage wheels, horses' iron shoes, and the march of human feet! Time, at Craigenputtock, was inconsequential. But here men and women seemed in a continual hurry, with a look of care and endeavor on every face. If human legs could not carry one fast enough on one's errands, ready for service on each thoroughfare lumbered huge omnibi, looking like painted corncribs mounted on four wheels. Sixpence was fare enough to carry one from one end of London to the other. And the cabs! They resembled upended open baby carriages, with the driver perched aloft where the handle ought to be. A stranger would think twice before trusting to one of them. The reins were handled by men who, most of them, resembled blackguards. They drove with the fury of Jehu along the congested ways. Even Ampton Street did not escape entirely from the din. Fruiterers and oystermen and piemen raised discordant voices in quite incomprehensible yells as they hawked their wares, and there were trundling wheelbarrows and dog

carts laden with miscellanies of goods. Sometimes, on Gray's
Inn Road, like a whale among the lesser fishes, a huge wagon,
drawn by six horses, would roll past, bound for the open country. Not till midnight did the metropolis relax, and even then
it breathed in stifled murmurs till dawn once more awakened it
to active life.

One evening, soon after Jane's arrival, she and Carlyle
walked over to Jermyn Street, where the Lord Advocate occupied a fine house. Jeffrey had been quite sick, but was better
now. The callers found both Mrs. Jeffrey and Charlotte away
listening to the debate in the House of Lords. For once they
were able to have Jeffrey all to himself in his own home—a
rare opportunity, for both in public and in private the little
man's life was now seldom his own.

When they returned toward Ampton Street, the weather had
changed to a damp, clammy night. The walk home through
the foggy streets was a foretaste of what London's inclemency
could be.

Jane had not reckoned on possible ill health. Sickness must
not mar the winter for her. With so much to do, it was shocking, here in London, to be indisposed more often than at
Craigenputtock. In Dumfriesshire, where each day of her life,
while the frozen months dragged on, too frequently resembled
all its fellows, and the only changes were those wrought hourly
by the wind which blew over the hills, she had weathered with
modest success far ruder buffetings of storm than those which
penetrated these sheltered city streets. But there was a relentless quality to these mists. Fogs so thick that one might put
them in one's pocket—they soaked one to the very heart, leaving no warmth or pith within. Jane found that her strength too
often deserted her. Carlyle blamed his wife's energetic packing
and galloping at the Craig in preparation for her winter's move:
all that fret, alas, was cause of her debility. Jane would not
admit that such things could down her. Yet there were many
days when she was compelled to rest on the couch beside her
husband's desk. That was no real hardship, of course. Outside
rolled the heavy breath of London: one's very nostrils filled
with soot. Under the brown mists, the smoke from a hundred
thousand ovens and hearths fell earthward from the chimneys

till the streets grew black. At the start of winter, while even fogs had novelty, Jane found amusement in groping along the thoroughfares, where torch-bearing spectres shouted through the gloom. But the sight of coach horses, in what should have been broad daylight, preceded by the dim shapes of men carrying flambeaux, soon lost its romance.

There were hours when she missed Scotland, Craigenputtock, and the presence of her own things about her. Most of all, she experienced an emptiness of heart when she thought of her mother at Templand, or the Carlyles at Dumfries. With Tom's family, though she had scarcely realized it, she had been developing an intimacy which made them as close to her as her own kindred—brothers and sisters and a second mother. But thoughts like these came to her only if she was quiet or unoccupied: situations rare with Jane unless illness held her captive.

When fogs darkened the streets, Jane lighted her candles at noon and hoped for visitors.

The rate at which company began to seek them out quite astonished the Carlyles. Almost a superabundance, thought Thomas, as he toiled over an essay due for the December issue of the *Edinburgh* (MacVey Napier had agreed to risk another article from Jeffrey's brilliant but dangerous protégé). All who came, Jane noticed, showed such respect for Carlyle. Several were obviously disciples, and listened to him as a prophet declaiming against the utilitarianism and selfishness of the age.

Even foreigners were calling at Ampton Street. Jane was quite terrified when a card bearing the name Gustave d'Eichthal was sent up to her as she sat at home alone one afternoon. She recognized the name at once. The man was a leader of a group of Frenchmen who were seeking to bring peace to a strife-torn world through a brotherhood of nations, and by a scheme calling for all property to be held in common for men's general benefit. Struck by certain of his articles, they had greeted Carlyle as a kindred spirit. Jane recalled the excitement which their message had brought to the Craigenputtock household, and her husband's conjectures as to the nature of these reformers. When he had written to Goethe of their communication, the old German had cautioned him against mixing with the likes of them.

But this warning was hardly necessary; from the start Carlyle had shown a rugged independence of all movements. He refused to ally himself with any 'isms, though he would not go so far as Goethe wished by cutting off all exchanges with these radicals in France.

Here, in the flesh, waited the writer of that earliest communication from the St. Simonians. What should she do, Jane wondered, in this embarrassing predicament? It was Carlyle he wished to see, not Carlyle's wife! What did she have to say to this utter stranger? Obviously he could not be kept lingering on the doorstep. In spite of her qualms, Jane asked him in.

A surprising radical and wild man. The first thing that Jane noticed was his gentleness. He was so trustful, so earnest-looking and sincere—a meek zealot ready to suffer for his faith. Before she quite realized what was happening, Jane found herself talking cordially and with animation to d'Eichthal who obviously was enjoying himself and not in the least impatient for the return of the man whom he had come to see.

When her husband at last entered, Jane was chatting as gaily with her visitor as though she were the experienced and accomplished mistress of some famous continental salon. Her success was in large part the result of a quite unstudied manner. She had simply been herself. The experience taught her confidence. She need not hesitate henceforth to take her part.

D'Eichthal came again. He brought others of his group to be introduced. He was also a friend of young John Stuart Mill, and sometimes arrived in his company.

John Mill was a person whom Jane had long looked forward to seeing. Through her husband's descriptions in letters she felt she already knew him well. When presently they met, a blush of pleasure mantled her cheek. It was thrilling to become acquainted with Carlyle's admirers. Cautiously she studied this boy, who, her husband thought, was one of the clearest-headed among the handful of his young followers. A slim, tall, rather elegant fellow, with a smallish face and neatly combed auburn hair. Rather lovable and sweet, one would say, if only he would be somewhat less earnest. His delicate, almost feminine mouth hardly agreed with the massiveness of his forehead. Highly strung, and nervous, clearly. There was a certain twitching of his eyebrow and lip when he spoke, noticeable especially when his face was tense with concentration. One thing she was surprised at: his modesty and shyness in the presence of women. Her blush, surely, had passed quite unnoticed by his bashful glance. Could such a quiet scholar ever dare to observe any woman or look her in the face?

Mill had no faculty for laughter. His precision and rationality were traits almost comic in their excess. If John Mill were to get up to heaven, Jane's husband wickedly remarked, he would not rest content until he had explored and explained it all. However, though lack of humor might be termed a defect, Mill was obviously loyal and affectionate. What more could one ask of a friend?

Jane had scarcely anticipated how exciting afternoons and evenings could be when the town began to fill up in November. The circle of their acquaintances grew ever wider and more interesting. Sometimes of course a rather ill-assorted miscellany of people gathered. When this happened, clashing opinions made the business of managing the company a problem. Yet in such emergencies Jane was seldom at a loss. She was learning to mix the oil and vinegar, the sugar, pepper and salt of humanity with remarkable skill. Never a dull flavor did she permit, but she tried to see to it that her spices would not bite the tongue.

"Charles Buller," Carlyle would exclaim when his former pupil dropped in of an afternoon, "you are the most genial rascal I ever met!" Jane knew that this young man was one of her husband's special enthusiasms. He expected great things of Charles. His wealth, his Cambridge training, his influential friends, his splendid physique and personal attractiveness formed an almost unbeatable list of qualifications for a political career. If only he would get over his habit of making a joke of everything! Of his quick intellect Carlyle had no doubt whatsoever. Jane could not help noticing how the blither spirits of the world were attracted to hard-working, generally serious Thomas Carlyle. They kindled his own spirit to a cheerier brightness, and in exchange they drew from him a greater strength and purpose.

Charles Buller's face was that of a mischievous seraph escaped from a canvas by Raphael and put through the best English schooling—an alert, quizzical, handsome, not quite grown-up countenance under its shock of waving hair swept dashingly across the forehead. His eyes under high arched eyebrows were set wide apart to contribute to the look of utter innocence which their mischievous twinkle so notably belied. His rather full lips had a slight delicate upcurl at the ends of the mouth which made it difficult for any watcher to take literally even such remarks as Charles was occasionally willing to advance in seriousness. As he entered the none too spacious door of her Ampton Street apartment, Jane had a moment of alarm—it seemed difficult to believe so big a man could ever squeeze through. He was six feet three inches tall, and his friends, joking at his size, insisted that he measured a yard at the shoulders.

Allan Cunningham was another big man: it was amusing to hear his Annandale accent getting ever broader under the infection of her husband's talk. Jane had long since given up the effort to break Thomas of his provincial dialect. He spoke it with such relish and affection.

These, and others, were the afternoon visitors—and of course, Jeffrey. There were weeks when he never missed a day. To have the Lord Advocate of Scotland trudging to their door was something of a novelty for good Mrs. Miles and her daughter. Evidently he took a lively interest in young Mrs. Carlyle, whom he referred to as his cousin.

His frequent calls did not begin till late autumn. Earlier his sickness and a misunderstanding had interfered. In October, he had sent a note of apology, explaining he could no longer visit nor receive visitors, so weary and ill was he after the day's obligatory business. But when his health improved, the Carlyles had already been swept up in the full current of their London life. Jeffrey was hurt by their neglect. He had called three times at their lodgings, only to find the occupants away. "I feel, or fancy," he wrote to Jane, "that you are cold or scornful to me and the things to which I am devoted—and this brings ice about my heart, and you do not care that it should be melted! Oh, the folly of these repulsions in such a world as this! But I will think no more of them, and am coming to see you."

When at last Jeffrey found the Carlyles at home, the old but weakened bond grew strong again. It was obvious that Jane was the primary attraction. But Jeffrey tried to make it clear that Thomas was equal partner in a triumvirate. "Does not Carlyle know yet that *you* is a *plural* noun? Or *dual* at all events?"

Jeffrey exercised for health. In Edinburgh, Comely Bank had made an excellent terminal for his walk. Here in London, Ampton Street served equally well. He was soon as much at home in Jane's drawing room as he had ever been while they were neighbors in Scotland.

To all appearances, London was treating him better than some of his letters had led Jane to believe. His spirits, at least, justified that supposition, though there were rumors that he did not succeed so well in politics as he had in law. With the Carlyles he was as gay as a lark and chattered with equal volubility. The barrier which, stone by stone, had been rising between the two men seemed crumbling away. Jeffrey's not quite abandoned efforts to shape Carlyle were sometimes an irritation, but the former editor was beginning at last to realize the hopelessness of the task. He had largely washed his hands of the affair.

Occasionally the thought crossed Jane's mind that it was rather surprising for Jeffrey to take no opportunity for presenting Carlyle to some of the truly distinguished men of affairs and letters with whom as Lord Advocate he associated. Not that Carlyle wished to meet them on the basis of an arranged introduction. Still, it was remarkable that Jeffrey never even suggested such a thing. What discouraged him, Carlyle could not imagine, nor did he greatly care. But neither husband nor wife realized how fully Jeffrey had learned his lesson. His notion of Carlyle had at last fashioned itself into a picture of him even more rugged, individualistic, and solitary than Thomas actually was. Yes, he would remark, he had praised him to Samuel Rogers. But to introduce his erstwhile protégé to the banker poet whose writings, in their sales, once rivaled Byron's, seemed never to have occurred to him.

Tom was still a trifle irritated at Jeffrey's insistence in keeping Jane's picture. Surely he did not deserve the honor of clinging to it so long. But Jeffrey's friendliness, the homelike way in which he comported himself—almost as though he were indeed an older member of the family—was disarming.

Edward Irving was their friend of longest standing now in London. But since Irving's wife believed she had reasons for discouraging intimacy between the two families, little effort was made to renew ties. Yet though Jane and Thomas rarely saw Edward, they could always hear about him through Eliza Miles, their landlady's daughter and a member of his congregation. They were fully aware of all that had transpired in his history since their last sight of him at Craigenputtock.

Irving's flock had long since moved from the Caledonian Chapel—a building too small to accommodate the crowds that gathered in the early days to hear the new-come orator—to a fine new building in Regent's Square. Dr. Chalmers, Irving's old superior in Scotland, had assisted at the inaugural service.

For a time all had gone well. But presently Irving, triumphantly set up in his new church, had noticed a diminution in the throng that came to hear him. This puzzled and distressed him. His early successes had led him to believe that he had been chosen by Divine Providence to be the instrument of a new spirit of religiousness which was to spread far and wide from London—just as once the gospel had gone forth to the North and South, the East and West, from pagan and unregenerate Rome. The first to drift away had been the fashionables of the city, whose presence had convinced Irving that even among the worldly and sophisticated his message was to take effect to the new glory of the Lord. Irving, in his lack of sophistication, had not reckoned on the propensity of society to chase after each new fad with the eagerness of hunters for treasure—fine gold or tinsel, it made little difference. He took a boyish pride in his powers of elocution. He could not see that his remarkable abilities caused both his triumph and his disappointment. When they became used to the novelty of his methods, when his archaic language and prophet's manner were no longer new, the fickle lords and ladies, the members of Parliament and officers of state, drifted away to other excitements and left Irving to the *bona-fide* members of his flock and to the expanding group of religious fanatics who attached themselves, because of his advanced doctrines, like camp followers to Irving's more level-headed compatriots. These enthusiasts could not be shocked when Irving spoke of Christ as a brother, nor when he insisted that almost any day God might walk the earth again for final judgment. The Bible foretold it. Irving had intensively studied the prophets. He had written books on *Revelations* and its secrets. For years the subject had furnished him with exciting matter for his sermons. But how would the immediate coming be announced? The clues to that great mystery were still to be found. Irving's brain, heated by his imaginings, kept in constant turmoil through his preaching, was ready to receive the final enlightenment.

Then he met a man named Hatley Frere. Like himself, Frere was deeply read in the *Apocalypse*. But Frere professed to see light where Irving still groped in darkness: the *Book of Daniel*, when rightly interpreted, unraveled the confusions of the present time and showed the day of new prophecy at hand.

Irving pondered what had been explained to him. His mind, intuitional, fervent, illogical, worked in the yeast of these new marvels. He placed himself under the tutelage of his inspired acquaintance, and before long was ready to accept what Frere foretold.

The times themselves had spoken; the second age of miracles was come. Who could doubt the authenticity of that divine cure which had taken place in the little village of Fernicarry? There a devout country girl, through prayer, had healed herself of a fatal consumption, then risen from her bed to utter prophecies in a strange voice under the spell of a divine seizure.

Irving and his followers clung to these portents with a solemn hope and an uncontrollable excitement. When the gift of tongues, so it was written, should come again to the world, the millennium would be at hand.

During the winter of 1831—that of the Carlyles' sojourn in London—Irving was facing the most serious problem of his career. The gift of tongues had broken forth among members of his own congregation. Small wonder, thought cynics—what with Irving's preaching and the influence of his writings. But Irving did not link cause and effect. Divine inspiration could come through God alone, and all that a mortal man in a position of responsibility could do was to verify divine authenticity. "The Lord prospers his work greatly in my church," he wrote to a member of his family, "several of the brethren have received the gift of tongues and prophecy; and in answer to prayer, the sick are healed and raised up again. The coming of the Lord is close at hand."

Yet should he allow these voices to speak out during public worship? With prayer and meditation Irving pondered his problem in an agony of indecision. Who was he to stop the voice of the Lord? He must surrender before it.

"Good Heavens! How *can* Edward Irving take in such *janners!*" exclaimed Jane Carlyle, horrified at the thought of the cult of prophets who gathered for nightly seances at Irving's house. She and Carlyle were sure that Irving's wife Isabella, instead of exercising a restraining hand, was pushing Edward further along the path which led to madness. Worse still, she fended off all her husband's old friends who were seeking to reclaim him. Carlyle had been rebuffed when the trouble first began. He must try again. They could not let Edward persist in this self-destruction.

Thomas agreed to do his best. On several evenings, now, Eliza Miles had come running home in tears from church meetings at Irving's, gatherings which had broken up in bitter wrangling, a majority opposing the "Tongues," the fanatic minority defending them. So Carlyle spoke to Irving with a vehemence amounting almost to anger, in his solicitude for his old comrade. Irving sat there, dejection in his attitude, his face buried in his hands. But he clung to what he believed in. Carlyle was forced to report that his mission had failed.

One day Jane and Thomas walked to Irving's house for an informal call. Irving himself greeted them. He had his youngest child in his arms and was tossing it playfully about in a bear-like manner which seemed to please both participants in the game. The Carlyles were delighted to find Edward alone. Privacy was almost a lost blessing with him. At any hour he was liable to intrusion. Soon, indeed, a muffled hum of voices let the visitors know that they had been mistaken in supposing the house deserted. A meeting of some sort was going on in an adjoining room. Innocent of its nature, the callers went on talking. Suddenly unhuman shrieks rang through the building.

"There is one prophesying, come and hear her!" said Irving, in a matter-of-fact tone. "There are the Tongues."

Jane and Thomas had scarcely credited the rumors which

Eliza Miles had been bringing home. Neither of them wished to see or hear further. But Irving insisted. So they mounted the stairs. What they beheld was almost unbelievable to them. They had never before seen religious hysteria. A woman surrounded by a group of wrapt listeners was howling like one possessed.

A feeling of utter revulsion swept over Jane. She must get out at once. She was on the point of fainting. Carlyle hurried her into the street.

One excellent feature about the writing craft, Carlyle told his wife: it needed very little equipment—a chair, a table, and paper. But for a while Thomas had some difficulty in establishing the table. With the restlessness of an Arab with his tents on the desert, he shifted about from place to place in the living room till at last he discovered the most favorable spot. After Craigenputtock, these quarters were decidedly hampering. He felt, he explained, as though he were tied up in a sack and could not get his fins stirring. But once plunged in his work, he and Jane hoped, these inconveniences would be forgot. Jane bore with his vagaries and migrations, and laughed at the idiosyncracies of writing men. Let us be of good cheer, Thomas declared, *nothing but ourselves can finally beat us!*

Through autumn and winter Carlyle was very busy. Two major essays grew under his pen—"Characteristics" for the *Edinburgh Review*, "Samuel Johnson" for *Fraser's Magazine*. These were the big guns fired for the defense of his beliefs and to keep his London castle free of debt. But there were lesser articles as well, and even verses: several of them new, others pulled out of an old grab bag and renovated for publication. More than ever before, his work was in the public eye—to the pleasure of some readers and the irritation of others. Enthusiasts, Jane heard, could recognize her husband's manner and thought in half a sentence of reading. When the *Athenaeum* published a stale thing written ten years earlier and submitted for what it would bring, the editors displayed the author's name in big letters as an incentive to purchasers. Tom, seeing it in their offices in the Strand, had walked hurriedly past with downcast eyes as if he had come upon his *alter ego* in the pillory. But Jane would not be a partner to such modesty. The growth of her husband's reputation meant a great deal to her and she was charmed when editors who had previously displayed no enthusiasm began to bid for essays. Rather like old-clothes shops, these journals, declared Carlyle, where one laid out one's wares and haggled for a price. A lot of that type of literary manufacture would be much too much; he refused to enter into any long-term contracts.

"Characteristics," as Jane might have expected from the fortunes of *Teufelsdröckh*, stirred up something of a fuss. Jeffrey had now and then confided his ideas about Carlyle to Carlyle's wife, not always with the happiest results. It was lucky that she knew nothing of the letter which he dispatched to Napier after reading this article. "I fear Carlyle will not do," he warned, "that is, if you do not take the liberties and the pains with him that I did, by striking out freely and writing in occasionally." That liberty, however, Napier had been expressly forbidden to take by the author. He might discard the entire article, if he chose, but, Carlyle warned, he must not treat it like a slaughtered fowl and pluck out all its feathers. "The misfortune is," Jeffrey continued in his capacity as power behind the editor's chair, "the misfortune is that he is very obstinate and, I am afraid, conceited." Jane would angrily have denied Jeffrey's charge had she learned of it. Opinionated and independent, of course, but not conceited. In London, Jeffrey went on, Carlyle had got among people who applauded him, nullifying the remedy of general avoidance and neglect which might otherwise effect a cure. "It is a great pity," Tom's old editor concluded, "for he is a man of genius and industry, and with the capacity of being an elegant and impressive writer."

Napier did not doubt for an instant concerning the genius. It spoke to one from every page. But his first reading of the article had left him confused as to its meaning. His mystification, when report of it reached Ampton Street, raised considerable merriment. Why, the sense was plain enough! The state of the world was deplorable, wicked, and unjust. For remedy, there must be long travail and the throes of new birth—that, or destruction.

When the issue of the *Review* appeared, however, Carlyle's friends understood the essay and encouraged Thomas to go forward. What if Napier were shocked once he fully comprehended what explosive stuff he had packed into his respectable *Review?* Leigh Hunt, whose *Examiner* article, written soon after the turn of the century, assailing the degenerate Prince Regent, was still memorable, was so delighted that he wrote an appreciative letter on the author's outspokenness and called on the Carlyles at their lodgings.

Thus, with work, new friends, and novel experiences, the months slipped by—Christmas season and New Year's of 1832. Not all of Jane's acquaintances belonged to the class that came for tea. The tradespeople who served her were part of her social world. She learned the history of each. She took a friendly interest also in the grimy little chimney sweep who took care of the flues, in the lamplighter whom she often met on his daily rounds, in the postman. On the latter's knock, she would drop her work and rush down to the door. A letter from her mother, perhaps, or news from Scotsbrig? Or Alick might be writing to tell how he and his wife were managing. Alick was bidding for a farm near Ecclefechan. His new-born daughter carried Jane's name, proof of the compatibility the two families had enjoyed at Craigenputtock. Most often merely the *Dumfries Courier* was Jane's reward for haste. But the newspaper told her more than what was printed in its pages. With canny thriftiness, to avoid the extravagant fee for letters (the penny post was not yet functioning), Carlyle and she had evolved the scheme of using the Dumfries journal, at its lower rate, as secret newsbearer. On its wrapper, in letters small enough to escape official detection, Tom's sisters could write "All's well," or send other messages according to prearranged code.

In late January a letter arrived from Scotsbrig. Jane and Thomas hid no secrets from each other. What came from either family both were privileged to read. She broke the seal. The writing was in Jean's hand. Idly she began to read. Then her heart pounded.

James Carlyle was dead.

Tom's old father had caught a severe cold. The toil-worn man —seventy-four years old—had lacked the strength to throw off what began as a minor illness.

Tears rose to Jane's dark eyes. No family lived in closer bonds of affection than those which held together the Carlyles. When Thomas, who had also heard the postman, came downstairs, he found his wife with her heavy news.

There was not time to return for the burial. Besides, Tom's mother, mindful of the difficulties of the journey and unwilling to interrupt her son's work, had bidden him not to.

No other man—and Carlyle had seen great ones now—could ever win so much of his respect as had this peasant father. One hope moved Thomas—to live worthily of James Carlyle. Should he and Jeannie have children, might those children be in the pattern of his father's spirit, so that its worth might carry itself honorably forth into new generations. Such a man, reared in poor Annandale, with no advantages and only his own character to fight his battles for him, was the true preacher of the gospel of freedom—of what man can do and be.

The grass in Hyde Park was losing its dun color. Trees were making leaf again and spring was actively returning. During the past winter, Jane and her husband had several times discussed the problem of where they should permanently settle. From the time she first thought of marrying Carlyle, Jane persisted in the conviction that the most fitting place for his career should one day prove to be London. Secretly she was hopeful that London would now become their home. But after she had joined him there in the autumn, she quickly perceived that for him the winter represented merely an interlude from Craigenputtock. He did not consider the time ripe for a longer test. His book had failed of publication. There had been only the meanest subsistence from writing for periodicals. The inferences were obvious. They must return to the moorlands. Lodgings, even of the best, were a poor substitute for a home of one's own, and the lease of a house could not yet be thought of.

So Jane and Thomas let it be known that they were going back to Scotland. Calls were exchanged and adieus bidden. Leigh Hunt came to say good-bye, Irving, and the others. All expressed the hope for a return at some not too distant day.

Amazing how one's possessions multiplied regardless of the admonitions of one's budget! An extra container for their goods was an absolute necessity. Jane was resolved that it should be no ordinary chest, useless once it had served the purpose of the journey. Poking about in the shops, she noticed an empty brandy barrel for sale at a good bargain. Clean, tight, and of ample proportions—just what she needed. It could hold such quanti-

ties of luggage, then be a water-barrel for the rains at Craigenputtock. So, to her husband's amused astonishment, she triumphantly made her purchase.

Like migratory birds flying to the Southland, they had come
before the setting in of winter. Now, in the closing days of
March, they returned where the swallows would be nesting in
the hills. The visit to London had left them poor enough in
cash, yet both were richer for the experience.

The coach in which they journeyed northward was a ponderous vehicle. From preference, Jane sat within and Tom—some
of the time—outside. When mid-day came, and a halt, they
dined, tête-à-tête like children at a picnic, on the lunch which
Jane had put up to save expense.

A brief visit to Jane's uncle and his family in Maryland
Street, Liverpool, then the voyage by boat to Caplegill, and
their feet once more touched Scotland. Before taking the familiar road to Craigenputtock, they were to visit Jane's mother at
Templand, and Carlyle's family at Scotsbrig.

At Dumfries, they found two letters: one from the continent,
from Dr. John, now comfortably supporting himself as traveling physician for the wealthy Countess of Clare; the other from
a magazine editor in London. Goethe, announced the editor, was
dead. Would Carlyle write a short eulogy for him?

Though long expected, this news and its way of reaching
them gave a heavy blow to the Carlyles. Thomas felt as though
he had a second time lost a father: Goethe, perhaps more than
any man, had been the guardian and shaper of his mind.

Goethe had died on the twenty-second of March, seven
months after his eighty-second birthday. To honor this natal
anniversary, Carlyle, with the aid of deputies in London and
Edinburgh, had sent a testimonial to Weimar bearing the signa-
tures of fifteen British friends. From Scotland, John Wilson and
Sir Walter Scott inscribed their names. Robert Southey, Barry
Cornwall, and other well-known men signed in London. Even
Wordsworth, though his opinion of his German contemporary
was privately low, added his name to the list. With the letter
went a medallion. Jane Carlyle had designed the seal. Round
it, in old German capitals, stood the inscription, *Ohne Hast
Aber Ohne Rast*—Carlyle's favorite text from Goethe. Such had
been the final gift to Weimar.

Chapter Twelve

A WOMAN'S arrival at her dismantled house is like an explorer's return to a bivouac in the jungle—there can be no foretelling what inroads time and nature will have made. Damp had penetrated the whinstone walls at Craigenputtock; a visitation of painters was a necessity. So Jane's first weeks were strenuous. But presently all was set to rights. Craigenputtock, without and within, was habitable and inhabited.

There had been a grand reunion of all the livestock. Harry, Jane's horse, neighed loud and long when he found himself back in his old quarters, as glad to be at home as Jane was to have him there. Nooly, the cow, munched the grass or lifted her slow, philosophic gaze to stare at Jane hurrying past on her rounds. A new flock of hens scratched and clucked in the yard, and produced eggs with such good will that Jeannie turned to the expedient of preserving the surplus in lime water against the days of diminishing returns.

What was it Goethe counseled? Do the duty nearest at hand, and the next will show itself in course. No one who lays that precept to heart, thought Jane, can ever suffer from the dull restlessness of boredom. It amused her to imagine how the fine ladies whom she had seen in London would conduct themselves here. Could they bake a loaf of bread? Could they ride to Dumfries and back again without disaster? Could they sweep and scour as she had done? Imagine a dame of fashion on these moors; the very church, her last imaginable resource, seven miles away over the stoniest roads! No place of amusement within a day's journey! The ridge of hills would seem to shut her off from every earthly bliss.

Jane fell easily into her old routine. Weather permitting, she and her husband took an hour's ride to begin the day. Tom saw the color returning to his wife's pale cheeks—her eyes alive and sparkling, her dark curls fluttering in the wind.

After breakfast, when her morning chores were done, there was usually time to wander in the small garden, gather flowers for the house, and inspect the livestock. Sewing and mending, reading and sometimes writing—there were more friends now who required letters—these and other occupations filled the afternoon. In the evening, if Tom was off on one of his mighty walks, Jane sometimes wandered alone near home as the evening star grew brighter and the constellations emerged in the gathering dusk to spangle its immensity with a million million points of light.

The charm of novelty had not yet worn away for Jane. How different was all this from Holborn or the Strand! If Carlyle could be satisfied here, and prosper in his writing (the lack of books, after such great plenty in the libraries in London, somewhat appalled him) surely she could be happy. Except for society, Jane told herself, she had everything that her heart desired. And after all her husband was as good company as one could wish for. If people she took pleasure in could hardly be expected, save by miracle, to visit, and the knocker hung idle for weeks, at least such quiet was better for the health and nerves.

A strange, shadowy existence; nothing actual in it but the food one ate, the bed one slept on. Hardly one's little daily round of life was real. All else—a dream of the absent and distant, of things past and to come.

Thus passed the first summer of their return to Craigenputtock. And after it, in eternal march, moved the procession of the seasons.

Though Mill and Leigh Hunt could not venture so far, there nevertheless were other visitors to break the solitude. One, especially, had surprised them. It was Sunday, the twenty-fifth of August, in the year 1833. Tom's brother John had just returned to Italy. Without his affable presence, the house seemed very lonely. The Carlyles were seated at dinner when they heard the clatter of a gig. Leaving the table, they hurried to investigate. A tall, spare, gaunt-faced young man, dressed in clothes of different style from those of either London or the provinces, stepped out of a battered carriage. His name, he said, was Emerson—Waldo Emerson. He had come from America. Were they by chance expecting him? John Stuart Mill, whom he had met, had promised to write.

The wanderer explained his mission. He had turned aside from the usual route followed by his countrymen in order to seek out the author of some essays, notably "Characteristics," which had deeply stirred him when he had read them in the periodical room of the Athenaeum, Boston, Massachusetts. They had been a new voice speaking.

Tom and Jane, recovering from their first surprise, welcomed the stranger. His coming was like a visit from the clouds. Such a journey to Craigenputtock, for such a purpose, Jane exclaimed, had not been undertaken since Noah's deluge. They insisted that Emerson spend the night. So the hired gig was dismissed with instructions to return on the following day.

Carlyle took the American for a walk over the Craig, and learned his history. On the moors and in the house they talked of many things, including books. Emerson, wishing to know the literary plans of his host, was told of the early misfortunes of *Teufelsdröckh*. But now, at last, James Fraser was ready to agree to run it serially in his magazine, though he would pay little enough for doing so.

That evening Jeannie wore the necklace given her by Goethe. Surely a man who had traveled so vast a distance on a mission like this deserved the acknowledgment reserved for the presence of genius. Emerson, watching Jane's animation, admiring her intelligence and imagination, rejoiced for the sake of his new-made friend. Truly, he was blessed in such a wife. She was a fitting partner for a man of Carlyle's gifts.

As for the host and hostess, they were delighted with the wayfarer. A lovable man, they agreed. Long after he had left they still discussed him. One characteristic, especially, was remarkable: his unity with himself.

What a strange feature of her husband's trade—he would write an essay which soon lost itself like a single drop of water in the great sea of magazine articles. Then, perhaps years later, the thought sent forth would return in unexpected guise. A stranger in a distant land might find it and bring it home as Emerson had done. Even in distant America, her husband's words were heard.

A second summer was over. Autumn would sweep across the hills, and freezing weather, raising a Chinese wall against the world. More and more these barriers irked Carlyle. Lack of intelligent men to talk to, lack of books to study—Jane listened with what sympathy she could to her husband's lamentations. Why was there not a royal library in every country town, he wished to know? There was a royal jail, sure enough, and a royal gallows!

John Stuart Mill, to Jane's relief, was helpful in the crisis. Thinking some day to write a history of the period, Mill had gathered a sizable library on the French Revolution. But when he learned of Carlyle's growing interest, he generously agreed to lend him books.

Goethe had been the strongest link in the already frayed chain binding Carlyle to German literature. With Goethe's death, Thomas was free to turn his attention elsewhere. More and more, Jane could see, his inclinations were shifting toward history and the huge subject of Democracy's emergence. His excitement was catching. She liked to keep posted on all topics that held him.

But during the autumn previous to the year of Emerson's visit, she had sighed inwardly when Thomas spoke of the imperative need for several months in Edinburgh. The books lent by Mill were not enough. "The grim prospect of another winter in this solitude," she explained to Bess Stodart, "is too frightful for my husband, who finds that it is absolutely essential for carrying on, not only his craft, but his existence, to hear from time to time a little human speech." Changes of routine had their vexations and their difficulties. These were hardly ameliorated if one lived with a man of Carlyle's temperament. The Edinburgh winter had gone badly for Jane. For the first time in the six years since marriage, a protracted interval of discouragement dulled the usual brightness of her spirit. The mischievous light in her eye was in temporary eclipse, and her cheeks grew pinched and thin. There were moments when she became indignant at herself for the failure of her energy and her enthusiasm. What right had she thus to squander time and make no progress? She must travel forward, not sit whimpering on a milestone, lamenting the roughness of the road. Long ago, a puzzled skepticism had stolen away her childhood belief in prayer. But her doubts had not banished the inner need for something outside herself to cling to. What Jane dreaded above all else, in ill health and despondency, was to become a burden to Carlyle and tiresome to her friends. Did it follow inevitably that one's dreams of life's ideal, running along the road of one's existence, should be crushed beneath the Juggernaut of realities? She was sick at heart and sick in body. The headaches that beset her eager spirit lasted, sometimes, for three whole days. Carlyle had never witnessed such agonies of pain.

In the autumn after Emerson's visit, there had been no need for another move to Edinburgh. A stroke of good fortune had come to Thomas in the shape of readily available books. Through the efforts of friends, the library of a big country house ten miles from Craigenputtock had been thrown open to Carlyle. The owner was willing to have him take away as many volumes as might be needed. Providentially, a large part of the collection lay in the very realm of Carlyle's exploration.

Two boxfuls soon arrived, the forerunners of many more. From the lot, Jane selected for her own reading Madame Campan's *Vie Privée de Marie Antoinette,* and Madame Roland's *Mémoires.* She also dipped into the autobiography of Madame de Staël.

Fortunate for Jane that she had reading of her own to occupy her. With such a quantity of books, her husband was racing through the supply like a consciously directed whirlwind. He had moved from Jane's century to the end of the eighteenth—she could follow him there or remain deserted in the present. For ten hours at a stretch he would be lost to immediate existence as the words before his eyes changed into the bloody pageantry of the Revolution. It was not mere articles that he was preparing. His hopes had turned again to the writing of a book.

Jane read near him or metamorphosed large balls of wool into scarfs and other garments. Her knitting needles, when she plied them, darted through her work with an almost inaudible click, so well had she mastered the art of keeping quiet. At last she would steal away to bed, the night retreating down the shadowed corridors before the little light of her candle. In the morning, over their breakfast, he would tell her of the visions he had seen—men and women, savage-eyed and wild, rushing through the streets of the Faubourg de St. Antoine to attack the Bastille, symbol of outmoded power changed to tyranny. Hapless, beautiful Charlotte Corday, riding as if in triumph in a creaking tumbrel to the guillotine which would shear her life away for the killing of Marat. Sampson, the executioner, had struck the cheek of the severed head, and an ominous mutter rose from the intent people—from the mob which was usually so ready to snarl approval of any wanton act of desecration by Sampson's bloody hand. Carlyle had deliberated in imagination with the shapers of the new Constitution during their hour of triumphant self-congratulation and had seen the smiles of men confident that they were about to cross the threshold of old oppressions into a bright new day of liberty.

Of such stuff were made the waking dreams of man—from these events had sprung the laughter and tears, the defeats and triumphs, of that frenzied generation.

Something would come of all this reading of histories and memoirs. A notable book, he promised, would emerge. Jane, hearing his descriptions, listening to the anger, the merriment, the deep sympathy in his voice as he told of his vicarious experiences, did not question the fulfillment of the hope.

By way of practicing himself in narrative, Carlyle began an account, half emotional in spirit, half historical, of the famous scandal of the diamond necklace—a brief dramatic parenthesis in the lull before the tempest of the Revolution. The theft of these highly valuable jewels through the supposed complicity of Marie Antoinette furnished a plot ideal for the purpose.

When Jane read what he had written, she had added reason for confidence. The action flashed before her eyes in words and images of extraordinary vividness. Like a painting in rich colors, yet with one great difference: the figures breathed and moved.

Jane was worried by the hours her husband kept. The candles which he used were her spies; their length told her how late he had stayed up. Thomas gave scant heed to the little clock which she had placed on his table. Sometimes, glancing at it, he would realize that time in the actual world was passing. He must take a walk by way of physic. Out he would go, alone, over the deserted moors, the very existence of which he had forgot in his concentration, only to return to the waiting books and further hours of study.

No disturbance, no distraction possible, in these gray, silent months of winter. Never a visitor to raise the knocker and interrupt Carlyle's labors. The few strangers who did appear were poor wandering laborers—Irish vagabonds in patched and tattered clothing. Jane never turned these miserable creatures empty-handed from her door. She could always spare them something from her supplies. Quiet by day, incredible quiet at night, save when the wind clicked together the brittle, naked branches of the plane trees and blew the withered leaves over the doorstep. In the morning, when one cleared a pathway through them, the rustle of the broom could be heard a furlong away.

As if to balance the frozen calm, a sullen tempest would sometimes rise to a crescendo of violence, knocking the slates from the roof, uprooting the trees, and spending itself at last in deluges of rain or sleet. After weeks of storm which blackened the peat moss and seared the heather a dull brown, Jane could hardly bear the sight of so much desolation. She could endure looking out only when the moon silvered the landscape with a magic garment. After the snows had fallen, Jane noticed, in the starlight, that the enclosure before the house was filled with hares driven in from the moors by lack of fodder. Their dark forms bounded and skipped over the ground as though in some fantastic, witchlike dance.

She drew some comfort from the thought of the ample peatstack ready at hand for heat and fuel. By keeping every fire blazing, it was possible, even in the bitterest weather, to be fairly comfortable within doors. Human warmth from outside was more difficult to obtain. So as not to upset him, his wife did not tell Carlyle how much, in her aloneness, she missed the friends who had peopled her little drawing room in London—the talking and the laughter.

Her piano, grotesquely out of tune and useless as a weaver's frame, had stood idle for many months. But just when there seemed to be little hope that she could play it again, a piano tuner, unexpected as a Negro at the North Pole, had come to the rescue. For five shillings six pence, he had rehabilitated the sick instrument. He recommended its removal from the parlor to the dining room where it would be safer from frosts. When the embers in the hearths blackened at night, water left in pitchers near the outer walls sometimes disclosed a heavy crust of ice on winter mornings.

After the piano was itself again, Tom once more could enjoy his wife's playing—the only music he really cared for. It had power to winnow all the bitter dust out of him when he was tired, he remarked half jestingly, and could make him for the moment a good man.

Would they attempt another winter at Craigenputtock? Perhaps not. Carlyle was again pondering the subject which had occupied their minds so often in the past: the question of where to make a permanent settlement. Should they think once more of trying London? Craigenputtock, of course, had its advantages. Its silences were unexcelled for writing. But even with authorship the sole consideration, there were obstacles in the way. At so great a distance from the offices of magazines, Carlyle was finding it increasingly difficult to market essays written to keep the pot boiling. It was easy, in correspondence, for even friendly editors to make polite evasions. Talked to in their sanctums, they could not be so noncommittal. Besides, literature written away from London had always a provincial look.

They must not forget, Jane remarked, that *Teufelsdröckh* had been written at Craigenputtock. Yet always, she added, they had been troubled by a hidden suspicion that the choice of this isolation, from the start, had been a mistake. Was it really justifiable to cut themselves off from human activities? The need for economy had been their chief excuse. Yet had they made their decision through wisdom or mere cowardice and an urge to run away? Life, a contracting circle, was hemming them in. Years of solitude would find them caught within a petty sphere; tethered like horses on a barren heath. With an objective before her, Jane declared, she felt she could leap six-bar gates; here there was no goal, only the profitless hardships of living on a remote hillside.

Because he was apt to change his mind as his work throve or languished, it was not easy to discover Carlyle's fixed determination. Of late, however, he had grown visibly and audibly restless. Nothing but the wretchedest, forsaken, discontented existence here, he muttered. The supply of books was once more running low. Far too much energy was used up, he declared, just in the effort to keep from exploding in fits of exasperation. During such moments of irritation he was prepared to rush incontinently from the spot like the waters of Loch Urr in the spring freshets. It was not good for him to stay longer in the Nithsdale peat-desert. Why continue in the wilderness like another John the Baptist? Better be a second Paul of Tarsus, and like Paul carry his message to the cities. He and Jane had been too long buried alive.

What brought the discussion down from mere hypothetical conjecture to the solid rock of fact was the conduct of their maid. Grace was her inappropriate name—Betty, Helen, all the rest in doleful procession, had left or been relieved of office. And now Grace wished to depart. After Jane's many struggles to discover servants who would stay at Craigenputtock, this latest defection marked the limits of endurance. "Let us burn our ships and get on the march!" Jane exclaimed. Why not bolt away themselves and end the problem? Why not plan at once for London?

Seeking light on houses, Jane wrote a letter of inquiry to an acquaintance in the city. No lodgings this time. No pepper-box affair like Comely Bank. They must begin their citizenship with a feeling of stability. Their place of dwelling must be adequate. Cheap in rent as possible, of course—very, very cheap—but substantial in construction, roomy and commodious. Possibly a house to meet their needs and pocket book could be found in one of London's suburbs. Rents were lower there, Irving had said, and one had trees and space for a garden.

By way of cash to finance their adventurous settlement, Tom had three hundred pounds in sight, no more. On their marriage day, eight years before, they had possessed as much. When Carlyle thought of past scant returns from literature, he could not down a sense of vague foreboding. But courage! the step they were taking was an obvious necessity. Jane, too, had her qualms. Carlyle was not in so grim a mood that he could not joke with her about her fluctuations. "Spairkin, Despairkin," he called her. To which she replied with spirit that she was no coward though the prospect of the move, with all the generalship entailed, roused in her a sense of desperation.

Cowardice was the last trait her husband dreamed of associating with his Jeannie's character. He had witnessed many tests of her fortitude and never, to his mind, had she failed them.

From his editorial office, Fraser wrote that *Dröckh*, now rechristened *Sartor Resartus* for its serial appearance, was exciting the most unqualified disapprobation among most readers of his magazine. It was even causing a loss of subscriptions. Never mind, the author told himself, no tide had ever ebbed without a turning. All in good time! There were already a few men, and one woman, too, his wife, who had put their highest stamp of approval on the work. In London they would manage somehow, though he would continue to write according to the dictates of his convictions—Jane herself insisted on his keeping his integrity. He would live neither dishonestly nor in vain.

Jane's friend, Mrs. Austin, had sent a letter about houses. They received word also from Leigh Hunt. In Chelsea, where he lived, he knew of possibilities. "How I enjoy the prospect of having such a neighbor!" Excellent Leigh Hunt! No people like their friends in London to cheer and fortify them.

In Scotland, the time for moving, with an inviolable compulsion, fell within a set period of the year—the three days of Whitsuntide, following the seventh Sunday after Easter. As well think of shifting Christmas to July as dream of leasing a house at any other season. The Carlyles did not know that in London such transactions were negotiated with less regard for precision. Hence, when they had made their decision, and the blackbirds, with returning spring, began to whistle in the copses, Jane and Thomas believed that not a moment should be lost. Tom must be off to look at houses, while Jane, at Puttock, should set in motion the machinery for transporting their Lares and Penates to an English home.

Carlyle trimmed the flower borders which he would not see in bloom, then, shortly after the first of May, he put out alone for London. He went reluctantly, mindful that on Jane's slim shoulders would fall the burden of the move. He was to stay temporarily in the familiar lodgings in Ampton Street. Could she have seen him as he approached the city on the top of the stagecoach, Jane, in spite of her distractions, might have laughed. Hunched on the roof of the coach in the drizzling rain, he stared ahead as the horses clattered along the pike. He was humming a melody to himself, over and over: the ballad "Fairest Phillis":

> Haste, haste, fairest Phillis
> To the greenwood let's away,
> To pull the pale primrose:
> 'Tis the first of the May.

But when at last he saw the smoky cloud hanging over London, and the city itself, he changed his tune. He broke into an ancient Scottish lay, a song full of battle and defiance. Grimly, under his breath, he chanted the bold words of a long-dead borderer:

> There's seven Foresters in yon Forest
> And them I want to see, see,
> And them I want to see!

His letters, franked by Charles Buller to save postage, gave Jane much news to feast on, as well as other sweeter fare. "What a time it seems since we were parted, though by the calendar it counts only some nine days! Oh, my Love, if I were to write all the loving things I have thought of thee, whole quires would not hold it. Blessed be the Heavens, I have thee to wife!"

He had seen many houses. He had also had encounters with two old friends. As he had walked through Kensington Gardens (she would stroll there often, he promised her, among its lawns and beech trees and along the margins of its lake, the Serpentine), as he walked there, a black-clad figure, more like a spectre than a man, had jumped up from a bench and clasped his hand in both its own. Irving! Tom had scarcely believed it possible, so pale and flaccid, almost like an effigy of death, had he become, and yet so flushed. Irving's one short laugh, as they talked, had been the horrid echo—not the equivalent—of the hearty peals of mirth which he used to utter when they were boys together in Annandale.

Jeffrey was the other friend. The Lord Advocate, now in

office no longer as a member of the government, was about to be made a justice of the high court of Scotland. He would presently give up his town house in London. When Thomas had called there one morning, he had been amazed at Jeffrey's tremulously amicable greeting, the strained effort which he made to revive the spontaneity of the past. He had been full of good wishes and kindliness, but so nervous and flustered that at the moment of parting he said "good-evening" at the door, though the sun had scarcely climbed to mid-morning.

Jane knew one cause of this embarrassment. It rose from a late misunderstanding which had widened the breach between her husband and Jeffrey. During the past winter the news had come to Craigenputtock that a professorship of astronomy at Edinburgh lay within Jeffrey's powers of appointment. The old observatory there had been modernized and equipped with fine instruments. Search was being made for a qualified observer. Friends who remembered Carlyle's proficiency in mathematics under famous Professor Leslie—he had been his crack scholar— were urging him to apply. But Jeffrey, aware of Carlyle only as a man of letters, was shocked at this presumption. The appointment went to another man.

Carlyle had been sorely disappointed. He had returned for Jeffrey's somewhat petulant, sputtering note of refusal and objection—of reproof on the old score of radicalism (Jeffrey had read *Sartor* in Fraser's)—a letter remarkably fair-minded and good-natured. Yet Jeffrey's attitude and tone had been unfortunate—Carlyle was hurt more deeply than ever he would admit. Had not his old editor of the *Review* days invited him to ask for favors? "Let me know whenever you think I can do you, or anybody you care about, any good." Those were his very words a short month before Carlyle's request. He had been relying too much, lately, on help from Jeffrey. He would not again commit that error.

One other corrosive was tarnishing the brightness of the friendship: Jeffrey's tutoring of Carlyle, direct or by implication, in the proper handling of a wife. Scarcely a sheet of correspondence passed without some hint or hit. In the very letter which administered a scolding for what Jeffrey deemed to be Carlyle's self-erected, perverse obstruction of his own best interests, there was a passing reference to Jane: "Who would not be provoked to see Titania in love with Bottom?" What should one make of that?

Jane had pondered Jeffrey's creed. Had she met it before she knew Carlyle, it might have influenced her more. Happiness was its chief good—it did not set great store by duty. Action and effort were justifiable only when necessary or agreeable. Bear one's lot, Jeffrey counseled, and await patiently the accidents of enjoyment which, along with life's sorrows, would surely come. A passive code, ill suited to a man of energy, or to an energetic woman either. Jeffrey had a disconcerting way of laughing at her schemes for active living, her restless mind, her notions of obligation. Though his attentions showed that he recognized her as a woman, he persisted in treating her, intellectually, as a clever, mistaken child. A child, he insisted, who should seek no goal other than her own happiness. Why, he asked, should she be so wayward as to set herself tasks which none required of her—tasks which only her own impulsions forced her to perform?

When he wrote in this manner, Jane would sometimes reply with a snappish letter. Then Jeffrey was always quick to make a humble plea for grace. How could one stay provoked with him? He was so lovable a man—amusing, sprightly, filled with such a genuine if ineffectual kindness. Jane, once her anger cooled, wished the friendship of all three—herself, her husband, and Jeffrey—to continue, if possible, for always. Wide divergencies of temperament and belief had not been able to destroy it. But now the most recent letter from her husband seemed to confirm the finality of the rupture. "So ends our dealing with bright Jeffreydom," he had written, "once so sparkling, cheerful, now gone out into darkness." But not perpetual darkness, Jane hoped—not darkness robbed of all possibility of sunrise.

Tom's reports on house-hunting were detailed and pictorial. Jane could imagine him storming over the city in pursuit of various clues. Sometimes he would miss his dinner and grow dyspeptical. Alas that such trials must be! Yet he was making fair progress. A house in Chelsea, another elsewhere, had survived eliminations and ranked at the top of his list. Carefully she weighed the advantages of each. That big, massive one, in Chelsea, which her husband and Leigh Hunt had discovered on the second try: three stories to it beside the sunk story, in every one of them three rooms, and in one corner a broadish stair with an old-fashioned balustrade. The apartments on the two upper floors would serve for sleeping quarters. And there were dressing rooms adjoining. Now that they were moving permanently to the city, they had discussed the possibility of separate bedrooms—more space, greater convenience because of Tom's late hours, and better rest since both were painfully light sleepers. Carlyle mentioned a china closet on the ground floor with shelves enough in it to hold all the dishes in the street. Excellent! Jane treasured her small collection of crockery and here was space for it to grow in. She wondered about the wainscoting he had described. Wainscoted to the very ceiling, was it? If so, she hoped the wood was painted. Should it be stained a dark color, hardly any number of candles would dispel the gloom, much less the paltry two which economy ruled as sufficient for each room. Might there not be pests in all that ancient woodwork? Room enough in the house, obviously, for Carlyle and herself, yet perhaps also for bugs! The river troubled her somewhat. Carlyle had explained that Cheyne Row, the street on which the dwelling stood, lay perpendicular to the Thames, fifty yards on the left. Would there not be fog in winter, damp and unwholesome fog? Thomas had written of Chelsea's isolation. That, she decided, must not be made a material point in their deliberation if the house had real advantages. Her husband owned an effectual pair of legs to carry him wherever he wished to go. As for herself, she had been fairly satisfied at Craigenputtock as long as all went smoothly. This outpost of London could be made to do. All she asked for was some of Tom's company. With it, she would find no lack within her own four walls.

Jane had intended to write her husband a long, affectionate letter. But her head ached. There would be little wisdom in driving herself unnecessarily beyond bounds, with final preparations for departure and the journey still to face. She dipped her quill for a last sentence. "God Almighty bless you, my Love," she wrote, "before many days I shall see your face again."

Chapter Thirteen

WHEN at last Jane was ready to leave, there was hardly time to let her husband know the details. "Tell me," he had written, "tell me pointedly which way you come and at what hour: I would not miss you for a sovereign."

Wednesday, the fourth of June, 1834. At the coach terminal in London, Jane scanned anxiously the faces of the waiting people. Not one bore a familiar look. Tom had failed to receive her letter, then? But Jane knew what to do. She supervised the transference of her luggage from the coach. To Ampton Street —she told the cabby.

When she reached their door, Mrs. Miles and Eliza were quite frantic with excitement. But her husband was nowhere to be seen. He had gone out, they explained, when he received no word from her that morning. Jane curled herself up on the bed for a little rest. She was drinking tea, the canary which she had brought from Dumfriesshire chirling away beside her, when Thomas burst in the door. Even before he reached the house he had known that she was there. Her songster had borne the tidings. From the street below, he had caught Chico's gay pipings.

Next day Jane set forth with her husband to inspect houses. A weird business—poking through silent, empty, darkened rooms. It tested one's inner eye to the fullest degree, this effort to imagine how bare walls might look if decently clothed with pictures, how yards of desolate flooring would appear once they were dressed in carpets and had tables and chairs on them. Rather like exploring many-chambered caverns of the earth, and guessing how they might look if one took the whim to furnish them.

Jane's first sight of the interior of the Chelsea house was not convincing. How big and echoing it seemed, how dreadfully impersonal! But as she looked at others her mind reverted to the first with increased liking. She began to see it brought to life with her own belongings. She would take for herself the bedroom on the story above the ground floor. Carlyle could inhabit the room directly over hers. Thus she could keep tabs on his sleeping; hear him if he stirred about. The head of her four-poster could slip neatly into the recess between the side wall and the built-out fireplace at the center of the north wall. Or perhaps it should go opposite the hearth, toward the south, against the partition dividing the room from the stairs.

The more one thought about that house, the better became its qualifications. Really, on final consideration, it seemed nearly twice as good as the others. It was sturdily built: a strong, roomy, durable affair, sure to outlive three races of the flimsily constructed modern dwellings which some of their friends had urged them to consider. "Look at these bricks," said Thomas, "not one of them is a lie." They were honestly made, and the plaster good. A house so built would stand till the trump of Doom. Even the three stone steps to the front door, hollowed by the tread of many feet during one hundred and thirty years of use, were a sign of durability. Curious, the steps leading into a house. The middle tread, where human footfall had borne down hardest, was more deeply grooved than the other two. Each tiny particle worn away from the solid material could tell its tale; had changed to the impact of human life.

The owner had kept the place in first-rate order. There was little need for extensive repairs. They could move in as soon as they wished. So Jeannie confirmed her husband's choice. They signed the lease.

Six days after Jane's arrival in London, the Carlyles entered their new domain. Jane had already acquired a domestic—Bessy Barnet, daughter of a gentlewoman fallen on evil days. Bessy had joined forces with them the previous night to be ready for the entry. They traveled by hackney coach from Ampton Street to the new address: 5 Great Cheyne Row, Chelsea. How everything should be fitted into the conveyance was something of a problem. Luggage, passengers, the excited, fluttering canary —all were bundled in till the carriage was loaded to the roof and beyond.

The Merovingian kings of old, rumbling in their bullock carts to occupy Paris, were merely forerunners and anticipators of this present history! Down Piccadilly rolled the argosy on wheels, past Green Park and into Belgrave Square. Chico, encouraged perhaps by the sight of leaves, after so many rows of brick and stone, burst into song. A good omen, Bessy Barnet insisted. Chico's mistress smiled. Such a tiny atom, yet he faced the world with so carefree a spirit! Many times during the course of this enterprise he had cheered Jane with his singing. He was better than the dove which had brought the olive branch from Ararat to Noah and his wife. The weather was gray and dampish, with never a sign of a rainbow, yet no drop fell.

The stretch of King's Road opened before them, leading southwest from the city. Presently they turned aside toward the river and Cheyne Row. By eleven in the morning, they were standing before their new threshold. The furniture had not arrived, but was promised for that day. Three carpenters, however, were waiting to attend to the few necessary alterations.

Jane mustered her little professional army and set it to work, then paused to give refreshments to the householders. A busy afternoon ahead of them; best to take some nourishment before plunging into the maelstrom. She opened and sorted the hamper of food which she had brought. Carlyle, fishing in his pockets, pulled out his matchbox so that Bessy could start a fire in the grate. Then he lighted a cigar to puff on while the first meal was in preparation. Nothing like a little smoke, from hearth or from tobacco, to flavor the atmosphere of domesticity. Three trunks were made to do for chairs, and a box lid with a towel thrown over it served as table. Thus, to a chorus of hammer strokes, they broke the first bread together. At two the vans arrived. All hands pitched in with vigor. Carlyle performed the duties of chief fastener-up of pictures. Bit by bit, familiar objects gave unfamiliar surroundings the look of a place seen once in a dream, now dimly recognized again. Hour by hour, where confusion had been, Jane was creating her universe from the rooms, furniture, decorations, and other equipment that were her artist's materials.

During the first few days they had led a sort of gypsy existence. There was even a gay charm, an amusing ludicrousness.

to this interlude when towels played the part of table cloths and a single dish and spoon had to do for an entire meal. But before the week was over, all household possessions had been sorted and fitted into place. The carpentry was done, such furniture as had broken in transit was repaired, the major tasks were finished.

When they rented the house, Jane and Thomas were aware that there was a flagged court in the rear and, supposedly, a garden. In it, a cursory examination revealed, grew a cherry tree struggling to ripen its fruit, and there were a few miserable rose-bushes. But the whole yard was so cloaked in weeds and tall grass that its possibilities were hardly to be imagined. While Jane managed her scourers and seamstresses within doors, her husband, like a pioneer exploring virgin forests, cleared away the outer jungles. He had bought a new set of garden tools to work with, and these he plied with such energy and good will that when Jane came to investigate there were noteworthy results. The tiny garden at Comely Bank, Edinburgh, had given them many an hour of relaxation. This one was better, and promised more. It would offer complete retreat, they assured themselves, and the seclusion of a cloistered monastery. When one stood in the little, sunken, paved court which lay next the dwelling, and looked outward, away from the house and its immediate neighbors, the garden beyond seemed truly one's own, safe from prying eyes. The high brick walls which bounded it on the two sides and at the rear gave a pleasant feeling of antiquity to the enclosure. The back wall, indeed, supposedly dated from the reign of Henry VII, when it had served as part of the boundary of a manor park. Over the bricks trailed grape vines, and a small walnut tree, companion to the cherry, offered a modicum of shade. Not a barren tree or vine in the tiny collection—all seemed determined to obey the injunction to be fruitful. Minute green clusters raised Jane's hopes for a bunch or two of grapes, and the walnut gave hints of coming harvest—a pennysworth of nuts, at least, or even more.

The garden itself lay some two feet above the courtyard. A low retaining wall kept the soil in place, and one entered by a white marble step in the center. From this step a straight little graveled path led outward for several paces, then turned

sharp left to within a foot or two of the sidewall, leaving space
for a narrow flower bed between wall and path when the latter
turned right again to the extremity of the plot. On the left
of this walk lay a square patch of greensward, and, next the
opposite wall, a broader flower bed.

Boxwood might be useful as a narrow edging for the walk,
and they would add new shrubs and blossoming things—a plum
tree, perhaps, and a willow, and spearmint and wallflowers.
Primroses, too, from Scotland, in good time. Jane had several
plans for swelling the ranks of the small green children in the
tidied beds. Carlyle planted the bits of jasmine and the gooseberry bush which he had brought from Craigenputtock. He
loved to wander in this little garden and to dig there. Here
he could saunter in his dressing-gown, and smoke a tranquil
pipe.

The Carlyles were getting ready to resume civilized living.
Jane, looking about her, took stock of her world and found it
good. Chelsea, also, was good, and London.

Bessy Barnet had been established in her ample, stone-
flagged basement kitchen—two rooms, front and back, each
with its open range. These were spacious fireplaces, in the middle of which, flanked by iron ovens, stood the ample grate,
with an adjustable barrier to regulate the space for fuel. A
blaze like Rome burning could be lighted below the broad
chimney breast, where the iron pot, on its swinging crane, could
boil and bubble over the flames. In the front kitchen, for water,
stood a pump and well, the shaft sunk deep in the Chelsea
gravel below the house. A larder big enough to hold supplies
for a company of soldiers filled Jane's and Bessy's heads with
thoughts of putting up preserves. Bessy was a treasure—cheery,
intelligent, and a good companion. One could easily forget that
she was a servant, and her mistress quickly did so, treating her
as a friend.

Bessy's kitchen was soon equipped for active use. It was complete, even to an amply-proportioned tinder box with flint and
steel. New inventions for kindling one's pipe or hearth were
beginning to appear, but Thomas liked to retain his Promethean
function as master over flame. It diverted him to manufacture

tinder from charred rags for the space allotted in the contrivance.

On the main floor, a long passageway ran from the rear of the house to the front entrance. Doors giving from it to the right led, one to the breakfast room with its single window facing east toward the court and garden, the other, further down the hallway, to the dining room with its two windows opening westward on the street. Jane planned to have this front room serve a double duty—for meals, and as a reception place. Here stood her sheraton table of handsome, shining mahogany. A figured cloth thrown over it, a knicknack or two, and it was ready for the eyes of callers. She could keep the double doors between the rooms flung wide open to make one spacious chamber. This gave a pleasant vista through the house, and led one's gaze past the rear window, where Chico's cage stood on its little pedestal, into a rectangle of open sky crossed by the branches of sundry trees. A carpet of bold design, hiding every inch of wood from back to front, would unify the general scheme. And the upper walls, above the paneled wainscoting, should be kept bright and cheery with a large-patterned paper— flowers, with wreathed stems and green leaves. The unpretentious marble mantel, the polished, slightly ornamental grate, gave an air of brightness yet of dignity to the fireplace in the massive projecting chimney that ran, with its paralleling twin in the next room, like a great inner column in relief, from top to bottom through the house, providing an open hearth for every important chamber.

On the story above, over the dining room, to the front of her own bedroom, Carlyle now had his study. This would also be the drawing room for intimate social life in possible leisure hours. Soon, Jane knew, he would wish to be at his new book— his history. He was waiting only till the hubbub of getting settled should die down. The large red carpet from Craigenputtock, tacked securely in place, lent its accent of familiarity. His books were on the shelf. His writing-table, with the ink bottle and the penholder which he always used, stood firm as Atlas to await whatever burden it was destined to bear. When he should sit at his desk, accustomed, friendly things, in quarters more spacious even than those in the whinstone house on the moors, would preside over him. The very trees outside his windows were benignant spirits—huge Scotch elms, growing in brotherly concord with the large pollarded limes that gave to Cheyne Row an almost sylvan appearance. Inside the room over the mantelpiece (the paneling set it off admirably) Carlyle had fastened a print of Belisarius, the Roman general, begging alms after his disgrace—a picture Jane was fond of because one of its incidental figures, that of a young Roman soldier, bore a close resemblance to her dead father, Dr. Welsh. Thomas valued the print for his wife's sake. On the opposite wall hung a small colored lithograph of a ragged old man, a professional scribe, seated at a make-shift table in the street, plying his trade of writing notes for illiterate pedestrians. For this picture Carlyle had grim affection—"He is a delightful fellow," he would say, "shows you literature in its simplest quite steadfast condition, below which it *cannot* sink!"

Jane's spare room, the large front chamber on the second bedroom floor, below the attic, stood waiting for the first guest to arrive. Back of it, directly over her own, as she had planned, was her husband's sleeping chamber. In the dressing-room behind, without fear of permeating the house with reek, he could smoke as often and as long as he might choose.

Jane luxuriated in her own private apartments. She could be as feminine as she pleased in their appointments. As for closets, Jeannie had never experienced such luxury—they were numerous enough to satisfy any Bluebeard. In this modest yet sufficient house, equipped with fragments of Haddington, Comely Bank, and the Craig, there would be room and to spare. When the family purse allowed it, she could add furniture of London make—supplementing her own old, handsome, weighty pieces with such cockneycalities as might from time to time be needed.

As Jane in her beelike flittings hurried from one end of the house to the other in the final stages of adjustment—opening drawers and closets and arranging her goods—she caught glimpses through the windows of a world of leafy regions. Meadows and trees, with only here and there a red, high-peaked roof showing through the foliage. When one looked out from the upper stories, one could scarcely believe that this was indeed London. The only incontrovertible symbols by day were the rounded dome of St. Paul's Cathedral, far in the distance, and the towers of the Abbey and other faint ghosts of spires. By night, one could see the glow from the myriad gaslights of the town. Air almost as good as that which flowed over the hills of Dumfriesshire, yet, near at hand and waiting, human life in multiple abundance.

How, by all that was miraculous, had she ever been able to put up with those years of solitude? Was it because she had not realized how incredibly lonely they were till they lay behind her, their like never to be endured again? Jeffrey, with a certain inconsistency, when news of their move first reached him, had not been able quite to reconcile himself to the thought of Jeannie coming to live in the smoke and stir of London; lost among the swarming millions in the huge ant-hill. Was it really the sphere for her? But he need not have troubled his head. She never doubted the wisdom of the decision. Here she belonged, and her husband too. The one slight disadvantage in their location, as Carlyle had warned, lay in Chelsea's remoteness from the heart of the city. But there were omnibuses in plenty, near at hand on Great King Street, with routes that led all through the town. Besides, Jane had determined to make good use of her legs. Though her husband insisted that she was no pedestrian, she quietly refused to heed his slanders. Had she not already more than once—all by herself and without benefit of buses—covered the five miles to the Strand and back?

Jane was beginning to gain as complete a knowledge of the region in which she lived as that possessed by Carlyle, who liked nothing better than to poke round in out-of-the-way places, where "gentlemen" and most certainly "ladies" were hardly expected to appear for exercise or pleasure. In their own quiet street, there was but a single uniform row of brick-built houses, old and ivy-covered, facing toward the west. Each dwelling had before it a stark cast-iron fence to safeguard unwary pedestrians against the risk of plunging into the narrow recess between house and sidewalk which gave light to basement windows. Ponderous, uneven, ill-laid sidewalks and curbstones—a peril to life and limb on foggy nights—lay between the railings and the street, on the opposite side of which scarcely anything in the shape of a building had yet appeared. Instead, a length of high brick wall, vestige of some nobleman's park in the days when Chelsea was a region of gentlemen's palatial residences, served as background for the trunks of the pollarded lime trees. Tranquil almost to somnolence, this retired street—it seemed hardly credible that the swelling tide of London should ever engulf Cheyne Row. Yet one or two ominous portents already had occurred. One morning Jane was shocked to observe a group of laborers hacking at the trees across the way. What could these crazy-headed cockneys be about? Hurriedly she went out to inquire. Some of the trees were already slaughtered, but the rest, by resolute argument with the man in charge, Jane was able to save, thus at least temporarily averting further devastation. Building operations of some sort, it appeared, required the execution, yet days had passed and nothing further had come of the business.

Chelsea kept about it much of the atmosphere of an old village. It lay, from west to east, along the banks of the Thames between Cremorne and the grounds of Chelsea Hospital, refuge of old and disabled soldiers—a waterfront of nearly a mile. Its boundary inland from the river hardly exceeded three-quarters of a mile at the widest point. Even its street cries and the goods which they announced seemed to differ from those in other parts of the town. The hucksters, somehow, retained the primitive quaintness and melody. "Shrimps as large as prawns!" chanted the old fishmonger in a long drawn cadence which a songmaker like Purcell might have set to music. Cowslips and primroses were still vended, and Chelsea buns were famous for their excellence. They were made at a bun-house which stood at the bottom of Jews-row, near the Chelsea Hospital, within easy reach. Swift and his friends had patronized this shop in former days, and praised its wares. Don Saltero's coffee house, described by Richard Steele in the *Tatler*, faced the Thames. The whole neighborhood, indeed, though now quite out of fashion, was rich in tradition and associated with many great names of the past.

From No. 5, one reached the Thames by turning left down Cheyne Row. Here, along the bank of the stream, lay Cheyne Walk, with fine old red-brick mansions—many of them fallen on ignoble days and mean enough tenants. Along this roadway flanked by a weed-grown bulkhead at the water's edge, and shaded by fine trees, Jane sometimes strolled with her husband to see the busy life on the river where plied a great variety of

small craft. Scows and barges, empty or heavy laden, moved up
and down, or lay on the banks in varied states of unrepair while
ducks probed with their bills among them in the mud. Awkward
sloops, built for heavy cargoes, waited at anchor, their decks
and rigging redolent with the odor of sea tar. Amid these working craft, like dandies among the farmers at the Dumfries cattle
fair, trim little sailboats wheeled and tacked, while now and
then, manned by athletic young men clad in white shirts, four-
oared racing barges skimmed lightly down the stream. Save for
the large pleasure boats of the wealthy, rarely seen on this
stretch of the Thames, the nobility of the river consisted of the
newfangled little passenger steamers that plied along the twisting water highway from Westminster to the pier at Battersea
Bridge and points beyond. For twopence one could sail right to
the Houses of Parliament. Side wheelers, these craft, on the
open decks of which one sat on benches that ran along the outer
rail and down the middle. They had thin high funnels supposed
to keep away the soot, which nevertheless often poured in greasy
clouds on the heads of the passengers. The pilots stood aft at
the wheel, directly over the rudder posts, as in the sailing ships
after which these vessels had originally been patterned. At night
as it plied the river, each craft bore a lantern in its nose, and
the sparks belching from the chimneys put to shame, through
very smoke and tumult, the chimera of old.

This was the river with all its life that flowed less than a bow-
shot from their door. Jane's walks by herself, for business or
pleasure, generally took her away from the stream, but sometimes she liked to seek it out. Especially she enjoyed standing
on Battersea Bridge, though the toll cost a penny. It afforded
so varied a prospect of the shores. A turn to the right down
Cheyne Walk soon brought one to it. Its ramshackle timbers
marched across the river on innumerable wooden piers that
looked like the ribs of bleached and forgotten wrecks cast up on
some lonely shoal. There were nineteen irregular spans in all,
the widest humping up above the level of the rest to give head-
room to the river traffic. At night a ribbon of gas lamps on this
bridge stretched like a glimmering chain of St. Elmo's fire across
the water. Rough laborers, hairy-faced boatmen, reeling drunk
after an afternoon of toping at one of the several taverns, eyed
Jane as she passed, but she never feared the likes of these. When

one of them, once, observing this young, attractive woman, accosted her, she withered him by the outraged glare which she shot from her snapping dark eyes. "Fool!" she said, and walked on. She later spoke with high glee of this small adventure. Yet the district, taken all in all, was as safe, if not safer, than more fashionable regions of London. Decent, quiet people lived round the Carlyles, and their silent attention to their own business was something Thomas could be thankful for. Thomas and Jane knew very little concerning their immediate neighbors, save that they were harmless. On one side lived two old ladies; the other house remained clothed in pleasantly noiseless mystery. The faint tinkle of pianos, far away, was occasionally heard, but never in threatening, swelling crescendo. Just as well not to be too intimate with the people on one's street; better to pass by with a cheerful, silent bow, or mere day's greeting. As it was, London grew acquaintances for Jane and Thomas as a field sprouts wheat, and the only seeds used were Carlyle's articles and their own personalities.

Jane was quick to notice the re-emergence, in stronger force, of a trait in her husband's character which she was aware of but had almost forgot during the last winter at Craigenputtock. He had in him, if he would give it freer range, the makings of a social character—tolerably social, at least. It amused Jane to observe the mingled awe and affection with which he was regarded by his friends among the younger men, and by some of the older, too, for that matter. Certainly the violence with which he spoke was sometimes terrifying, though she knew he could be gentle as a lamb.

After her long sojourn in the wilderness, Jane was eager to reap the harvest of friendship which the city might yield. Not just the half-literary, half-sentimental acquaintanceships which flourished at every hand for the delectation of the wife of a rising author. These were weeds, even nettles, to be treated with caution—though of course an innocent flirtation, when the gentlemen were amusing, was rather fun. What she hoped for, however, were real intimacies—genuine friendships—with women and with men. Suppose she had developed misanthropical tendencies during her exile in the desert, and could not live in amity with her fellow creatures? The notion troubled her, though a silly enough fancy. She was amazed by the attentions

paid her. These people were unbelievably kind! Their insistence
on calling her "sweet" and "gentle" and, of all things, "endear-
ing," amused her, for she had no illusions about her temper.
Cynically she sometimes told herself that true friendship was
nonexistent. Middle-aged discretion, surely, taught this lesson
to check the ardors of one's young enthusiasm. Yet in her heart
Jane believed that there was no treasure to equal friendship:
without friendship, the soul perished.

The sums she allowed herself for clothes would hardly have
sufficed to keep a barmaid happy, yet word went round among
her London acquaintances that this Mrs. Carlyle who had come
from some wild place in Scotland was a very well dressed young
woman. Jane watched the city fashions with discernment, and
sought for style, not fad. The enormous bustles affected by
women in this year of the Lord 1834 baffled her wish to believe
in feminine intelligence. What absurdity to stroll about with a
huge false bottom! Fashionable ladies strove to measure three
yards in diameter, and even the servants aped them. Eliza
Miles told of her maid going out on Sunday with kitchen
dusters bunched monstrously under her skirt.

Jane's own trim clothes and new bonnet satisfied her taste.
The hat especially, of her own manufacture, had an air. A little
brown feather at the front gave it jauntiness, and the crown was
pointed like a sugar-loaf for piquancy. Not that clothes really
mattered—yet it was a pleasant feeling to know that one passed
muster.

What had happened to that pleasant, entertaining Mr. Hunt
who had watched with such solicitude and encouragement while
she and her husband went through the early throes of getting
settled? Both Jane and Thomas were ready to welcome his calls
as they were now welcoming those of other friends. Yet so considerate and polite was Leigh Hunt that he would not come
near them without express invitation, for fear he might disturb.
This reticence must be done away with. Carlyle, it is true, felt
certain misgivings lest such propinquity—Hunt lived round the
corner at No. 4, Upper Cheyne Row—might lead to entanglements. But surely there was little cause for worry. Several times,
now, Carlyle himself had sought out Hunt for walks and Hunt
had accepted with alacrity. He should call more often, Jane let

it be known; they would always be happy to see him. Like other women who met Leigh Hunt—he was very attractive, in a harmless enough fashion, to the opposite sex—Jane had been drawn to him immediately. She began asking him in once a week for a cup of tea. On such occasions he would linger, talking in his brisk, fanciful way, till after the supper hour.

Jane was not disturbed when Leigh Hunt dropped into the habit of stopping more and more frequently, toward evening, at No. 5, Cheyne Row. Always he appeared scrupulously dressed—at home he enjoyed a certain negligence—his long, once black hair brushed for the occasion and almost tidy. His favorite position was by the hearth, where he would stand with his elbow propped against the mantelpiece, his thin lithe body leaning slightly toward the wall. Yet there was no hint of lassitude about the man. A sensitive, optimistic schoolboy—past fifty years of age. One of the most innocent creatures imaginable, though his hair was graying and his face ploughed with many sorrows and disappointments. No one who studied him could doubt his unconquerable elasticity of spirit. He had dignity, too, as well as youth and hope. He talked in a grave, sweet voice, or listened in respectful silence to what his host or hostess might be saying. Jane and Thomas were somewhat puzzled by his extremely dark complexion. Could it be that there was a trace of African in him? But his cupid's bow lips seemed to contradict this supposition.

Jane rarely played or sang for visitors, but Hunt could persuade her to abandon her reticence. He knew by heart the words of many of her Scotch tunes. Early in the acquaintanceship he had discovered her gifts for conversation—his own were brilliant; full of many unexpected turns of witty insight. Mrs. Carlyle, he reported to his wide circle, was an eloquent woman, in fact a woman of genius. Hunt's disciples were quick to pass along the word. They praised her deft art as raconteur and began to refer to her as a British Madame de Staël.

These evenings which Hunt spent with the Carlyles always ended with the ceremonial of porridge. He had learned to like it at his first supper with them. Mrs. Hunt, he declared, should serve it henceforth at Upper Cheyne Row. He would insist that she do so. Insistence, the Carlyles soon realized, did not get very far with Leigh Hunt's wife. She was a very vegetable of a woman, rooted deep in lethargy. If he wanted porridge, he must find it away from home.

A tiny bowlful was all that Hunt would take. They had a special little plate for him to suit his appetite. In Italy he had dined with Byron, who enjoyed unusual dishes though he was a careful eater because of the threat of stoutness. He had known Keats intimately: Keats who delighted in choice foods. But porridge, Hunt would say, with a chivalrous bow to the hostess, was a noble, excellent, frugal diet. Then he would bid goodnight, with apologies for the lateness of his stay. Surely he was taking advantage of their hospitality, he would exclaim with a little laugh. Why, he was becoming a regular fixture, as though a Lar or a permanent Household God!

One thing soon was obvious to Jane. Hunt's views and her husband's were totally at variance. Like Jeffrey, he talked much of happiness as the highest good, though fate, to all appearances, had brought him little enough of it. Along with his dead friend Shelley, he believed in utopian reforms that Carlyle insisted ran counter to all the laws of human nature and lacked the least particle of common sense. But his charm did not suffer through disagreement, and his ideas, in such hands as his own, said Carlyle, were surely harmless enough. Thomas classified him as a mendicant minstrel of ancient days, strangely washed ashore out of time's ocean into a century he should never have belonged to. Pleasant to listen to him, but rather like taking draughts of perfumed water. A kind of talking nightingale, said Jane. In various ways, Hunt surely had nightingales on the brain. He insisted on Carlyle's tracking out into the country with him to hear them sing, though never a one had lifted its voice while the two men tramped together.

With all his enthusiasms and his optimism, Hunt was a man who evoked one's pity. Jane and Thomas knew how ruthlessly his debts thronged in upon him and crushed him down. He never heard a knock on the door without the fear that a bailiff stood at the threshold to haul him off to prison. Every farthing that he earned came from his pen. Through the test of his own experiences, Carlyle knew exactly what that meant. Without the help of his thrifty wife, his own financial structure might long ago have suffered complete disintegration.

Hunt's domestic establishment was the millstone round his

neck which threatened to drown him, yet swim with it he must.
An incredible household; unutterable! Even Carlyle lacked
words adequately to describe it. The drawing room, so called,
in which were carried on all the multiple functions of domesticity, looked like a scene in a madhouse. It was a tidy woman's
nightmare. Six or seven rickety old chairs, as if suddenly halted
in the midst of a violent hornpipe, clustered together in attitudes of fatigue and dissolution. Dust clothed the table save
where the scrape of a dish had rubbed away a channel like the
track of some huge snail. And under, over, and upon everything
lay a confusion of litter—books, papers, egg shells, scissors, even
a wad of nibbled bread. Mrs. Hunt, the presiding deity over
this petty chaos—a large, unhealthy-looking woman with a passion for indolence—lay much of the time asleep on a mound of
pillows. Poor woman, she had for years been the victim of disease. Pitiable, of course, yet what of her husband? Four or five
gypsy-looking children with nondescript clothes—each one in
fact in a varying degree of lack of dress—took care of their own
needs and their mother's. The younger ones, with their dusky
complexions and dark eyes, possessed a strange foreign beauty,
but Percy, the eldest son, on whose narrow shoulders fell the
chief burden and practical management of the household, looked
sallow and peaked: underfed, as indeed he was.

How aid Leigh Hunt without offending him? The man had
a gentle pride on which the heavy feet of charity must not be
allowed to trample. Yet a sovereign or two, now and then, was
an obvious, in fact an imperative need. Not that Jane and
Thomas could readily spare one—but no matter. So they tried
an experiment, coupled with the vaguest, most impersonal hint.
At the corner of the mantelpiece, just where Hunt always rested
his elbow, they occasionally left a bright and shining gold piece.
From· time to time the money would disappear.

Though Leigh Hunt had scruples against borrowing, his wife
had none. She was the perfect sharer, ready to take the most un-
borrowable things. She had asked for one of Jane's brass fenders
for some reputedly vital need and when its owner sought to get
it back, the effort had been harder than extracting copper from
the mine. Mrs. Hunt would dispatch her slut of a servant on
the harpy mission: tumblers, teacups, porridge, even a few
spoonfuls of tea were requisitioned—"Missus has got company

and happens to be out of the article." Out of a penny in her purse, more likely!

Sometimes the mistress herself came foraging. These raids began to drain away most of Jane's reservoir of patience. She was very busy, she excused herself, very busy—painting.

"What?" brightly inquired the lady, "is it a portrait?"

A portrait? Great heavens! A large wardrobe, which Jane, through her own efforts, was making presentable.

The children were easier to endure. Jane liked children, and these queer little waifs, with their fantastic wildness and quaint, poetic thoughts, were appealing. They were always so cheerful! They would run into the house to tell her of some trivial adventure met while roaming the streets or countryside. "A good joy," they would call it, and Jane, in high amusement, adopted the phrase.

No denying it, Leigh Hunt's was an establishment to be associated with on cautious terms—with its sordid collapse and utter hugger-mugger. How the master of this house could emerge from it dressed so neatly, with just the slightest hint of the dandy, and with such blithe chivalry of manner and an air, even, of repose, was a mystery for which the Carlyles never found the answer.

Hunt was working on some tragedies. Surely the stage would reward his efforts with success! He liked to have Jane's and Carlyle's opinions on these vital works that, somehow, should mend his fortunes. Unless the reader was his wife, Carlyle hated to be read to. His own eyes could follow the lines of a book so much faster, and he grew restive when forced to listen. But Hunt was so eager in his invitation that it was impossible to deny his wish. Out they would go, at the appointed time, to hear the latest act. Those were evenings when Hunt's drawing room grew almost quiet in the dim light of a single candle— the children, asleep, curled up on the chairs with the torn upholstery. Then the playwright would begin. Bombastic, neo-Elizabethan verse sounded rich and choice and filled with the music of poetry under Hunt's expressive voice. This man had heard Byron recite his lines, and other poets. Though she was reading less and less of it, poetry still charmed Jane's ear and moved her heart. Even Carlyle was pleased and forgetful of his growing prejudice against both plays and verse.

Sometimes an evening at the Hunts' would be given over to music. Leigh Hunt played the piano and sang with grace and spirit. One night he offered the entire repertoire of melodies from the *Beggar's Opera*, bringing out the charm of the verses without damaging their quality of earthiness.

Carlyle responded with gusto to the performance. He would pay any amount of money, he declared, if only he had himself been taught. Jane's eyes flickered with amusement.

"He never sings but when he is in absolute despair!" she drily remarked.

Tom joined in the laughter.

But more usual were the evenings given over to conversation. Then Tom's deep rumble would break in repeatedly on Leigh Hunt's gleaming, perishable fancies. Hunt was all light and air, his talk an iridescent flight of soap bubbles. Little chance of its surviving unpunctured in the buffeting, hot breath of Carlyle's tirades against the follies of mankind when Thomas became eager on some topic which stirred his almost painful emotions. Hunt preferred the Cavaliers to Cromwell: an incomprehensible error, a heresy against all rules of duty!

In the midst of his volcanic eruptions, it was difficult not to take Carlyle very, very seriously. Hunt grew pale under these castigations of his opinions—these fiery sunsets that consumed his tender, rose-colored visions. He was sorry, he hinted, to see a man ruled thus by his Scotch Presbyterian background. Why, that was a thing he was everlastingly grateful for—Carlyle retorted—and resumed his thunder.

Strange that Hunt's visits to the house were beginning to grow fewer! Was it his grief over these clashes? Jane would see what could be done: Hunt was a good man, regardless of his butterfly beliefs. She would send him a note explaining that Carlyle had finished his day's work and counted on him, as of old, for a visit. "I cannot make you as happy to come to us, as we are to have you come!"

In response to her plea, Hunt called again. Jane was waiting in the familiar drawing room. Impulsively she jumped up and kissed him as he entered.

On his way home—the family had moved from Chelsea to Kensington—he revolved in his mind some words of verse. Keats, Shelley, and he, in those glorious days at Hampstead when they were young and with the world before them, had often competed in extemporaneous riming. Those two, of course, were far greater poets than he—world conquerors, he thought of them. Yet sometimes his own quick mind had beaten their agility, and composed, in these jovial bouts, very creditable verse.

The rondeau was complete, now:

> Jenny kissed me when we met,
>   Jumping from the chair she sat in;
> Time, you thief, who love to get
>   Sweets into your list, put that in!
> Say I'm weary, say I'm sad,
>   Say that health and wealth have missed me,
> Say I'm growing old, but add,
>   Jenny kiss'd me.

Chapter Fourteen

*T*HOUGH fellow residents of London, the Irvings and Carlyles, as far as sociability was concerned, might as well still have been parted by the length and breadth of England. After the chance meeting in Kensington when Thomas was searching for houses, Edward had once more vanished into the maelstrom of his portentous career. A baleful enchantment held him—he was plucked at by contending forces: intense, fanatic belief in his doctrines; intense disapproval of him and them. Carlyle's renewed efforts to seek him out had failed. Always he was put off with one pretext or another—Irving was sick; he was not at home.

But though they had not enjoyed a satisfactory talk with him since his call to welcome Jane on her winter's visit of 1832, the Carlyles remained keenly aware of Irving and his fortunes. Before they had abandoned Craigenputtock, disquieting reports continued to hover about like rooks flying overhead at dusk. And now, in the city, gossip flocked even more thickly in Edward's troubled skies.

Irving had been expelled from the Scottish Kirk in 1833. This deprived him not only of his right to function as a minister; it barred him forever from membership in the Church of Scotland. He had been summoned to Annan for his trial, before the Presbytery which had originally ordained him. In the eyes of these orthodox ministers, his entire course of action and belief was against him—his traffic with the latter-day prophets, his hope for the second coming, even his popularity among the masses to whom he preached.

"Remember where you are, Sir!" cried one of his judges, when Irving made an impassioned speech in his own defense.

"I have not forgotten where I am," said the accused man, "it is the church where I was baptized; where I was consecrated to preach Christ; where the bones of my dear ones lie buried!"

A shrieking and clamor, in the language of the inspired tongues, rose from one of the ministers present, who had been smitten, some believed, with the divine gift of prophecy.

"Hear that!" said Irving, as if he had won vindication from Heaven, and indignantly withdrew from the assembly.

After his expulsion, Irving lingered for several days in Annandale. He would continue to preach, he said, in the great name of the Lord. The country people remained full of zeal for him and he was followed by great crowds. Jane and Thomas got ample reports of one of these meetings, for Carlyle's sister Jean and other members of the family had listened. Gray, haggard, toilworn—he had seemed to Jean's sympathetic eyes as he spoke at Ecclefechan. An immense black cravat, one of his eccentricities of dress, but useful now for protection against the cold, was spread over his broad chest. He stood on a table under the branches of a plane-tree. It was in March, and flurries of mingled snow and rain were being driven by the wind over the huddled attendant throng. Irving, his cloak tossed by the storm, his long hair—he wore no covering for his head—in disorder, raised his eloquence above the creaking of the branches and the strong voice of the gale.

That spring and summer he had preached elsewhere before the people, with a conviction and fervor that thrilled the naïve and the skeptical alike. Now and then, from the crowd, the weird sounds of the prophetic voices would break in on the discourse. Then Irving would stop and, with rapt expression and attentive ear, would listen as if to catch from these unintelligible tongues a divine message foretelling Christ's descent to deal out judgment on earth.

Jane and Thomas, hearing these things, scarcely knew what attitude to take. Incredulousness, amusement even, and bitterness moved them as they thought of Irving. But chiefly, they felt pity, and the wish somehow to stop this self-betrayal. What astonishing contradictions marked the past! How tragical had Irving become! Strange indeed this man's career. Stranger still when he returned to London.

The fanatical supporters who had led him into this tumult had founded an independent church, in Oxford Street, to which they moved themselves, their beliefs, and their deposed minister. But when Irving, after his trial at Annan and his preachings in the countryside, returned to these rabid faithful, certain prophets among them showed themselves tyrannical despots to the man who had defended them. In the name of "The Power" who guided their voices, they passed an interdict forbidding Irving to exercise any priestly functions among them. He could not hold service, he could not administer the sacraments, he was forced to take a humble place in the congregation while others carried on the work. Because he believed that these voices expressed divine will, Irving, though broken-hearted, bowed his head and obeyed the prohibition. He had returned from his martyrdom in Annan—so he regarded his trial—to receive, not honor, but this indignity and humiliation. He would utter no protest. For weeks he sat mute till other voices prevailed, and he was reinstated. By command, he was awarded the office of chief pastor, with the title "Angel over Christ's Flock in London." Yet this elevation gave him small control. His church, named Catholic Apostolic by its directors, was ruled by the Voices, and whatever these might order he felt it his duty to do. The Apostles who managed affairs interpreted the words of prophecy, and on them they based their decrees.

Though Irving, worn by his troubles, was sick and in no condition to travel, he had been dispatched, in January, 1834, to Edinburgh, on a mission to a recently established branch of the new church. When he returned, his once great strength had deserted him. He coughed frequently, and though he would not complain, it was apparent that he was troubled by some malady of the lungs.

He had already drained his cup of sorrows—yet again and again it had been filled to the brim. One by one his children— he was a devoted father—had sickened, till only a daughter was left. When a son died a few hours before service, Irving had felt it his duty, in spite of his grief, to preach. His sermon, on the text from David, "I shall go to him but he shall not return to me," had a heart-breaking pathos which those who heard it remembered for years.

The Carlyles had been told of the failure of Irving's health. But they counted on his tremendous strength to pull him through, and there were rumors, indeed, that he had recovered. But Thomas, when at last he was allowed to see him, could make no very encouraging report to Jane. He had found Irving lying on the sofa, unable to rise though he had tried to. Edward spoke of pain on his right side. A rasping, thick cough broke repeatedly from his lips. Isabella, his wife, haggard too, sat beside him, refusing to leave the two men alone though Irving had begged her to go. Her conduct explained the failure of past efforts to see Edward. In her misguided zeal, she had kept his old friends from him by various subterfuges, admitting to her house only those who were connected with Irving's church.

This meeting took place in August. In September, Irving was well enough to make a visit to Chelsea. Sunset was at hand—the afternoon damp and cloudy. Edward had found sufficient strength to ride his bay horse to Cheyne Row where Thomas and Jane greeted him in their ground-floor sitting room. He was going soon to Glasgow, he explained, on a mission for his church. The prophets had ordered him to the north again, to do a great work in his native land. He had come to say farewell.

Irving was only forty-two, but he had the look of an old man. Jane and Thomas were shocked by his flaccid, wasted, sunken face. His eyes were full of the old friendly light, but in his glance there was an unquiet fever, a look of bewilderment and pain. At the temples, his hair, once raven black, was now white. The ghost of his old laugh was a haunting thing.

Much to their relief, he would not speak of his church. Appraisingly he took in the details of the room in which they sat: the little touches which made it so homelike, the ornaments, the tasteful appointments and furniture.

"Ah, yes," he said to Jane, "you are like an Eve; make every place you live in beautiful!"

It was dark outside. He rose to go.

Imperative for Irving to be taken from these coils which bound him! If only they could induce him, on his return from Glasgow, to visit Italy for the recovery of his health!

In December, Jane and Thomas learned that Edward Irving was dead. The inevitable had happened, then, though shocking to think of. What a man he might have been had he remained a preacher in Scotland where first he had prospered. Within this huge confusion of a place—London—there were influences which had taken fatal hold of certain qualities of Irving's. Scotland had sent him forth a Herculean man. In England, the gross atmosphere of adulation began his decline, the strange vagaries to which he had fallen a prey had wasted him and broken down his judgment. While it was yet the midseason of his day, he had sunk overwearied and had perished.

Jane's feelings on Irving had undergone many changes. First there had been a little girl's admiration for her handsome, athletic, brilliant tutor; then the fascinating discovery that they were equals in the same generation. After that: attraction, repulsion, contempt—but also, briefly, a passionate love. Carlyle and Irving. She could have married either man. She had not chosen Irving.

Chapter Fifteen

*E*VER since the day in early summer when she dismissed the last of her genii from the house—the carpenters who raised bookcases and dust, the upholsterers who clipped and stitched and littered the drawing room with their rubbish—Jane had cause to be thankful. She could enjoy the satisfaction of knowing that her husband was busily at work on his next book, and what was even better, contentedly at work. Experience had taught her that no matter how situated, Thomas could not be relied on to admit that he was at ease. Even after changes initiated by himself, there were flaws in the expected felicity. But at last, in Cheyne Row, he acknowledged with a positiveness excluding qualification that London was the place for them. The gloom and acerbity which he had shown from time to time at Craigenputtock had abated. Jane was filled with thankful optimism. Her spirits found the wings they for a time had lost. This new volume would fend poverty from the door and bring her husband a wider fame. Carlyle would henceforth be healthier and happier than he had been for years. Her own strength was not failing her: there was no repetition of the illness which had plagued her on her first visit to London, two winters before.

Marvel of marvels, under her supervision, Carlyle agreed to the acquisition of London clothes for himself. Was not this frock-suit too giddy?—he objected, as the tailor set the pins and Jane looked to the cut. But tactfully his wife, speaking of warmth and comfort, silenced his protest. When he emerged from the shop in his stylish coat of rifle-green, he had the appearance of a smartly dressed man. A cloak of brown cloth, with a snug fur collar, would keep out the sharpest weather. To match the cloak, Thomas had even consented to a brand new hat. Jane's triumph was complete.

What pleased her most was the attitude of his London

friends. Like herself, they expected the forthcoming book to be a thrilling accomplishment. How different from the bantering reproofs of Jeffrey; the cold indifference of Edinburgh! To these London disciples her husband was a leader; not a dangerous though gifted man who needed chastening. His views, to them, were not radicalism, but the truth. Here, in his growing circle, Carlyle's indignation at injustice among men, his anger at the degradation of labor and the aristocratic contempt for work, found ready ears and sympathetic minds. What if "Sartor," in *Fraser's*, had met with lack of understanding and hostility? Mill had praised it, Charles Buller, and others. Even America responded, for Emerson had written in encouragement and exhorted Carlyle to proceed fearlessly since men in the distant ends of the earth were giving heed.

Hard to say precisely what the financial returns from the new book might be. At least Fraser would print it without cost, though he would promise nothing more. If only he could get it written to his own satisfaction, Carlyle felt, he might gain enough reputation to permit his lecturing for pay—the sole occupation for writers which seemed to promise a fair return. What if other hopes had failed? The more that possibilities diminished, the easier the choice of a future path.

Jane's husband was holding fast to his sore-tried confidence— he would not be shaken loose. Indeed, the pair made a joke of their difficulties and laughed in the face of the enigmatic future. Gleefully they chanted the words used by a Sans-culotte Deputy in reporting from his province to the convention at Paris. *"Tout va bien ici,"* he assured the leaders; everything prospered, everything was following the right principles—save for one particular: *"LE PAIN MANQUE!"*

On Monday, September 1, 1834, Carlyle had begun the actual composition of his history of the French Revolution. During his voluminous reading he had taken few notes. Notes bound and constricted him. He would rely on his retentive memory to preserve what he had learned. An immense amount of preparation had been accomplished; an immense quantity remained still to be done. Mill had lent him more than a hundred books and in the libraries of London were hundreds more.

This work of his must be different from the run of histories. Most were no better than dried thistles for pedant chaffinches to peck at. Out of this huge plot, this epic of humanity, he would make an artistic picture, but beneath its poetry and symbolism would lie revealed the truth. The story of man's heroic refutation of sham lay at the heart of the Revolution. To show graphically this casting out of old beliefs, this banishment of hereditary privilege—vital once, but at last dead and stinking—*that* was his duty as historian. He saw the Revolution as a tract for the times, a vast factual reality illustrating what he had already tried to shadow forth in the allegory of *Sartor*. His book must also reveal the grandeur of the truly heroic individual, the maker and shaper of the destinies of men.

Carlyle had moved his workshop from the room upstairs to Chico's domain with its outlook on the little garden. He wrote with a terrifying intenseness. His long legs, feet encased in stub-toed, comfortable boots, twisted and tied themselves into knots under his chair, defying all laws of human anatomy. And as the chapters were finished, Jane glanced them over. More readable than *Sartor*, she told him. Daily the stack of sheets grew higher at the writer's elbow. The beginnings of a book forbid all hopes of its ever ending. But when he passed the middle of what was to be the first volume, Thomas could at last believe that presently he would finish it.

It was hard, of course, having a husband visible in the house, yet as removed from her as though he were at Craigenputtock. Physical absence might be almost easier to bear than thus living excommunicated. Yet there were respites to look forward to, during which his voice and personality would return, breaking the spell that held them. These came when his day's work and his exercise were over. Generally he walked alone to rest his thoughts and satisfy his need for rapid motion. But when he returned, in the winter twilight, and she, too, often, from some excursion of her own, there was never a lack of things to tell each other. Jane had calls to talk about, and people. How strange a contrast to the Glaisters hillside, the only visible life a flock of grouse, the black-faced sheep, and melancholy curlews! Those scenes lay thousands of years in the past.

Though Carlyle lived in his book, there were intervals of leisure, even, for friends and for the city. When Jane had come to London as a winter visitor, during the Craigenputtock years, the town with its multitude of human faces had seemed a waste wilderness, each blade of grass a man or woman, but impersonal, undistinguishable. Now the city had turned into a peopled garden. Not even his Grace the Duke of Wellington, Jane declared, could have a choicer group of friends. As for his Majesty the King, he needed to beware of all who came near him. Not so with these acquaintances—they called because they wanted to and gave invitations in the same spirit. Clever and entertaining persons, too. With her own home as background, Jane found society better than ever—even the persons who had begun to call at Ampton Street took on an added excellence. She was wonderfully well hefted in London.

Chelsea's remoteness was not such a handicap as she had feared. If she did not feel inclined to make an excursion by omnibus, there were friends and to spare within the circumference of a mile. And distance meant nothing to masculine callers.

On Sundays, sure as the ringing of church bells, John Stuart Mill would appear from Kensington to take Carlyle for a walk. Once during each week or oftener he came down for a friendly visit. All day he was busy as an official at the India House. But any evening might find him thumping the brass knocker at the Chelsea door. He was as full as ever of useful information on the French Revolution and eager to give Carlyle the benefit of his knowledge.

After the Carlyles had been living in Cheyne Row for several months, Mill, who liked to bring his friends to call, introduced a certain Mrs. Taylor. Rumors about her had already reached the Carlyles. They knew that she lived with a husband somewhere in Kensington, but they were scarcely prepared for the vivacious little apparition that burst on them. Not above twenty-five years of age at the most, a will-o'-the-wispish creature—beautiful too—who flashed and shimmered in the room, casting her brightest rays rather obviously on the two men. Jane she evidently regarded as a country girl who required only a stray spark or two to keep her happy.

Jeannie did not greatly mind. In fact, she was sufficiently dazzled by these occasional rays. Mrs. Taylor was something new among London experiences. When she invited Jane, with a flash of a smile, to pass a day in Kensington, Jeannie readily

accepted. Indeed her susceptibility made her respond with eagerness. Here, perhaps, was just the sort of warm, vibrant creature
whom she could really love.

The more Jane saw of Mrs. Taylor the more complex she
found her; a little terrifying, even! Jane noticed a passionate
sadness on her face in its rare moments of repose. Several times
she and Thomas went to dine at the house in Kensington. Mill
was always sure to be there, though Jane could not see that the
husband minded or even noticed. He was an older man—dull,
unsuspecting, and given to jovial hospitality. Nobody paid much
attention to him; he served as background for his wife. Because
of her, there was always brisk company at the Taylors':
laughter-loving, witty men, though rarely any women. There
you might run into Charles Buller, whose cherubic looks and
wickedly amusing conversation lent wings to even the airiest
persiflage. Or Fonblanque who edited the *Examiner*, and other
noteworthy men. Frightful, this dining at eight, instead of an
earlier, more reasonable hour, grumbled Carlyle, thinking of
the day's work ahead of him as he and Jane returned, after
midnight, from a party at the Taylors'.

Mrs. Platonica Taylor, they dubbed their hostess. All very
high and noble, of course, this attachment with Mill, yet a
dangerous experiment with an unpredictable future. The more
Jane thought of it, the less she liked it. She was no prude, but
she had her own ideas on marriage and what she saw at Mrs.
Taylor's did not accord with them. Moreover further acquaintance with the lady brought unpleasant revelations not suspected
at first meeting. Mrs. Taylor's condescension, for one thing, was
becoming a bit thick. At last Jane refused longer to act the part
of child to Mrs. Taylor's sophistical tutoring. So, greatly to
her surprise, John Mill's friend discovered herself brought up
short by a seemingly innocent remark of Jane's. She had swallowed it down like a hungry fish, only to feel, too late, the hidden barb. Henceforth she became more circumspect. This Mrs.
Carlyle was not so self-effacing as she seemed.

Much of Mrs. Taylor's vivacity sprang from violently forced
mannerisms. If she wished to sting or be uncivil, she spoke in
the most honeyed and affectionate of tones. And if she really
wanted to say something kind, she did so with a hard, unyielding

voice. "Come down and see us," she remarked to Carlyle on the occasion of the first invitation to dinner, "you will be charmed with our house, it is so full of rats."

"Rats!" exclaimed Carlyle. "Do you regard them as an attraction?"

"Yes," replied Mrs. Taylor (voice soft, so as not to mar her climax), "they are such dear innocent creatures."

Carlyle grunted.

But chiefly, what about poor Mill? Jane and Thomas were convinced this Mrs. Taylor business was become a matter of more and more questionable benefit to him. They said nothing, and did nothing, yet was it kind thus to stand idly by? Mill, with his rich auburn hair and gentle, pathetic expression, was such an unsophisticated creature. And now Mrs. Taylor was wrapping him up like a cocoon. Poor Mill, he was surely spellbound. Before mustering the courage to glance at Mrs. Taylor, he had probably never looked any female creature in the face, not so much as a cow. But once he had gazed into those great dark eyes—eyes full of questionings, full of comfort too, and skillful flattery—he was lost, drowned as deep as if he had fallen into a bottomless well.

Mrs. Taylor was jealous of all his friendships. When strait-laced acquaintances began to cut him for his association with a married woman, Mrs. Taylor seemed neither to mind nor care. But it was hard on Mill. The Carlyles refused to let these vagaries interfere with friendship. What he did with his private life, of course, was his own affair.

Taylor, goaded to action at last, separated from his wife. She lived now at Kingston-on-Thames. This was further for Mill to travel, although pleasantly secluded. Thomas and Jane saw less of him, though he did his best to visit them with customary frequency.

At No. 5 Cheyne Row the ultimate objective was to get Carlyle's *History of the French Revolution* successfully written. The grand immediate concern was to finish the first volume. Only a few days more, and he would be through with it. Some five months of hard labor had been expended in actual composition. When he started writing, two volumes, he hoped, would be sufficient. But how compress the record of so vast a cataclysm?

Three volumes, it was clear, would be necessary. Yet with the first almost finished, with the hard struggle of getting underway successfully over, there was no longer cause for apprehension. In the earlier stages, with so much concentrated history still before him—every day itself a history—the task had seemed almost too difficult. It had shrunk now to proportions a man could face.

He could scarcely believe so many weeks had gone. But to Jane this passage contained no such element of silent, unmarked flight. Carlyle had driven himself hard—she knew—perhaps too hard. At night, when he should have slept, she could hear him toss in his bed in the room above her. Presently, muffled thumps. He was getting ready to solace and calm himself with a smoke. Only tobacco could quiet the wild horses of his brain. She recognized, to every least creak of the stairs, the course of his midnight journey. In the darkness, groping carefully so as to make as little noise as possible, he would explore his way past the landing by her door. Then down to the kitchen basement. He knew just where to reach for the tinder-box, the flint and steel which were kept there. In the silence she could hear him strike a light for his pipe. Sometimes the door to the courtyard would stir on its hinges—a mild night, evidently; he was going outdoors for a look at the sky.

How could she prevent him from overworking? With his wire-taut nerves, overwork was a constant threat. From the earliest days his health had been a cause of worry to her. At Craigenputtock, much against his will, she had taken him on regular visits to the doctor at Dunscore. He would not go alone.

Yet of late there seemed less cause for alarm. He was secretly enjoying the writing of this book. Though overstimulating, the present occupation had its virtues as medicine. He found nothing so profitable as to be left alone with his *French Revolution*. He was even willing to admit—for him a startling confession—that the book pleased him better than anything he had thus far written. Jane emphatically shared her husband's belief. When he sometimes remarked that its outspokenness gave it no chance of being liked by any existing class of readers, Jane smiled. Carlyle's obstinate refusal to be really hopeful concerning his work was sometimes grotesque. Had not a publisher's reader said that the author of *Sartor* could some day become a popular writer? Popularity in the sense of that possessed by the latest fashionable novelist, like Bulwer-Lytton, was of course the last thing that she wished for him. But he would and must become esteemed by men and women with more than an egg-cup-full of brains in their heads. These would buy his books and give him an honest living.

Yet the fact remained that during the past two years up to this month of February, when the first volume was nearing completion, Jane's husband had not turned a single penny through the craft of literature. Well for them that the new work would soon be finished. Even if it yielded scant financial returns, Carlyle was at least hopeful of the book's general effect. It should serve to make future ventures more lucrative.

The *History* had been announced for coming publication. If only he were further along with the whole project! Yet courage! They had some £300 in reserve with which to front the world.

A splendid feeling—this sense of breaking through. Even in the stiffest trials, when the book, with terrifying perversity, absolutely refused to get itself written, Carlyle had not quite despaired. Discouraging moments, of course, but they had passed. At last he had triumphantly committed to paper the opening canto of this prose poem of the Revolution. There it stood as it had actually taken place—vital, alive.

Though Mill protested that his help could be of small value, he had been given the manuscript to read. Perhaps, thought Mill, he could draw attention to a few defects of style—if they were eccentricities merely, and contributed nothing to the vividness of the author's method. The work was not one to be tampered with; Mill felt sure it was destined to be among the great productions of the age.

Not since many years had Carlyle felt so sure of himself, so free and in right tune.

It was the afternoon of March 6, 1835. Thomas and Jane were having tea. Like a diligent bookworm, Carlyle had been boring all day through stacks of material, preparatory to beginning the second volume of the history. No callers had dropped in. The householders at No. 5 Cheyne Row were enjoying a quiet chat in a solitude almost like that of Craigenputtock.

A knock at the door—Mill's short rap, as familiar and recognizable as the postman's. Friday; not Mill's usual day or hour. Perhaps he was returning the manuscript. Jeannie ran impulsively forward. But it was not Mill who entered the room; it was Mill's ghost. On his face was a nightmare look, an expression one could not forget as long as one lived. Full of quick solicitude, Jane demanded to know the trouble. But Mill, scarcely articulate, waved her toward the street. She must go speak with Mrs. Taylor who was waiting outside.

Great Heavens, had he run off with the woman? A multitude of conjectures flocked through Jane's mind. But Mrs. Taylor, strangely acting too, offered no light. Jane returned to the room.

The truth was out. Except for one or two pages, every scrap, every particle of her husband's manuscript had been destroyed, burned by a careless servant in Mill's lodging. The servant, Mill explained, had believed the leaves to be so much waste paper, and used them for lighting the fire.

Jane had not seen her husband's face at the breaking of the news. The incredulity, the numbness, the wild pain in her own heart told her what he with an even greater intensity must be suffering. The shock of it was like an undeserved sentence of death. Yet there he sat, comforting John Mill! He was thinking of Mill's distress and hiding his own. The heroes in that lost volume had scarcely seen their efforts more ruthlessly blasted or faced sorer trials with greater courage.

"But such a thing never happened before!" groaned Mill—refusing to be consoled; witlessly refusing to keep silence or withdraw.

"Yes, though," answered Carlyle, "Newton and his dog Diamond."

"But Newton went mad over it!"

Carlyle's voice could be so gentle. "Well," he replied, "we shall hardly be so bad as that."

For three incredible hours Mill sat in the room—returning again and again to the subject when Thomas and Jane sought to divert the talk. Would he never leave them to themselves? His reiterated account was confused; its details unconvincing. Could such an accident possibly occur in the house of a writer and editor like Mill? A grim suspicion flickered through Jane's mind. Much more likely in the house of a woman once the wife of a wholesale druggist—Mr. Taylor's profession.

Shortly before the clock struck twelve their caller finally thought of leaving. When at last the door closed behind Mill's back, Jane, in her distress, hardly dared to meet her husband's look. He had just reentered the room after seeing the calamitous visitor safe on the way.

"Mill, poor fellow, is terribly cut up," he said in his husky voice—deep now, and tired—"we must endeavor to hide from him how very serious this business is to us."

A rush of affection and pity swept over Jane. She threw her arms round his neck.

What could she say? She hardly knew, but she had all her sympathy and comfort to give, and the strength of all her love. She had her belief in her husband and her conviction that nothing could defeat him. She was ready, as always, to stand beside him through any fortune or mischance.

They sat talking till day was almost at hand. This book was to have been their last cast of the dice in the game of winning subsistence from London. But now the future seemed ominous as the shadows which threatened the guttering stubs of the candles in the room.

Carlyle turned to his wife. "It shall be written again," he said.

But his nerves made warfare on his courage. Little sleep that night, or the next. Little on the third either. Jane could feel in her own breast the stabs of pain, of hopelessness and despair, that assailed him. She could not persuade her husband to eat. All food turned against him. He spoke of the fantastic nightmares that troubled his fitful rest. In his dreams he saw his dead father; his sister Margaret too, also dead. They came from the grave like corpses, swollen and defaced.

Yet on the very morning the blow had fallen, he was writing a letter to Mill. "How are you?" he inquired. "Is there anything I could do or say to alleviate you?" He was buying new books of reference, he explained, and a better sort of paper to write on. "Thus, far from giving up the game, you see, I am risking £10 on it. Courage, my Friend!" To divert Mill's attention, he commissioned him to seek out some needed volumes.

"Thanks to Mrs. Taylor for her kind sympathies," he added. "May God guide and bless you both!"

He would have preferred to refuse all help, but Mill insisted on one act of compensation. Money could not recall the lost spirit of the book; at least it could make recompense for labor. Carlyle would not accept the £200 which Mill sent. But finally, more to comfort Mill than help himself, Thomas kept £100, a sum equal to the housekeeping expenses during the five months of the manuscript's creation.

In the days immediately following the accident, Carlyle was on the point of writing his family about it. But Jane counseled him to delay awhile. Thomas was grateful for this advice. Better to let them know only when he had launched a second time into the task and could tell them that already the book was in process of reconstruction.

As for his friends in London, none save the publisher, Fraser, should hear of what had happened.

In time the news leaked out, but not the culprit's name. Mrs. Austin, in Mill's presence, remarked that only one course lay open to a man guilty of such wicked carelessness—he should go home and shoot himself.

As he settled again to work, Jane, in anxious silence, watched her husband. He did not plunge at once into the recreation of the annihilated manuscript. Instead he finished what he had just been writing—the opening chapter of the second volume. This done, he goaded himself to recapture what was lost. Not the merest scrap of a note or reference did he have by way of help. His daily readings and past study had been his only guides. To make way for the rest of the pageant, he had swept his mind clear of that part of the history which he had at last committed to paper. Now he must people it again as best he could.

By sheer force of will he drove his pen over page after page of the new-bought sheets. Hour after hour he worked, without relaxation. Yet when he read what he had written, disgust sickened him. He drew his quill through every line.

At last, however, the start was made. Very different, he bitterly declared, from the original, but perhaps no worse. Jane was relieved to see him go out for his first real walk since the disaster. But the glimmer of hope had come too soon. Not one word more would get itself satisfactorily on the empty paper.

A short distance away, a little beyond the nearest roof, a man on a scaffold was building a wall. Without volition, with an effort, even, to check his wandering eyes, Carlyle's glance rose from his idle pen to stare resentfully at the laborer. The mason was even singing at his work! How could any mortal man rest content in such a bile-spotted atmosphere as this, with everything in the universe plunging into regions of the inane? Jane longed to help Carlyle. Even to this innocent wall-builder, she was ready to slaughter any person who caused her husband the least irritation.

Totally idle, not a sentence written, Carlyle sat wrathfully eyeing the laborer. Row after row of bricks, in steady advance, inched upward as the man stuck to his task. He would slosh a splash of mortar upon each just completed layer, then, block after block, the next tier would rise. Each brick, as it settled into place, received a final stroke from the butt of the workman's trowel by way of benediction and farewell.

Carlyle remained motionless, hunched over, deep in thought. Like this very mason, his father James at Ecclefechan had plied his trade. James Carlyle's houses would stand for years as monuments of a good man's industry.

Tom roused himself, tensely erect. He was the fool, and not that singing laborer. What a priceless idiot, to sit there by the window, whining and complaining! His little house of cards had fallen to the dust. He would build it up again, word by word, its images new and fresh, its construction better than before. Nothing, not even that house yonder, though it might serve for generations, could last forever. But valor could, and faith. What counted was the spirit with which one labored. Up then, and be cheerful!

Carlyle left his desk. He washed his face and hands. He would relax, then start again. In spite of ill fortune, the book would be a good book. Its vicissitudes would give it greater rightness and truth.

For a week or more Carlyle rested. He took long walks. To divert his mind he read floods of trashy fiction, snorting with laughter at its absurdities. Then he returned to his place by the window. The distant wall had grown many feet, firm and sturdy and well built.

Chapter Sixteen

JANE could not help regretting that her husband allowed so little time for acquaintances. It had always been so: in Edinburgh, at Craigenputtock, and now in London. His nature, as she knew it at its best, was designed for human companionship. Yet save when he forgot himself, he was all too apt to begrudge as wasted the hours spent in sociability. He would not cultivate friends.

It was not from lack of opportunity. Large numbers of well-wishers were always ready to flock about him. Not a few of these might become intimates if only he would permit it. When, in spite of obstacles, a warm, close bond presently began to form between her husband and a new youthful member of the circle, Jane watched the portents.

The young man's name was John Sterling. Miracle of miracles, he was a clergyman of the Church of England. Her husband, with his contempt for dogmas, rarely took to members of the clerical profession. What made this friendship all the more agreeable was its inclusiveness. Jane had part in it as completely as did her husband. Furthermore it brought in not only John Sterling but all members of his interesting family. John's father and mother showered her with attentions; they invited her on visits to the country; they were delighted with her and gratified by her regard.

John Sterling was only twenty-eight when the Carlyles first met him, yet his years were already packed with a full career. At Cambridge he had distinguished himself as chief speaker among the group of able young men who belonged to the Union, the debating society of the University. He had wandered over Europe and lived in the West Indies; he had dared espouse the cause of the Spanish Revolutionists (an adventure which cost some of his friends their lives); finally, under Coleridge's influence, he had entered the church. A singular clergyman, the

Carlyles thought him. They were not at all surprised when Sterling, after ardently performing his duties for eight months, as ardently abandoned office, convinced that the keys to man's regeneration were not held in the palsied hands of the established church.

John's mother was a gentle, self-effacing woman—young-looking, and still beautiful, though seriously ill. But she never complained of her health; few realized that she suffered from a dangerous heart ailment.

John's father Edward was chief leader-writer and editor of that powerful trumpet of England's might and conscience: *The Times.* He had once held a commission in the army and had still the bearing of a clean-washed, sharp old military gentleman, in spite of his effort to assume completely the guise of respectable man-about-town. Though he knew so much, there was an Irish candor about him, a total lack of subterfuge, which greatly amused Jane and Thomas. Genial, energetic, and irrepressible, he made it his practice to drive round London, mix in society, and visit all the clubs. He enjoyed stirring up the prodigious fuss that swirled and eddied wherever he went. By this simple device he heard what every manner of man was saying on each topic of the day. Then at night, in his study, he became the voice of England. His skill in reporting and shaping current opinion made him by all odds the most successful journalist of his time. In his editorials, he boomed and delivered broadsides like a British man-of-war. "The Whirlwind," the Carlyles named him, or "The Thunderer." That last title seemed destined to stick to the august *Times* itself because of Sterling's opening salvo in one of his leaders—"We have already thundered forth this opinion!"

His rumbling and his lightnings never frightened Jane. In fact she had tied his bolts to her apron-strings and made them tame. His opinions on national affairs might be sound enough—in print they were violently convincing. But in the scale of common sense his views on the intimate details of existence were often grotesquely out of balance. Jane took delight in puncturing his balloons. Down he would sink, after sharp fencing and cutting, only to soar again, blown up by another monstrous notion. But in spite of her tactics he was unreservedly her slave. He relished her banter, and never seemed to mind being a target for shafts which were generally, it must be admitted, quite deserved. Sometimes Jane was mystified by this strange attraction which lay in her for all the blood of Sterling. There was no understanding such things. She was sure that she had taken a hundred times more pains to please other persons of her acquaintance. The phenomenon held not only for the males. Its magic extended even to the wives—both sons also were married. The elder Mrs. Sterling was as kind as an ideal mother. But the tie which held the men was amazing—they stood ready, with quixotic chivalry, to meet Jane's every wish. They acted as though each, individually, were married to her. Jane was very slow to ask for favors. She detested burdensome or selfish women. But she found pleasure in the realization that these men, if it lay within their means, were ready to perform any service which could bring her health or happiness.

Anthony, John's elder brother, was a stunning fellow. He was more reserved than his parent, yet irascible too, and full of sparks. Like his father he had become a soldier and was now a captain. There were few manlier men in London—a person it did one good to look at daily by way of tonic.

Though Anthony was attractive—no woman would deny his claims—John was the choicest member of the family; a prince among his companions. Yet in spite of his incisive mind, his gifts, his great potentialities, he was something of an enchanted princeling. He was so very restless, so incapable either of tranquillity or effectual motion. A personality combined of sheet lightning and the aurora borealis—beautiful, but lacking in direction.

Carlyle was uncertain as to what course in life these energies ought to pursue. Jane was surer in her analysis. John was a poet, she knew, a splendid poet. He had just finished a long poem—an allegory of the union of the ideal and the actual. It held a mirror up to his own fine spirit.

To Jane he admitted privately that as he composed he often had her husband's approbation in his mind. "Carlyle will be pleased with that," he would tell himself.

But Carlyle was becoming steadily further estranged from poetry. In her conversation Jane rarely mentioned the topic to him now. More and more he was turning to what he called the great realities of life—facts and the truths behind them. With its infinite riches, prose, not tinkling verse, was a diviner language for expression of vital things. He loved Sterling and was solicitous of his future. But these efforts in verse seemed a waste of time to Carlyle. He preferred to read the able essays, signed with the symbol £, which were beginning to appear in the pages of *The London and Westminster Review*.

John owned a feminine quickness and delicacy of perception. But these gifts were backed by thoroughly masculine power. From his intuition he could build a shining adamantine fortress of argument. He enjoyed debate with his friend Carlyle. But he was always glad when he could draw Jane out. In her mind he found a compatibility which placed them on an equal footing. He admired her zest. He spoke approvingly of what he called her "youthful enthusiasm," a description which both amused and pleased her. Her letters, he told his friends, were the wittiest he had ever received.

Sterling agreed with Carlyle in everything—except opinions. There he stuck to his guns. He would not compromise, though many persons, to keep the peace, spiked their own cannon when they called at Chelsea. It was beautiful to hear him speak. "Hopeful"—Jane christened him. Tall, well-proportioned, slight, he filled the room with his engaging presence. His face—keen, gray-eyed—combined strength and delicacy, energy and refinement. Ostensibly a clergyman, said Jane, but more like a creature from heaven.

It was shocking to realize how ill he was. Very pale, he sometimes looked, in refutation of the impression of health conveyed by his slim, athletic frame. His doctor had warned him not to spend another winter in England. Before leaving for Bordeaux, he wrote Jane a long letter. It was all about his future and the plans he was making. But Jane saw that its light tone was forced, and the striving at gayety distressed her.

Would she and Thomas ever see him again? Consumption of the chest was a fatal scourge. She had never known a man or woman, once afflicted, to get well. Carlyle insisted on remaining optimistic. Had Sterling not recovered from his latest seizure, when for weeks no one save his family could see him and his many friends had been so apprehensive?

Over the sofa where Sterling had rested on his last visit hung

Albrecht Dürer's woodcut of Christ bearing the cross. John's gift. Whenever the picture caught their eyes, they thought of him, brave and hopeful, carrying his own burden on the continent.

The infinite variety of people which the town afforded captivated Jane. From Christian gentlemen to heathen Chinee— the range was enormous.

Political fermentation on the continent—a devil's brew which seethed with increasing turbulence, casting its froth and scum, and some of its finer essences as well, to the very shores of Great Britain—terrified many Londoners. Might not an ill wind some day blow too much of this gathering vapor across the channel? These fears never troubled Carlyle. He enjoyed shocking the ears of conservative hearers with diatribes on the wretched state of England. A land almost too rotten for revolt! But change within must come, or decay and putrescence.

For Jane the disturbances abroad brought interesting new acquaintances and the chance to brush up on her languages. During her first visit to London she had met noted radicals. Now, with equal impartiality, she was on the friendliest terms with a sample or two from the aristocracy. Just for the music of it, a speaking acquaintance with exiled Italians was worth the cultivation. Count Pepoli, for instance, one of the handsomest and best-mannered of men. With his little bows, his amusing continental ways, his animated, tuneful speech, he was welcome to drop in, as he did, twice a week or so to make Jane's thoughts melodious for the rest of the day. He knew scarcely a word of English, but Jeannie's struggles through the whole of Dante, under the tutelage of John Carlyle, had lent proficiency to her tongue. Count Pepoli vowed he was astonished at Jane's skill. A divine talent! he would murmur in admiration. "Ah, graziosa! Ah, bella, bella! Ah, ah!" When she met a young and fascinating Bolognese noblewoman, Clementina degli Antoni, eager to exchange both friendship and instruction—Madama Carlyle to teach English, the Contessa, Italian—Jane was charmed by the arrangement. The Contessa was the woman, Jane remarked, to make any husband faithless, including Carlyle. So graceful and so witty, an enchantress if ever there was one! Everything about her, Jane declared, was contrived to fascinate the heart of man. Promptly she invited the countess to dine and watched with amusement her husband's marked politeness.

With Jane the countess was soon at the stage where such phrases as "carissima amica" flew through the air like turtle doves. As for Jane's Italian, Carlyle insisted that his wife progressed amazingly, though she replied, with an expressive shrug in the best continental manner, that the mingled chatter of English and Italian, when she and the contessa met for lessons, was something truly remarkable; "una confusione siccome nella Torre di Babele!" Thomas roared with delight, his struggles with the French Revolution momentarily forgotten. His clever Jeannie had just the right accent; her vehement pronouncement rang like silver in his ears.

Jane's London housekeeping had reached a maximum of technique, upset only if the current maid-of-all-work, as was to be expected where one could afford to pay very little for servants, proved to be unbaked potter's clay and foundered in a horrid pudding instead of bearing up according to the promises of her credentials. Carlyle's friends often remarked that he must be a very unusual man who understood the art, unknown to them, of living on next to nothing. But Thomas generally gave credit where it was due. His thrifty wife—she was the magician. Hers was the gift that carried them along while not a penny was coming in and the new *History* was in the making.

It had been a sad day, late in their first summer at Chelsea, when Bessy Barnet had left because of complications in her family. To school a raw, totally ignorant girl (they came cheapest so), yet not upset her husband's routine, was Jane's repeated household problem. Once trained, they could command higher wages elsewhere, and like as not fled incontinently away. Yet Jane's average for holding servants was high; better than that of many of her friends who could afford liberal remuneration.

Jane's standards never dropped because of human imperfections. She kept her household banner high, nailed to the mast even in storm and disaster. Few establishments, with cook, housemaid, and manservant, were better kept than hers single-staffed. Jane knew how everything should be done, and rather than have a duty bungled, she attended to it herself.

Cleanliness was Jane's passion. Without this virtue few servants could last in her house. She had her notions, too, about
employment. The obligation of housemaid to mistress, and vice
versa, she regarded as sacred. She never stood for airs, in herself or in a servant. Jane liked to get her maids from Scotland.
She understood their temperaments better than she did the
cockneys (though presently she could also manage these), and
her husband liked the rolling "Rs" of good Scots talk about the
house. On the average, Jane paid her maids twelve pounds a
year, with a bonus of one pound ten for "beer money" which
they could drink or save as they saw fit. She furnished all the
tea they might require in the kitchen (not a universal custom)
and the sugar to go with it. In London, one engaged servants
by the month. Jane did not believe in any term so short as that.
It gave too great an opportunity, she thought, for maid and
mistress to fly asunder in any moment of ill humor on either
side, when, had they been bound together for six months, they
would have been forced to make the best of it. In the end they
would probably find themselves better off and more contented
than had they parted company. Repeated change, Jane declared,
was not good for the soul.

As for duties, her servant cooked the meals, but Jane was
ready to help with the housework. On Carlyle's behalf, there
were special instructions which she transmitted to each incumbent. Her husband knew less and less about the household
and noticed things only when they went wrong. "Trouble him
with as few questions as possible," she warned. If they took pains
to please him, all would be well. "And if he look fussed or
cross, never mind so long as you are doing your best." Above all,
keep the kitchen in order! When Mr. Carlyle went down to
light his pipe, his sharp eyes would be sure to notice irregulari-
ties. One other thing, if the sound of a street organ should be
heard (more and more they were invading Chelsea) the servant must rush out and bid it move along lest it disturb the
master's labors.

Before she learned the ropes, Jane's major problem in
London was the marketing. By purchasing her supplies from
shopkeepers whose good will she cultivated, she presently was
able to avoid the town's worst atrocities: milk as blue as a china
dish, eggs ready to become chickens, and potatoes watery and

sodden at prices ten times higher than those in Dumfriesshire. As
always, Carlyle's diet, because of dyspepsia, was a grave concern
to Jane. She taught her servants to prepare the dishes he could
eat: broth, minced mutton browned before the fire, chops, and
rice pudding.

No truer, more skillful, gleg little Goody ever existed—
Carlyle boasted—she was worth any twenty London wives all
put together.

Jane had little respect for women who minimized or pretended to ignore the part played in their lives by domestics.
Servants, she protested, were a most important, a most fearful
item in a woman's existence. She thought, talked, and wrote
about them, Jane readily admitted, as much as some women
did about their lovers. Her maids were never mere soulless
automatons; she considered them always as human beings. In
London she had gathered and observed several rare specimens.
Anne Cook, from Dumfriesshire, was a famous importation.
She was clumsy as a calf, but full of assiduity, good-nature, and
an Annandale primitiveness which brought spasms of amusement to her master and mistress. There was about this wild
Caledonian a quality which made the Cockney mind pause in
astonishment. The porters from stores who came to the house,
even the polite visitors above stairs, knew not what to make of
her. Broader Scotch than hers was never spoken in greater
London.

Anne's perfect incomprehension of anything resembling ceremony amused Jane every time it disclosed itself. Once, when
this maid had cut her finger, Jane was helping her to wring
out a sheet. But Anne was scornful of her mistress's effort; the
task was far above her strength.

"I shall get at it by practice," Jane insisted, "far weaker
people than I have wrung sheets."

"May be sae," remarked Anne, with a disparaging glance at
her employer's slight figure, "but I ken-na where ye'll find any
weaker, for a weaklier-like cretur I never saw in a' my life!"

Like a grouse on the moors, Anne lived her life on nature's
plan. Her notions on early rising would have unstrung any
London servant. Four-thirty was none too early. She resented
only her inability to wake up at the desired time. Carlyle's

sleepless ways had not deserted him. He often wandered about the halls in the hours before dawn. One evening, Anne, having observed this idiosyncrasy in the master, decided that in it lay the solution to her problem. So she remarked confidentially to Jane, "if Mr. Carlyle bees any uneasy through the nicht, and's ga'an staverin aboot the hoose, will ye bid him gae us a cry at five in the morning?"

Anne was a rare gem, but perhaps the choicest of them all was Helen Mitchell, Kirkcaldy Helen, who stayed with the Carlyles, off and on, through nearly twelve years. Helen, Jane insisted, was the strongest mixture of philosopher and perfect idiot that she had ever met with. Her conduct in either capacity was equally unpredictable and bizarre. After some of Helen's more violent escapades, Jane had made a determined effort to sever relations. But it was never any use. "What would become of you I should like to know?" Helen would ask in a tone of affectionate contempt when Jane told her to leave. "Fancy you ill and me not there to take proper care of you! I think that would be a farce!" Whereupon Helen's mistress would capitulate.

When Jane suffered from one of her ripping, tearing headaches, Helen had a way of bending over and stroking Jane's face as though a little sick child lay suffering on the bed. Once, Jane noticed, Helen's cheek was wet with tears.

Helen's faults and virtues were strangely mixed. She was a great reader, but not always discreet in her choices. She read the master's books, but she also thoroughly enjoyed the mistress's letters. When she could remember to, Jane took good care to seal what she had written. Helen considered herself a member of the family and entitled to share in all its secrets: a forgivable sin, perhaps no sin at all. But she had one serious fault which caused her mistress real distress. From time to time, one could never be sure when an outbreak might occur, she would take violently to the bottle. A long interval of good behavior, then Helen would again fall prostrate under the dictatorship of gin.

Helen possessed other appetites, but hardly so disrupting. She was very fond of kippered herring. One morning, while Jane was ordering the dinner, Helen asked if she might have a red herring all to herself. "My heart has been set on it this good while back," she pleaded. So modest a petition was quickly granted, and Jane thought no more about it.

After the meal, Jane became aware of the fact that her maid was lighting the fire in the upstairs parlor. It was impossible not to notice. Every stroke of the poker bore the weight of uncontrolled rage. What ailed the creature, wondered Jane—had the herring disagreed with her?

After Helen returned to the kitchen, the hubbub continued till Jane was ready to believe that her maid was having another seizure of whiskey. But she was sober when she appeared with the tea tray, though obviously distraught. She planked down her burden as though minded to demolish dishes and table at one fell stroke, and a look of thunder brooded in her face. Jane ignored the symptoms and remarked coolly, "a little less noise, if you please." At that, Helen cast her glance aloft with the look of a martyr, but said nothing and went below. The uproar continued in the kitchen.

Jane hurried down the stairs. Helen stood belligerent, a broom grasped firmly in her hand. The cat, usually a fixture in the place, was inexplicably missing.

"Where is the cat?"

"The cat?" said Helen grimly. "I have all but killed her."

"How?"

"With the besom."

"Why, for goodness' sake?"

"Why?" Helen's rage became explosive. "Why, indeed! Because she ate my red herring! I set it all ready on the end of the dresser, and she ran away with it, and ate it every morsel to the tail."

Poor Helen! Had she eaten no dinner at all?

"Oh, yes, I had mutton enough, but I had just set my heart on a red herring!"

In spite of interruptions, the Phoenix-like rebirth of the burned volume of the *French Revolution* was almost in the final stages. A most persistent round of parties had broken in on Carlyle's efforts. At last he had struck. He refused to go anywhere, even to the simplest cup of tea. Jane did her best to fend off callers. In the evenings, if he was not working, Carlyle rested. No more heart-breaking job than the present one had

ever come within his experience, nor was ever likely to. Not till
he had really grappled with it had he realized how near this
task bordered on the insuperable. At times the thought struck
him, ill and miserable, that in this dogged pursuit of a writer's
career he was perhaps on the wrong track. Why not quit literature, with a vengeance to it! Better, almost, to turn to sheep-
herding.

In his gloom, he thought often of Jane. Her hopes of him
had been so high, her faith so great. She had endured trying
vicissitudes beside him with never a murmur of disappointment
or complaint. Should all this end in defeat? Never, if he could
help it! He would finish the book. After that, if fate demanded,
they could plan another life. In the dim background, as a last
resource, hovered the thought of America. Ever since the visit
to Craigenputtock, Emerson, from a place named Concord,
Massachusetts, had been writing letters of encouragement.
When he learned of the catastrophe which had overtaken the
History, and of Carlyle's financial plight, he suggested a tour
of the lyceums of America to reap a harvest of dollars through
lecturing. His proposal had been backed with figures and the
promise to help. He had also hinted that Carlyle might edit
a new literary journal in Boston which a group of energetic
people were on the point of founding. Stranger still was news
that youthful New England (not represented by the staid
professors at Harvard, of course, but by keen young graduates)
was falling head over heels in love with *Sartor* through treasured copies of *Fraser's Magazine.* Could the work be brought
there as a book, Emerson was sure it would sell. But Fraser,
approached with the idea, had almost fainted at the thought,
so Thomas let the matter drop.

As Jane stood watch, Carlyle pressed doggedly on. Two
manuscript pages a day in his fine writing—equivalent to some
four or five in print. She read each chapter as it was finished.
Good, she insisted, very, very good. This book, surely, could
not fail to sway men's thoughts.

Her husband, alas, was working far beyond his strength; of
that she was certain. His face had grown yellow, his eyes
bloodshot. They seemed to retreat ever deeper under his bushy,
projecting brows and massive forehead. Sleep had practically de-

serted him. Jane worried to hear him prowling in his room at
five in the morning or earlier. A little black speck, he said, flit-
tered like a signal of distress in the vision of his left eye. But
he would not heed the warning though his nerves were jangled, his body and mind alike hag-ridden and weary.

Jane's headaches returned. But quietly, unobtrusively, she did
what she could to aid her husband with his intolerable load.
Ill health was not the only threat. Their money was diminishing, with no immediate replenishment in sight.

Yet Jeannie was not discouraged with her bargain. An old
suitor had called on her, a man who after ten years in India
had returned with more thousands of pounds than she and
Thomas were ever likely to possess in hundreds or dozens even.
Yet the sight of him with his wealth did not make her doubt
the wisdom of her choice in husbands. She could wish Carlyle
a little less yellow, a little more peaceable—that was all. In
every other respect, she told herself, she was satisfied.

One chapter more and the thing would be finished. "We shall
sing a *Te Deum* and get drunk!" said Jane. For the last mentioned ceremony they had excellent facilities. An acquaintance
had just sent them a hamper of the finest old Madeira wine.

On the rainy afternoon of Monday, September 21, 1835,
Carlyle wrote the last page of the new first volume. In what
now appeared to him a state of detestable enchantment enduring for six long months he had labored like a man painfully
accomplishing zero. But the thing was finished. What was to follow would be like child's play in comparison.

The new manuscript, he felt, was not so well expressed, perhaps, but more compact: not *very* much worse than the original
volume.

Better than the first, insisted Jane; a little less vivacious, perhaps, but more carefully thought out and firmer in the joints
and sinews.

Chapter Seventeen

*T*OM was looking forward to a recuperative pause in
Scotland. There had been talk of Jeannie's going with
him, but when Mrs. Welsh agreed to visit her daughter these plans were abandoned. Another year would do as well.
A vacation in the North, suggested Jane's mother on arrival,
might plump Jeannie up a bit—she was so woefully thin. But
Jeannie protested that country air and country fare would
hardly counterbalance country dullness. With the ill-fated manuscript finished, and Carlyle ready to be off for the recovery
of his health, Jane already felt in better spirits.

Mrs. Welsh did not take very kindly to London or its ways.
She refused to share Jane's belief that a little exciting social
talk was more advantageous to well-being than medicine and
rural breezes. Jane dutifully showed her the grander sights of
the town. At the British Museum, they looked at the sculptures
plundered from the Parthenon. Mrs. Welsh, however, was
more thrilled by a glimpse she caught of the king and queen,
William IV and Adelaide. A beggar woman hurrying past with
ragged, cobwebbed shawl gave the news that the royal pair
were about to inspect the Chelsea Military Hospital. Jane was
on good terms with many of the derelicts of her neighborhood.
Her unobtrusive charity had won their friendship and in exchange they passed on to her any likely bits of gossip which
they thought might interest. So Jane hurried her mother off
to see the royal spectacle. Mrs. Welsh's burst of patriotic enthusiasm amused her daughter. To Jeannie and her husband,
crowned heads were an anachronism. Poor princedom, so storm-
tossed in these grave years of reform bills that brought little
reform, of taxes on food that struck directly at the hungry
workers! How frost-bitten and anxious she appeared—the
Queen hurrying past, curtsying to the wretchedest looking
rabble which Jane had ever seen gathered together in Chelsea.

Adelaide behaved as though in fear of her royal life. Jane felt a touch of compassion for her in the part she had to play. It was said that she had been hissed, some days before, while attending the theater. Might this be the beginning of the end for English royalty? In similar fashion had the change occurred in France, as Carlyle had recorded in his *History*. Would Victoria, the Princess Royal, ever sit on the British throne? Poor child, she was like a canary bird in a cage, looking out on a gathering tempest.

Mrs. Welsh, Jane perceived, had made up her mind to dislike the London friends who came to Cheyne Row. Though Carlyle was away, there had been no diminution in the stream of evening callers. But only one of these really met with Mrs. Welsh's approval. This visitor was Count Pepoli. She had been so charmed with his manner that the grand hindrance to conversation between them—he knew little English; she no Italian—bothered her not at all. She presented her tartan scarf to the Count when he admired it, bestowing her gift, said Jane, in a manner *molto graziosa*.

Meanwhile, from the North, came Carlyle's letters. His first, from Annan, sounded quite encouraging. "You will come back strong and cheerful, will you not?" Jane pleaded. "I wish you were come, anyhow. Don't take much castor; eat plenty of chicken broth rather."

Jane had amused herself writing a long, excessively *spiritosa* letter in Italian to "mia adorable Clementina," the Countess degli Antoni. Why not send a note in the same language to Carlyle? "Caro e respettabile il mio Marito!" she began. But her impetuous thoughts tumbled over one another with such rapidity that English words soon jostled on the page with the foreign ones. "Try all that ever you can to be patient and good-natured with your *povera piccola Gooda*, and then she loves you and is ready to do anything on earth that you wish; to fly over the moon, if you bade her. But when the *signor della casa* has neither kind look nor word for me, what can I do but grow desperate, fret myself to fiddle strings, and be a torment to society in every direction?"

Carlyle received her gay, tender, appealing letter in one of his self-condemnatory moments. They were complicated, injurious and self-injuring states of mind—moods sufficiently difficult to deal with. "My poor Goody," he replied, "it seems as if she could so easily be happy; and the easy means are so seldom there." The thought of work yet to be done before that despicability in three volumes, *The French Revolution*, should be ready for the press, still hovered like London murk over his head. She was depending on cheerful looks from him to bring happiness to herself? "For God's sake do not, or do so as little as possible!" He had little cheerfulness to give, he said, with his heart feeling as if it were drowning in floods of confusion and obstruction.

Jane might have been painfully discouraged by this letter had there not been in it one or two little hints which she could expand into confirmation that he was really a good deal better in health and spirits than some of his remarks implied. He was bilious the day of writing, he confessed. He loved her more than words could say, or her own imagination could tell her. And tucked away in the letter, as in the days of their courtship, was a message of reassurance and counsel for Jane about her mother. Mrs. Welsh's visit, Carlyle knew, had lasted beyond the margin possible for peacefulness. Mother and daughter were getting on each other's nerves. "Hadere nicht mit deiner Mutter, Liebste"—Mrs. Welsh was ignorant of German—"Trage, trage; es wird bald enden." Don't quarrel with your mother, Dearest. Be patient, it will soon end.

During her husband's absence Jane had made one great discovery. It concerned her own position in London. She had not failed to notice that the stream of callers at Cheyne Row had experienced no drouth though Thomas was away. There could be only one conclusion: these visitors to Chelsea came there as much because of her as because they wished to see her brilliant husband. This revelation, so unexpected, warmed Jane's heart. She was not a vain person—no one had ever accused her of vanity. She was proud to be Carlyle's wife. But also, she had a secret yearning to be herself.

Back again, Carlyle plunged into the vortex of his *French Revolution*—into the last two-thirds which was to have been such child's play in its completing. Yet when he sat down to his desk his mind was confused, his spirit feckless. Discouraging in the extreme—that mountain ahead, still to be moved! But once he had heated himself into the old fever of composition, he discovered to his joy that he could still write as of old. All natural work now; no recreating of burnt stuff, surely the miserablest of all human punishments—enough to break the heart of any man. His health was better; he was getting along cannily.

The very atmosphere in which he wrote smelled of revolution. Europe was wallowing in the after-birth of Democracy. And the child itself was painfully feeble and ailing. Further sprinklings of foreigners, political refugees of all complexions and persuasions, were descending in ever increasing volume on the master and mistress of the house at Cheyne Row.

Jane had a tender heart; she lacked the power to turn waifs of any kind from her door. In her first days in Chelsea, the number of animals in distressed circumstances that had imposed themselves on her country simplicity had been quite amazing. Thomas ironically advised her to put an advertisement in the window, "House of Refuge for Stray Dogs and Cats." Jane soon found that she should alter the sign to read, "political exiles." Or why not "General audit office for all the miseries of the universe"? Certainly the weaker of these foreigners were always ready to pour their troubles into her ears. Personal woes or national, she must listen to them all.

These strangers enjoyed coming to her house because it offered them the lost pleasures of domesticity. They came also because they could speak their own languages in its hospitable parlor. The Carlyles did not possess the usual British aversion to every tongue save English. French, German, or Italian, they stumbled along in each with a fair degree of fluency, though the more exacting of their callers declared themselves shocked by the outrages on grammar committed at Cheyne Row.

Many of these men cast out from the continent made little appeal to Jane's husband. They murdered his precious time and he was glad to turn them over to his wife. Their alien ways, of course, were curious and interesting but could hardly make amends for the faults in the men themselves. The aristocrats, in Tom's opinion, were usually drones, and the revolutionaries shrill and impractical. From a few, however, real instruction could be had, and these he welcomed. To talk with men whose parents' lives had been shorn away by the guillotine, or men whose fathers had been instrumental in the severing, brought greater vividness to the panorama of the Revolution.

By far the best of the Frenchmen who visited Chelsea was Godefroi Cavaignac, son of a deputy who had voted in the Assembly for the execution of Louis XVI. A man of determination, pride, and unbounded courage. Since he was an old acquaintance of John Stuart Mill, who had met him in Paris, the Carlyles had known of Cavaignac and his exploits several years before they encountered him personally. He had been active in the movement which produced the French Revolution of 1830. A man of irresistible power and indomitable will, intense in everything, including his atheism. "I don't like those who believe in God," Cavaignac would say. "It is generally a reason for doing nothing for man." He believed in human progress and considered it a duty to struggle for its sake against all obstacles. He was still an active revolutionist, eager to overthrow by force the corrupt régime of Louis Philippe, erstwhile President of France. Louis Philippe's assumption of the crown had banished Cavaignac to England. He was now biding his time for a propitious moment to tumble the pasteboard king from his throne.

By 1835, Godefroi was a choice member of the Carlyles' inner group. There was something leonine in this Frenchman's face and manner. Calm and noble when not excited, he could become terrifying when aroused. Foreign aristocrats in London trembled to meet him. Yet among honored acquaintances, no matter what their belief, he was serene and courteous—a fine Bayard soul, though a republican, with a body to correspond. Jane, watching him in her drawing room, felt that he possessed the dark, half-savage beauty of one of Milton's rebellious angels who feared neither heaven nor earth. Yes, Cavaignac was a hero who fought and spoke and wrote with passionate intrepidity, who was ready to dare or suffer, to live or die, without disturbing himself about the personal consequences. A paragon who defied all men and honored all women—a thorough-going man, worthy of love and honor.

Carlyle had great regard for Cavaignac. Jane found him one of the few men she had ever met who drew forth her unqualified respect and admiration. The longer she knew him, the more attractive he became. So intense did her feeling grow that she presently realized there was in it a quality which might lead to infatuation. If one loved one's husband, such things were dangerous.

Punctually on New Year's day, Godefroi Cavaignac always gave Jane some little present to honor the season. At her impetuous thanks, spoken in his own language, his stern face would relax into a smile; into a burst of mantling joyous humor. "You are no Scotswoman," he would say. "Soon you will be a woman of France!" Sometimes he dispatched a messenger to her house with tickets for a performance at the Gallic Theatre. Thomas was never eager to attend—there would be fatigue and headache in the morning and a working day ruined. But out of respect to Cavaignac, he would go. And when the play happened to be *Figaro*, even Jane's critical husband was satisfied and enjoyed the performance.

The never ceasing revolutionary plotting of their friend dismayed the Carlyles. The fine, chivalrous, foolhardy, gallant man, waiting for the moment to come when he could at last blow Louis Philippe and his régime into perdition. With Godefroi's fiery spirit, there was no telling how his life would end.

Godefroi seemed always supplied with funds and willing assistants. In that respect he differed greatly from the majority of these plotters. The only possessions left to most of them were their wrongs. Yet how could one help sympathizing with them, and honoring them too, when one saw them with waiters' aprons over their only suit of clothes, emptying slop-pails for the salvation of the world? They dared to be men and to face adversity bravely for the sake of their convictions.

Carlyle's efforts were bringing their reward. He was splashing down in large masses of color the overpowering spectacle of revolution. A queer book, he said to Jane, one of the strangest that would be published in the century. A study of men's souls through the shapes of their outward actions. A savage book, unwelcome, as had been all his writings, to conservative England. Yet so must the story be told if the book should have the truth within it. He had dared to look King and beggar in the face, he had dared strip away the outer clothing to search beneath. He had shown the glorious heights, the horrible depravities within men's hearts—their baseness and their might. The book would be *Sartor* without the allegory, presenting, through flesh and blood which had lived and died in violence, a tract for the times. Nor could the story that he was recording be wholly completed though the first great revolution was over. The struggle must go on, perhaps through many generations, till Ragnarök—till the final bright emergence, after blood and fire, of a cleansed and tempered world.

While Adam toiled, Eve spun. As her goodman plowed his field, Jane strove to keep her house together. When she was in fair health, the burden was supportable. But when she grew ill, the present became heavy as a millstone. It was so easy to become depressed and out of sorts. In April, 1836, Carlyle finished the second of the three projected volumes. John, back from the continent, was in London. Before grappling with the problems of the final book, Thomas went swashing far and near on long walks with his brother. But for Jane there had been little respite. Her well-being had suffered under the long strain, and she was in need of change. Brief stays with friends in the country near London were not enough. When she spoke of a month or so in Scotland, her husband encouraged the proposal. He was not unaware of her dispiritment. The bitter style of mockery of which he knew her capable rose too easily to her lips. But Templand would cure her. She must look out of the windows there and see the green earth and its flowers, the arching sky beautiful overhead. This world, he assured her, could not really be a place of hopelessness. No, emphatically there was hope for all.

On Saturday, the ninth of July, Carlyle saw her off. Only one passenger besides Jane sat in the coach as the horses clattered out of Holborn. She stole a peep at him. Certainly a quiet seeming individual, who ought not to add to the discomforts of the trip. Jane had convinced herself that she was a poor traveler. She looked forward to the journey with considerable dread, and the thought, under the circumstances, of having to talk with strangers did not appeal to her. But her fellow-passenger uttered never a sound. They left town in uninterrupted silence. In the flat country just outside London, the horses moved at a good pace, and the vehicle lurched and rolled with disquieting violence. Not uttering a word, Jane's fellow-passenger folded his greatcoat and made a cushion of it for her back. Then he produced three lemons from a pocket and handed them to her. They were a safeguard, he explained, against carriage sickness. She was to suck them, one after another, through the day. Having performed his humanitarian service, Jane's companion once more sank into himself.

When night drew on (no more people entering the coach) Jane had a whole side along which to stretch out. Stoke Goldington, Northampton, Brixworth, Leicester—the villages and towns dropped away. Loughborough, Kegworth, and the highway once more visible in the dawn. At Derby, one hundred and twenty-six miles from London, Jane's fellow-passenger left. There was fine scenery along this section of the route, with hills beyond Ashbourne which made the horses labor. Manchester was less than forty miles distant. Her first halt was to be Manchester, where she would rest a day or so with Carlyle's youngest sister Janet, recently married to Robert Hanning, a small shopkeeper in the city.

Suddenly Jane discovered that she had come away without Janet's address. How could she have done so stupid a thing? She fancied herself seated disconsolate on her trunk like a deserted orphan. But even before the coach had stopped, Robert's cheery face popped in at the window. Soon the hackney cab which he had summoned deposited them in front of Janet's home, the living-quarters right above the shop itself. A busy, noisy street, Jane noticed, with a public house next door.

Being weary after her almost sleepless journey, she soon retired. But when she tried the bed, her back and sides misgave her. Hard as a deal board, and it had a hump in the middle right where there should have been a hollow. While Jane attempted to adjust herself round this obstruction, growing every moment more wide awake, her worst fears began to be realized. All through the night, in ones and twos and threes, drunk or merely happy tipplers emerged from the near-by jerry shop and went roaring home. To add to Jane's distress, she felt welts rising, big as hazel-nuts, on her sensitive skin. Bugs! Or fleas perhaps? Janet was an orderly housekeeper, but one could never tell about beds inherited through marriage. John Carlyle, who had gone on to Scotsbrig, was to be the

Hannings' next guest on his way back to London. In London, he would claim Jane's guest room. The possibilities were ominous. "O Darling," she wrote to her husband, "thank Heaven that we are without bugs;—and see that John's window be kept open, when he returns; and order Anne to take down his clothes and shake them in the Garden."

Her next move was to Liverpool, where she was planning to visit her aunt and uncle, the John Welshes, and their family. She traveled thither by that new marvel, the Manchester-Liverpool railway. The line, first notably successful thing of the kind in all Britain, had seen six years of service. Already several horrid accidents had occurred. But Jane was determined to try it. Soon London itself was to become the railway's southern terminal, and the stagecoach days would be ended.

She mounted into one of the iron-wheeled carriages behind the locomotive, a hissing, puffing monster with an entire French Revolution within its boilers. As she sat waiting, Jane became very uneasy. Of course the other passengers seemed to be taking the experience calmly enough. Yes, but once the train started, how could one ever get it stopped? For once Jane did not relish her powers of imagination. Yet when the railway coach at last got under way, Jane could find little difference between its motion and that of the horse-drawn one in which she had come from London. Odder still, she did not seem to be going any faster, though the changing panorama of trees and houses framed in the window told her that the train's passage was more like flight than earth-bound travel. Thirty-four miles covered in an hour and a quarter! It was scarcely believable.

Since she wished to surprise them, Jane had given her relations no precise word as to the time of her coming. But soon she was regretting her impulse. She had not taken account of the strangeness and confusion awaiting her at the Liverpool station. In a stagecoach, one's trunk was a fellow-passenger, in sight whenever one wished to be sure of its presence. How different by train! With so many travelers, and so many pieces of luggage, one's possessions were like needles in a haystack. Jane's sharp glance—she peered about as though searching for a lost child—spotted her trunk among the hundred others with which it had been tumbled. How could one ever get it out? Jane's polite, quiet-voiced inquiries were lost in the hubbub. Resolutely she pressed forward into the heap.

"You must take your turn, Ma'am, you must take your turn!" an official called to her.

"Stand out of the road, will you?" Jane exclaimed, determination in her voice. "There is the trunk before my eyes; and I will lift it away myself without troubling anyone!"

At that, the official took notice of the energetic little cyclone bearing down on him: "For God's sake give the Lady her trunk and let us be rid of her!"

The driver of the waiting omnibus snatched Jane's luggage from her hands and heaved it aloft. He would pass within ten yards of her uncle's house, he said, when she gave him the address. He was even better than his word; he deposited traveler and baggage at the very door.

The family were within at their dessert. When Jane entered, they bobbed up in astonishment. Such laughter and ebullience in their greeting! These Welshes were more than kin; they were kindred spirits—Uncle John, his two daughters Helen and Jeannie, and a string of boys besides. Jeannie Welsh, called Babbie for pet-name, was eighteen years younger than her cousin Jane, and Helen younger by twelve. But the three were like girls together.

John was her favorite uncle. A genial, affectionate, impetuous man, he was her mother's brother: the Welsh name ran on both sides of the family. But though habitually cheerful and friendly, he had a roar in him like a lion if he became provoked. He was a person of extraordinary integrity, and had made heavy sacrifice to the demands of honor. When his partner had failed in business, through no fault of John's, and plunged the firm in bankruptcy, Mr. Welsh assumed every penny of the obligation. During seven difficult years he built up a new business, and on the eighth, he invited the creditors to a dinner at his house. The family plate, which had been locked away since the misfortune, reappeared bright and gleaming on the table. Under each man's cover lay a draft meeting to the full his individual claim. "Pocket your checks, gentlemen," exclaimed John Welsh, "and let us drink Better Luck for time coming!"

Ever since that day Mr. Welsh had prospered and now lived in considerable luxury.

Before setting out for Manchester, Jane had felt ill enough. The excitement of the train journey had scarcely brought improvement. She was tired and thirsty and longed for tea. But she would cause no trouble to her aunt by asking for any, and when a plate of strawberries and cream was thrust toward her, though she looked at the offering with alarm, she ate up every morsel. Incredibly, this diet not the least suited to a semi-invalid nevertheless agreed with her. Before quitting Liverpool, after a day and a half visit, she had consumed six platefuls. Verily, mysterious were the ways of life!

Jane was to take the boat from Liverpool to Annan, but the waves were rough that day so her uncle would not hear of Jeannie's going by steamer. The boilers of the ship, he said, were weak; there was real danger in heavy seas. Over his niece's protest he insisted on her traveling to Dumfries by coach, and to settle the argument bought and paid for a place in the night mail. To top his considerateness, he even remembered that this was July 14th, her birthday (an anniversary which her husband had let slip into oblivion) and presented her, on parting, with a beautiful warm shawl. Eight guineas' worth of shawl, at least! The weather had turned suddenly cold; there could have been no more appropriate gift.

The coach set Jeannie down in Dumfries at half past eight in the morning. Since the steamboat by which she had announced that she was coming was not expected before eleven, Jane was sure her mother could not yet be there to meet her. So she saw her trunk deposited at the King's Arms, then sat down to wait in the lobby.

A woman was coming down the stairs; Jane could see her skirts. Her mother. Such a fluttering and embracing and happy crying! Even the Boots at the Inn, Jane reported cheerfully to her husband, was affected by this moving scene and spoke in a plaintive voice for the rest of the morning. Mrs. Welsh was in her very best mood. She overwhelmed her daughter with kindness. Jane had scarcely set foot within the house at Templand before her mother gave her a birthday gift, a purse which she herself had embroidered. What's more, it was filled with sov‑ereigns.

Jane had several commissions to keep her busy in Dumfries‑shire. Anne Cook, the servant, had younger sisters there. For

these Anne had bought some London dolls, and Jane had promised to see to their safe delivery. Carlyle also had an errand or
two. Would Jane call at Robert Shankland's, the Thornhill
tailor, and choose for him a pair of winter trousers? They must
be wide enough, her husband cautioned, and long enough, and
not too heavy, and above all, of a dun color. Carlyle was on
his guard against his wife's quiet determination to have him
dress like a man of London. He abominated cockney tailors.
For another winter, at least, he need have nothing to do with
their snippings.

Would she also have the cobbler make him a pair of shoes?
He had the last, Thomas was sure. Carlyle's toes were extremely long—like roots of trees, his brother Alick had once
described them. Right fitting footwear, with his zest for walking, was a serious necessity, and he loved those best which resembled most a farmer's broad-toed boots.

Carlyle's hats were Jane's special sorrow. He insisted on
their being large enough to let the air circulate within them.
As a result, he looked like a candle snuffed beneath an extin-
guisher. By way of added horror, he insisted on the widest
possible brim, and his tastes in color were extraordinary. The
latest he had bought was a staring white that made it as con-
spicuous as a woman's lace parasol. Jane had almost burst into
tears when, for the first time, he wore it home.

His news from London, fortunately, was reassuring. A hundred pages more, and the book would be finished. He was not
working all night, he told her, indeed not at night at all. Instead, he took his walks then. This made for better writing. An
unrested horse or author could not perform worthy labor. He
had toiled so hard before, he explained, largely because the
book had held them too long on a grindstone and should be
kicked out of doors as soon as possible. "Hope, my little Lassie,"
he encouraged her; the ordeal would soon be over. "Drink new
milk with a little brandy in it; tolerate the country gossips;
possess your wearied soul in patience; and come back to me
rested and well, and *all* will be well." Did she have Cavaignac's
manuscript for translation? He trusted so; it would keep her
occupied.

But Tom's letter found Jane in the usual embroilments that

rose between herself and her mother toward the end of every visit. Mrs. Welsh had her own notions of how to manage everything, including her daughter's health, and Jane could be equally resolute. Her mother insisted on dosages of medicine which Jeannie did not believe in, and when for the sake of peace she swallowed them, they effectively upset her. Her mother, as always, was generous enough. She would give Jane everything on earth, and do everything—except the thing asked for. Brandy in milk? It was no drink for a modest woman. In cooking one could use it, but not in milk. Jane meant to have her reports to Carlyle sound amusing. But she was no longer enjoying her stay, and her letters contained as much ruefulness and acrid mockery as fun.

A message from a woman friend had informed her that Thomas was in good spirits. "I am exceedingly happy to hear it," she wrote to him. But the phrase did not deceive her husband. He knew too well whence she had filched it. It came from his own translation of a novel by Hoffmann in which the words are spoken by a character in a state of wrathful storminess.

Carlyle's sensitiveness had never been able to accept with equanimity Jane's irony. When this mood was on her, he was apt to magnify its significance and read too deeply its implications. The strain of work he was under made a calm reception of her present attitude even more difficult. The first letter that he had received from her ended affectionately enough with a plea for him not to overwork. "Go to bed in time," she wrote, "and take your meals regularly;—and think of me as kindly as you can." The last one bore no signature. It ended with the words: "You do not say that you miss me; but I hope it is out of self-denial, not indifference."

The trip had failed, then, in its purpose? A visit to her mother was always such a risk! He urged her to return. At least he could offer quiet at Chelsea. "I wish to heaven I were better, cheerfuller; but I take heaven to witness I will be cheerful as I can. I will do what is in me, and swim with myself and thee. I do not think the waves can swallow us. Open thy heart out again to me; have hope, courage, softness—not bitterness and hardness—and they shall not swallow us."

Anne Cook, busy with her cleaning and scouring at Chelsea, had begged the master to ask a favor of Mrs. Carlyle. Would she bring a pair of trim Scotch brooms or scrubs from Dumfriesshire? While Jane was wondering just how she could run to earth one of the itinerant vendors who traded in them, a boy came to the door, offering for sale exactly two of the coveted objects. Jane snapped them up on the spot. She would bear them to Chelsea like a banner.

After a brief stop with her relations at Liverpool, Jane began her homeward journey. On the last day of August, towards evening, she took her place in the London Mail. She had a headache. It somewhat dismayed her to find three passengers already occupying the vehicle. There would be no lying down that night. But luckily, at the very next stage for changing horses, two of the passengers alighted and she was left with a single *vis-à-vis*. There would be a side for each.

Her fellow-passenger was evidently a lawyer. While there was light, he read sundry long papers to himself with the pondering air of that profession. No trouble from that quarter, obviously. At Litchfield, which they reached at five in the morning, they had breakfast—muddy coffee and scorched toast. Near two in the afternoon there was a halt for lunch. Jane did not feel hungry. Instead of eating, she retired to comb her hair and bathe her hands and face with a cooling wash of vinegar. While engaged in this solacing operation, she heard a rumbling in the street and the sound of hooves. The Mail! It was leaving without her! Her luggage was on top of it; she had left her purse in the pocket beside her seat. Not even sixpence to pay for the vinegar she was using! With hair streaming behind, face half dried, and the towel fluttering like a signal of distress, Jane dashed for the courtyard. Why were inns made on so devious a pattern? They were worse than the cavern of the Minotaur. Jane scuttled down misleading hallways and blundered through wrong doors. At last she came out at the public room of the inn, where the barmaid stared at her in bovine amazement.

"Is the coach gone?"

"The coach? Yes."

"Oh! and you have let it away without me? Oh! stop it, cannot you stop it?"

Jane, words and hair trailing behind her, rushed out into the street—and barely checked her mad career in time to avoid dashing her brains out against the coach, which stood tranquilly by the door without even a horse hitched to it. She clutched her head. In her hurry she had quite forgot her bonnet. Shame-facedly she went back to finish her interrupted toilet. What she had listened to with such alarm must have been the passing of some other heavy vehicle.

When Jane arrived at the *Swan with Two Necks*, in Lad Lane—the booking and parcel office for the London Mail—she looked in vain for Carlyle. She might have known that he would miss her! Or perhaps he had gone to the wrong inn. She hailed two porters who took her luggage on their backs. With Jane as leader, the little procession began a march for Cheapside and the Chelsea omnibus. The first bus to arrive was almost full, but Jane managed to clamber in and get her baggage safely poised on top. As the vehicle rolled off, Jane's thoughts of her husband were not fraught with charity. The omnibus became more and more crowded. Soon it would halt for no more passengers.

Just in the thickest traffic of Fleet Street, a commotion arose outside. The horses stopped. Some idiot, at risk of life and limb, was evidently determined to force his way inside. "No room, sir!" shouted the driver. Jane, raising her eyes to the center of the tumult, saw under a broad-brimmed white hat the face of her agitated husband. He looked so pathetic and amusing that she could not help bursting into a shriek of hysterical laughter. The driver still would not let him enter, but happily a passenger got out a little further on, and Thomas squeezed in beside his wife. He had been delayed, he explained, and while hurrying along the street had recognized her trunk on the top of the omnibus.

When she found her home in good order, her husband fairly well, and Anne attending to business, Jane quickly rallied her volatile spirits. Like Carlyle, she had her periods of depression, but these generally puffed away when life grew active and interesting. Even her threatening headache folded its somber wings and fled away as her husband and Anne, scurrying about, fried her a mess of bacon and plied her with tea. She was glad to be home. She was glad to see the holes in the stair-carpet all neatly darned. She was glad to luxuriate in her husband's attention. Plainly he had missed her. Her flight into Scotland had produced at least one good result: it made her take to London with new relish.

There were various blessings to be thankful for. The family purse was looking fatter and the *Revolution* almost done. Fraser had accepted for his magazine Carlyle's story of the Diamond Necklace in which he had first seriously tried his hand at historical narrative; his essay on Mirabeau, written during a pause in work, was coming out in Mill's *London and Westminster*. In America, much to Carlyle's surprise, an edition of *Sartor*, with a preface by Emerson, not only had been printed but was completely sold out. Such funds as had been realized went to the publishers, but Emerson was hatching schemes for an American edition of the forthcoming *History* which should outwit the book pirates in the United States who published without recompense to the authors the writings of British men of letters. There were certainly prospects for money enough to keep the Carlyle household solvent in London for another year.

The spectre of destitution sometimes haunted Carlyle's dreams. But Jane could even find excuse for joking on this grim enough subject. "I have always a sort of lurking assurance that if one's bread ceases it will be possible to live on pie-crust," she remarked. She was thankful that her mind refused to take seriously the idea of starvation. Who that had fingers to use and brains to direct them had ever lacked for food? Only as a last resort, Carlyle agreed, would they quit London or entertain the notion of going to America.

Chapter Eighteen

IN DECEMBER, old Mrs. Carlyle had written from Scotsbrig, "I will be glad to see you both here to rest awhile when the fight is over." The struggles of the past few years had been indeed a battle, a war with destiny itself.

Friday, January the 13th, 1837. Carlyle had taken no time off that day. A few lines more and he would finish the third and last volume of the history. All through the gray, damp afternoon (a rather tepid one for the middle of winter) he remained steadily at his desk. He was writing upstairs in the drawing room, Jane seated near him. It was evening now, though a faint light still revealed the shapes and shadows in the street. Anne Cook came in, bearing two bowls of porridge—the clock was striking ten. Carlyle looked up. "Thank God, it is done, Jeannie," he said.

On first release from this three years' burden, they hardly knew how to act. A great thankfulness filled their hearts, yet because he was so tired, Carlyle had to struggle not to give way to tears. It was finished; it was over with.

"What they will do with this book, none knows, my Jeannie, lass; but they have not had, for a two hundred years, any book that came more truly from a man's very heart; and so let them trample it under foot and hoof as *they* see best!"

"Pooh, pooh; they cannot trample that!" Had she not read every page and seen how splendid it was?

Next day Jane saw little of her husband. He was trying to walk off the feeling of strain which still possessed him. What dish that he would like should she prepare for his dinner? Bread pudding was always acceptable. When he returned, after twenty miles' tramping far and wide in the city, he ate his meal with relish. His health was better than could have been expected. The nerves and sinews of that lean frame of his must be stubborn and unbreakable as wire. Carlyle was sometimes astonished at his own toughness.

Even before the last word had been written, the presses had begun work on the manuscript of the *History*. Carlyle took, and gave, extraordinary pains with his proofs. Up to the neck in a heap of reference books and clippings, he checked and corrected with a thoroughness equivalent almost to rewriting. A single glance at the numerous alterations could shock into sobriety the most drunken of typesetters. Two printers were busy on the volumes; the book should be out by April.

January and February of the year 1837 had been especially wicked months. Because of a virulent epidemic of influenza, manufactories, shops, publishers' offices, all were understaffed, many closed, while every other man and woman lay sniftering at home. The season of unhealthy weather had opened in December with a heavy fall of snow. Though Jane knew the imprudence of her conduct, she had not been able to resist the impulse to take a walk in the frosty streets. How strange the city looked under its dirtying white mantle! Cautious residents, noses blue, shuffled along wrapped to the ears in heavy cloaks. Gardeners who generally plied an active trade in the suburbs and town itself till New Year's or later, cheated of their work by the severity of the cold, were begging now for help. She had noticed five in Cheyne Row. They had elevated a huge cabbage-stock on a pole as emblem, and were bawling out their plea: "Poo Gawnas! Poo Gawnas! All froze out!"

With January had come oily, yellow-black fogs. These had been too much for Jane. Shortly after Thomas wrote the last word of the *History*, she was down with the influenza. When influenza caught Jane, Carlyle was apt to describe her illness as merely a slight cold. But if he succumbed, he sang a very different tune. It plagued him—he insisted—in every nook and cranny of his being: in bone, muscle, head, heart, soul, body, and spirit! Yet when she would not rally as expected—instead remained day after day in bed—Carlyle grew apprehensive. His poor Goody! She seemed weak as a sparrow. Jane could not muffle her cough; she knew her husband, busy with his proofs in the upstairs parlor, was listening on the other side of the wall. He did his best to play the rôle of nurse, but Carlyle's nursing, with printers knocking at the door, was satisfactory neither to the book nor patient. When Jane's doctor called —the same man who kept John Sterling precariously alive—he was none too reassuring. Not till April, when the weather improved, did Jane grow better. The threat, for the time being, was removed.

What a comfort, Jane declared, that the *French Revolution* had got itself finished before she was lamed by illness—at least that the writing part of it was completed. Seeing it through the press was quite bad enough in itself, with a tag-raggery of printers' devils driving her husband from pillar to post. "*Quelle vie!* Let no woman who values peace of soul ever dream of marrying an author!" Especially if he were an honest author who did his work under the rod of conscience. "Should I state such a sentiment openly," Jane added, "I might happen to get myself torn in pieces by the host of my husband's lady admirers, who already, I suspect, think me too happy in not knowing my happiness."

These admirers included such stars in the firmament as Fanny Kemble, whose name was on the tip of many tongues in London. None who had seen it could forget the debut of this niece of the celebrated Mrs. Siddons. Miss Kemble was just sixteen years old when she played Juliet at her father's theatre. Not merely had she packed the house and charmed the town with her acting. She had cleared away, during her first season, the entire debt on the building, a sum amounting to over eleven thousand pounds. Since that winter of 1830, success and the adulation of young men had persisted. She followed up her triumph in London with a tour in the United States, coming back as Mrs. Pierce Butler, wife of a prominent rich Philadelphian.

Urged to do so by her brother John (a friend of Charles Buller), she had read *Sartor* on its appearance in *Fraser's Magazine*. A precocious girl, fond of radical thinking, she became one of that early small minority who admired Teufelsdröckh immensely. When she presently met the author she was quick to tell him of her enthusiastic approval. She knew *Sartor* almost by heart.

Not easy to resist that bright vivacious face, with its look of a little girl just grown up! Fanny's expression of almost too great naïveté was counterbalanced by a pair of mischievous dark eyes. Her wise, serious forehead, under a profusion of dusk hair, gave her the look of a young bluestocking and critic. When she took to bursting in on Carlyle and his work at non-calling hours, he did not grumble too violently. In fact the part she played as guiding sylph and arbiter of feminine dress amused him. In Fanny's presence he could even forget to be outraged at human vanity. He had seen her recently at a soirée. She had been a veritable gliding, billowy ocean of lace and broad-cloth. All the women that year were imitation oceans. These soirées were not composed of persons, Carlyle snorted; they were agglomerations of dressmaker-dummies! Certainly women loved to rush between extremes—seas of material at one moment, then trim as boys the next. In these multifarious guises, one could lose one's very wife at a party.

Fanny Kemble had a way of bolting gaily into the Carlyle house, dressed in riding-habit, a jaunty cap on her head, a dapper little whip in her hand. Jane, glancing from the window, noticed wickedly that no horse stood below. Anne Cook had been dumfounded when first she opened the door. Was it a leddy or a gem'man she had admitted?

Jane grew somewhat restive under these precipitous descents. She made a tiny effort to like this admirer of her husband, but it would not do. Fanny Kemble, she told herself, cultivated too much the atmosphere of the greenroom. She had a heart all tossed up into blank verse: blank verse, too, of the "fish—be it ev-er so salt, is ne'-er too salt for me" variety. Not enough honest naturalness about her. She spoke of things having a "ba-wd effect," and she stuck to her musical utterance even when she talked of commonplace things.

Fanny remarked how sorry she was that the Carlyles lived so far from her part of the town. Were it not for the distance, she would call more often. Jane had no quarrel, this time, with the geography of London. The two women were separated by more than the width of the city. Miss Kemble's interest lay in the husband. Jane was merely the wife of Thomas Carlyle. On occasion, when Fanny could not help noticing some amusing remark of Jane's, she dismissed it as sauciness. What Mrs. Carlyle might say was really of little moment; probably she was quoting—probably these flashes were only a pale reflection of the brilliance of her husband.

Jane felt very differently towards Harriet Martineau, and Harriet Martineau had an attitude towards Jane not the least like Fanny Kemble's. When the Carlyles first met her, Harriet was rising to the crest of the wave of fame which was to carry her onwards so spectacularly throughout her energetic life. Her stories, each patly illustrating the needs for social reform, were already highly popular in London. She had just returned from a whirlwind tour of the States during which that whole broad land had been compressed, catalogued, and made ready for explanation within her facile, opinionated, yet liberal mind.

Another feminine admirer of Carlyle, Jane Wilson, had introduced Harriet at Cheyne Row. Miss Wilson and her brother lived in fashionable, conservative Eccleston Street. They were opulent Church of England people—scrupulously orthodox in the secularities no less than in the spiritualities of their creed and class. Yet regardless of this formidable background, they had taken to the Carlyles. That was a peculiar thing about the Chelsea house in the early London years. In spite of the heterodox, outspoken opinions of the master of No. 5 Cheyne Row— religious, social, political—people of entirely opposite views could enter with enjoyment and without offense. Jane's deft, unostentatious diplomacy was largely responsible for this phenomenon. She could snuff the fuses of all but the most explosive arguments.

A shame that Harriet Martineau was so deaf! Even though she wielded an ear-trumpet which might have served the Angel Gabriel for a horn she missed much of the conversation. But if she did not hear what you had said, it bothered her not at all. She simply carried the talk with her and one jumped aboard as best one could. She would sweep her trumpet from side to side, picking up the clues, then rattle away in highly entertaining fashion.

Miss Martineau was a veritable giantess in stature, yet distinctly good looking, Jane thought, in spite of her height. She was close to Jane's own age, thirty-five or so. Tom's wife liked her calm, steadfast gray eyes, her warm-heartedness and sincerity. Of the famous females she had so far met, Harriet was by all odds the best.

Though not convinced as to her qualifications to write with bold assurance on spiritual and social questions, Carlyle, too, approved of Harriet. She had such guileless, easy, friendly ways. And certainly she was an efficient woman of business. He was glad to benefit by her advice in the management of his literary problems.

For her part, Harriet so enjoyed her first visit that she saw to it that the experience was frequently repeated. She reveled in the talk of both husband and wife. Mrs. Carlyle had at first seemed a quiet, self-effacing little thing, but soon opened up amazingly. Harriet was an ardent feminist. She liked to see women shine. Jane Welsh Carlyle was the right sort; there was a flash of genius in her.

When Harriet wished to dine at Cheyne Row, she never hesitated to invite herself. Because of her new book, America was frequently the subject of the conversation. Did Mr. Carlyle realize how great was his influence there? Every word that Emerson wrote about it in his letters to Chelsea must be regarded as gospel truth. His scattered articles had met the needs of the best minds in New England—minds weary of cant and mechanical morals; minds seeking something truer to rest on. But the triumph of *Sartor Resartus*, she declared, was the most interesting news of all. The edition of the book which had appeared in America had acted on its public with wonderful force. At this point, Harriet, quite aware of the lean finances at Cheyne Row, put into Carlyle's hands a sum of money. It was modest enough, she apologized. She had obtained it, she explained, by importing from the New World twenty-five copies of *Sartor* which she had sold, at a profit, to friends in England. Carlyle was visibly embarrassed. He squirmed uncomfortably in his chair. But finally he pocketed his gain.

Some time later, when Harriet called, she found a gift awaiting her. Out of the small revenue brought by the American *Sartors*, its author had purchased two signet rings—one for Jane, one for Miss Martineau. Each was engraved; the first bore his wife's, the second, Harriet's favorite motto.

This would never do! So Miss Martineau imported and disposed of another parcel of the books. She took to a wineshop the few sovereigns she had gained by the second transaction. There she invested them in French brandy of the best quality. Triumphantly she gave the hamper to Carlyle—this time no transmutation would be possible.

Turning his eyes toward the long-necked bottles, Carlyle, with a shout of laughter, exclaimed that at last he had got a reward for his labors. Jeannie at once invited the good Harriet to dinner. After the meal the three sat round the fire. While Jane and Miss Martineau were discussing literature, Carlyle mixed a toddy. The two women were speaking of the rewards of honor and reputation open to an author. Thomas pricked up his ears. He held out to his guest a glass of brandy and water.

"Here, take this," he said, "it is worth all the fame in England!"

The proofs were done to the last galley. The *French Revolution* was coming from the presses. Already several friends had their advance copies. From Edinburgh, Jeffrey had written in acknowledgment. This new book, he declared, would bring Carlyle honor, though written in the Carlylean style and manner against which he had protested in the past. Jeffrey's was a handsome admission. But Carlyle was not yet ready to believe sanguine prophecies. The struggles he had gone through in the past three years had left him dusty and shrunken as a cinder with flame temporarily burned out. The added strain of some lectures, undertaken for a little ready cash, had further dulled him. All he could think of was an escape to Scotland. A summer in his native land would be the best restorative.

When he was ready to start for Annandale, Jane would not accompany him. Jokingly she put him off. Having neither published nor lectured, she felt no need to refresh herself with Scotland's breezes. Furthermore, after last year's bellyful of traveling, she declared robustly, she wished no more of it for quite some time to come. She had a catlike attachment to her own house, and a preference for London above all other localities. It was a very jewel of a place. If one wished to be solitary, that could readily be managed. If one were gregariously disposed, one might have society to all lengths and of every possible cut.

She plunged heartily into the maelstrom of London life, and the whirling, glittering, changeful sights and sound of the last weeks of the London season before the city emptied itself as its inhabitants sought refuge in the country from summer dust and heat. She went to the opera. Carlyle's friends did not neglect their calls. And she dispatched long reports of her activities to her husband at Scotsbrig. "It is a pity, and perhaps not a pity," he wrote, "that so lively a pen did not turn itself to writing of books. My *coagitor,* too, might become a distinguished female. May after all, who knows? But perhaps we are better as we are, probably just as well." Jane had not much encouraged his past efforts to make her turn author. She still went occasionally to her desk, but she would never let him see what she had written. With some casual excuse she would put him off, then tie up her notebook under his nose. She had shown some bits of her scribblings to close friends, he knew, but further than that she would not go. She would not write a word for editors.

In England, in Scotland, in far away America, thinking men and women were reading the *French Revolution.* Not one penny had yet been realized, but fame in copious measure. There was praise; there were emphatic protests, too. The author was accused of violent partiality. The wild originality of the style repelled many and gave the critics attacks of literary indigestion. Hallam, the historian, found the early pages so abominable that he could read no further. A wonderful book, declared Emerson, that would last a very long time. It was like reading history by flashes of lightning, Jeffrey remarked when he closed the final volume. Sir William Hamilton began the first chapter at three in the afternoon and became so fascinated that he did not lay the book down till four the next morning. Old Walter Savage Landor, who had seen a long procession of masterpieces during his life-span, called this one the greatest in his time. Southey read it over and over. Young Charles Dickens, whose *Pickwick* had been reviewed in the same issue of the *London and Westminster* that contained Mill's enthusiastic praises of Carlyle, was fascinated by the historian's work. He would base a novel on it, a tale of two cities. Young William Makepeace Thackeray had reviewed it most favorably in the *Times*—Jane had sent the notice to Scotsbrig to cheer her husband.

But Carlyle tried to close his ears to praise. He had an active horror of conceit. He took his lonely rides, he walked, he smoked. He read his Goody's letters, and sent letters of his own to Chelsea. But the sodden, tired note was still in them, though he had earlier said his health was mending. A trip to Dumfries and Templand had jangled his nerves. His vivid report of his discomforts caused Jane to burst out crying. Her head was aching when she read his note and the pain upset her sense of proportion. He was no better, she told herself, than when he had left her. She wanted to kiss him back into a state at least resembling cheerfulness, but the length of a kingdom lay between them. Possibly just as well. Even with the best intentions, she might have quarreled with him instead.

An entire summer in London can grow oppressive. In August the Edward Sterlings persuaded Jane to join them on a carriage tour to the Malvern Hills and down the Valley of the Wye to Chepstow and home again. Jane had not intended leaving the city, but when Colonel Sterling wished her company he could usually get it.

They *did* Tintern Abbey, as Jane appropriately characterized this pursuit of the picturesque, and inspected castles, ruins, and cathedrals by the score. Old Sterling was a cyclonic traveler whose final conclusion on nature, no matter how beautiful, was that it was all humbug: "strip the soil a foot deep and it would be a vile black mass." Jane's own opinion of the sophisticated landscape of a resort like Malvern was not enthusiastic. Genuine, unrefined country was one thing—but this man-exploited scenery was a bore: a theatre-setting through which one dawdled on the backs of donkeys, gazed through sea-green arbors at mansions big and little, and was haunted by the everlasting smell of roast beef.

Traveling with the Sterlings had its drawbacks. During the intimacies of the tour, Jane better understood why the couple were so anxious to have her along. They were fond of each other, but with old Sterling so given to argument, and his wife filled with a soft resistance in defense of her own ideas, an arbiter was essential. Jane furnished the sugar and ginger that blended the mild alkaline solution of Mrs. Sterling and the tartaric acid of the husband into a more agreeable and lively mixture.

Jeannie could usually humor the old man, though she did

not check her tongue for they both enjoyed baiting each other. Only one thing really troubled her. The Thunderer showed an inclination to monopolize her at the expense of his wife. This tendency grew more and more pronounced. He had cast out hints that the tour should be prolonged—why not skip over to Dublin, or to the Isle of Wight? But Jane, sensing what was in the breeze, objected. She would descend from the rocketing balloon, she declared, even if it had to be by parachute. Mrs. Sterling wished to linger with some friends at Clifton, but his Whirlwindship spun all the faster at the thought— these persons were bores, he protested, and not to be endured— no stimulus in them. Furthermore, he should do his duty by poor Mrs. Carlyle! She had expressed a wish to be back in Chelsea before Carlyle's return. Why could his wife not make her Clifton visit alone? The old fox, Jane realized, wanted to drive her back by herself, leaving Mrs. Sterling to follow as best she could. So Jane frowned on the suggestion as too ungracious a plot.

The trip had been amusing, but this hithering and thithering and shifting of purpose fretted one to fiddlesticks. At Worcester, Jane had collapsed. A headache was bad enough in itself, but to succumb to one in a friendly stranger's house was even worse. The travelers were the guests of an acquaintance of the colonel, venerable Archdeacon Singleton, a rounded prelate of twinkling wit and gregarious good humor—the beau ideal of an old Abbot. Jane had been forced to take to bed and miss the fun. Before retiring she had swept a glance over a sumptuous banquet the like of which realized one's sublimest ideas of a convent refectory.

Throughout the night the great cathedral clock bonged every quarter of an hour, giving Jane the strangest dreams between sleeping and waking. When morning at last came, the entire establishment seemed bent on destroying her with solicitude. Was there anything she lacked? No, thank you, nothing! All she wanted was to be left alone. Whereupon old Sterling himself appeared outside her door, and demanded, in a tone of loud pathos, if she knew how exceedingly sorry he was for her.

She was glad when she could again be on the move. She hated to linger in houses where she had made a nuisance of herself. Most of all, she was glad when the tour was over. She was eager to set Cheyne Row in order for her husband's return. He was such an unbelieving creature! She must convince him what a great success his book had become.

"O, my Darling!" she wrote on the way to London, "we will surely be better, both of us, *there* again; effervescing even: —don't you think so?" They had not seen each other for over twelve weeks.

Chapter Nineteen

VARIOUS mountains were now coming to Mahomet. It was not always easy for Jane to tell their altitude or even to distinguish them from the foothills. Nor could she be quite sure just when they might appear.

One of Jane's accomplishments was the brewing of orange marmalade. The poetry of preserves, Thomas described it— clear as liquid amber and delicate as nectar. Jane bestowed infinite pains on its manufacture. An important item was the state of the fire—brisk and steady to make the large pot boil at a constant rate. The kitchen hearth sometimes failed her. To avoid this hazard, Jane once lugged the large brass pan from the depths below to the parlor hearth where the flames were vigorously dancing. The kettle, responding to this Promethean heat, went all aglow. Up bubbled the concoction, up and over. The thickening sugar sprang into a blaze.

A ten pound fine was the penalty in London for a conflagration in one's chimney. With the present state of the Carlyle finances, so much money burned away would be a very serious matter. Desperately Jane extracted the pan, but the fire and smoke would not at once die away.

At her shriek, Carlyle came galloping down the stairs. His eye at once took in the situation. With great presence of mind he rushed to the chimney, let down the iron valve behind the mantel, and effectually starved the smoldering flue. Meanwhile, with no rightful place for escape, the smoke from the now scattered and beaten mixture of coals and marmalade eddied in clouds within the room. Carlyle was just opening the back window to let the stench and vapor out when a thunderous banging at the front door made him and Jane leap almost out of their skins.

The fire engines!

But it was not the fire engines; it was two callers—an elderly man and woman.

Jane struggled to recover her poise. Who could these strangers be? She had never laid eyes on them before and in the excitement Carlyle had failed to make introductions. At last the realization came—Robert Southey, Poet Laureate of England! Jane recognized him now from her husband's characterization. A spare, whiteheaded man with amazingly long legs; a walking pair of fire tongs, as Thomas had said. His complexion was a perfect barometer for his emotions. When he had greeted her, an amiable pink blush, like a young girl's, suffused his cheeks, yet if any thought angered him, the rush of blood to his face darkened it till it assumed a hue of purple rage. The woman was Miss Fenwick, in London from the Lakes where she was a neighbor of the Wordsworths. Old and crooked-backed, but pleasant and a first-rate talker. The *French Revolution* had brought the honor of this visit. Admirers, old and new, were flocking to the door.

More and more frequently, the Carlyles were bidden to drink tea and attend soirées. Jane even tried her own hand at one of these affairs. The actuality of the thing had descended on her before she quite realized it was there. It was so easy to make casual plans. But as the time drew nearer, Jane wished she had never begun the venture. Her husband refused to bless the event with his approval. There were, he declared, soirées in great plenty during these months of the season: enough and to spare. Little need to raise the fuss of such a thing about one's head. But Mrs. Welsh, down from Templand on another visit, was there to help. Jane gave her a free rein with the preparations.

The day arrived. Mrs. Welsh was stirring about on the main floor where breakfast and dining room, with the doors between flung open, made an excellent large chamber for the party. Carlyle had vanished, though he promised to reappear with the guests. Jane was busy in the kitchen and elsewhere about the house. Her nerves were taut. With only a general housework girl for maid, there were emphatic disadvantages to entertaining on so grand a scale. One could almost agree with Carlyle that the entire project was a questionable undertaking.

She heard her mother calling, so hurried to the dining room. On the table, becomingly arranged, were dishes of confectionery and cakes. All about gleamed candles, making the place quite splendid. Not till that moment did Jane realize that her mother had secured these extra contributions. Mrs. Welsh watched her daughter, expectant of her praise.

What would the guests think? All knew that her husband was poor. They would believe that she was an extravagant woman, bent on ruining him with rash expenditures. In a few moments they would be at the door. Hastily she cleared some of the bonbons from the table, and she blew out and removed two of the candles.

Mrs. Welsh burst into tears. She had barely stopped crying when the first guests entered. Soon twenty or thirty persons— big and little celebrities or just plain people—were rattling away in lively talk. Carlyle had appeared, as scheduled, to perform his part. Really, the affair went off in a shining manner. But Jane, who had the tenderest of consciences, was not happy. She regretted the flare-up with her mother, whose sole impulse, she realized, had been one of generosity. She took the two candles which she had discarded. Carefully she wrapped and put them away.

Carlyle, smoking a pipe after the last guest's midnight departure, prayerfully remarked that he hoped the house had witnessed the last of such affairs. Jane never tried a second soirée.

Far better she enjoyed giving intimate little dinners for a few choice guests, guests who could be selected with an eye to lively conversation. Jane did not always assemble little groups known to be compatible. Sometimes she tried the wildest mixtures, to her husband's infinite dismay, till the event itself once more confirmed her agile skill as ring mistress.

Among the exiles who found pleasure in visits to Chelsea was Alexis François Rio, a Bourbon royalist of the most purple hue. He had fought Napoleon in the Vendée and was the enemy both of usurpers and of those who supported democracy. Because of the *French Revolution*, Rio had expected Carlyle to be a republican savage. Instead he found the historian a friendly, likable man, an idealist in spite of his worship of facts. The more he saw of Thomas and his wife, the more delighted he became with them. Jane had taken to him at once. He was such an engaging enthusiast in spite of his martial experiences. Innocently she asked him if he knew his fellow Frenchman, Cavaignac.

"Ah, who does *not* know Cavaignac by name," Rio answered with polite volubility, "but I, you know, am a victim of *his* party, as *he* is a victim of Louis Philippe!"

Jane was charmed with these ramifications of political dispute.

"Does Cavaignac come here?" Rio had asked.

"Yes, we have known him long."

"Good gracious! How strange it would be for us to meet in the same room. How I should like it!"

"Well," said Jane, "he is to dine here on Monday."

"I will come; good gracious"—Rio's English was excellent, but had its limitations in the matter of expletives—"Good gracious, it will be so strange!"

Jane counted over her crop of exiles. Too bad, on such short notice, that she could not include the Italian Mazzini. She would ask Latrade, a revolutionary Frenchman, to make it a completely Gaelic party.

"Mercy, Jane, are you distracted?" exclaimed Carlyle, anticipating nothing but bloodshed at such a feast of enemies. Jeannie refused to let herself be shaken. She would rely on providence and the quality of her dinner to preserve the peace. To the leg of mutton already ordered as background for some capers she had purchased she added a beefsteak pie, a dish sure to soothe the fiercest tempers.

The day for breaking bread and tasting salt arrived. So did Rio, at the early hour of half past three. But no Latrade, no Cavaignac. At four, Latrade entered. He brought some news of the still absent guest. Two of Cavaignac's friends, it appeared, were about to fight a duel; Cavaignac had gone to see if he could part them. Another half hour dragged by. Then a carriage halted at the door. But it was not the fiery peacemaker. Instead, Mrs. Macready, wife of the actor, and Macready's sister, entered. Was ever hostess or beefsteak pie in a worse predicament? Nothing for it but to invite the unexpected guests to join the feast.

When the remains of the dinner, mutilated and cold, were going off the table, Cavaignac came in, his hands full of papers, his mind full of the duel. Carlyle waited for the explosion. Instead, Rio and Cavaignac got on amazingly. Jane had the satisfaction of watching all her guests walk peacefully away. Nothing like beefsteak pie to conquer political hates and passions!

Mazzini's earliest visit to Cheyne Row had occurred in the year 1836. His face, Jane thought at the time, was the most spiritual she had ever looked on. Then for almost two years he had dropped below the Chelsea horizon. Thomas and his wife were glad to welcome Mazzini back when at last he reappeared. They never quite grasped the significance of his long withdrawal. But then, they had never quite understood the Italian revolutionary. With new acquaintances it was his practice to be secret and subterranean as a mole.

At the time of the first call he had just reached England. He had come to London as an exile with a price on his head. In his native Piedmont, a sentence of death awaited him because he had dared to conspire for Italian unity and independence under a republican form of government and had plotted to throw off the yoke of Austrian dominance. In other countries of the European mainland, because of hostility to his democratic notions or fear of autocratic, monarchistic Austria, he had met with persecution and threats of imprisonment, even of death. He was like a wearied young stag hunted out of his own land into unknown perilous terrain, only to be beset by fresh packs of clumsy, relentless dogs. England alone offered a precarious hope of refuge. Mazzini had arrived in a personal crisis of absolute poverty. He was struggling under an emotional burden as well. All reasonable hope which he had entertained before that Italy was to be saved through the efforts of the young men whom he had organized under his banner had now been shot away. His own attempt at open insurrection had ended in tragic and ridiculous failure, and the powers of reaction were in complete control in the governments of the little Italian states that stood in the way of his conception of united Italy. Harassed and depressed, pitting against the realization of failure only the desperate hope that his country might still be saved through some miracle of faith, he had been loath to make his presence known outside the tiny circle of his Italian compatriots in London. And he resented as time lost all efforts made by his few friends in the city to bring him more into association with the right sort of British men and women. All visits, he declared, lost him half a day in precious time and upset him for the other half. He needed every moment for his affairs—his voluminous correspondence with fellow conspirators, his scheming for his cause, his efforts to keep his own body and soul together by means of various business enterprises and by the writing of essays and reviews. "Tomorrow," he informed his mother by letter to Italy, "I am compelled to see a Mr. Carlyle, author of many works and recently of a History of the French Revolution which has made a great stir here in England." This duty done, he had retreated once more to his squalid lodgings (he hated them, but could afford none better) off Tottenham Court Road.

Poor, unknown, highly sensitive, highly idealistic, he was damaging his health and spirits, in his earlier years in London, through his mode of living. Active, open fighting in behalf of his aims for Italy was denied him. Nothing to do but bide his time; nothing to do but plunge, as he always did in exile, into ceaseless, soul-racking conspiracy.

His own wants were few enough, but the cost of propaganda for Italian independence was very great. Though the child of well-to-do people, he could not rely on their whole-hearted support. His father was none too sympathetic toward his son's radical ideas. What money was advanced to Mazzini was quickly spent—on the cause, or to support other exiles sometimes better off than he.

What bound his followers to him was their knowledge that he sought nothing for his own sake and never spared himself either toil or danger. That—and the charm of his personal appeal. Belief in his unfaltering integrity sent men to imprisonment, torture, and death—perils he was always ready himself to face. The injustice of men roused his deepest resentment; he believed oppression should and could be done away with. Why were he and his fellows exiles? By what right? What code of laws justified the verdict against them? Where were the witnesses? Who dared offer defence? Their sentences were not supported by common right or public law. A tyrannous usurping State ground Italy in the dust and Italy's defenders, scattered far and wide in alien lands, were given over to the mercies of political expediency. The Monarchies, the ruling autocratic heads of government, in exiling Italian patriots from the fatherland had exiled them from humanity. Everywhere they were regarded with suspicion. But look out!—Mazzini warned all tyrants. Yet a little while and humanity would reply with no uncertain voice to a damnable persecution. "You strike down a few men, but the *idea* escapes your blows. It is immortal. It gains a giant strength in the fury of the storm. From day to day it penetrates and incarnates itself more deeply in the conscience of humanity. The peoples themselves thrill to it. When you have emptied your anger and violence upon a few individuals who are only its forerunners, it will rise before you in all its democratic majesty. It will sweep over your heads like the sea over the sand, and destroy even the memory of your resistance!"

As to the sentence of suspicion and persecution on his and his fellows' heads, its shadow hovered ever larger over England. At first Mazzini's presence there was hardly noticed. But soon rumor spread his name across the kingdom. He was a dangerous agitator. He was fomenting discontent among the youth of Italy by contraband writings and through secret societies. Was he not promoting every insurrection in the Italian Peninsula? Would his efforts confine themselves to his own land? Respectable England became incensed. There were ugly rumors of his cut-throat ways and his encouragement of assassination.

Ever since that first meeting, Mazzini had been disturbed in mind about Carlyle. The historian had asked him for his address and invited him to call again at Chelsea. But he hesitated to reveal his place of living—partly because of its squalor, partly because he had a compelling wish for privacy. So he put Carlyle off with polite evasiveness. The request to call again he really intended to comply with. But delayed by one thing or another, the second visit seemed destined never to come off. Carlyle lived at such a distance—four or five miles away. Mazzini hated to walk. In their letters his family urged him to exercise for health, quite in vain. Winter had arrived and still the invitation to Cheyne Row had not been honored. He would go tomorrow—

but something always prevented. Bad weather would furnish an excuse, or his own indisposition. How could he venture on foot through all the mud? And to travel by carriage would be too expensive.

Presently Mazzini's conscience began to tease him acutely. Had he not been guilty of a discourtesy? He had been negligent; impolite! What could he say or do to justify himself? Nothing, probably! Should he visit after this long delay, Carlyle would receive him coldly. Better not go at all.

Just when his rationalization had achieved this stage, Mazzini was asked by a London editor to write a detailed criticism of the *French Revolution*. He did not wish to, but he needed the cash. He was running heavily into debt. There had been times when he had not felt the weight of a single shilling in his pocket. He was beginning to ask himself whether he should ever succeed in getting out of his difficulties. Yet the wretched business of this review would make of him a minor Judas. This man had been polite and kind to him, and he was about to damn his book! Its very philosophy, he believed, was radically false. It worshiped might; it worshiped the power of the individual. This charge he was bound to level against the *History* in his criticism.

To cap the misfortune, Mazzini accepted an invitation to dinner only to find out, when escape was not possible, that Mr. and Mrs. Carlyle would be fellow-guests. Cordial ties would be renewed; then, in ten or fifteen days, out would come the unfavorable review!

But the horrid spectre which Mazzini had been laboriously creating in his mind proved to be a very harmless ghost. When it was explained to him, Carlyle had laughed over the whole thing. The invitation to call was renewed and Carlyle himself dropped in to see Mazzini after worming from him the secret of his lodgings.

The ultimate result was that Mazzini found himself becoming a more and more frequent visitor at Cheyne Row. He was asked there for dinners and for tea. These Carlyles seemed bent on drawing him out of his shell. He resented this, he told himself; but still—he went.

The wife was very good; certainly *gentilissima*. As for the husband, he was an excellent man and a potent genius. Of course two thirds of this Scotsman's opinions differed from his own with no possibility of conversion on either side. Even Madame Carlyle sometimes astonished him with strange foreign notions and manners. One afternoon, while he was waiting in her living room—Mazzini was quiet as a moth in flight— Mrs. Carlyle had entered without awareness of his presence. She had been greatly startled when she noticed him silent in a corner. He had thought her out of sorts when he first observed her, though in conversation she was friendliness itself. When he left, she presented him with a little phial of Cologne water that she held in her hand. He could not imagine the cause of this impulsive gesture. Certainly these British ladies treated him with gallantry!

Mazzini had no way of knowing just how the Carlyles looked on him. They were used to exiles and did not take them very seriously. He had no suspicion of the fact that Mrs. Carlyle, especially, regarded many things about him as amusing, especially his struggles with the English language. She delighted to quote odd circumlocutions of speech to her husband amid shrieks of mirth. But the better she learned to know Mazzini, the greater became her respect, her admiration and sympathy. Not for his opinions—these she generally refused to consider seriously (she had listened to so many exiles)—but for the man himself and the spirit she found within him. Impossible to resist the spell of Mazzini's countenance; his deep set, penetrating, hypnotic eyes. His calm smooth forehead accentuated the air of an ascetic and zealot who had sacrificed logic for faith. There was about him a look which might have made even an agnostic pray; the face—thoughtful, meditative, and sorrowful in repose—of a highly intellectual, highly spiritual, highly idealistic priest. Yet there was fun in him too, when he could be made to forget the griefs of Italy. This was the side of him Jane loved to bring out, and she approved also of his tenderness and humanity. He could be even playful, telling a story or hitting off, with a shrewd, graphic touch, some person of their acquaintance. Yet he was never unkind, and there was a respectful gentleness in his manner toward women. His social theories insisted on equality of the sexes and he was a staunch advocate of political enfranchisement.

This young chief of *Giovane Italia*, of Italian youth, Jane presently acknowledged, was more than that—he was the finest of Italian men. Would such a powerful, original mind waste itself in conspiracy and exile? How widely his thoughts ranged over all subjects; how deep and broad was his spirit!

Mazzini would knock at the door with the softest possible rip, tip, tip, and glide into the house. A beautiful little man, Carlyle named him, full of sensibilities; a man of sterling veracity and nobleness of mind. Surely one of those rare persons—they came but singly into the world—who could without exaggeration be called martyr souls. Not a genius of compelling skill in international affairs, Carlyle insisted—rather, greatness should be conceded to him in spite of his lack of insight into the politics of men.

Naturally, when Carlyle and Mazzini met in the drawing room, Jane could be sure that sooner or later there would be argumentative pyrotechnics. These grew so tiresome! Mazzini's program for the Young Italy Association which he headed was to link together the strife-torn, severed fragments of the Peninsula into a single fatherland, a free Republic. Incredible, even comically so, though tragic also, Thomas declared these views to be. The wish of most Italians to get out from under foreign domination was understandable and could be sympathized with. But this insistence on a Republic as sole means of bringing about the desideratum was preposterous! Carlyle's even qualified approval of Democracy was steadily lessening. There was little wisdom in the people, however much one might agonize over their wrongs. Giving the rank and file the vote was a feeble remedy, if a remedy at all. As to united Italy, even the wisest Italians expected merely a nation of several governments, joined perhaps in some kind of Federation.

But Mazzini, in spite of Carlyle's heavy artillery, clung to his own position. He had amazing powers of tenacity. The idea of one Italian state, he declared, had always lain in the minds of the greatest Italians, from Dante onwards. It would yet be realized! He refused to have his ideals trampled and would make a little uproar of his own in defence—his voice, usually soft and musical, shrill with earnestness. Or he would lapse into a melancholy silence and refuse to be prodded into further rebuttal. This last attitude never quite suited Carlyle, who, Jane was aware, sometimes took a stand for the sheer fun of disputation. In the midst of what, in its fury and thunder, sounded like the most trenchant denunciation, her husband's voice was often ready to break into that uproarious laughter which accompanied his final mental dig into the ribs of his adversary.

Of course Mazzini *was* given to high flights and a passion for abstractions. Jane was ready enough to admit as much. Yet it was cruel to tease him. For him these arguments were sure to pass beyond the realm of casual fun. So she would sometimes interrupt with a quiet remark of her own. Mazzini had suffered and made sacrifices for his cause. Carlyle must remember that, and be considerate. Whereupon her husband, taking the reproof meekly, would drop his banter—at least for the time being.

Inevitably, Mazzini became Jane's friend rather than her husband's. Not that he did not like Carlyle. For a time, even, misled by some of his early writings, he had cherished the hope of seeing him an active crusader for the rights of man—but soon he told himself that this was impossible. Sad, very sad, to observe a person of such power so full of contradictions! Carlyle desired progress, yet showed hostility to all who strove for its realization. He foretold great changes, great shifts in the social, religious, and political order of the world, yet insisted in the same breath that the revolutionists keep their hands off these movements.

Mazzini's sense of humor got no relief when he was listening to Carlyle. Everything that was said, if it concerned Italy, he took to heart. But in spite of what he had to endure if Carlyle were present, Mazzini continued to be a partner in a growing intimacy which had thus far no parallel in his life in England. Though he felt it a duty to his cause to avoid personal entanglements, his inner nature was capable of very strong attachments. Indeed, it craved them overwhelmingly. "Who knows if in this island I shall find someone to add to that very small number of souls whose approbation I desire," he wrote to his mother. Mrs. Carlyle, he hinted, might in time be such a person. He knew that she had republican sympathies, regardless of her husband's equivocal attitude. Thus far, he explained, he had not revealed to her much concerning his nature: "I have not expressed a thousandth part of my sentiments—some judgments on authors and insignificant things have formed the whole of our conversation; yet there is a strange sympathy that attracts me to her, and it seems to me that she esteems my heart more than our slight acquaintance would permit."

He felt the need of sharing with some one, intimately, his hopes and aspirations. Perhaps Jane Carlyle was the woman.

Chapter Twenty

*R*EALLY, thought Jane, unless he could get hardened in this trade of lecturing, Carlyle ought to discontinue it. No gain or éclat that it could yield was sufficient compensation for the martyrdom it brought on him, and incidentally on herself as witness and sharer of his torments.

Thomas had first become a public speaker in the spring of 1837, shortly before the publication of his *French Revolution.* Harriet Martineau, the Wilsons, James Spedding, and other friends had cooked up the plot through which, they hoped, some easy cash might be obtained by the struggling author. A shameful waste that such marvelous talk as his should be poured forth so prodigally in the restricted sphere of his own drawing room. Harriet was aware that Emerson had invited him to gain a swift profit on American lyceum platforms. The thing could be done as readily in England.

Though his need for money was acute, Carlyle had agreed reluctantly to the proposal. His attention during the early months of 1837 centered on proof-reading the *History.* He was unwilling to believe the scheme for speaking promised much. Five hundred circulars had been printed to announce the course. How in the world could such a quantity even be distributed?

But Thomas did not adequately recognize the enthusiasm of his backers. "As it is Carlyle's first essay in this kind it is important there should be a respectable number of hearers," wrote Spedding to another friend, Richard Monckton Milnes.

Milnes was the very man to attend to that. He was one of the choice company of young gentlemen from Cambridge whose other luminaries included Charles Buller, William Makepeace Thackeray, handsome Charles Brookfield, who everybody said would some day be a bishop, and Alfred Tennyson, author of several little books of verse which his friends insisted showed the greatest promise though the world in general chose still to ignore them.

Buller had brought Milnes to call soon after the Carlyles established themselves in London. He had been calling regularly ever since. It was impossible not to like Dicky Milnes. Carlyle, busy at his desk, had tried to fend off the shower of invitations which the young man precipitated on him, but to dodge them all was impossible. Richard's smiling, bland face was always popping up. He was a man easy to see and to talk with. Jane and he got along splendidly together; there was an instant sympathy between them.

Richard took a wicked pleasure in rousing Carlyle's argumentative spirit, baiting the hook with some often preposterous notion just for the fun of seeing Thomas worry it. He was one of the few persons who could tease Carlyle with impunity—a really dexterous villain who pricked into him with all kinds of fly tackle to make him bite. Yet one look at Richard's good-natured face, and Carlyle's ire would cool at once.

"I often think, Milnes," his friend Charles Buller once remarked, "how puzzled your Maker must be to account for your conduct." Milnes was famous for his dinner parties. He had a way of getting together people who were as oil and vinegar, as wolves and tigers to one another, just for the pleasure of rousing then quieting the hubbub. Because of this propensity, Carlyle had playfully recommended him for the post of Perpetual President of the Heaven-and-Hell Amalgamated Society. If Christ were again on earth, said Carlyle, Milnes would ask him to breakfast, and the Clubs would all be talking of the good things Christ had said.

Milnes was a man of many nicknames. For his serenity and smiling self-sufficiency he was referred to as "the Cool of the Evening." "Bird of Paradox," a London wit had called him, hitting off at once his plumage and his speech. He knew every one in London, and every one knew him. He was only too glad to give his share of help to Carlyle's enterprise, for he admired him immensely.

As the day for the first lecture crept nearer, Jane watched its approach with a growing terror. Her husband simply refused to make any preparation. The subject was the familiar one of German literature. He would deliver these talks extemporaneously, he explained. He pretended to be calm as he worked on the final proofs of his book, but Jane was not deceived. She was a delicate seismograph for his emotions and recorded every tremor. Only the sharp bayonets of absolute necessity at his back could ever drive him into the lecture hall. Would he remember to say "Ladies and Gentlemen" to that audience of fashionables which the sponsors were promising to assemble? "Fool-creatures come here for diversion" would be a far more typical opening.

On the 27th of April, Jane had seen her husband dispatch to the printers the last revise of his book. Exactly two days left in which to prepare.

She could not muster sufficient courage to attend the first of the series. Her greatest effort was to get her husband there on time. He must not be allowed to poke and dally till half past the last possible minute. She even meditated setting ahead all the clocks and watches in the house to insure his promptness.

A little drop of brandy in water, measured out carefully by her hand, and he was off. He had scribbled out some notes by way of sheet anchor in a gale, but intended not to use them if he could avoid doing so.

Toward tea hour he returned. The audience, he declared, had been amazingly humane. His sponsors had pressed on him a pocketful of coins, the first rewards for his effort. From the lot he selected two sovereigns, one for Jeannie, one for her mother down from Scotland on a visit. "Buy some little gift as handsel of the novelty!" he exclaimed.

Subsequent lecture courses, during the next three years, had met with even greater success. And the financial returns had been a Godsend. But when a series impended, Thomas acted like a man seated on an ant hill. In the spring of 1840, though her husband was an old campaigner now, Jane could see little improvement in the way his nerves responded. The lecture hall was a cockpit, and he the poor rooster forced to crow and struggle against his will. Goaded by his uneasy anticipations, he fell into the bad habit of waking up at four in the morning to wander about the house like an unlaid ghost. The only thing that momentarily soothed him was breakfast, but four-thirty or so was hardly a convenient hour for one's domestic ménage. As escort, during a lecture period, he became a total loss, finding it necessary to refuse all invitations. He regretted this circumstance, but what else, he lamented, could he do—a hapless dyspeptic in a rising tumult of nervousness till at last his duties ended?

In February of 1840 his friends began their usual pleas for another series. Not till April did he finally consent to the proposal. Jane knew what to expect as the result of the decision. If she wished to bring her husband through without explosion, she must be vigilant in quelling all possible sources of disturbance till the last word should be spoken. Trivial nuisances could prove as upsetting as major ones, and one never knew from what quarter they might arise. There were those new residents in the house next door, for instance. When they first moved in, they had seemed harmless enough. During the winter, it was true, muffled sounds had revealed the presence of a piano, yet under the circumstances its playing could be endured. With the coming of spring, however, windows were flung open, and the music, like the winds of Aeolus, penetrated everywhere. Worse yet, these neighbors kept a parrot. In fine weather the bird was hung outside in its cage. Jane was dismayed to hear it emitting its raucous shouts in the adjoining courtyard. Carlyle, she knew, was seeking inspiration for his talks and would surely take notice. She had not long to wait. Presently her husband was storming up and down the room. With that infernal racket going on, he exclaimed, he could neither think nor live! A quickly written, tactful little note sent at once next door, and Jane had the satisfaction of watching the parrot borne away to subterranean depths whence its screeching, thin and faint through the intervening masonry, was scarcely audible. But suppose there should ever be less amenable neighbors?

Jane had largely conquered her nervousness at watching her husband perform. She would sit with a friend or two in an inconspicuous part of the hall and observe the show. This time he was to speak on Heroes and Hero Worship.

Carlyle never lacked a distinguished, fashionable audience. The present was the choicest of them all. In both directions from the building the street was crowded with carriages. Jane had noticed among the stylish equipages one bearing the royal arms: some member of young Queen Victoria's household, actually, in attendance!

To a curious outsider, there was something strange and moving in the sight of this man, totally lacking in the usual graces and mannerisms of the skilled lecturer, holding the attention of these Lords and Ladies and noteworthy people by the sheer force of his personality and earnestness of his convictions. They sat spellbound as that wild Annandale chant went gollying forth across the room. He spoke in the language of a poet, as a mover and compeller of men. His deep-set eyes, gray-violet in their shifting color, flashed in his rugged, strong face. There he stood, like an inspired child, devoid of all artifices, while the thoughts rose kindling from his mind and took their flight over the assembly.

Some of the things he said shocked many in his audience yet they heard him to the end. His defence of Mahomet as a true man and prophet was disconcerting to hearers who traditionally had considered the founder of Islam an impostor. The modern utilitarians, declared Carlyle, with their doctrine of virtue by profit and loss, dispensed a beggarlier view of man and his destinies than Mahomet. "No!" shouted some one among the listeners. Necks craned to find the source of the interruption. It was Carlyle's friend, John Stuart Mill, who had broken in. The lecturer continued as though he had not heard.

Thomas might be as modest as he wished about these *Hero* lectures; Jane saw no need to curb her own satisfaction. She was bursting with pride at her husband's success. Just to look at him had given her pleasure. With a strong light from above shining down on him he had appeared surprisingly handsome. And all these men so attentive; these women taking notes! A friend had sardonically remarked that it was dates, not thoughts, they were recording, and these, in all likelihood, quite wrongly set down. But no matter. Their approving admiration was what counted. She had listened to persons on all sides of her—people who did not know who she was and therefore might be believed—praising the lecturer to the skies. Amusing, delightful, frightening even, to catch these fragments of conversation! "He's a glorious fellow," exclaimed one man, "I love the fellow's very faults!" "Aye, faith, is he; a fine, wild, chaotic, noble chap!" And when acquaintances began to praise her husband to her as a man of genius, she remarked with a little half scornful laugh, "They tell me things as if they were new that I found out years ago."

But Jane was thankful when Carlyle, after *Heroes*, made up his mind never again to speak in public. A detestable mixture of prophecy and play-actorism, he called the function. Her memories of her husband's agitation stayed vividly with her six months after the final series was over. "No lectures to be this spring," she wrote, "or ever more, God willing!"

Yet it seemed a shame that what her husband had spoken should fade from recollection. These *Hero* lectures must not be wasted. After delivering them, Carlyle had set them down on paper with the aid of newspaper reports and his own notes. Jane commandeered the manuscript, and bore it off to Fraser. Thus far her husband had never received immediate recompense for his books. Payment, if it came at all, followed years after printing. Jane was bent on instant returns; one hundred and fifty pounds was her demand. Fraser looked pained. Carefully, with his bookseller arithmetic, he demonstrated that no edition of the lectures, no matter how priced or issued, could bring one shilling more than £150 by way of net returns. What, he asked with a look of blank pathos, remained for the publisher? "Plainly nothing," said Jane, "which I regard as a clear intimation of Providence that no such character should exist."

The best part of this £150 must not be eaten up by Fraser's profits. She would try some other consequence of the Fall of Adam in the shape of a book dealer. If all turned out to be unreceptive to the notion that both they and the author could benefit, or were averse to printing the volume for virtue's own reward, why then let these *Heroes* retire to a shelf till some blessed new order of things arose in the dominion of booksellerdom. She and her husband were no longer so closely pursued by the wolves of beggary; they no longer had to face the prospect of jumping down the gaping throat of carnivorous booksellers as sole alley of escape. Carlyle's final speaking engagement had brought him over two hundred pounds. With that return he was quite content.

One result of Carlyle's increasing prominence, an outcome hardly anticipated in its fullest possibilities, had to do with his standing in London. Literary-fashionable society was claiming Thomas for its own. He had become a lion, a form of human creature that he had always regarded with the gravest suspicion.

Jane took this "rising in society"—this recognition by select individuals of the aristocracy—as an honor due her husband. She was amused and pleased when flunkeys pounded thunderously on the door with requests for Carlyle's presence at a coming grand affair. All this was new and entertaining. Before the novelty wore away, Thomas admitted even to experiencing the faintest trace of snob triumph—he the son of an Annandale stonemason in demand at these houses of nobility and wealth. Jane listened with quizzical attention to his descriptions of these affairs—characterizations often disapproving enough in tone, though it was noticeable that he continued to accept at least some of the invitations precipitating on him. A most noteworthy party—that at the Chancellor's of the Exchequer. Carlyle had gone, he protested, for the curiosity of the thing—but also for the honor, he admitted. Strange indeed: a man who disposed annually of the whole revenue of England shaking hands with a man who had scarcely cash enough, at times, to buy potatoes and onions for himself. There had been high dames and distinguished males simmering about in the genial light and brilliance of the ornate rooms, and the air was electric with the sound of noble names. Carlyle discovered with some incredulity that he had lingered till after midnight. He had dined at Holland House—Lady Holland a kind of hungry ornamented witch peering over at him to see if he were worth adding to her menagerie. At Bath House, the city residence of William Bingham Baring, son of the first Lord Ashburton— a man reputed to have gained more millions of money by commerce than had ever been made before—he had met Baron Bunsen, the German ambassador, and various Lords and Ladyships, several of them auditors at his last public discourses. Between twelve and one he had escaped to quiet Chelsea. Little good in all this, he told Jane. Politeness had forced him to sit and talk for a very long while with Lady Harriet Baring, his hostess. Not very beautiful to look at, but one of the keenest creatures, Tom admitted, that he had ever chatted with—full to the brim with mirth and spirit. She had kept him conversing an hour or more upstairs to escape from the German ambassador who was a bore. A clever devil, certainly, this Lady Harriet, *belle laide* but full of wit—the person coming closest to a dame of real quality of all whom he had so far met.

These soirées and dinners among the great, where one was flattered and stared at, he protested, could become weariness itself. As for Jane, she had no ambitions that way. As the lion's wife, she was sometimes included in these early invitations. But when it was only a sea of faces she went to swim in, she found nothing in the business for her. What she looked for always was human friendship, and this she accepted gratefully wherever she could find it, in any walk of life. Her first adventures with West End sociability had depressed her—the true spirit of humanity seemed so foreign to it. There was woeful lack of heart and health. And unless one could thrive on other things in the atmosphere and gain more substantial nourishment than that provided through mere chitchat, one was like to stifle or starve.

Only when here and there these high-born faces became known friends did Jane's lack of interest vanish. Presently, because of what she herself had to offer, human companionship began to develop even within this gilded sphere. Hosts and hostesses—Lord Lansdowne and others—who had invited her out of politeness to her husband, discovered with some amazement the legitimate appeal of Mrs. Carlyle's own claims.

The epidemic of high social notice had begun in most spectacular fashion. One day Jane was aroused from her meditations by the clatter of horses down Cheyne Row. Then a footman's cannonading volleyed at the door. Would Helen have presence of mind to open in the face of such a knocking? Jane hurried to the window to take a peek through the blinds. There before the house stood one of the most resplendent equipages she had ever beheld—a gorgeous sky-blue and silver chariot from whence emanated a peacock figure of a man. Jane could hear the patter of Helen's footsteps in hurried retreat. The silly girl had been so startled by all this magnificence that she had fled in confusion to the kitchen. Luckily she had left the door open so that the visitor could enter.

It was Count D'Orsay, London's Prince of Dandies, whom Byron had called one of the few living specimens to gratify one's ideal of a French aristocrat before the Revolution. Jane had observed him before, bowing to the ladies at one of her husband's lectures. Impossible, indeed, to live in London without catching rays from this splendid comet as it swept from one constellation to the next in the town's most brilliant society.

One of her husband's admirers, young Henry Chorley, a journalist employed by the *Athenaeum,* was with the Count. Jane, hurrying to cover Helen's retreat, was struck by Chorley's manifest confusion. Apprehension as to what effect his man of genius and his man of fashion would produce on each other had quite unstrung him. His jaw worked nervously, his face, under its thatch of red hair, was a mirror of apprehension.

But Thomas and the Count got on famously together. In sly amusement, from the vantage point of the sofa, Jane watched the meeting: this Phoebus Apollo of Dandyism facing the prophet of Sans-culottism. There was Carlyle, in his dusty, gray-plaid dressing gown, at ease in his favorite tub-chair, looking blandly and approvingly at the Prince of Dandies, while the Prince of Dandies, resplendent as a diamond beetle, approvingly and blandly returned the gaze.

Jane had never seen such fantastic finery of dress: sky-blue satin cravat, yards enough of gold watch chain to hang a man with, white French gloves, two glorious breastpins fastened together by a chain—these were but the outer garnishings. D'Orsay's coat was cream shade, his waistcoat blue velvet, his trousers light buff. He was as gay in his colors as a hummingbird, and equally trim. His auburn hair, rich and abundant, was as carefully groomed as the headdress of a girl awaiting presentation at Court. There was a certain sexlessness about his beauty which Jane found, on first appraisal, rather disgusting. But this repulsion quickly vanished before the strength of D'Orsay's masculinity of person and of character. He was a tall fellow, six feet three, and built to match his height—a perfect tower of a man. Had he been born twenty years earlier, he might have become one of Bonaparte's most dashing marshals. His manners were the reverse of effeminate. There was about him a *bonhommie* and rough sarcasm surprising in such a porcelain figure. Noticing a bust of Shelley in the room, he remarked contemptuously: "Ah! It is one of those faces *who weesh* to swallow their *chin!*"

After hearing the excellent lectures, he had been eager to know Carlyle—that explained the call. The history of the Revolution was a splendid epic. The Madame Crawford of the Rue de Clichy, he added, where Marie Antoinette hid her Varennes coach, was his mother's cousin.

When the sun chariot had rolled away, Helen emerged from the vantage point where she had been observing the splendor.

"A *most* beautiful man and most beautiful carriage!" she exclaimed in rapture. "The Queen's was no show i' the worl' compared wi' that! Every thing was so grand and so preceese!"

Chapter Twenty-One

*J*ANE found her husband very uneasy in the winter of
1841 and during the following spring. He was getting
up steam for a new book, a process always full of hiss
and sputter. She had developed a certain immunity to his unease
and restlessness. He was constantly talking about dashing away
somewhere for a change of scene, yet would not get in motion.
He was speaking, too, of quitting the city for good to settle in
some countryside remote from all mankind. The absurdity of
this yearning, Jane reassured herself, lay in the probability that
if ever he took to any such refuge, he would be on the verge of
cutting his throat after six months of it. With all his pretended
detestation of London, the town and what it offered was as
essential to an important element in his personality as it was
to Jane's whole being. Yet fly from it, at times, he must. That
was necessary, too. His portmanteau, half packed, had been
standing on a chair for the last four weeks, with the tag, Mr.
Carlyle, Passenger ———, but the rest was blank. Whither?
If only he would make up his mind!

While he delayed irresolute at home, an unexpected visitor
arrived. During the previous year, from Lancashire, Carlyle
had received a letter sent by an admirer of *Sartor*—at last available in an English edition. The signature was unknown to
either Jane or Thomas: Geraldine Endsor Jewsbury. She wished
advice, she wrote, from the man who had emerged out of doubt
—the Everlasting No—into the mystical belief set forth as the
Everlasting Yea. During childhood, she explained, she had discarded her orthodox creed. She had never gained a fresh one
to take its place. Could the author of *Sartor* aid her? Carlyle,
always sensitive to such requests, replied kindly, as best he
could. Both Jane and he had been impressed with the ingenuous, anxious appeal. On the spur of the moment, they invited
Miss Jewsbury to stay with them if ever she came to London.

In March the questioner had appeared—a small, eager little thing whose confiding, impetuous ways fairly bowled Carlyle over. His first impressions told him that here was one of the most interesting young women he had met for years. Jane was more reserved in her estimate. Flighty, erratic, impulsive creatures who clung as though one were a sweet to be devoured filled her with misgivings. Yet it was hard to resist Geraldine, even though she was incredibly romantic and had a mind teeming with half-formed plots and novels.

Miss Jewsbury was much too fond of that indecent French writer, George Sand, Carlyle remarked on further acquaintance, modifying his earlier enthusiasm. He wished, privately, that his Jeannie would show less taste for this same reading—it was nothing short of a new Phallus worship, with Sue, Balzac, and Co. for prophets and Madame Sand for virgin.

After Geraldine departed in a flurry of raptures, Carlyle resumed his uneasy meditations on where to go. April had arrived; high time to be off to the country.

Ever since the start of their acquaintance, Richard Milnes had cherished the intention of getting Thomas to pay a visit to Fryston, near Wakefield in Yorkshire, where Richard's family lived. Better go, urged Jane. Well, said Carlyle doubtfully, if Milnes really wanted him, he should stop at Chelsea to tell what the possibilities, limitations, difficulties, laws, and conditions of the enterprise might be. Taking a hint, Milnes did so—and successfully bore off Carlyle.

As Thomas drove away, the last look on Jeannie's face—sad and careworn—troubled him. Yet when Tom had been a day or two out of the house, Jane, rested and once more in a sparkling humor, was writing him brisk, lively, affectionate letters. This was his first visit to a palatial country house. She could picture him, from his descriptions, coursing about like an awkward bumblebee trapped by accident within finely appointed, enormous rooms. An amazing place, an amazing life, Thomas reported—champagne, silver dishes, and four or five embroidered lackeys standing like tailors' dummies about the rooms. But it was clear that he was enjoying himself and his hosts him. The tone of his letters was reassuring. "Dear bairn," he called her, and "my lassie." Her first note, he said, had been borne to him at breakfast by a flunkey in a red-quilted coat, who walked solemnly round the table with a salver, laying by each plate such offerings as the post had brought. Two reviews of the new *Heroes* book, one saccharine with praise, the other denunciatory, had caught Jane's attention; she sent both to her husband. Amid bursts of laughter, Carlyle read part of the objurgation aloud to his hosts and their guests.

"But does Mrs. Carlyle send you this?" asked one literal-minded hearer whose sense of humor was not strong enough to overcome her amazement.

"Ah, yes, the wicked gipsy!" answered Mr. Carlyle with evident satisfaction.

From Richard Milnes', at Fryston, he went to Headingley, near Leeds, where lived an even wealthier friend, James Marshall. Because of abominable late parties, Carlyle objected, rest in these gorgeous houses was out of the question. "This morning I had a fair chance, had fallen asleep again, and was afar in sweet oblivion, apparently for hours, when the visage of a flunkey at the foot of my bed roused me. 'What o'clock?' '*Af pas seven*, Sir.' 'When is breakfast?' '*Af pas eight*.' Flunkey of the Devil!"

Carlyle's restlessness had not been stilled when he came back to London in the first week of May. In June he was off again for Scotland, this time with plans for Jane to meet him later on. She was to go North by way of Liverpool, where she would visit a Mr. and Mrs. Paulet, friends of Geraldine Jewsbury. They lived at Seaforth, outside the town. Geraldine she would also see while in Lancashire. She would then join her husband in a visit to Mrs. Welsh at Templand.

Jane traveled by boat from Liverpool to Annan where Carlyle was scheduled to receive her. "Sail prosperously," he bade in his letter, "come jumping up when I step upon the deck at Annan Pool!"

There were other guests at Templand when the Carlyles arrived, and a crowded house. At three in the morning, Thomas, after a sleepless night, got up and dressed. He would go to Dumfries, he said. If he stayed longer in that dwelling, he would be miserable for the day and cause only misery to others. Quietly he stole out into the pallid light of the July dawn, yoked the gig and drove away.

Jane received a note from him to help with such explanations for her mother as she might choose to offer. But most of what he wrote was for her eyes alone. He had reached Dumfries, he reported, in better shape than she perhaps had anticipated. He had even won some hours of rest. "Would to Heaven I could hear that my poor Jeannie had got to sleep! I have done little but think tragically enough about my poor lassie all day: about her, and *all* the history we have had together." He hoped his going had not disturbed her. Perhaps she had lain ill with a headache. "Write, write!" he begged. "Adieu, my hapless, beloved Jeannie! Sleep and be well, and let us meet not tragically."

They had leased a cottage on the North coast of the Solway Firth for the month of August. Ever since the end of winter, Carlyle had been looking forward to this period of quiet in the country. Jane had agreed to take part in the experiment. But its near approach daunted her. She did not share her husband's need for isolation, for the murmur of eternity in the waves, the sight of empty green fields. He must have solitude, he announced, to get his inner world once more in order.

When a book was imminent, Carlyle's mood resembled that of a brooding hen which knew not where to set or even what to lay. The subject was to be Cromwell, but the spirit of the thing was still embryonic. A history, probably, rather than strict biography; a work like the *French Revolution* though this time with but a single hero. Might not the whole grand problem of leadership be illustrated through the character and acts of the Great Protector? A mighty subject, truly—vast and difficult as the French Revolution. The lonely shore of the Firth was the place to battle with the manifold complexities of the problem.

Jane knew the symptoms and their import far too well to be at ease in their presence. She had lived with them through *Sartor* and through the *History*. Well, her husband's growls and wrestlings were the inevitable consequences of genius. She was ready to endure them, for its sake, as best she could. But if only he would not set up such a caterwauling! And then, when the book at last would be finished, like as not he would regard it merely as a disease thrown off. If she were to praise it, and insist on its excellence, he would again cloak himself in the dun mantle of incredulousness.

Jane's meditations blended uneasily with the moaning of the waves at Newby. From the very beginning, as far as she was concerned, she entertained grave doubts on this place of her husband's choosing. A lonelier spot on earth could hardly be discovered. Nothing but sky and water, with the sea ten yards from the door. Behind lay an oat field, and neighboring their cottage were fishermen's huts. A three-day storm of wind, roaring above the thunder of the waves, had ushered in their stay. When the skies cleared, the view was magnificent enough: the troubled water, and beyond, all Cumberland, blue and shining in the August sun—Helvellyn, Skiddaw, and a thousand peaks. But far too often for Jane, that month, there was gray tempest and the monotony of storm.

She had set to work at once to make the house, with its alien furnishings, livable for herself. She had even brought her maid along, and Carlyle was optimistic of results. Why, the place had been created for them! They had a gig for transportation. They could drive, he said hopefully, and have excellent swimming on the pebbled beach. Jane tried the water just once, and bruised her ankle on a jagged stone. That ended her halfhearted interest in bathing and she left the sands to her husband for his lonely walks and swims.

He would see nobody and discouraged visitors. He quite realized that this deliberate policy of isolation, in a district inhabited by old friends, would give offense. Regrettable, he admitted, but what other course, in his present state of health and nerves, could he pursue? There had been far too much profitless sociability in London. Here at least he could protect himself against the menace.

As for Jane, she set her heart like flint against this style of rural living. Newby bored her to extinction and she had made up her mind to experience no good from it. Before the time scheduled for their departure, they left the place. Jane's secret campaign had won the victory. In his innocence, Carlyle sadly admitted this venture in Paradise had proved a failure for himself and Jane. A visit to Harriet Martineau at Tynemouth, and they were home. Jane watched her husband with a knowing glint in her eye. He was purchasing new carpets for the stairs and library. She heard no more talk of the possibility of quitting London.

That winter the Carlyles entered into terms of intimacy with John Forster, an explosively energetic young barrister far too busy with his literary interests to have any time for law—an able, self-assertive fellow who was substituting for a legal career the more congenial pursuits of journalist and critic. A noisy man, was Jane's first impression when Forster burst overwhelmingly on her. But soon she was ready to admit that there was body and substance behind his foaming vitality. Presently he entered the select company of men and women who were recipients of Jane's most sprightly, confidential letters. One met convivial guests—Charles Dickens, William Macready, and others—at the choice dinners he gave at his bachelor establishment in Lincoln's Inn Fields. An ursine, stocky man, bushy-browed and shock-headed, whose tread reverberated through the house, and whose voice echoed upstairs and down like a trumpet blast.

Two friends of his, the publishers Chapman and Hall, men of enterprise and means, had purchased the moribund *Foreign Quarterly Review*. Forster was to be the new editor, at least till the journal should become re-established. He at once began stirring actively about to raise a corps of first-rate reviewers. Who better fitted to appeal to for help than Jane Welsh Carlyle? If it could be done at all, surely Mrs. Carlyle was the person to urge noteworthy men to write for the struggling magazine.

Jane was greatly surprised to be pitched on for this function —quite a novel experience, to become midwife for a journal. But she began the quest at once and soon attracted powerful contributors. Then having done her bit, she withdrew, declining the honor of remaining the siren behind the editorial chair. She had no intention, she explained, of becoming like Tasso's Armida, in the poem *Jerusalem Delivered*, whose feminine wiles lured away so many of the principal knights from the enemy's camp.

Though several of her friends regretted this reticence, it was Jane's fixed determination to shun connection with literary matters. Was she not sacrificing her talents, they asked? "One writer is quite enough in a house," was her stock reply, and none could shake her from it.

But though she would not herself write for publication, she

could not wholly escape the rôle of literary adviser. Friends and acquaintances, even strangers, sent her manuscripts of various sorts. But Forster's hints that she should add herself to the circle of distinguished critics that he was assembling she persisted in ignoring.

Chapter Twenty=Two

*J*ANE'S partings from her mother were always trying. Together, their disagreements far too often made visits unpleasant; separated, each worried about the other's welfare. Jeannie's pause at Templand, before the hapless experiment of cottage life on the Solway Firth, had followed the pattern of earlier days.

That autumn, as the Carlyles were on their way back to London, Mrs. Welsh had come to Dumfries to see them off. The three of them visited the shops in town to purchase farewell gifts. There were tears in Jeannie's eyes, and in her mother's, but neither would cry lest the other be upset. At such moments of farewell, the obstructed intense affection between them came nearest the surface.

They had gone to the house of Tom's sister till leaving time. Mrs. Welsh would not linger to see them go. She preferred to retain the memory of a cheery, casual parting. From the living-room window they watched her out of sight round the corner of Dumfries High Street.

In London, through the winter, Jane's thoughts turned often to Templand. Though she was at a loss just how to remedy it, she did not approve of her mother's aloneness there since the death of old Mr. Welsh. Could she be persuaded to live nearby in London? She had never really taken to the city. To have her become an inmate of No. 5 Cheyne Row might be an even more risky venture, yet perhaps the only course. Somehow she must give her mother, now that old age was approaching, the care and love she had too thoughtlessly failed in during past years. They must discuss plans more fully in the coming summer.

Her mother's letters, thus far, were cheerful enough. But January and February can be wicked months in Scotland, months crowded with sickness and discomfort. Her mother, indeed, had admitted that she was not well, though she gave the impression that there was nothing to worry about. But sometimes Jane had a foreboding heart. Should she go see for herself? Yet precipitously to do so might accomplish more harm than good. At least she would ask her husband to write privately to Dr. Russell, Mrs. Welsh's physician, for a report.

On Saturday, February 26, Jane received another letter from her mother. Like the earlier ones, it was written in good spirits, though unlike its predecessors, it contained very little personal news. Jane took alarm at once. Anxiously she waited for word from Dr. Russell. There could be no post on Sunday. When Monday and the letter came, Jane was herself ill in bed. Mrs. Welsh, the doctor wrote, had indeed been dangerously sick; was sick yet, though there was no need to give up hope.

Jane realized that her mother had been shielding her. She got up and dressed for travel. She was in no condition for the journey north, declared her husband, trying to allay her fears. But his wife would not listen.

Blustering, rainy skies hung, dank and chill, over London as they made their way toward Euston Square Station, where Jane would catch the night express for Liverpool. Thomas helped his wife into a railway carriage. She would send him a message later if there was need for him to come. He stood hesitant on the platform, waiting for the train to move. Close beside the window she could see his tall figure in the smoky air, his face, anxious and distressed, lighted by the flaring lamps. The words of hope with which he sought to comfort her were lost in the confusion. She sat quite silent, white-faced, looking ahead into the darkness. With a hiss of steam, the locomotive gathered momentum. Just time to wave a mute farewell; the journey through the night had begun.

The rhythm of the ties beat cruelly into her brain as the express moved across the hardly visible landscape—houses first, dim in the rectangle of the window, then farmlands soaked in rain. As the hours dragged interminably by, Jane presently noted a change in the turmoil of her mind. Hopefulness, which she had thought extinct, was still waging war on her fatalistic mood. Her mother had rallied from other serious illnesses; sixty was not really old. As the factory chimneys of Liverpool grew taller in the morning light, Jane clung desperately to her feeling of suspense: kinder to her than despair.

She took a cab for Maryland Street where she would get news. "Your mother is dead," they told her. Her cousins, Helen and Jeannie Welsh, put her, almost delirious, to bed. For weeks she lay very ill. Grief, bitterness, and self-reproach struggled within her, dissipating her small reserve of strength. Even the sleep-inducing medicines which she was given brought only temporary relief. When Carlyle, who had set out at once from London after receiving word of his mother-in-law's death, reached Jane's bedside, he was shocked. He had watched her in many sicknesses. Never before had he seen her so miserable, so low and wretched.

Carlyle presently went on to Templand. His letters kept Jane posted on the details of the closing of her mother's small estate. The lease on the house was to be terminated, the furniture sold. That was how Jeannie wished it. Might it perhaps not be advisable, Carlyle hinted, to keep the place? They could use it as a summer retreat. But Jane, in her present state of mind, shrank from the thought. What was Scotland to her, with her mother gone? So Carlyle said no more about it.

With Mrs. Welsh's death, the house on the Craig which Jane had deeded to her mother before marriage was once more hers. Just prior to the auction at Templand, Carlyle offered another suggestion to his wife who was now almost well enough to leave Liverpool for London. "Once or twice today it strikes me, if you did not so dislike Craigenputtock, might we not carry all over thither, build them together again, and avoid the sale? But this, I am afraid, is rather wild." He did not propose actual settlement at Puttock. The place, he hoped, might serve for occasional visits, needful to inspect the tenant and keep the farm in order.

Jane, distraught, unable, unwilling even, to banish from her mind the sick thoughts that troubled her, could scarcely finish Carlyle's letter. She hated the spot; loathed it! Was her husband seeking to torment her? She wrote him a bitter, stinging reply.

Carlyle answered with sorrowful contrition. Surely she must

know that he could not deliberately intend anything harmful! "Do not tear yourself to pieces," he begged, "do not fret yourself about that note." Craigenputtock, he assured her, was just a passing fancy and had not come to mind again. Since she herself liked Chelsea, she must pay no further attention to his own difficulties. London, after all, though his health and nerves might suffer, was the best place for him. It was the one spot on earth, he said, where he could enjoy something like the blessedness of independence. If the city at times became insupportable, he could always run to Scotland to recover.

On his return, Carlyle found his wife still thin and pale. This long despondency worried him exceedingly. She continued so disheartened, so weary of the world in general, that it was terrifying to observe her. When she could possibly do so, belying her nature, she avoided company and lived within herself. She had fallen short of every duty, she insisted; she was useless and a burden. Carlyle thought he saw in her mood the dispiritment of a buffeted, tired, sick mind. Surely she was no judge of herself! "Courage, my poor little Jeannie"—he repeated—"Courage! We must hope for gladder days." The sight of woe always moved him. In its presence, he could be as gentle as her father had been. If only, he told Jane, she could rouse up those splendid faculties of hers in some task worthy of herself! She was allowing too much time for painful reflection.

What, Jane answered, was there for her to do? Surely not join the ranks of scribbling females on whom he often vented his contempt? She set her standards higher than those which governed the likes of them; higher than could lightly be achieved. There was philanthropy, of course. Yet humanitarianism as a trade was futile—he himself had said so.

Life was such a quandary! What *did* women want? Most of them would never know. The majority, like herself, if they did not have to work for bread and had no children to care for, let themselves be dominated by a pack of trivial cares that devoured their working and their sleeping hours. Yet the greatest crime of all, perhaps, was thought. Too close analysis could ruin happiness or intensify despair.

Surely, surely, Carlyle insisted, his Jeannie would see her way through this present darkness. Had his own nature been other than it was, he said with humility, had he taken life less hard, life might have been kinder, too, for her. But alas, he was what he was, though he would do his best never to distress her. Even in the grimmest rocky wilderness of existence there were blessed well-springs; there was an everlasting guiding star.

With gentle tact, he sought to lead her once again into her accustomed mode of life. He urged her to renew old friendships. The Sterlings took her on a trip to Windsor, and there were other excursions.

On July 14, 1843, Jane would end her forty-second year. Always, on the anniversary of her daughter's birth, Mrs. Welsh had made holiday. At Templand there was always a feast and rejoicing. For Chelsea, on that date, there would be a cheerful note and welcome gift.

Jeannie Welsh Carlyle had much of the child about her still. She could look forward with the enthusiasm of her teens to birthdays and the surprises which they brought. But this year there would be no celebration at Templand, no letter for Cheyne Row. The day would be wae indeed, thought Jane, a day like all the rest—empty and sorrowful.

Carlyle, to his wife's puzzlement, was very mysterious the night before—as jumpy and nervous as though he had some great crime to hide. What was this? Awkwardly he was thrusting a package on her. Within, from one of the fine jeweler's shops in London, lay a handsome bottle for smelling salts! Jane could hardly believe her eyes. A poignant, confused emotion swept over her. Imagine! her busy husband, who disliked nothing in the world so much as buying anything, had ventured for her sake into that shop to make so feminine a purchase! Carlyle, who believed anniversaries to be such nonsense, was acting as though today were the greatest in the year! Jane hardly knew whether to laugh or cry.

From that time forth no birthday of hers ever passed unrecognized.

Jane finally decided to accept the invitation. She liked the Bullers; why not come out of hiding for this journey into Suffolk? Old Mr. and Mrs. Buller were staying at Troston Rectory with their youngest son Reginald, the parson there.

On Thursday, August 10, she set out for Bury St. Edmunds, seventy-five miles from London. At Bury the family would meet her for the drive to Troston. She had resigned herself to a fatiguing journey after her early morning departure. Surprisingly, the trip was not half so tiring or dull as she anticipated. Really, it was good once more to be about. Her husband, occupied with his friend Oliver Cromwell, would be well enough off at home. What's more, he would not remain without company. Her little cousin Babbie Welsh, who had come from Liverpool to be with her during her illness, had agreed to stay as housekeeper.

At eleven, she nibbled a small Ghent loaf which she had brought, sampled a biscuit, and sucked some barley-sugar which Babbie had pressed on her. At two, she finished the rest of her small provender. A well-dressed man in a gray jacket, observing her, solicitously handed her a glass of water. Helpful gentlemen, assuredly, had a way of popping up on one's travels. Jane gratefully accepted the offering. The water was refreshing, even though pervaded with a faint reek of onions.

She arrived at her destination early, three instead of five, but fortunately Mr. Buller and the carriage were already waiting, and Jane, after cordial greetings, was soon on her way to Troston. The region had become more wooded now, and lusher. As they drove along, Jane noticed many parks and fine manor houses. The rectory itself proved to be an ideal setting for a wealthy man-of-leisure cleric such as Reginald. Surrounded by tall, cool trees, with green fields all about, it impressed Jane as a compromise between a country parsonage and an aristocratic villa. In absurd contrast, the small dilapidated church lay close at hand and beside it slumbered a quiet churchyard. After the horrible London cemeteries, it was a relief to see a tranquil place like this where the wicked really ceased from troubling and the weary were at rest. Jane found the spot not in the least depressing in the mellow afternoon light. Just so, under the blessed sunshine, would drowse the churchyard at the little Scottish village of Crawford, and her mother's grave.

Mrs. Buller received Jane with an affectionate embrace—a flattering spontaneity from so reserved a woman. "Dear, *dear* Mrs. Carlyle!" she exclaimed, and the way she said it was convincing. She welcomed Jane as a daughter of the house. Precious indeed were one's friends! In her self-exile Jane had forgot just how precious. She felt as though she were being received

again into familiar sights and sounds after wandering confused
and alone in regions of nightmare.

In her bright, large room, Jane put her clothes away and
took stock of her surroundings. Certainly as exotic a chamber
as she ever hoped to see! Mrs. Buller's tastes, acquired during a
long residence in India, were individual enough to strike one
dumb with amazement. Little as Jane cared for expensive deco-
ration for its own sake, the display impressed her. Her bed was
of bamboo—shaped like a tent, with curtains of embroidered
cloth from India lined with a strawcolored material. At the
windows hung draperies to match, and on the floor lay the
strangest carpet Jane had ever in her life beheld. In its center
were two white swans kissing each other among the reeds. This
scene was in the heart of a hexagonal field covered with pagodas
and Indian trees, round which, in turn, wandered a border of
green and rose-colored dragons braided by the tails. From the
fantastic bed into which she had climbed, Jane was able to see
her reflection in the ornate mirror. Could that small, thin, large-
eyed, sober-faced woman be Jeannie Welsh Carlyle? She looked
at herself with disapproval. That glass must be made to reflect
a livelier image.

Jane was still a bit uncertain; still testing her course. Her first
whole day at Troston was marred by a headache, and unaccustomed rural noises—braying of donkeys, barking of dogs—
troubled her sleep at night. But the rectory was a delightful
place; its inmates perfect hosts. They made you feel as though
you were in your own house—the very quintessence of hospitality. The forenoons were her own to do with what she pleased.
She could walk from the living room right into the garden
through the tall French windows. She could write. She could
read. Mr. Buller had a great assemblage of French novels
(Carlyle despised such literature, though occasionally he would
read it) and these Jane eagerly sampled. New packets came
from time to time to replenish the supply.

"A very bad stock, this last," she remarked one evening.

"Yes," replied Mr. Buller, raising his eyebrows, "when
French novels are decorous, they are monstrous stupid!"

Reginald, though a slothful young man with a bulging waist-
line, was an early riser. Every morning at eight Jane could hear
the houseman knocking at his door. Disobeying Mrs. Buller's

injunctions to sleep late, she would get up at the muffled signal. She enjoyed the luxury of dressing without hurry. Not for months had she combed her hair with such deliberate pains till its broad bands sweeping down from her forehead shone like blackest jet. Her small, well-shaped head looked trim and thoroughbred again, the style of hairdress accentuating her natural dignity though her returning vivaciousness—never suppressible for long—guarded against any hint of severity or restraint.

Breakfast came at nine. The family dined at three. Drives and various excursions filled the afternoons. When high tea was over at eight, Mr. Buller would rattle his box of chessmen. "When you are ready, I am ready." Jane might be writing to Carlyle or to her cousin Jeannie Welsh or dipping into another French novel. But soon pawns, knights, queens and bishops would be marshaled in battle array. On the first evening, because she had neglected her game along with other interests during the past six months, Jane played somewhat listlessly. "I *do* wish you could improve a little!" said the victor complacently. That remark by Mr. Buller was the only goad Jane needed. She was determined to let him see what she could do if she chose to. So she mustered all her tricks, and before he quite realized what was happening, her opponent found his king a prisoner in checkmate. Thenceforth, though he prided himself on his skill, he had sore thrashing of his brain for every game he won, and the series finally ended in Jane's favor.

If one accepted the temporal hospitality of the parson's house, one was more or less obligated to acknowledge his spiritual dominion by attendance at his church. Jane, standing beside Reggie one evening in his dilapidated place of worship, was shocked by the symbolism before her eyes: this ancient crumbling house of prayer—and its modern incumbent placidly vegetating in the rich soil of the country living that had come to him! Long ago she had lost her outward faith, but the need of her emotional temperament for something to replace it at times positively ached within her. The spectacle of Reggie, shepherd of the sheep, gave ironic acuteness to the pain. Here in this parish lived four hundred and fifty souls that might be considered worth the saving—and Reggie was the means of rescue! Anything so like the burial place of revealed religion she had never seen, nor a rector more fit to read its funeral service. Yet one could not blame him too much—at least he was sweet-tempered and kindly, though nothing further removed from the inspired man of God could be found in all the parishes of England. As for what passed under the guise of his opinions, Jane dared not look at his mother when Reggie spoke. How Mrs. Buller, forced to listen to such pompous drivel, kept herself so serene and cheerful was an enigma beyond Jane's solving. It was a mercy that Mr. Buller was so deaf.

Jane had told Reggie about her young cousin in Chelsea. Unlike his flashing brother Charles, Reggie was the victim of an almost unconquerable shyness. Yet he summoned courage enough to hint that Miss Jeannie would be most welcome to join Mrs. Carlyle at Troston. Attractive, lively little Babbie, Jane reflected, might do very well for and with Reginald. And where could one live more comfortably than at Troston? But alas, there was the vicar himself with his multiplying stoutness and his habit of taking snuff. Literally, he peppered and salted himself with it. No, Reggie counterbalanced the inducement; Babbie must make a better match.

Yet Jane was forced to admit that Reginald improved on acquaintance, especially when he had overcome his terror at her being feminine. Indeed he waited on her in exemplary fashion. Poor Reggie! Jane questioned if ever before he had lavished so much attention on any woman besides his mother.

So, out of consideration for Reggie, Jane ventured to church on her first Sunday at Troston. The congregation consisted of the servants at the rectory, and some thirty or forty poor people. Somewhat to her discomfort, the latter stared at Jane as though she were a visitor from Saturn, and they shuffled about like a bewildered herd of cattle. Above them stood Reggie in his white vestments, praying and giving out the psalm in a loud, sonorous, perfectly cultured Church of England voice. Just as he finished announcing the hymn, a shrill thin note, something between a squeal of agony and the highest bleat of a bagpipe, echoed from the far end of the moldering church. In great astonishment Jane turned round but could not discover the source of this disturbance. No special intrusion of the devil, apparently, for the congregation, bursting into a noise which resembled singing, joined forces with the invisible instrument. "A clarinet,

Madam!" respectfully murmured Hesketh, the butler. Perfect servant, Hesketh, always prepared to fill one's wants.

Very little faculty is needed for reciting prayers tolerably well. But the sermon! That was quite another matter. "It's none of his," Mrs. Buller whispered with perfect candor. Obviously not! He read his borrowed tract as though it were not even English. It might as well have been a Chaldee manuscript. The sound bore not the slightest relation to the sense. Reggie paused only when he needed breath—even when that happened at the very center of a word. In the midst of this performance a small infant suddenly interrupted. "Away, mammy! Let's away!" it screamed as if possessed. All the while a larger child was punctuating the discourse with loud volleys of whooping cough.

In a little square enclosure Jane noticed a portly character with a wand some five feet long which he swayed about majestically as though it were a sceptre. Hesketh again obliged with a ray of enlightment.

"To beat the bad children!" he confided.

"Are the children here so bad that they need such a functionary?"

"Ah, they will always, them little 'uns, be doing mischief in the church. It's a-wearisome for the poor things, and the rod keeps them in fear!"

Jane's glance strayed to the walls to study the inscriptions. Two white marble tablets were noticeable: the first told of the virtues of a deceased wife and her husband's sorrow, the second bore an inscription for a young girl dead of consumption. There were also a sword and sword belt hung on the tomb of a young soldier killed while fighting Napoleon in Spain. And all these persons—the graven lettering declared it so—were to be raised through Jesus Christ. This was the resurrection and the life; this the beautiful promise. Yet even as she read the words, her ears were mocked by the droning voice of Reggie, God's vicar. The Gospel of the Lord made into something worse than the cawing of rooks! Jane's feelings rose to her throat as if they would choke her. Never, never again, would she bring herself into that building misnamed the place of worship.

But next Sunday, when Reggie asked her if she were attending and she answered in the negative, he looked so wae that her compassion betrayed her.

"It's a nice pew, that of ours," remarked Mr. Buller from its depths. "I read most part of the *Femme de Qualité* this morning." A sudden afterthought struck him. "Don't tell Mr. Reggie this!" he begged.

As for Jane, she managed to sit in cool indifference through the service. To rest pampered pious knees, there was a goodly supply of cushions available. From these, in the pew's fastnesses, she made herself a sort of Persian couch, wickedly removed her bonnet, and stretched out for pleasant daydreams. Before she realized the fact, a slight rustling and the words: "t' Father, Son, and Holy Ghost . . ." warned her that church was over.

Reggie was better on the excursions they took together or with the elder Bullers. They had gone to Ampton one evening, a beautiful deserted place belonging to Lord Calthorpe. She and Reggie clambered over a high gate with spikes on the top— Jane had forgotten the lassitude of the past months—and enjoyed a stolen exploration through the lovely gardens. They rested in a summerhouse which could have served as an Arabian Nights pavilion, then looked through the windows of the house at the luxurious furniture, fine books, pictures, and statues assembled by the owner. Every appointment for ease and comfort, yet Lord Calthorpe, having taken some aversion to his expensive toy, had not set foot in it for years. This royal park and its delicious mansion on the one hand, and on the other, squalid towns full of paupers, vices, and disease! And yet one was asked to believe that a benignant spirit ruled the world.

Charles, the charming, distinguished Charles, was coming to visit his mother and father. In anticipation, the house had been in a bustle of excitement for days. From her stay with his adoring family, Jane observed there was an uncertainty, a fly-by-night quality about Charles. He was supposed to arrive directly after the close of Parliament, but instead dashed off to Addiscombe Farm, the summer home of Lady Harriet Baring. Lady Harriet, Jane was aware, exercised a spell over the best men in London which might have made even Circe envious. She was indignant when she heard that Charles had failed to arrive at Troston because of Addiscombe. Why did he need to go there just when his parents wished to see him? As if he had not been flirting with Lady Harriet all through the London season! After Addiscombe, Mrs. Buller explained, he had gone to Havre, poor boy, to be near the sea. Charles's health, his mother insisted, was very delicate. Then, just when they were sure of his visit, he had popped off to Lady Harriet's again.

Jane wished his mother would not take these disappointments so as a matter of course. Through this neglect of his parents, Charles was laying up a score of remorseful memories in future years. Had not her own experiences taught her as much?

But now he was coming! His mother had put the house into apple-pie order. His father had searched far and wide for a pointer dog for him to hunt with. Mr. Buller set out alone for Bury St. Edmunds: Charles always brought such a quantity of luggage, and a valet besides—there could be room for no one else to go along.

Mrs. Buller had put on her most becoming cap and gown in which to welcome her son. No Charles—only Mr. Buller got out of the carriage. Jane could see the tears in Mrs. Buller's eyes. Impulsively she flung her arms around her neck and kissed her. "Oh," said Mrs. Buller with a smile, "I am not disturbing myself—I am merely sorry that Mr. Buller had the long drive to no purpose."

They sat down to an unusually lavish dinner. "The fatted calf, you see, Mrs. Carlyle," remarked the old gentleman, "but *no* Charles!"

"My dear," said his wife gently, "I thought you had grown *philosophical* about Charles—as *I am?*"

That evening, Jane played three games of chess with Mr. Buller, instead of the usual single one. She would do what she could to help while away the disappointment. Late in the night, after reading in bed, Jane was just dozing off when a horse in the nearby paddock neighed with all its power. "The devil fly away with you!" muttered Jane. Then there was a rumbling in the darkness. "More thunder," Jane thought—there had been a heavy storm the day before. But next followed a great opening and banging of doors, and finally something in creaking boots entered the room adjoining hers. Charles, of course! He had arrived at last.

Next morning, Jane breakfasted with Mr. Buller before the prodigal came down. Though rain poured outside, all faces within had a look of sunshiny gladness. After the anxieties he had caused, Charles hardly deserved so unqualified a welcome! In a spirit of revolt against the extravagant homage he received from all people, especially women, Jane kept to her room that morning, and did not go below till summoned to dinner.

She was bound not to relent before his charm. He sensed her grumpy mood at once. They were standing together at the hall door, looking out into the dripping world of the garden.

"I will shoot a hollyhock!" Charles suddenly exclaimed. "Wait, Mrs. Carlyle, till I fetch my gun, I *must* shoot a hollyhock!"

Hesketh brought the weapon. Charles took careful aim; a thunderous report echoed through the house. In the distant bed a tall stalk nodded over at the middle, then hung there as though burying its head within its breast. Charles flung down his gun. Pulling a large knife from his pocket, he ran up to the shot plant and severed its neck at the wound. Then he sped back to the house to present the trophy, all dripping, to Jane. She exploded into uncontrollable laughter. The huntsman, with his alert cherub face, joined in. They were friends again at once. Mirth, honest mirth between comrades, was the very wine of life.

From the first day of Jane's visit, the Bullers had been insistent that Carlyle, too, should join them. But with Jeannie Welsh at Cheyne Row, he seemed contented where he was. In fact he was dilating rapturously on the excellent care he was receiving. "Little Jeannie comes down in the morning, in a kind of shawl dressing-gown, almost with the air of a little wife, to make coffee for me!" Oh, yes, Jane knew that seductive dressing gown! Teasingly she sent a letter to her cousin: "If there were a spark of jealousy in my disposition I would have taken out my seat in the next Bury coach immediately after reading that sentence, and returned in all haste to put a check to such dangerous illusions!" "I hope you will think of me a great deal," Jane wrote to her husband at the outset of her stay, "and be as good to me when I return as you were when I came away—I do not desire more of you."

Since he would not be going to Lady Harriet's—he had been asked there along with Charles but had declined—perhaps after all he could be induced to come to Troston. Jane tried him again. Presently she learned that he would arrive. Troston lay in Oliver Cromwell's district; he really ought to see it. He was thinking of taking a walking tour over that part of Suffolk—at Huntingdon, Oliver was born; at St. Ives he had farmed; the cathedral town of Ely had elected him to Parliament.

Jane was not too sure of the wisdom of these schemes for tramping all over England—more and more she was developing her tendency to baby her husband. But when he arrived, Mrs. Buller, like a prudent fairy godmother, equipped him with a horse to aid in his explorations. After a four days' absence, he returned one evening drenched to the skin by a thundershower but full of talk and vigor. He had seen enough, he exclaimed, to fill three octavo volumes.

A few days later, Carlyle and his wife came back to Chelsea. Jane had been away from home during five recuperative weeks. Her husband was convinced that she had prospered beyond all hope. The change marked her first reawakening to the sight of life since her mother's passing.

Chapter Twenty-Three

*J*ANE was still dubious about Oliver Cromwell. Judging from the splutter which her husband was making, the life of the Lord Protector was destined to be a particularly toilsome subject and Oliver himself a cantankerous old beast. Thomas, Jane explained to friends, was seeking inspiration from a human shin bone and some teeth dug up at Naseby battlefield. These were the gift of Edward Fitzgerald. Certainly Fitzgerald was a strangely peaceable, gentle, dreamy-spirited young man to be the donor of such gruesome trophies. The explanation was that his family owned the battlefield. When Thomas heard of Fitzgerald's knowledge of the district—he had himself not been able satisfactorily to locate the scene of the conflict—he begged him to establish the exact site by searching for the common grave where the soldiers had been buried as they fell, one hundred and ninety-seven years before.

Fitzgerald did not exactly enjoy his assignment. This skull-rummaging was a revolting business. Cromwell's new biographer, what's more, would doubtless make a mad book out of these civil wars. Edward had not liked the *French Revolution;* this new work promised to be just as violent. But he liked Carlyle though not his histories. And he promised to assist.

So he hired a farmer to begin the excavations. That night the man had reported the discovery of skeletons. Next morning Fitzgerald would himself go look. Meanwhile let them lie exposed under the full harvest moon after their long hiding. He thought with a shudder of that warm fourteenth of July when the battle was fought, and cavaliers and roundheads had plunged to earth pell-mell. Then the country people buried the corpses in a long ditch so shallow that the stench crept horribly through the soil and the putrid matter oozed over the ground for yards. During several years, according to legend, the cattle cropped the rich turf very close above the mound.

Thus Carlyle got his proof: an ancient bullet, the shin bone, and the teeth. He had been tremendously excited at Fitzgerald's discovery—the thought of the opening of that burial-heap blazed luridly in his imagination. There were the very jawbones that had been clenched together in deadly rage many generations ago! And now, Fitzgerald had reported, the local plowmen used the mold to fertilize their turnip fields. That, too, was part of history.

Ever since his gift, Fitzgerald was a welcome visitor at Cheyne Row. A shy man, he preferred to smoke a pipe alone with Carlyle rather than chat in the drawing room. Jane would watch them disappear, bearing their clay churchwardens—half a yard in length—and an ample jar of tobacco. Up they would go, through two stories of the house, into the little dressing room at the rear of Carlyle's bedroom.

It was just as well that Mrs. Carlyle could not listen to the heresy Fitzgerald sometimes preached. He was a man who loved green boughs and the country. In the spring, from Carlyle's window, the two could look below on several nursery gardens, the almond trees in them filled with blossoms. Beyond, bare walls of houses, and over these, roofs and chimneys, roofs and chimneys, with here and there a steeple—the whole of London crowned with smoky darkness like vapors in a dream. Then Fitzgerald would seek to persuade Carlyle to leave this sprawling city. At such moments Thomas looked wistful—but perhaps not wholly wistful. London had its inducements, too.

Since the days of the lectures, the news had spread even more widely that at No. 5 Cheyne Row, in the quite unfashionable suburb of Chelsea, lived a remarkable pair of human beings whom it was fascinating to know. Dickens, author now of *Pickwick, Oliver Twist, The Old Curiosity Shop,* and other books, came often. Jane liked to watch his alert, sharp face, that looked as if made of highly tempered steel. He was a man of indomitable cheerfulness—a type Jane and Thomas, despite their often darker outlook on the world, had a gift for attracting. His eyes, large, deep blue, and very keen, glanced under eyebrows which he manipulated as though acting in pantomime. His features had a quite remarkable mobility. He shuttled them about in an extraordinary manner as he talked. Dickens wore his hat tipped jauntily to one side. No man looked or acted less like a professional writer—a fact which Jane welcomed with relief. No man ever told a tale so drolly, nor, far more uncommon, relished another's story with equal heartiness. Carlyle had his favorite anecdote to tell. A solemn clergyman had been administering ghostly consolation to a dying man. When he finished, very successfully to his own mind, and was leaving the room of the supposedly rescued sinner, the parson was startled to hear him ejaculate: "Well, thank God, *Pickwick* will be out in ten days anyway!"

Thackeray, too, was a caller, though married now and burdened with heavy cares. His wife, after the birth of a third daughter, had failed completely in health, and—people said— was in gravest danger of permanent insanity. For a time Thackeray had sent the children to Paris with their grandparents. When they came back to London, Jane was assiduous in helping their father obtain a governess.

Old stand-bys and new, they thumped the brass knocker at No. 5 Cheyne Row. Of late years the ranks had been swelled by hitherto unknown admirers, many of them Americans sent by Emerson. Some of these were pleasant, some delightful, some Jane found insufferable bores. But however much she might make fun of these open-mouthed worshipers, she took a secret pride in the expansion of her husband's fame.

Lord Jeffrey, now a Judge in Edinburgh, dropped in at Cheyne Row whenever a vacation brought him to London. Year after year he came, unwilling to let Jane and her husband slip away. Anne Cook at first had been mystified by these appearances. She had introduced him as Lurcherfield till Jane explained his title. "But wath *is* a 'Looard' then?" she demanded, perplexed, "what diz't duih?"

Clever old man, mused Jane with affection—still full of his quick-witted talk, his sprightly, airy ways!

Why could not Jeffrey, thought Carlyle, grow serious as he grew older? Did he deem it proper, at his age, still to affect the same light manner?

Jeffrey was not always discreet in his greetings. But he was approaching seventy, Jane past forty; there could be no thought of nonsense. Still, it was sometimes most embarrassing! His years gave license to his demonstrativeness. Jane long remembered the time when she was entertaining a shy young foreigner and Jeffrey had burst in. Not only had he kissed her, one kiss after another, right on the lips, but when this display was over, he had seated himself on the sofa beside her, stroking her hair, patting her face, and fondling her hands, all the while exclaiming in the most tender tones, "my darling Jeannie! my sweet child! my dear Love! ! !" How explain to the youth that this was merely a sort of paternal greeting? After one highly significant look, the embarrassed visitor had shrunk behind a newspaper to cover his confusion. Jane could almost see his blushes through the sheet.

Mazzini, John Forster, Cavaignac—these, and many others, were old stand-bys. They had met another Forster, too, William Edward, a prosperous and able young Quaker of Rawdon near Leeds.

Jane would never openly have admitted it. Yet people acquainted with the gossip of London were remarking that many who came to sit in admiration at Mr. Carlyle's feet remained in devotion at his wife's. For most persons she had an extraordinary power of attraction. Not for all, of course. Some were shocked by what they considered to be her unfeminine, unwifelike presumption in entering into the conversation, especially when the topic was one supposedly beyond a woman's sphere. Was it not shameless thus to state her own views, at times even opposing those of her husband? But her warmest admirers could never get enough of her talk. Her understanding, her powers of sympathy, always present beneath her brilliant, often mischievous, sometimes wickedly sarcastic manner, increased their adulation. They regretted her tendency to let Carlyle do most of the talking when both were together in the drawing room. Dinner partners who sat beside her were usually first impressed by her gentleness of manner. Sometimes they never penetrated beyond that surface. More often, they discovered presently her humor; more rarely, they felt the barb of her sharp wit. To most, her caustic trait was a thing of rumor rather than an experienced reality. Untroubled, they enjoyed themselves under the spell of her entertaining conversation and quizzical bright ways. Carlyle was delighted with his wife's successes. At Craigenputtock he had foreseen these eventualities; now Jane's position was one of the things that reconciled him to London. The jealousy exhibited toward her by some of the women amused him, and he was pleased at the attentions she received from the men.

The claim for Mrs. Carlyle's genius was an odd, subterranean thing. Someone, like John Forster, would be heard to remark that she possessed a greatness rivaling her husband's. Someone else, like Charles Darwin, would admit no such honor for her. His elder brother, Erasmus, had long been faithful at her shrine, but not he. Charles had a cautious, painstaking mind. Jane bothered him. Before seeing her, he had heard so much about her. After the meeting he found himself in doubt. Was she quite ladylike, he wondered? It was high treason, he admitted, but he could not muster the admiration expected by his brother Erasmus.

The two Darwins, though they had traits in common, also had divergent characteristics and their lives had followed different paths. Ill health since his early childhood had doomed Erasmus to patient idleness. Though he had studied medicine, he never practiced, but his interests leaned more towards literature than science. He lived a solitary bachelor life in his simply furnished, somewhat ascetic London house on Queen Anne Street—its distinguishing feature the splendid library which it contained. There was nothing of the bookworm in his nature. He was a widely read, highly cultured gentleman with a certain superficial intolerance that added spice to his talk and set off his peculiar brand of humor. A kind of gay scorn characterized his manner, pathetic and appealing when one knew the man well and recognized the checks imposed on him by his bodily infirmities. Never really bitter, and the gentlest of men, he was capable of a sardonic turn which delighted the Carlyles. But his chief virtue, in Jane's eyes, was his chivalry and the sweetness and patience of his nature. He was the best friend she possessed in London—the likest thing to a brother she had ever known in the world.

There was about him a peculiar combination of liveliness and repose which was restful to a temperament like Jane's. Even his stutter was no real hindrance. "Don't you find it very inconvenient stammering, Dr. Darwin?" a busybody once inquired. "No, sir," Erasmus replied, "because I have time to

think before I speak, and don't ask impertinent questions."
Erasmus always thought before he spoke and what came out
was always worth considering.

Practically, he was very thoughtful of Jane. When she and
her husband left Cheyne Row during a summer, he guarded
their table silver for them in his house. His carriage was always
at Jane's disposal. She and Erasmus sallied forth on many a
shopping tour—no trivial help, since otherwise her sole reliance
lay on omnibuses. His little dinners in Queen Anne Street were
always in the best of taste, and he was himself a valued guest at
the small parties at Cheyne Row. In December of the year of
the Troston visit, she had given a Christmas feast for Erasmus
Darwin and Tennyson. Erasmus had come bearing a quite unexpected gift. He had heard Mazzini mention to Jane that she
should wear a shawl about the house. The result of the chance
remark was a handsome fluffy white scarf of lamb's wool.

That winter had brought no serious return of Jane's ill health.
It was fortunate for both, because Carlyle was having an immense tussle with Cromwell. Somehow, in spite of the bones
from Naseby, the book refused to get itself on paper. But after
several false starts, Thomas had at last worked himself into
the red-hot mental state necessary for composition and was again
scribbling furiously. Jane glanced over the litter of papers on
the desk. What on earth had this attack on the present day to
do with Oliver Cromwell? When she asked her husband to
explain, she learned to her utter amazement that the growing
manuscript was not Cromwell at all. No, Oliver was not even
begun. This was something applicable to the immediate hard
times; his indignant thoughts on the blindness of the governing class had burst through the gathering matrix of Cromwell
to demand expression.

But when the mysterious book came out, in the spring of
1843, Jane was ready to admit that it was worth the effort.
Past and Present was its title; a great book, she declared, cal-
culated to waken up the soul of England if England still possessed one. All London was buzzing about Carlyle's forthright
utterance. It was upsetting the complacency of Jane's more easy-
going friends and delighting her husband's admirers. The most
practical and satisfactory thing, they said, that he had yet

written. Very dangerous, insisted Milnes, if it were to be turned into the vernacular and generally read. Even so, it would, of course, be transformed into speeches and leading articles by the rising young progressives of the House, who would thus, without acknowledging their source, gain a reputation by expounding the Carlylean doctrine of the right to work at just wages—a right which challenged the validity of governmental *laissez faire*, requiring instead a forthright, energetic policy. They could emphasize or attack, according to their leanings, Carlyle's ripening belief that control by popular vote was largely unavailing; that what was needed was the commanding hand of a strong, just, authoritative leader.

During the rapid manufacture and detonation of this gunpowder *Past and Present*, Jane saw rather less than usual of her husband. But she had not lacked diversion. Perhaps one could scarcely call so intense a being as Geraldine Jewsbury a diversion. Jane had rarely lived through a more phenomenal experience than the thirty-three days of Miss Jewsbury's visit.

It had all come about through Geraldine's manuscript *Zoe*, an unfledged novel which the authoress had sent to Chelsea for Jane's criticism. Jane had laid the parcel aside on its arrival, since her husband had just finished his own book and wished her opinion on it. But when she presently got round to Geraldine's novel, she had something of a shock in store for her. This girl, obviously, was a far more profound and daring speculator than she had fancied. Not even George Sand could equal some of her best passages. But the manuscript was a hopeless jumble—an extraordinary mixture of sense and nonsense, of insight beyond the stars and blindness before the very tip of Geraldine's nose. *Zoe*, in its present form, Jane decided, should never be published—decency forbade! Not decency in the common meaning of the word—though there were lapses even in that department. The trouble lay in the fact that the hero's career was made to hinge on the victory of modern skepticism over conventional belief. The great unthinking public would be scandalized by such a dénouement. She could not permit this young woman to court destruction by thus exposing herself without reserve as though living in a world in which the fall of Adam had never taken place. So she wrote a careful letter stating her objections. The result was a temperamental outburst from the aggrieved author. This was soon followed, however, by a penitent apology. Jane read to her husband a few sentences of this reply—Carlyle had not greatly deviated from his early opinion that Geraldine, in spite of all, was a rather good soul.

"You should ask her to come up here for a little while," he remarked, "it might be of great use to her!"

Jane was so taken aback at such a proposition—when her husband was busy with proofs—that she stared at him in amazed silence.

"Why," said he, "you seem *doubtful* about it—she is very easy to do with, is she not? and you like her company?"

"Oh, as to the *doing with*, I have no misgivings about *that*, but . . ."

"But what?"

"Why, I am afraid that having her beside me from morning till night would be dreadfully wearing!"

"You had Jeannie beside you from morning to night—what would be the difference?"

"Jeannie! Jeannie was not always in a state of emotion; dropping hot tears on my hands, and watching me and fussing me as Geraldine does!"

"Oh, as you like! Only I think it would be a kindness to the *poor lonely girl*—and that her company might be useful to yourself when you have so little of mine!"

Jane lay awake that night trying to decide. A little of Geraldine, of course, would be very enlivening. But much of her? Nothing could be worse! Yet Carlyle *was* very exclusive because of the pressure he was under, and the scheme *was* of his suggesting. Yes—but then Geraldine had within her a complex spirit of intrigue. Jane had observed that failing on earlier occasions. Might she not prove to be a somewhat perilous commodity for a married pair to invite into their home? Not that she could seduce Carlyle's affections—Jane told herself she was not the least bit jealous of him, despite his feminine admirers; he had far too deep a habit of preference for her over all other women—yet Geraldine might cause mischief in other ways.

After weighing the pros and cons, Jane finally wrote bidding her come. A perfectly ecstatic acceptance by return post was the answer. Jane felt somewhat provoked with herself for not sharing Geraldine's transports. The best she could do was to look forward to the visit with a certain dubiousness. She had been careful not to mention that the invitation originated with Carlyle. If Geraldine, with her romantic nature, were to hear of that, there could be no foretelling the consequences!

Geraldine, arriving on the dot, began at once to gush from her bottomless well-springs. At first Jane attempted rational talk. Hopeless! Geraldine's notion of dialogue made her conversation so artificial that Jeannie felt as though in a play.

The sole amusing feature of Geraldine's visit was to watch her casting nets for the men. Not one was let slip past—her snares fell alike on the married and unmarried. But Jane noted with malicious glee that she made no slightest execution. Indeed, some of her intended victims, such as Mazzini and Erasmus Darwin, manifested a positive aversion. Thomas she hardly saw at all. Since Geraldine's arrival, he had taken to sitting upstairs in the evenings as well as during the day. If Miss Gooseberry— Carlyle's name for her—continued to linger, Jane feared that she herself would lose her husband's company save at mealtime. Yet nothing, not even incivility, had power to drive her from the house. Carlyle's disillusionment was rapid and complete. "That girl is an incurable fool!" he remarked. "It is a mercy for her she is so ill looking!"

Geraldine had tried every measure on Carlyle, from the most unctuous flattery to the device of stretching herself on the hearth rug at his feet and pretending to fall languorously asleep. Afterwards Thomas confided to Jane that the one thought which had crossed his mind was to notice how remarkably like an old snap-wife she had looked, sprawled out in this fashion.

At the end of five mortal weeks, Geraldine departed. An invitation for another visit lured her away. That evening, Carlyle returned to the parlor. "Oh, my dear," he said to Jane, "what a blessing it is to be able to sit here in peace without having that dreadful young woman *gazing* at me!"

Jane felt a little ashamed of herself for having treated her guest somewhat unkindly. She was amazed to receive, soon after Geraldine's departure, a note from her which was veritably dripping with good will. For months, with scarcely a reply by way of encouragement, these letters continued—sometimes coming twice or thrice a week. Could this absurd affection be really genuine? Jane capitulated. A second time she was forced round to the opinion that Geraldine was an amazing clever young woman. She even resumed her help with *Zoe*. Greatest concession of all, she took the pains to seek out a publisher for it. Carlyle had prophesied the attempt would be hopeless, yet the first house to which Jane offered the novel had accepted it. Jane was surprised at her luck and Geraldine's. Here she had at once obtained a contract for half profits, while her husband's *Sartor* had to be hawked through the trade for years before it could so much as be printed free of cost to the author.

Negotiations with the publisher and alterations in the manuscript, Jane soon discovered, took up a large part of her time. She might just as well have written the book herself and had something to show for her trouble.

While her husband was occupied with *Past and Present*, he was of course far too busy to take part in outside engagements. A complimentary ticket of admission—"one gentleman and one lady"—had been left at the door for a public lecture on a topic of lively current interest: the iniquitous corn laws that forbade importation of grain to England unless the cost of the domestic product mounted to starvation prices. Much to Jane's amazement, Carlyle invited her to go. But after she accepted, he hesitated, as though he had forgotten something.

"Very well," he remarked, "but *I* cannot go with you—I promised to go to Lady Harriet tomorrow evening. Can you get any other man?" Jane was silent for a moment, thinking. She would have liked to suggest Mazzini, but recently her husband had shown a tendency to froth at mention of his name—Mazzini's pervasive activities with his revolutionary movement were deep in his disfavor. Thomas himself resolved the difficulty by suggesting Mazzini as an escort. He showed Lady Harriet's letter to Jane—it was addressed from the Barings' town house. She was ill, Lady Harriet wrote, and allowed to go nowhere in the evenings—to do nothing save talk. Would not Mr. Carlyle come to help her wile away an evening? There was nobody—really nobody in the world—she liked so well to speak with as himself.

Surely a seductive little note, thought Jane. Yet Carlyle protested that he regretted the promise he had made. Of course it was an act of charity demanded of him. But what a shame it should conflict with the lecture!

A very innocent, naïve man, her husband.

Jane had never met Lady Harriet; never so much as laid eyes on her. But she was frequently enough reminded of her existence. Had not Lady Harriet been the chief cause for Charles Buller's delaying his visit to his family? Had she not showered kindnesses on Mill till Mrs. Taylor had yanked the poor young man away from the sphere of her Ladyship's influence? These were just individual soldiers in the imposing troop of Lady Harriet's admirers. When a clever, striking, reputedly haughty woman like Lady Harriet began to appeal to the charity and piety of a simple man like her husband, Jane felt sure, the appeal had not the ghost of a chance of failure. Lady Harriet had obviously not forgotten the Cheyne Row address, as Carlyle feared she might after his refusal of her summer invitation to Addiscombe. There had been several winning little communications since that time, in fact regular flights of charming letters, Jane observed with a shrug. Carlyle, indeed, had quite ceased to excuse himself with Lady Harriet on the score of being busy. He was calling, now, regularly once a week, and there were excursions on Sundays to the Barings' Addiscombe retreat outside the city.

Jane told herself that she was really pleased to have Thomas find a house in London to which he enjoyed going. Geraldine Jewsbury, during her visit, had of course professed to be scandalized. Jane could see this response grew from simple envy —she had been chagrined because she could not win similar attention from Carlyle. As for her own feelings, Jane believed that she could not possibly be jealous.

Yet the topic of Lady Harriet fascinated her; she could not get Lady Harriet out of her mind. "You better see a little into the thing with your own eyes," remarked Mrs. Buller. So she arranged to have Jane call for tea on the same date that Lady Harriet was to come.

Jane was surprised by what she found there. Lady Harriet was immensely imposing—a regular winged-victory of a woman! Beside her, Jane felt like a little child. With her plain, stoutish face, rather shapeless nose, and broad almost masculine forehead, she might easily have been one of the ugliest women living. Instead, Jane decided, because of her cordiality of expression and the alertness of her face, she would almost be called beautiful. Where was that hauteur which people spoke about? Jane could discover no slightest trace of it. Meeting her thus informally, who could ever guess that she came from one of the proudest strains of the hereditary aristocracy—the eldest daughter of the sixth Earl of Sandwich? Her marriage with the immensely rich, though less blue-blooded house of Baring, had roused the envy of many Peeresses wedded to better pedigreed but far less wealthy husbands. This woman, by resources and position, could gain anything she might wish. But Jane, at this first meeting, perceived no dictatorial manner about her—only a certain brusquerie which, far from being offensive, contributed to one's interest: an outspokenness rising not from pride but from exuberance of spirits and the absence of affectation. Unquestionably she was brilliant: the wittiest woman, Jane admitted, that she had ever met. No wonder Carlyle enjoyed her company! Of course she had many aristocratic prejudices that rather grated if one possessed democratic leanings. How in the world had Carlyle managed to swallow this bias whole, without gagging?

A very lovable spoilt child of fortune; really, almost a first-rate woman. A little adversity perhaps—even a good whipping from her wealthy husband—might make her perfect. But as to adversity, how could one encounter that when married to a Bank? And as for Lady Harriet's husband, Jane understood him to be the kindliest, most self-effacing of men.

"Something in her like a Heathen Goddess," Jane exclaimed to Carlyle on her return. He readily agreed.

Yet was her husband's friend a coquette? Jane could not make up her mind on that question. Before meeting her, she had believed so. Now she was not sure.

And what had the noble Lady thought of her, she wondered? During the afternoon she had noticed Lady Harriet's eyes stealing long and searching glances in her direction. The next letter Thomas received—he showed it to her at once—gave Jane at least a clue. "I meditate paying my respects to Mrs. Carlyle—so soon as I am again making visits—she is a *reality* whom you have hitherto *quite suppressed*."

Chapter Twenty=Four

JANE was having her portrait painted. Not for her own sake, but for a refugee's. An Italian, his name was Spiridione Gambardella. He had been introduced at Chelsea by a letter from Emerson. Fleeing Italy, he had gone first to America in the hope of making a living as a painter but, finding the new world blind to his art, had come to England to try his luck. With his tropical manner and strange appearance—a perfect image of the god Pan save for absence of horns and goat's feet—he was an excellent if unconscious court jester for Cheyne Row.

His first portrait was of Thomas—a commission ordered by the American sponsor—but it proved to be a failure. A grotesque caricature, it gave not the slightest hint of Carlyle's true personality. The picture could be improved, the artist insisted. For several days he would admit no one to his studio to see it. At last Jeannie was summoned to make an inspection. Without a word—an unusual display of restraint—he set the portrait before her. Just at the meeting of nose and brow, Gambardella, for some reason of his own, had put a small triangular patch of light. This gave the victim the appearance of smelling something to which asafetida was as frankincense and myrrh. For a second Jane looked at the thing with what gravity she could muster. Then she turned to glance at the painter. Both exploded into laughter.

Carlyle had absolutely no knack for sitting, explained the artist. "But we must not tell him so, it would vex him, and the poor man has done the best he could! Just let it pass for *my* want of talent, and I will do him a picture of *you* to make up to him for his lost time!"

So Jane had found herself becoming a portrait. Gambardella was a relentless worker, and insisted on sittings many hours in length. But though he tortured his subjects, he carefully saw

to their wants. When he detained Jane past her hour for dining, the artist produced a large paper bag full of rusks, a string
of Italian figs in the shape of a hoop, and drinks in infinite
variety: Guiness's porter, Scotch ale, Indian ale, cider, and a
potion with a quite incomprehensible Italian name.

Through the backing of the Carlyles and others, Gambardella was rapidly becoming something of a fashionable artist.
He had enlarged his quarters, and was even planning to engage
servants of his own rather than relying on those of his landlady. He had been laughed at by Lady Morgan, he explained,
for having his door opened by a maid with a baby in her arms.
More style was due a society painter; he must have a man
servant, and an attractive, useful girl. "The lodging house
gu-ls," he declared, "were vile creatures who left finger marks
on everything." This gu-l, he added, should wash his brushes,
mend his linens and even make costumes for his models—"out
of very rich *stoffs!*" Most important of all, the gu-l must have
a "beautiful fo-m" so that she could serve him as a model
whenever he needed one.

How, inquired Jane, was this paragon among gu-ls to be obtained? Oh, said Gambardella airily, he had inserted an advertisement for such a creature in the *Times*. Jane looked incredulously at his face. Could he not see what his rash course
would lead him into? She asked to be shown the advertisement.
Gambardella, proud of its English wording, handed over what
he had written: "Wanted a very genteel girl to do *very genteel
work*—not under fifteen nor exceeding eighteen years of age."

Next day Jane returned to the studio for her sitting. Her
knock brought Gambardella himself to the door. His hair was
rumpled; his eyes glaring; a wild look of perplexity and anger
made his face more comical than ever. He was far too agitated
to explain what had been happening, though Jane at once
guessed the trouble. Presently his sputterings grew more coherent. Since eight that morning, gu-ls had been trooping to
the door. They had come at first in threes and fours, but by
nine, he declared, a troupe of fifty or more had rushed up to
demand admission. The people of the house were furious, and
had presently declined to answer the door, forcing him to attend to it himself. As Jane, trying hard to look sympathetic,

listened to this recital of woes, further applicants kept interrupting. Three to four hundred women, he averred during lulls, had already called that day. Most had been creatures of detestable ugliness, with not a single "beautiful fo-m" in the lot —"vile wretches calling themselves *eighteen*, who were *thirty*, if they were a day!" He had received numerous letters from the country from women eager for the place, yet not a single writer had made the least inquiry as to the nature of the "very genteel work."

For the present, Jane had to abandon Gambardella to his fate. There was nothing else to do. With so many distractions, painting was out of the question.

Next afternoon she found the stream of applicants had abated. A mere twenty showed up during her sitting. Somehow Gambardella had placated his landlady—she had consented to usher them one by one into the room. Of those Jane saw, most were certainly unattractive enough. But three, at least, were very pretty, though all quite definitely revealed their trade. One had pretended hesitation at sitting as a model, but when Gambardella gravely proposed interviewing her parents on the subject, she hastily replied that they were both ill in bed and not to be seen. The last of the three was really pitiable—a gentle, innocent-looking child, not more than sixteen, brought by a witch-faced she-devil like a sheep to the slaughter. Gambardella dismissed the procuress, and the pair went off to seek a less scrupulous customer.

That night Erasmus Darwin called at Cheyne Row. He had got wind of the artist's predicament. "Have you found Gambardella a mistress yet?" he inquired.

Jane helped the unfortunate victim of the English language to concoct a more explicit advertisement. Till this flood of fallen women could be turned away, there would be no finishing the portrait.

Gambardella was a temperamental painter. He gave orders to the girl whom Jane's efforts at last secured—respectable as the Archbishop of Canterbury though better than he in "fo-m" —that under no circumstances was he to be disturbed. To make doubly sure, he locked the studio door. Presently there was a knock. A gentleman below, the girl announced timidly, a Mr.

Sterling, who had insisted that his name be sent up though she had told him nobody was at home. Thunderer Whirlwind Edward, of course! Ever since he had known her portrait was being painted, he had been bursting with curiosity to see it, and now had come puffing all the way to Michael Place. The old fool had long been nagging her for a picture of herself. He was a dear silly old thing, but so impetuous!

Gambardella, angry at having his *fiat* disobeyed, repeated his injunction that he would see no one. The girl delivered the message, but soon returned, reporting that the caller would not depart. Should she show him up? "No!" roared Gambardella, thoroughly aroused. "No! I repeat to you, stupid woman as you are—I am not at home!"

A pause.

Then the maid's frightened voice crept again through the bolted door. It was Mrs. Carlyle, not Signor Gambardella, whom Mr. Sterling wished to see for a few minutes, she explained.

"Are you mad?" screamed the artist, perfectly furious now. "Go back, you vile woman, and repeat that I am not at home!"

To Jane's dismay, Sterling, who really should have known better, began to ascend the stairs.

The Italian looked as though ready to commit murder. Naturally he regarded his studio as the residence of a private gentleman, and here was this barbaric Englishman treating the place as though it were a public shop. He opened the door to face the intruder.

"I wish to see Mrs. Carlyle," said the old warrior in a tone of forced politeness.

"I am engaged, Sir. I am painting—I desired my servant to tell you I was not at home!"

"Sir, it is Mrs. Carlyle that I wish to see!"

"Sir, I tell you I am painting—I am engaged—I have a sitter!"

Bang went the door in Sterling's face. Silence; then a heavy tread clumping down the stair.

Gambardella snatched up his brushes and set furiously to work. No go; his hand still shook with rage. He tried again—in vain. He laid down his palette and took a pinch of snuff. Then he glanced at Jane. Her expression was too much for him.

His anger, like a sudden tropical storm, vanished away as both burst into laughter.

When the portrait was ready for its finishing touches, the artist drew off to survey what he had accomplished. Then with ineffable selfcomplacency he remarked, "It looks too young! I must put in some wrinkles!" As for Jane, when she gazed at this smirking, gazelle-eyed likeness of herself, there was only one way she could describe it. It had the look, she declared, of an improper female doing a St. Anthony's ecstasy.

Gambardella's row with Sterling would surely alienate the old man, Jane feared. But she did not reckon on the degree of his dependence on her. She was distinctly relieved when he reappeared at Chelsea quite as though nothing unusual had happened.

Summer and winter, his carriage, like Erasmus Darwin's, was at her service. A true newspaper man, old Sterling knew all the best places in the town to stop at for refreshments. Together he and Jeannie would halt at Grange's, during a shopping tour, for some cake or cherry bounce. Sometimes it was rather difficult to curb his extravagance. He insisted once on pausing at Howell & James's, London's exclusive fashion shop, to buy her a couple of guinea pocket handkerchiefs. The ownership of these quite flabbergasted Jane, whose frugal dress allowance permitted no such luxury.

Old Sterling dropped in as often at her house as at his favorite club and made himself as much at home. One forenoon he had arrived with a lamentable ·account of his wife's illness. Jane felt very sorry for him, and tried to ease his grief. Presently, in the midst of his story, the old gentleman fell silent. She turned to look at him. His features were pinched together, his mouth open—he was fast asleep. After a quarter hour or so, he started up.

"Gracious God, have I been dreaming?" he exclaimed.

"You know best," remarked his hostess, "I only know that you have been asleep."

The culprit was profuse in his apologies.

If more encounters could pass thus tranquilly, it might be easier to keep the peace. Sterling could be brutally insolent when he lost command of himself. Without the least provo-

cation, during a call, he fell afoul of Carlyle's *Past and Present*.
Jane knew perfectly well that he had not even read the book.
Yet there he stood, uttering the most monstrous impertinences
about it! She made a spirited rebuttal, then dismissed the critic
with the remark that she would not receive him in her house
till he had learned better manners. Two days later his carriage
was again rolling down the street. Old Sterling drew in his
horse a few doors away, and came on foot to the portal. Though
the maid begged him to come in and rest himself, he would
not do so. Instead he handed in a letter expressing the most
abject contrition. And as soon as he had gained Jane's forgive-
ness, he became more of a fixture than ever.

She rather wished that he would be less histrionic. John
Sterling had suffered another hemorrhage of the lungs. The
Carlyles had long been seriously worried over him. His pil-
grimages to the continent were proving of little avail. And in
England, he never showed the least discretion, doing the mad-
dest things. This time he had prostrated himself by lifting
tables to spare his servants trouble. For two days his condition
had fluttered between life and death. In order not to agitate
his mother, whose state—her heart was failing—required the
utmost tranquillity, only his father was to be told of John's
latest attack. The Carlyles had been asked to break the news to
him. Jane was prepared to be very sympathetic with the old
man. But his theatrical fuss was almost too much for her.

"No!" he exclaimed, clapping his hand, as he supposed, to
his breast, though it rested far closer to his stomach. "This heart
must not break yet! I cannot afford to sink under my griefs!—
I have five orphans depending on me."

Jane stared at him with dry-eyed disapproval. "Bless me!"
she exclaimed. "You had better see the end of it—they are not
orphans yet!" Finding that he meant to see his son at Fal-
mouth, she strongly advised him not to go. The thought of that
apoplectic bull in a sickroom was something to be shuddered at.

"Do keep yourself quiet if you can," Jane urged. "It were
the greatest kindness you can show."

And for this, more in the nature of a reproof than a comfort, he had called her his "Angel of Consolation!"

John grew better. It was Mrs. Edward Sterling who presently died. Jane had been called by the sick woman to say farewell, but each time she went she found Mrs. Sterling delirious or unconscious. She hated to see her thus—a horrible last remembrance. On the evening of the day that Mrs. Sterling died, Jane walked back from the house with Anthony, the oldest son. Allan Cunningham, a close friend, was also with them. Both men tried to speak of inconsequential things. How people tortured themselves, mused Jane. Surely manhood did not require that one should make conversation about the effect of St. Luke's steeple against the blue sky when one's heart was full of death.

Jane had not yet seen old Edward, but she could imagine the state he would be in. So she went next day to see if she could be of help. Poor old fellow, he cried with his head on her shoulder like a deserted child.

She did not at once revisit the house, thinking it better to stay away till after the funeral. She was surprised, next day, when her husband called upstairs to her: "My Dear, here is old Sterling been to seek you, *roaring and greeting!* You must go away in the carriage with him somewhere and keep him quiet."

To be thus bottled up beside him, in his small barouche, he weeping all the while as they drove through the streets, was an ordeal. Dry-nursing this big obstreperous infant of an old man had its drawbacks. Yet how could one withhold comfort and sympathy? But when Sterling's visits became a daily occurrence, Jane began to wonder.

"You will see that in a few weeks he will be back to his Carlton Club and all his old haunts," his son Anthony remarked, "and the past will be for him as if it had never been." At first Jane was scarcely willing to listen to this heartless, realistic comment. Presently she was forced to concede its truth. There could be no doubt of it: he was stretching out his grief in order to exploit her compassion. Certainly it was gaining him kinder treatment than he might otherwise receive! In what was supposed to be the very depths of his despair, he had asked her to go away with him to the Isle of Wight. Jane had not at once said no, in her simplicity. But the last drive together gave her a brand new set of thoughts on the matter.

One day the Thunderer came to the house in great excite-

ment. He seemed positively bursting with pride; he had just
composed his wife's epitaph. The fire of the creative spirit
glowed in his eye, and this was the result:

"For thee no gaudy, monumental shrine;
Hester, a Husband's riven Heart be thine!"

Chapter Twenty=Five

*J*ANE had practically ceased making inquiries concerning the state of Oliver Cromwell's health. Since the publication of *Past and Present,* her husband was floating on a sea of literary doldrums, interrupted from time to time by violent contrary winds and heat which, on subsiding, left Thomas and Oliver in exactly the same positions as before. What Carlyle needed was another rest, but as usual the problem of when and where to go delayed his departure. His objections to city life had beaten so long on Jeannie's ears that she had reached a point almost of indifference as to whether they lingered there or not. Whereupon Thomas, inexplicably, developed an attachment for No. 5 Cheyne Row and spoke in terms of procuring a life-time rental. The solution of the whole problem, he declared, lay in providing a decent room to work in. Why not a good-sized study at the back of the garden? The drawing room, too, could be made more adequate. Why not throw the upstairs sitting room and Jane's bedroom into one sizable chamber? Should that be done, they could even have a soirée now and then.

Jane looked at her husband in genuine alarm. Was he ill, to talk thus wildly about soirées—he who had raised his arms in horror at her single attempt in that direction? Soirées every fortnight, and with but one maid servant? Besides, where should she sleep if her bedroom were gobbled up to provide sufficient place for the realization of these grand ideas? Jane was thankful when Carlyle at last made up his mind to leave for Wales and Scotland. "I hope that you'll go somewhere during my absence," he remarked. She must not stay in London all the summer. Why not accept Edward Sterling's invitation to the Isle of Wight? Or did she not wish to go again to Troston? But then the house and its problems entered his head and he agreed that someone should remain there to see to the alterations.

According to final plans, Jane's bedroom was to be spared. But she herself had determined on a cleansing which would put to shame even the efforts of Hercules with the Augean stables. When Jane made up her mind to clean house, she plunged in with appalling zest. These renovations, when of her own devising, were creative work to Jeannie, and, like creative work, were carried out with consecrated passion. Long since, Carlyle had learned the wisdom of moving out from under when his wife was bent on raising one of her earthquakes. Even Helen, accustomed to these bursts of energy, could be amazed. "No use stopping Missus if she had anything on her mind. She was an example! Was there anywhere another lady that could stuff chair-cushions, and do anything that was needed, and be a lady too!" In the tumult of an earthquake, Helen was invaluable. Her remarks mitigated the rigors of the most strenuous day. "Take care, that ane's the Maister's *Sartor Resart!*" she would say, taking down a book from the shelves for dusting and handing it to Jane, "a capital thing it is,—just *noble* in *my* opinion!"

Before the cataclysm began, Jeannie, thoughtful of her neighbors, did all she could to placate No. 4 Cheyne Row, to her left, and No. 6, on the right, by sending messages of apology for the hubbub she was about to be raising. Then, at six in the morning, her genii appeared—a painter, two carpenters, a paperhanger, and three nondescript apprentice lads. Their entrance was Jane's signal for jumping out of bed. She began her day with a shower bath—a practice indulged in sometimes even in midwinter. Nothing like a shower to freshen one for the noise and dust and strain of the undertaking! The contrivance for it —a perforated tank—would sometimes fail to work, no matter how hard Jeannie tugged at the chain. But in such emergencies, Helen was always ready to assist by emptying over her mistress a pitcherful of cold water.

By the time Jane was dressed, the workmen would be ready to start. Then Jane took charge at once—suggesting methods of procedure and keeping a sharp eye open for slovenly labor. In the bedrooms, the paint needed scrubbing and the ceilings must be treated to fresh whitewash. All the carpets required to be beaten. The upstairs drawing room was to be entirely repapered. In the dining room and back room, there was to be intensive cleaning, though the old paper must be made to do after a renovating process carried on by diligently scrubbing the walls with crumbled bread. The apprentices were set to work pumicing every floor. One lad consoled himself at his task by lugubrious singing, but like his work, his song was never ending. He could just manage a bar or so of "Evelyn's Bower," then the air would disintegrate into a jumble of sharps and flats, to vanish quite away at last. Each time it died, the boy would try again, always with like results. When this music became intolerable, Jane took issue with the lad. But her approach was far too gentle, and merely increased the nuisance. He had lately been repeating over and over the first measures of "Love's Young Dream."

"How happy you must feel," Jane began, "that you can sing through that horrible noise you are making."

"Yes, thank you, ma'am, it sounds pleasant to sing at one's work, doesn't it ma'am?"

"Oh, very pleasant; but it would be still pleasanter for me, at least, if you would sing a song from beginning to end, instead of bits here and there."

"Thank you, ma'am, I'll try!" And alas, he did.

Because of the smell of paint (old Sterling had prophesied it would be the death of her) nights were something of a problem. One could not close the windows. The setting was a paradise for thieves, but Jane refused to worry. Far better to adopt Erasmus Darwin's principle and lay the silver on the lobby table to make it easy for robbers and avoid personal molestation than to turn one's house into an armed camp. Jane did however take one precaution. Beside her pillow she laid a policeman's rattle. With that, if there were need, she could unloose the very devil of a noise. And under her mattress she hid the sharp Italian dagger which Mazzini had given her.

Though Jane could muster the energy of an Amazon, she was far too good a general to dissipate her strength in the routine of a common soldier, especially in so long a siege. With her own hands she erected in the garden a kind of gypsy-tent, constructed of long poles, clothes lines, and an old brown carpet. Under this contraption she placed an arm chair, and there she sat with a small round table beside her laden with writing and sewing materials. Of course this odd-looking structure roused infinite curiosity among the neighbors, who kept peering down

at it. Jane amused herself composing a little speech with which
she might address them. "Ladies and gentlemen," she would
say, "I am not here to enter my individual protest against the
progress of civilization! nor yet to mock you with an Arcadian
felicity which you have neither the taste nor the ingenuity to
make your own! but simply to enjoy Nature according to my
ability, and to get out of the smell of new paint."

She was sometimes rather provoked by the solicitude of her
women friends, who asked her how she got along, through such
upheavals, without a man. She could manage very well, thank
you! And if she wanted men for company, she had no lack of
such. Her special group of male attendants never failed her.
Her Sunday morning's congregation, she called them, from
their habit of turning up on that day. They would find her
seated by her stocking-basket, diligently mending the goodman's hose. Jane was at her best in a small group, especially
when her husband was not there to dominate the conversation.
Her knack in spinning tales from the little occurrences of daily
life delighted this audience—she could tell a yarn about a broom-
handle and make it entertaining. And few were her equals in
hitting off a character. Though they hardly realized what was
happening to them, she pumped her acquaintances to their very
depths on matters biographical and autobiographical, and thus
gained for her use the private history of half of London. She
took a mischievous delight in treading on the toes of the conventional proprieties, and could say the most audacious things
with a look of demure unconsciousness. She was a naughty
woman, said some persons. "Spirit of soot," or "Creosote," Carlyle laughingly named her. Yet because they felt her to be
sincere, her band of admirers—the Sterlings, John Forster,
Dickens, Mazzini, and all the rest—rallied to her defense on
any imputation that she possessed too sharp a tongue. Most of
them had reason to be grateful for her tenderness of heart,
and had experienced her willingness to be of assistance in time
of need or illness. She was also mistress of the art of dealing
out little flatteries. She never was extravagant or indiscriminat-
ing in her use of this elixir so unconsciously craved by men. Her
most telling employment of it was made with what seemed to
be a happy inadvertence. She could prick conceit with the deftest

of needles, then mend the wound again if the victim deserved healing. Keen observers were often struck by her powers of apt quotation. She could fit into the texture of her conversation a scarcely perceptible allusion from her reading, or perhaps a deliberate, amusing misquotation from Dante or Milton right down to Dickens's latest—suitable phrases were easily and naturally at her command to spice her speech. What interested and amused Jane, and what she liked to talk about, was the passing show of life—its humor, and sometimes, its tragedy.

During earthquakes, her claque was especially faithful. Its members would seek her out in the whitewash-spattered house or find her resting in the garden. "You look as if you needed to go to Gunter's and have an ice!" Erasmus Darwin would remark and spirit her off. Or they would bring new friends, and these she welcomed even though the furniture was all huddled into a corner of the room and the whole house in a mess. One stand-by, John Robertson, a member of the editorial staff of the *Westminster Review*, thus brought young David Masson—a fellow Scot who edited an Aberdeen newspaper. Masson had come up to town to view the Lions. Robertson at once placed Jane on the list of those deserving inspection.

Masson saw before him a fragile little lady resting for the moment on the sofa. Curiously he examined that drawn, pale countenance framed by its black hair smoothed on either side of the forehead. Mrs. Carlyle's eyes, soft and lustrous, were of a haunting gypsy darkness. He was puzzled by that face. What did it remind him of? There was a strange resemblance to something he had lately seen. Presently it flashed upon him— Voltaire! a distinct likeness to the portraits of the young Voltaire! And the brilliance of her style intensified the illusion.

As the two men left, Mrs. Carlyle apologized for the absence of her husband. Masson must surely be disappointed at not seeing him. "Eh! what a real shame in ye to say *that!*" the young man exclaimed, pumping her hand up and down till Jane winced. If ever she came to Aberdeen, he told her, he'd assemble a crowd to welcome her in the marketplace and they'd give her a grand cheer! Jane was amused by his fervor. But she enjoyed the compliment.

During the summer of her major earthquake, Father

Mathew, American evangelist, was preaching to the lost wretches of the slums of London. John Robertson, knowing of Jane's interest, took her one afternoon to hear him. At five they rumbled off by omnibus to Mile End, Whitechapel, where, on a large piece of waste land near a Catholic cemetery, Father Mathew was to speak. Jane had never seen a religious meeting without its fringe of scoffers—but here there were no scoffers. The crowd, massed before the high, narrow, improvised platform, stood—thousands strong—in hushed, respectful silence. Steps led up at the front of the scaffolding, but the press there was so dense that Jane and her escort had to approach from behind if they were to get near enough to deliver the letter of introduction they had brought. Attracting a policeman's eye, Robertson handed in the note which was in turn passed on to Father Mathew.

While another speaker was addressing the throng, the evangelist came to the rear of the platform and glanced down to where Jane was standing. How good, how simple and sure was his expression! All her suppressed fervor, all her doubts and puzzlement rose chokingly within her. More than anything in the world, she wished to draw strength and reassurance from that benign countenance. The day before she had been joking and laughing, wearing the mask she could so well assume. Now she was melting and tremulous. Father Mathew reached down a hand to her. Instead of letting go after clasping it, Jane gripped it tighter. A bit of rope, dangling like a festoon from the platform, caught her notice. Using it to raise herself by, Jane managed to fling her body up on the platform to be near the evangelist. He made her take a chair on the scaffolding where she watched him administer the pledge. A hundred or so unfortunates came up. Those faces, Jane knew, would haunt her throughout her life. Such concentrated wretchedness she had never before seen, though her own quiet charities in Chelsea had brought her in close touch with misery. And in Father Mathew's expression, she thought, the mercy of Heaven itself was laid bare.

She was a very silent companion for Robertson on the journey home. That night she could not sleep. The pale countenances she had seen hovered before her eyes—and Father Mathew's smile. Next morning, from her deepest feelings, she wrote the evangelist a letter, and with it she sent a copy of her husband's *Past and Present*. He, too, this husband of hers, was a man of compassion who knew the struggles, the despairs of the poor; who sought to awake the conscience of the governing classes to their obligations! Like Father Mathew, fame and reputation meant nothing to him. He composed his books from a deep and active sense of duty, as a man would perform an arduous good action. Critics might call him misanthropical; yet surely no man was less so! Beneath his rough surface lay an inner, painful sensitiveness. He wrote because of his passionate concern for his fellow man, though the words were often despairing and the thought clothed in bitterness. His grim face, when it relaxed into a smile, had Father Mathew's kindness. If he walked the world like a soul in torment, his response to life could be explained by his extreme susceptibility to suffering and to wrong.

By mid-August, the house was beginning to recover from its earthquake. All summer Jane had fended off her husband's return—he could never stand the confusion. Even she, though she liked to watch results, had been sometimes aghast at the mess of noise, dirt, and wild dismay. What thin-skinned people they were, Jane mused—she and her husband—to have their lot thus cast together in a bruising world! With Thomas away, she could see him more objectively, unhampered by the fuss he stirred up over his books. He had remembered her birthday with a letter and gifts, and she replied with a dozen kisses as though she were still a romantic girl. He had visited her pensioners at Thornhill —Old Mary, and Margaret Hiddlestone, formerly her mother's charges. How thoughtful he could be! She would welcome him back to a fresh new house and a renovated study. All these operations, furthermore, had been carried out at minimum expense. To save cash, she had herself done some of the glazing and painting. And to secure possession of these improvements over a longer term than the usual short lease, she had gone to old Morgan, the lawyer who controlled the property, and asked for a five-year rental. Her husband was out of town, she explained, and could not come himself. "Better as it is," said the agent, glancing at Jane in her trim muslin gown and silk bonnet, "do you think I would have written to your husband's dictation as I have done to yours?"

Jane looked with pride at her results. What could give greater comfort than redecorated, cheery rooms? Of course, there were some finishing strokes still to be done—books to be replaced on the shelves, window curtains to be hung, and a deal of needle-work. But this could all be managed in good time before her husband's return.

"I was just standing this morning, looking up at the corner of my bed, ye ken," remarked Helen casually, "and there what should I see but two bogues! I hope ther's nae mair?"

Bedbugs! In her immaculate house, now in its final stages of scouring? Jane rose in a perfect frenzy. "Good God! you hope?" she exclaimed. "How could you live an instant without making sure?" Hurriedly she went to Helen's room to see with her own eyes. She pulled away the curtains from the wood. There, sure enough, were the two Helen had spotted. But far worse, darkly moving about in a joint which she could not get at without a bed key, were many others.

What troubles people had in this world, thought Jane, merely in protecting themselves from the inferior animals! "Tiny beings," Mazzini called them with becoming reticence. In an old London house, in spite of one's best vigilance, they *would* creep in—creatures with or without legs, winged, wingless, crawling on their bellies or skipping about in unbreakable armor. She summoned one of her handymen. Together they tore the bed apart, then gazed in dismay at the alarmed colony which their spying revealed. "Pretty strong!" remarked the workman.

Jane flung pailfuls of water on the stone floor to drown any possible fugitives. After a pogrom of all the enemies visible, she and her assistant, taking the bed completely apart, carried the pieces to the garden and steeped them in a tubful of water. *That* should leave not a bug alive to tell the tale! When the bed was once more ready to be assembled, Jane, to make doubly sure, painted all the joints.

Another discovery had resulted from these investigations: the woolen mattress was swarming with moths—literally, it was being eaten away from under Helen! Nothing to do but rip the thing apart and set all the wool to boil and dry. Positively amazing to see what a vast quantity of stuffing was contained in a mattress, once one had set it all afloat! It overwhelmed the finite mind with a sense of the impossible. Yet somehow she managed to get it cleaned and housed once more between its covers.

In the middle of October, Carlyle returned. Always, Jane hoped he would come back to her rested and well. Often she was disappointed. Nervous indigestion still had him in thrall. The problems of Cromwell still harassed him. As usual, he was drinking oceans of castor oil by way of remedy and swallowing quantities of his favorite blue pills. Yet despite his condition, he found words with which to praise her industry. His new library really pleased him and Jane was hopeful he could settle down to writing.

But on the third day, the young woman next door began practicing on the piano. Carlyle jumped up in distraction, declaring he could neither work nor live in a house constructed as at present. Carpenters were immediately summoned to make new alterations.

Jane was in despair thus to find herself once more in a regular mess after just having brought to an end three months of confusion. Up came the carpets which she herself a few weeks earlier had painstakingly nailed to the floors. Down came a partition in one room, and up went a new fireplace and chimney. Window boards stuffed with cotton were ordered, and as these would prohibit airing, zinc ventilators were to be set into the walls. Helen, instead of exerting herself, appeared to be struck with temporary idiocy (small wonder, thought Jane) which rendered her incapable of useful action, and Carlyle himself, dismayed at sight of the uproar he had raised, wrung his hands and tore his hair like the sorcerer's apprentice who had learnt magic enough to make a broomstick carry water but had not the counterspell to stop the floods. He could not sleep in his altered surroundings, and went prowling about the house, to his obvious hurt, though Jane, lying awake listening, dared not meddle with him.

After a forenoon of papering the broken parts of the plaster and an afternoon spent in nailing down the carpets—a job Helen never could be relied on to do satisfactorily—Jane looked ruefully at her blackened and irritated hands. And *he* worried about expenses! When they had lacked money, Jane recalled, she never grudged her own work. But with the small inheritance from her mother—Jane had turned it over to her husband and would accept none of it for herself—there was no need for scrimping. Surely, in this emergency, it would have been good sense had he told her to get a carpenter to do the carpets. Geraldine Jewsbury had written from Manchester, "My dear child, you ought to know your value better and not to allow your life to be worried away for no earthly good—it is a sort of quixotism you have for sacrificing yourself."

Maybe—but a writer like her husband could not hold his genius as a sinecure. Jane watched him shift from room to room like a domestic wandering Jew in his effort to settle himself for work. At last he admitted that no mere room could answer his problem. The trouble lay in the book itself—he simply could not get into the subject. He had filled great masses of paper, but they would not read as they should. Through three long years, this monstrous embryo of a volume had been a continual misery for him. And poor Jane, he thought, how dismal all this pother must be for her! These books were none of her choosing, yet she bore so patiently with him and them!

He buckled down to the task. Some of the material he wished to use lay in the custody of the British Museum. He had never succeeded in obtaining the least concession from Panizzi, keeper of the books. Instead he had to carry out his researches in the cavernous general reading room. Among such a promiscuous assembly of readers, concentration was well-nigh impossible. Some had iron heels to their boots, and went clanking like felons down the passageways. The worst trial of all was the man with the bassoon nose—as Thomas had christened him. Every half hour he blew his horrid trumpet, till Carlyle's head throbbed to distraction. A hundred museum headaches were the toll of Cromwell. The trumpeter was an idiot, Carlyle presently learned, sent to the reading room by his friends to keep him occupied. His entertainment consisted of making extracts from the volumes, and otherwise piddling away his time.

Such were the uses of a library in England!

But the manuscript was growing. Jane could at least take comfort from that. December had come. Sitting by the hearth,

Jeannie was peaceably darning her husband's socks when she was startled to see him appear in the room, a great bundle of papers in his hand. His face looked grim as the spirit of Presbyterianism. Silently he walked to the fire and thrust among the coals the bundle he was carrying. A never to be published *Life* of Cromwell roared up the chimney.

Through Jane's mind quivered a moment's terror at thought of the ten pound fine they would have to pay should the wad of papers kindle the flue.

Presently Jane got an explanation. During the night, said her husband, he had decided to take up the whole damnable subject from a quite new tack. The pattern of the French Revolution *History* simply would not do. Instead, he would bring out an edition of Cromwell's speeches and letters.

Jane's emotions were a mixture of exasperation and pity. Poor Carlyle! He had said to her, with a naïveté altogether touching, "They may twaddle as they like about the miseries of a bad conscience: but I should like to know whether Judas Iscariot was *more* miserable than Thomas Carlyle who never did anything *criminal*, so far as he remembered!"

Jane had often heard her husband declare that to write a good book a man needed to have a blazing, burning interest in his subject. Yes, but there were many different sorts of blazes!

Chapter Twenty=Six

*J*ANE was scarcely feeling up to the mark after these upheavals. She eschewed most parties that winter, and relied on callers to keep her in touch with the world. She
was even planning to stay away from Mrs. William Macready's
combined birthday and Christmas celebration for her daughter
Nina—Jane was a Macready godmother—till the insistence of
the hostess forced her to reconsider. "My dear," said Carlyle,
surveying his wife, "I think I never saw you look more bilious;
your face is *green* and your eyes all *blood-shot!*" A comforting
beginning to an afternoon's festivities! But Jane, once determined to go, would not change her mind.

William Macready was away on a tour of America. All his
friends seemed animated by a single purpose: at least somewhat
to compensate his family for his absence by a lively display of
general gaiety. Dickens filled the rôle of magician with John
Forster as assistant. If the bookseller trade should founder,
Charles need never lack for bread, thought Jane, watching him
convert a heap of bran into a live guinea pig, turn ladies' handkerchiefs into candy, and perform other conjuring feats. The
grand climax was what looked to be the utter ruination of a
gentleman's hat. Into it Dickens first broke several raw eggs.
Then he added flour and other ingredients with which, he explained, he proposed to make a plum cake. Thrusting the mess
right into the flames, the magician presently tumbled from the
quite undamaged hat a steaming pudding before the very eyes
of the astonished children and equally astonished grownups.

After the show there was dancing. Jane considered her
dancing days over, but not so Dickens. He pleaded with her to
try a waltz with him. Only by keeping up an effervescent stream
of nonsensical chatter with John Forster and Thackeray was she
able to put him off. But soon all were at it; old Major Burns,
son of the poet, whirled past like a good-natured cyclops, his

sole undamaged eye twinkling merrily; Thackeray, with his gigantic frame, was capering about; indeed the grownups quite outfrolicked the children.

After supper the celebrants waxed madder than ever—pulling crackers, drinking champagne, and proposing toasts. Then someone suggested a country dance, and before she realized what was happening to her, Jane found herself seized round the waist by burly John Forster and plunged into the thickest of the round.

"For the love of Heaven let me go! You are going to dash my brains out against the folding doors!"

"Your *brains!!* Who cares about their brains *here? let them go!*"

Jane quite agreed. After all, the pleasantest company lay among those who snapped their fingers at restraint and felt themselves unbound by ceremonial and convention. She was thoroughly enjoying herself. Excitement was her surest form of rest.

On New Year's Day, Jane glanced out the window. Snow on the red roofs, and on the bare branches of the poplars, and an icy mist falling. Who would come to be her "first foot"? She still attached great significance to the omen, watching the portents—she admitted—as Roman Augurs watched the flight of birds. Scarcely had she dressed when she heard a soft rap at the door. Mazzini! . . . She hurried down to meet him. There he stood, his shoes oozing moisture, big drops of sleet hanging from his mustache. Would the man never learn to take care of himself? "What on earth could tempt you to come out in a day like this?" she exclaimed. But he looked so pitiable in his wet clothes that she quickly stopped her chiding.

His indifference to health had often caused her anxiety. Some time previously he had been afflicted by an abscess in his cheek of really terrifying proportions. A fever had developed from the tumor, forcing him to stay in his lodgings. Throwing convention to the winds, Jane had gone to his rooms to nurse him. A strange thing, she thought, that the stupid world should consider it disgraceful for a woman to act as nurse at a friend's lodging if he happened to be a youngish bachelor!

Mazzini, though he pretended to pay little attention to Jane's advice concerning his health, nevertheless was grateful. But what he wished most from her was an understanding sympathy with his revolutionary schemes in Italy. He knew her husband looked with contempt on them. He counted on a more heartening response from the wife. He had given her a ring with the watchword of young Italy—*ore e sempre*—engraved on it. This ring, he noticed, she always wore. In his frequent letters to his devoted mother in Italy, he sometimes mentioned—always discreetly—"La Carlyle," as he called her. Her husband, he reported, was a good man but, like almost all writers, lived only in his ideas; in his mind rather than in his heart. He was a person restless by nature, and inclined to discontent. La Carlyle had no children and felt alone in the world. She was a woman of most sensitive nature—too intense for her own good—and of responsive sympathies.

Naturally Mazzini's mother grew somewhat alarmed at her son's remarks. He always insisted that his devotion to the cause must exclude from his life intimate ties with women. But word and fact had not always agreed. How did he feel towards this woman whom he described as black-haired, dark-eyed, vivacious, and still youthful? "Lest her being still young may make you suspect more than the truth, know that I do not love her except as a sister for the excellent qualities of her heart, for the love she bears my country and my ideas, for the good that she wishes me, and for the affection shown my friends and to all who interest me." Her own regard, he reported, was Platonic: "She loves me as a sister would, with a friendship that is a woman's and exalted, but still a friendship. And so it will always be between me and women who are not free, and especially when I am a friend also of her husband and he a friend of mine." But in London, among his compatriots, significant glances were exchanged, and muted whisperings.

Jane, regardless of such things—busy, too, with the other members of her congregation—persisted in her enjoyment of Mazzini's company. People were idiots to make a fuss over an honest intimacy between a man and woman! Her husband, sensible creature, never objected. As with all masculine friendships, he was glad to have her amused. So she gave Mazzini little gifts—a writing set, a pair of slippers. And she took an active interest in his charitable enterprises for his destitute countrymen in England. But to his continued disappointment, she refused to espouse wholeheartedly the cause he lived for—the struggle for Italian unity and independence.

He had established in London a school for Italian organ boys. Jane was always ready to enter into deep consultations on its management. Though she had helped to plan it, she did not attend the school's first anniversary. Her husband had looked so thundery on the whole business—as if the education of organ boys were something closely approaching a felony—that Jane, for the sake of peace, had stayed away. But she made every effort to win donations from her wealthier friends.

One day Jane, Erasmus Darwin, and Mazzini were having an intimate fireside chat. His friend Sismondi, remarked Mazzini, had once been nearly lapidated.

"Nonsense!" exclaimed Jane. "You should say *stoned*, there is no such word as lapidated in that sense."

"Let him alone," remarked Darwin, "he is quite right, *lapidated* is an excellent word."

"Do not mind him," Jane said to Mazzini, "he only wants to lead you into making a mistake."

"But are you sure?" inquired the Italian, "in the Bible, for instance, does not she call it lapidated in speaking of St. Stephen?"

This femalization of the Bible so delighted Darwin that he gave a sovereign to Mazzini's school.

Carlyle sometimes remarked that Jane had no bent at all for pedestrianism. Mazzini on the contrary wrote plaintively to his mother that La Carlyle had walked him almost to death —ten miles at a stretch and in the wretchedest of weather. But though he would never admit it, the exercise was saving his health. To him, an Italian, walking for pleasure was a fantastic notion. La Carlyle sought out the weirdest places, also—Battersea Bridge, to watch the shipping, for instance, though the wind blew damp and cold. Sometimes she carried him off on all-day excursions. They set out, once, for the top of St. Paul's Cathedral. As they went down the river by steamer toward the heart of the city the great dome dominated the skyline. But in the busy streets themselves, St. Paul's was completely lost. The ten or so people whom they asked to discover it for them considered the question a joke. But at last, not twenty steps away, they saw the huge building mounting skyward before their eyes. Accompanied by an old woman who acted as guide, they climbed the stairway to the dome. Bothersome individuals, these custodians with their memorized speech on each object one was supposed to notice! Presently, scandalized to find them so inattentive to the things she declared most interesting, the guide left them alone for three-quarters of an hour. A diabolical wind up there, thought Mazzini—his companion apparently was enjoying it—but the view *was* impressive. All those red smokestacks and pointed, tiled roofs looked like the flames in Dante's purgatory suddenly cooled and turned to stone.

Not long after coming to London, Mazzini had abandoned his miserable lodgings for better quarters in Chelsea which Jane had discovered for him. Before the move, his dislike of walking had interfered with his calls. Now he dropped in frequently—two and three times a week.

It was very cosy, sitting for hours in the snug upstairs drawing room, one's heels on the fender, the conversation running easily along, now lively, now in sober mood. Once in a while her caller brought a pocketful of figs cured in wine, and these they would nibble as they talked. Or Jane would get some gingerbread from the kitchen.

At times Mazzini came to the house with an expression as radiant as though he had seen the fulfillment of his dearest wish for Italy. The inward joy would bring beauty to his face and a sunny flash to his eyes like that of the first waking of Pygmalion's statue. All these hopes, Jane felt, were doomed to utter frustration. He a conspirator chief! She would make as good a one herself. What could be more out of the rôle of conspirator than his telling her all his secret operations, even to the places where insurrection was about to break out and the names of those organizing it? She never asked him about such matters; on the contrary, avoided the subject as much as possible. Yet he insisted. Jane did not realize that with men he was secretive as a clam—she alone was privileged. So she knew the various subterfuges and disguises under which he handled his intricate correspondence and the aliases under which he hatched his plots. When he needed it, she let him use No. 5 Cheyne Row as an address at which to receive letters. Two months be-

fore the appointed hour, she had been told the secret of an
impending outbreak. Once he had come to her with the information that he was about to persuade an Italian frigate, now in
an English port, to mutiny and carry him to Italy.

"And with one frigate," asked Jane, "you mean to overthrow
the Austrian Empire?"

"Why not? the beginning only is wanted."

Jane threw up her hands in despair. But in general, because
he liked it, she allowed him to believe that she sympathized
with his cause. Jokingly, she had once hinted that she would
accompany him to Italy as a fellow conspirator when he started
his next revolt. Alas, he had taken her more than half seriously! One or two of his schemes appeared to her as utterly preposterous. An inventor named Muzzi, he announced, had discovered the way to steer balloons as readily as one managed a
steamboat. For two thousand pounds, said Mazzini, he could
buy the secret for Young Italy. Jane gazed at him with incredulous wonder. Had he entirely lost his senses?

"You mean that you would invade Italy in balloons?—that
the Association would descend on the Austrians out of the
skies?"

"Exactly! And I confess to you—you may think it childish—
but there is something of romance, something which flatters my
imagination in the idea of starting up a nation in a manner
never before heard of!"

"*A la bonne heure*, my Dear! but if it be decided that we are
to begin the war by personating the fallen angels, adieu to *my*
share in the expedition."

"Now why so?" There was a look of grave astonishment on
Mazzini's face, "It was just in reference to *you* that I felt the
greatest preference to *this means*—to think that you would go
without incurring the physical suffering of a sea voyage, and all
the dangers—what shall I say?—of being sunk perhaps by a
volley of cannon from the shore! and then there would be
something so new and so—what shall I say?—*suitable* for *you*,
in descending as it were out of Heaven to redeem a suffering
people!"

Surely the man was joking! Jane glanced inquiringly at his
face. It was radiant with enthusiasm. How infinitesimally small

was the line of separation between highest virtue and the beginnings of madness! Even when his schemes were fantastically grotesque, it was a desecration, a crime, to deride Mazzini.

All his plotting kept him in a constant fever. When plans miscarried, he became frightfully dejected; sad beyond all words. He would come to the house looking as though he had been boiled in tea leaves. Jane would do her best, at such moments, to cheer him up. If Carlyle were also present, and in an argumentative mood, her task was not the easiest imaginable. Stirring restlessly about from mantelpiece to table, lounging now in one chair then the next, springing up again to pace the room, Thomas would loudly contradict every word Mazzini was saying. At these displays, Jane would be hurt and vexed. Surely that husband of hers had not the least consideration for Mazzini!

Following her practice with other close friends, Jane had long been writing the Italian intimate, affectionate little notes— invitations to tea, requests that he call because she felt unwell and could not go out, even confidential letters when she was depressed or troubled.

One day Mazzini came to Chelsea with a very grave face. Did she know, he inquired, that the British Government was prying into all his mail? He had scattered poppy seeds in letters addressed to himself, and found the grains missing; he had placed a hair under the seal, and found it gone. There could be no doubt whatsoever.

Mazzini was troubled, not for himself, but for others. If certain of his letters reached the Austrian Embassy through the British Government, the lives of fellow-plotters would be imperiled. But Jane did not care so much about the fate of exiles quite unknown to her. What made her wild was the thought that Sir James Graham, England's Home Secretary, and his assistants, had been grinning smugly over some of her most intimate letters. Henceforth, in writing to Mazzini, she must be more circumspect! After the first shock was over, she took delight in penning saucy little asides to the spies: "Mrs. Carlyle would be particularly obliged to the embassy to lose no time in forwarding this letter."

When Mazzini had sufficient evidence assembled, he revealed, through a friend in Parliament, the British Foreign Minister's devices. In an effort to divert attention, the Home Secretary had thereupon raked up the old accusation that the Italian patriot was little better than a common assassin.

Knowing her husband's disapproval of his plotting, Jane was astonished to see him kindle in wrath at these slurs on Mazzini's name. In an outspoken letter to *The Times*—a glorious letter, she thought it—Carlyle attacked the Foreign Office in no uncertain terms for its violation of the rights of privacy. Mazzini, he affirmed, was a person of veracity, humanity, and nobleness of mind.

Whether Carlyle had desired it or not, one result of the communication to *The Times* was to draw Mazzini—hitherto an obscure exile—into the brighter rays of public notice. British friends gathered round him in increasing numbers—a veritable Mazzini cult. His time was less and less his own, or even Italy's. And Jane, too, saw less of him now. He could find other, more whole-hearted sympathizers with the cause.

Chapter Twenty=Seven

ON THE 26th of August, 1845, Cromwell had finally got himself completed. Work on the book, in Jane's opinion, had lasted far too long. Another man like Oliver would be the death of her husband. As for herself, she found the burden of forebearance sometimes intensely irksome. There were periods, she admitted, when she and her husband must have made a grim enough pair.

Carlyle, his publisher, and Jane—all three were surprised that the success of *The Letters and Speeches of Oliver Cromwell* should prove to be so great. With it, Carlyle's literary fame reached its zenith.

Helen Mitchell, noting the acclaim, turned inquiringly to Jane: "Master, Ma'am, is the cleverest man as is?"

"We fondly hope so," answered the mistress of the house.

Surely the English were a singular people to receive with comparative indifference a book so interesting as *Past and Present,* and then to bestow on *Cromwell* such a cordial reception! Jane was delighted at the thought of at last escaping from the Cromwellian atmosphere she had so long been breathing. The Puritans, she had long ago decided, were not much to her liking.

She was not alone in her disapproval. Edward Fitzgerald, who had furnished the inspiring bones from Naseby, considered the Roundheads quite intolerable. What a brotherhood in comparison to Omar Khayyam and Omar's boon companions! Of course Thomas would not care a straw about Omar either, so Fitzgerald was on his guard not to speak of the tentmaker in his presence.

But Edward Fitzgerald could not stay away from Carlyle— a lovable bear if only he would forget his everlasting Puritans! One night at Cheyne Row (Jane had not intruded on the men) had been very, very dull—Oliver had emphatically ruled the conversation. Fitzgerald was delighted to escape at last into the street. Though it was ever so late, a hand-organ was still abroad, vigorously playing a dance air. The lover of the Rubaiyat pricked up his ears. Had Jane gazed at that moment from the window, she would have seen an innocent enough spectacle. There was Fitzgerald solemnly revolving down the pavement to the strains of a polka till he vanished out of sight at the corner.

Carlyle, staring in amazement, uttered a groan and shut the door. That's what comes, mused Fitzgerald as he twirled on his way, when one gets possessed of a great idea. Once within the brain, it grows like a tapeworm and finally consumes the vitals.—What a thoroughly nasty comparison! Fitzgerald was amazed at himself. Hastily he turned his thoughts to sweeter things.

Unlike Fitzgerald, Carlyle's wife could not blithely polka out of reach—not while that hapless child, her husband, needed tending. Jane's mind was flexible as a whip-lash. Yet through it one fixed idea ran like a rod of iron. She was morally certain that to leave Carlyle alone in Chelsea would some day be fatal— he would eat harmful food, he would scald himself to death with the tea kettle, he would set the house on fire. There was simply no telling *what* he might do!

Actually, he managed very well on those few occasions when he stayed behind while Jane made summer visits. He would write under an awning in the garden, a tray of books at his elbow. When friends called—Robert Browning, Tennyson, any of the group still lingering in the city—he poured them tea with a competent hand and relished a genial pipe.

Helen Mitchell, under Jane's tutelage, had become an expert in attending to his diet. When competently fed, Thomas Carlyle throve as well as any man despite his biliousness. Young David Masson, studying his ruddy face, was of the opinion that this gifted Scotchman with the strong features of a peasant and wiry loose-knit frame would live to be a man well over eighty.

After a summer of visiting—Carlyle was still absent on his own wanderings—Jane returned to the city in time to be present at some theatricals got up by Dickens and his energetic lieutenant, John Forster. Jane was not enthusiastic over plays by amateurs, but Forster put in such a vigorous plea for her attendance that she finally decided to appear.

She was much amused at Macready's jealousy over the goings on, but she could not help sympathizing with him, too. There had been a tremendous puff of the thing in *The Times*, a golden blast of praise such as William himself seldom if ever received. As for the actors, they were in such a state of jubilation and excitement, poor things, that they seemed ready to make the fatal plunge of turning professional—a step, Jane was sure, which would bring them face to face with sad reality. She refused to share in the hysterical jubilation.

The play was Jonson's *Every Man in His Humor*, and the scenery and costumes, professionally done, were not in scale with the unprofessional acting, so that the production tumbled disastrously between the allowances one made for amateurs and the critical view induced by the sumptuous staging. Little Dickens, got up in black and red as strutting Captain Bobadil, would have been unrecognizable to the mother that bore him save for his voice, which almost burst in his throat because of his effort to make it sound like the speech of a man six feet tall.

Jane found greater diversion in the intermission than in the actual performance. As she was threading her way through the crowded aisle from her place in the dress circle to the private box where her friend Mrs. Macready was sitting, she nearly bumped into a tall man leaning against the wall like a caryatid, his head almost touching the ceiling.

"Alfred Tennyson!" she exclaimed in joyous surprise. "I did not know you were in town!"

After they had shaken hands, the poet asked when he might call at Chelsea.

"But Carlyle is in Scotland," said Jane.

"So I heard from Spedding already, but I asked Spedding, would he go with me to see Mrs. Carlyle, and he said he would."

Jane enjoyed the society of poets and kept up with their writings. Though she liked Browning, she much preferred Tennyson. She had once read *Sordello*, but had never been able to make out whether Sordello was a man, a city, or a book. After her latest earthquake, young Robert had committed a slight error in judgment for which Jane had not entirely pardoned him. She was pouring tea one afternoon, and needed the brass kettle that was boiling on the hearth. Since Thomas gave no sign of moving, Browning sprang up and carried it over. But instead of resting it on the tea table, he held it in his hand while he went on talking. "Can't you put it down?" suggested Jane. He did so—on her brand new carpet. She cried out in alarm. Sure enough, when Browning raised the kettle, there, burned into the immaculate material, was a round, angry stain. Carlyle came to the rescue of the embarrassed caller. "You should have been more explicit!" he said to Jane.

When Tennyson called as he had promised, shortly after the play, he found the house well garrisoned with men. He had left a dinner party early and driven up by cab for a tête-a-tête which obviously was not to be. John Carlyle, Tom's lazy, good-natured brother, turned at last into something of a sponge, emerged from the kitchen where he had been smoking. And George Craik, a journalist, was also there, talking in the parlor. While Jane poured tea—regretting that Tennyson had not found her alone—Craik prosed and John babbled and the evening was wasted. Alfred hung on till eleven, then left, since Craik obviously intended to sit him out. George Craik, reflected Jane, would probably sit out the Virgin Mary should he ever meet her.

But Jeannie got her chance another evening. Carlyle was not at home and she had settled herself before the fire when presently she heard a carriage drive up and men's voices at the door. In came Tennyson, with a friend of his, Edward Moxon. Alfred was always dreadfully embarrassed with women. He entertained for them, she knew, a sense almost of adoration mixed with a feeling of ineffable contempt. Adoration, probably, for what they *might be*—contempt for what they really were.

Jane, determined to put him at his ease and get the most good of him, plotted to make him forget her womanness. She produced pipe and tobacco, brandy and water, with miraculous results. Though he professed to be ashamed at polluting her room, Tennyson smoked like a Liverpool locomotive. Quite unconsciously, he began talking as though the partner of his conversation was a clever man—not a mere female. Jane was immensely flattered. How irritating it was to have men pitch their conversation to the level they supposed to be pleasing to a woman's taste! How delightful was Alfred's present lack of conformity to the rule!

Shortly before midnight, Alfred left. When Carlyle returned at twelve to find Jane in an atmosphere of smoke so thick that one could cut it with a knife, his astonishment was considerable. Had she been using his cigars?

Alfred was a singular compound of manliness and helplessness. Jane sometimes wondered if he would ever marry. Really, he needed a woman to take care of him! She had thought of her attractive cousin Babbie Welsh as a possibility. Certainly Alfred was handsome enough to win any woman's heart. And he was a real poet too, though the vulgar public had even yet not mustered sufficient perception to recognize him as such. One needed only to read "Ulysses," thought Jane, to be convinced of his genius. There was a suggestion of the Romany strain, of gypsy blood, in his appearance. He had beautiful waving dusty black hair—never combed yet never tousled to an unbecoming degree—large, deep-set slumberous eyes: eyes full of gloom and darkness yet kindly too. His mouth was delicate, petulant, and moody, and he wore a slight frown on his high forehead, with tiny perpendicular wrinkles above the bridge of his classic nose. Certainly a beautiful figure of a poet—strength and delicacy blended in sculpturesque perfection. He should make some woman an enchanting husband!

Yet what normal woman could endure the atmosphere of tobacco smoke he always made about him? Most were not yet educated to the aid tobacco brought in soothing their men into a state of domesticity. Let them smoke and they could be taught good manners! Jane was proud of her own husband's considerate technique. He would sprawl on the hearth-rug at her feet and dexterously blow up the chimney the gray, wavering clouds that gathered from the fiery core of his long clay pipe. Alfred (he was always losing it!) had a small, blackened old brier that he puffed on, gossips reported, nine hours out of every twenty-four. No better man than Tennyson to smoke a pipe with, declared Jane's husband. He preferred Alfred's smoking to his poetry. "There he sits upon a dung-heap surrounded by innumerable dead dogs!" he once snorted, referring to his friend's interest in creating modern adaptations of ancient

Greek themes. Tennyson, when he heard the phrase, tried hard not to be provoked.

"I'm told that is what you say of me!"

Carlyle gave a loud guffaw. "Eh, that wasn't a very luminous description!"

Jane Carlyle had long since steeled herself to her husband's contempt for poetry. There were times when she almost persuaded herself that she shared his feeling. But deep within her lingered the love for poetry which had so influenced her girlhood, now keeping alive, under the armor of her realism, the romantic spirit which was essentially part of her being.

Alfred was far from well off, though he had never lived in real poverty. Should he not have a pension from the State? Lean men never yet grew fat on verse. A hundred and fifty pounds yearly: surely Tennyson was worth that sum to England! These poems of his, Carlyle admitted, showed within them the pulse of a real man's heart: strong as a lion's, yet gentle, loving, and full of music.

"Richard Milnes," he said to that eminent member of Parliament and perennial caller at Cheyne Row; "when are you going to get that pension for Alfred Tennyson?"

"My dear Carlyle, the thing is not so easy as you seem to suppose. What will my constituents say if I do get the pension for Tennyson? They know nothing about him or his poetry, and they will probably think he is some poor relation of my own, and that the whole affair is a job."

"Richard Milnes"—Carlyle spoke with a solemn face—"on the Day of Judgment, when the Lord asks you why you didn't get that pension for Alfred Tennyson, it will not do to lay the blame on your constituents; it is you that will be damned!"

Sometimes, when Tennyson called, it was not to chat with Jane or Thomas or smoke a pipe in the garden (he kept one there in a special niche). He came instead to lure Carlyle to the Cock Tavern, near Temple Bar, a favorite eating place. Tennyson's choice of food was sometimes trying to a dyspeptic —one pickle, two chops, two cheeses, one pint of stout, and one of port. Or he would fetch Carlyle away for long walks through the night.

Alfred was one of the few persons for whom Jane would play on her piano. Carlyle would ask for some of his favorite Scottish ballads. Did Alfred know the tale of Macpherson's Lament? Macpherson was a highland robber and a fiddler. On the gallows themselves, he played his farewell. Then he held up his fiddle. "Has the Macpherson any clansman?" he shouted. No one answered; no one dared to. "Any kinsman, any soul that wished him well?" Silence from the crowd; no one to claim the minstrel's instrument. Macpherson smashed the fiddle under his foot—the noose round his neck—and sprang into space. That was the story.

Jane sang and played the air—a tune rough as hemp, but wild and strong. She could see Alfred's face grow darker, his lip quiver.

Chapter Twenty-Eight

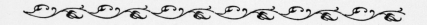

*M*RS. ANTHONY STERLING had fallen ill. Jane did not greatly care for the woman, yet in sickness one must play the good Samaritan. It was raining, but she set out for the Sterling house to see if she could help. Too bad the Sterlings were so ill-matched a couple! They rasped on each other like a pair of files. A sad mess, Jane decided—she proud and petulant toward him, he cold and argumentative with her. A husband and wife who felt like that could hardly be expected ever to become reconciled.

Jane felt sorry for Anthony. He was really a splendid fellow, though not the equal of his brother John. She enjoyed his calls and considered him one of her warmest friends. He acted at Cheyne Row quite as though he were a member of the family.

Jane thumped the knocker. When the servant came to the door, he gave a start as though he had seen a ghost. A strange look passed over his face, and he appeared hardly willing to let her in. What ailed the creature, Jane wondered? But Anthony's conduct was still more peculiar. He beckoned her silently to the library, then silently shut the door. Did Jane know, he asked, that his wife had gone out of her mind?

"Good gracious! do you seriously mean that she is gone mad?"

"Yes, she is at present in a decided state of monomania—which the doctors say the slightest contradiction may drive into hysterical frenzy."

"Monomania? And what is her particular *idea?*"

Anthony drew himself up in military fashion. "Her particular idea," he said, "is that I have fallen in love with *you*—that *you* are a dreadful person and that I ruin myself in making you presents."

Jane was thunderstruck. Such a predicament had never occurred to her. After Anthony's revelation, she felt positively ill. As for gifts, she could think of none. Oh, yes, now she remembered; Anthony had once brought a large crockery jug to the house! But Mrs. Sterling was insisting that he had presented her with the new piano at Cheyne Row and the new dining-room carpet! Anthony, noticing Jane's pallor, tried to make her take some wine, but she refused. She even refused the offer of his carriage to bring her home.

When she told Carlyle, he laughed uproariously—simply would not take a serious view of the matter. It was a judgment come upon her, he remarked. Next morning at breakfast, while she sleepily drank her coffee, he exclaimed, "Just to look at you there, looking as if butter would not melt in your mouth, and think of the profligate life you lead!" He had a new nickname for her now—"Destroyer of the peace of families." But Jane saw nothing to be amused at. Poor Anthony was having the very devil of a time at home. His wife, having been informed of the visit, had rushed into the hysterical state which the doctor had foretold. Anthony could not leave her room without her shrieking that he was off to take a walk with Mrs. Carlyle. Even when the frenzy abated, the jealousy remained.

Jane heard all sorts of tales. Mrs. Sterling was combing the hair of one of her little nieces—a daughter of John Sterling— when the child's brother suddenly exclaimed, "Oh, that is very pretty! That is just the way Mrs. Carlyle wears her hair!"

"We do not speak of that person here!" said Mrs. Sterling with emphasis, throwing down the comb.

The worst of it was that Anthony—though less frequently than before—persisted in coming secretly to Cheyne Row, like a man sneaking off to rob a hen-roost. Such conduct, Jane felt, placed her in a very false position, and Anthony also. He should make up his mind to one of two things. He ought to explain to his wife: "These people are my friends and I *will* go to see them reasonably—and there is no wrong in my going—and so *you* had better just reconcile yourself to the idea of it, or go mad again, if you like that way of it better!" Or he should come to Chelsea and say: "You see I am oppressed by a distracted wife —she is my wife, however, and I must consult her whims before all else—and so since I cannot see you any more without pain for her, farewell and God bless you!" The trouble, Jane was sure, lay in the circumstance that the woman could not view her husband's friendships rationally and allow him liberty to gratify his inclinations. But then, of course, Mrs. Sterling could make no claim to rationality. Alas that she was as she was: it distressingly complicated existence! Jane saw but one thing to do. If matters did not mend, she must tell Anthony Sterling to keep away.

Yet for a long time the impasse persisted.

At last Jane received a note from Anthony. She must not be surprised if his wife should come that day to call. Jane could hardly believe what he had written. She put on a bonnet and threw a shawl across her shoulders. She had a clear conscience, yet, for Mrs. Sterling's ease of mind, she might as well convincingly look the part of an old woman.

Mrs. Sterling, on entering, began some meek words of apology—she was so sorry for her past attitude; she would have come long ago had she believed that Mrs. Carlyle would be willing to receive her. Jane looked at her in wonder. Could she, in her position, be as brave? Doubtful, to say the least. Before Anthony's wife could go any further, Jane cut her short with an impetuous kiss. A wave of relief surged over her with the realization that henceforth she would no longer be a cause of misery to the poor woman, no matter how unintentionally so.

Jane was becoming increasingly independent of her husband's summer plans. She was learning to throttle her sense of duty and scurry out from under in order to preserve what tranquillity was still left her. When she was tired and alone, she was apt to think too much and analyze too complexly. Her horror of analysis was surely justified—it drove people into such perplexity and set riddles that lacked solution. Why did she have these gnawing, aching attacks of melancholy? Were they not trespassing more and more frequently, and with an overwhelming pressure? What caused them? The petty cares at home—the house to be kept quiet as a tomb, Carlyle's woes to be listened to, a mountain of socks to be darned? Was it lack of hard work to perform: not drudgery, but work that merited the doing? Had she let her best years run to waste, productive only of tares and nettles? For days, for weeks, she told herself, she had experienced not a single moment of gladness.

Yet her cordial welcome of the friends she liked best, her lively repartee, her zest, half belied the thoughts she entertained in solitude. And mere acquaintances who watched her in her drawing room in Cheyne Row decided she must be a very happy wife.

At the Macreadys', once, Mrs. Macready chanced to speak of the blues that sometimes oppressed her.

"Every one, I suppose," Jane said comfortingly, "have their own fits of depression to bear up against, if the truth were told."

"Do you say so?" remarked Macready's sister. "Oh, no, surely! Some people are never out of spirits—*yourself* for example. I really believe you do not know what it is to be ever sad for a minute. One never sees you that you do not keep one in fits of laughter."

Jeannie amazed even herself. Surely she must have within her a superhuman gaiety of spirits! But at times she had a different answer. She had been acting, she reasoned. One could not, in company, play a death's head at the feast. The required part must be selected from comedy.

A wretched weariness had driven her forth in recent summers. Carlyle would not miss her—he had his Lady Harriet to go to whenever she summoned. Jane was more troubled about herself than she cared to admit. She had made up her mind not to talk of her difficulties to her husband. But at last her determination broke down in a violent outburst of weeping. Carlyle was aghast. His wife must go away at once for a rest— she must visit the Welshes in Liverpool, or the Paulets at Seaforth, or any other friends she might wish to.

Nothing could have pleased her better. Instead she had first to go to Addiscombe Farm at Croydon for a promised four days with Lady Harriet—the very place and person, in her immediate mood, Jane longed most to avoid. The invitation in itself was an anomaly. Jane's intuition insisted that Lady Harriet, in spite of recent friendliness, did not like her and never would.

As usual, the Barings' house was spilling over with fine company—people whose main objectives were brilliant repartee and the wearing of fashionable clothes. In her agitated state, Jane did not feel the least bit in the humor for such diversions. And the mental effort she was forced to make cost her heavily in sleep. Lying awake—hour after hour—on the thronelike bed of the room to which she had been assigned gave her plenty of time, time and to spare, in which to think.

Ever since her husband had drifted into intimacy with Lady Harriet, Jane had been studying her with scrupulous attention. This was the place, and Bath House in the city, that drew him away. Not only did he call on Lady Harriet; he wrote her, Jane knew, many familiar little letters. She had been shown some of them by her husband; some, but not all.

"I could not see you," he had written; "they tell me you are not well, too. The housemaid said you were better; but did not seem to know much about it. Why will you dine at seven o'clock and waste yourself with the frivolities of this generation? Are you of no value to anyone, then!" And he had closed with a kind farewell: "Good night! The old Chelsea clock is striking midnight: the Sun is right under our feet, and wet winds are blustering,—and the quantity of insane confusion in this World is very great. Shall we ever have wings, think you? *Ach Gott!*— I send you blessings as ever, and the best good night. *Ewig,* T.C."

Jane kept telling herself that this diversion with Lady Harriet was good for him. But she sometimes twitted him about it, hoping he would see below the fun that sheathed the point of her remarks. There seemed to be no limit to the dominion of this intellectual Circe over men. Carlyle never by any chance, so far as Jane could see, denied a wish of Lady Harriet. If she wanted him, he was ready at her call—at Bath House, at Addiscombe, or at the Grange, her father-in-law's luxurious mansion near Winchester. And only fancy being able to drag him to the opera, and have him dress for the occasion! Yet somehow Lady Harriet had managed even that. Her fascinations surely qualified her for the title of most skillful coquette of modern times.

In these troubled waking thoughts, as Jane tossed on the cambric sheets with their rich borders of lace, in this unfamiliar room at Addiscombe, it was hard to avoid visions of a dubious future; hard not to see spectres. The thought of Mrs. Anthony Sterling's plight hovered in that darkness, and the ruin of Jane's youthful hopes for a life-long, understanding partnership with Thomas.

Carlyle was still away in Scotland when Jane returned from her summer's excursion to Liverpool and Manchester. She was therefore surprised when a note, in Lady Harriet's familiar hand, reached Chelsea, addressed, not to her husband, but to herself. With lively curiosity, she tore it open. Lady Harriet would be in town for a few days. Would Mrs. Carlyle come to see her? She would send her brougham to fetch her.

Here, truly, was a somewhat unexpected turn of affairs. Rather incomprehensible, in fact! Could Lady Harriet possibly consider her a worthy substitute for Carlyle? Jane stuck to her unconquerable persuasion that Lady Harriet not only did not like her, but never could.

At two in the afternoon, the Barings' carriage stood waiting at the door. Jane was soon walking through the lofty halls of Bath House, galleries hung with priceless works of art by Da Vinci, Giorgione, Van Dyck, Rembrandt, and a host of other great painters. At the far end of the big house, in a large dressing-room on the top floor, Jane found her hostess resting on a sofa. For two hours the women chatted, then Jane, so as not to make her visit too long, departed, though urged to remain for dinner. No one could have been more gracious and agreeable than Lady Harriet. Really, it had been a quite delightful call!

In November had come a request that the Carlyles spend the Christmas holidays at Bay House, another estate belonging to the family, on the south shores of Hampshire. The sea, through the immense ranges of windows, looked chilly and bleak enough, but inside, the rooms were warm and comfortable, and everything was as magnificent as money and taste could make it. Yet life in such a place, as these people lived it, would in the long run be suicidal. Nothing to do, day after day, save dress, talk, amuse oneself, eat, and try to sleep. Jane marveled that so intelligent a woman as Lady Harriet could endure without interruption this idleness, pleasant as it might be for a short while. Even the brief snatch of it which she was sampling palled at times on Jane, though the vacation from material duties at home was very welcome.

She decided that she had been mistaken in several conclusions about her hostess. Lady Harriet was *not* a flirt—not the least in the world a coquette. Her character was built on the grand scale—far above such lightness. If all the men lost their senses over her and fluttered about her as though she were a Queen Bee, how could Lady Harriet help that? Yes, she was full of sincerity, and had, Jane convinced herself, an excellent heart. If only she could break through the golden cobwebs of the high position in which she was entangled she would be not merely the most amusing and gracious lady of her day, but the best woman of her times as well. Surely, with this person of good sense and perfect good breeding, one ought to be able to avoid collisions, no matter what the circumstances. Of course Lady Harriet had a passion for controlling people, and she a passion for not being ruled. But that, if other things did not interfere, was an obstacle to friendship not impassable with the aid of mutual forbearance.

Jane was almost ready to drop all reservations. How unexpected, how delightful to find a close friend in Lady Harriet! Jane had friendships with many men. But heretofore, though a few women had almost filled the need, a really intimate attachment with a member of her own sex had not yet been experienced by her in London. Perhaps now she was on the brink of its realization.

Throughout the winter, the stylish brougham waited many evenings to carry Jane to Bath House. Carlyle's own visits there had diminished. With Lady Harriet well entertained, there was less excuse to go. Together the women chatted, played chess, or read German. Pleasant notes from Lady Harriet arrived more frequently for Jane as the friendship ripened. She even asked Jane to come to Rome with her for the winter. And what she said she meant—Jeannie now had not the slightest doubt of that.

Lady Harriet was one of the least demonstrative of women. But then her little acts meant infinitely more than Geraldine Jewsbury's pink oceans of gush. If she liked you, she said nothing about it, but one sensed the fact because she made every association with her so pleasant. People who tired her, Jane had noticed, she quickly discouraged. It was easy to understand one's footing beside her: she would blow one up with gunpowder rather than be bored in one's company.

Jane, though the fact itself meant nothing to her, was amused to see the miraculous increase in attention which she received from the smaller gentry since Lady Harriet had taken her up. She had been unable to resist the temptation to answer with a touch of acid a sugary note from Lady Monteagle, who had not before been heard from during more than a year.

But with the coming of spring, Jane's hard-won tranquillity deserted her. The slug tracks of doubt once more trailed across her mind. Circumstance, in part, was at fault. Just when she thought she and her husband had cast off forever the incubus of Cromwell, it settled once more on their backs. The book's success required a second edition. Unwillingly enough Carlyle pitched headforemost into the vortex of rewriting. He was again so hard at work that he seemed scarcely aware of his wife, and once more he sought his relaxation, not at home, but in calls at Bath House.

Lady Harriet, at the end of March, was to move to the farm at Addiscombe. She had invited Jane to come for a long visit. Should she accept? She was in two minds about it. But finally she went. Lady Harriet's conduct was exemplary throughout Jane's stay; wholly devoid of caprices or anything the least bit questionable. One gesture had been quite unexpected—she had greeted Jane with a kiss of welcome. And she kissed her again at parting.

Every Saturday Carlyle rode out to Croydon and stayed till Monday. But whom did he come to see?

As summer approached—the new edition was nearly finished —Carlyle's restlessness returned. He had been searching for a home in the country—for the summer or longer—though Jane could not see that he had any real intention of acting on his impulse.

June that year was excessively hot. Yet Carlyle, for all his talk, seemed unprepared to make the actual move to quit the city. The weather, her husband's indecision, his faithful squiring of Lady Harriet—the impact of these and other matters on her too high-strung spirits were threatening Jane with a major crisis.

At last, not waiting for Carlyle, she flung off to Liverpool, leaving behind her the taunt that he could go if he liked to

Addiscombe; it was all one to her. He had established a small permanent wardrobe there—he better use it!

The first weeks of July with the Paulets at Seaforth House brought Jane diverse letters. The first came from her husband. "We never parted before in such a manner," he wrote, "and all for—literally nothing." Her precipitate going had left him bowed under the saddest mood he had been in for years. "I suppose you fancied me happy at Addiscombe. Alas! I was in no humor for anything of that laughing nature." Instead he had delved for hours among old papers. "It was a day of the resurrection of all sad and great and tender things within me —sad as the very death, yet not unprofitable, I believe. Adieu, dearest—for that *is*, and if madness prevail not, may forever be, your authentic title."

Another was from Mazzini in answer to a note she had written him. Indeed, he wrote her twice—long, beautiful letters: "Whatever the *present* may be, you must front it with dignity, with a clear perception of all your duties, with a due reverence to your immortal soul, with a religious faith in times yet to come, that are to dawn under the approach of other cloudless suns." She must be calm, he urged. She must dispassionately re-examine the past and send back to limbo the ghosts she had conjured up. Was not the immediate moment, after all, a trial that would soon be over? A devotion to duty, he remarked, was the course that had often saved him from despair—that, and a trust in God. "For I now most coolly and deliberately do declare to you, that partly through what is known to you, partly through things that will never be known, I am carrying a burden even heavier than you, and have undergone even bitterer deceptions." She must rouse herself. She must be strong—strong for the sake of the parents she had loved and for those persons whom she now loved or esteemed. "Some of them are deeply, silently suffering, but needing strength too, needing it perhaps from you. Get up and work; do not set yourself apart from us. When the Evil One wanted to tempt Jesus, he led Him into a solitude."

The fourteenth of July was approaching—her birthday. In

her confusion of mind she was tormenting herself with un-happy thoughts. A poignant desire was swelling in her—more than anything else in the world she yearned for the reassurance of a birthday letter from her husband. Were all her doubts mere phantoms? And after that parting, could Thomas write again in the spirit of his old affection? Possibly she had treated him with injustice, had made herself an added millstone round his neck at the very time when he most needed understanding and sympathy? True, in his latest note he had spoken of her goodness and watchful affection. She could herself not think of her conduct thus. Yet perhaps he would forgive, and write.

The night before her birthday was a bad, wakeful one for Jane, and she rose despairing of all things. At ten, the hour for letters, she slipped away to go, alone, to the Postoffice. But her hostess, and Geraldine Jewsbury, down from nearby Manchester, saw her and joined her for the walk. How she wished they had not come! But the letter would be there and her companions would merely delay a little the actual joy of reading it.

Jane reached the window. Not one, but two letters were handed out. Eagerly she took them. The writing was not familiar; neither was for her. Because she was so tired, Jane felt ready to burst into tears, but somehow controlled herself. Once in the house she shut herself in her room—a tumult of wretchedness in her heart. Was he so out of patience that he would no more write at all? Had he gone to Addiscombe and found no leisure there to remember her existence? Was he ill and could not write?

"Mrs. Carlyle, Mrs. Carlyle!" some one was calling, "are you there? Here is a letter for you!" Jane flung open the door. It was from her husband. The post-mistress, having overlooked it, had sent it out now.

No love note was ever received with greater thankfulness. Yes, she must try to believe what he said there, believe it now and ever more: that with all her faults and follies, she *was* dearer to him than any earthly creature. He had sent a tiny card case as a gift. It bore his kiss, he wrote; would she kiss it too?

What a pother she had made over this incident—this matter of the letter! Really, with the set of nerves she possessed, she was unfit for living in such a world as this! Why, her hand still shook so that she could scarcely write to thank him, as—lovingly, gratefully—she did at once. She must lie down now, and get some rest.

Four days after her birthday, Jane and her friends from Seaforth spent a weekend at Speke Hall as the guests of its owner, a Mr. Brereton. Never in her life had Jane seen a more fascinating, ancient manor. It was so dead-old, so rickety and crumbling, that she would scarcely have been surprised had Queen Elizabeth and all her Court walked through the portals of her bedroom in their winding sheets for a cozy talk with her about the other world. The place had its private ghost, of course, a white lady with a baby in her arms which she was always on the point of tossing into the moat. Behind the tapestries in some of the bedrooms—fortunately not in hers—there were screech owls that snapped their beaks and chattered all night long in a way to make the blood freeze.

The other members of the party had already gone to bed. With curiosity Jane poked about beneath the drapery in her room, hoping to find a secret door or passage. She was enjoying the excursion with characteristic zest, and her own particular adventures. At last she tapped on woodwork that gave forth a hollow reverberation. Jane felt quite like the heroine of a romance of mystery and horror. Somewhere, surely, there must be a concealed lock or spring. She pushed gently against the wood. All at once the panel gave. Jane opened it with caution. Holding her candle before her, she peered into the gloom.

Strange! Here was a narrow cell with shelves of new wood in it. What could that vague, dark object be, above up there? Cautiously she stretched her hand towards it. Her own bonnet! Somehow she had managed to penetrate into her closet!

At Seaforth, there were further letters from her husband. "I do not go to Addiscombe today, nor tomorrow, nor indeed for an indefinite, perhaps infinite time to come. To the lady I have, of course, told nothing, except that you are very unwell. But she seems to have discerned pretty clearly for herself that our intercourse is to be carried on under different conditions henceforth, or probably to cease altogether before long." Lady Harriet, he added, appeared quite ready to conform to this arrangement; seemed, indeed, more indifferent to the matter than he had quite expected. He too, if needs must be, was ready to comply, though that it should be required, he added, struck him as rather a perversity of fate. Lady Harriet and her husband, he remarked in closing, were about to make a tour of Scotland. They had suggested that he join them from his mother's at Scotsbrig. But there was little likelihood that he would do so. Circumstances must decide.

When he stopped off at Seaforth on his way to his native Annandale, Jane learned that her husband had accepted the Barings' invitation. He had not wished to, he insisted. He was hoping, indeed, that rain would prevent the trip. Could she not believe that the prospect gave him not the slightest pleasure? Their farewells at Seaforth were quite as distressing as had been those in London.

A woman with plenty of solid fat, a woman with an unlimited supply of mirth and all the good humor in the world: that was the type, Jane decided bitterly, that Carlyle should have married—not a person as sensitive and thin-skinned as himself.

What had now come to pass?—reflected Thomas. Farthest from his thoughts had been the idea that conduct of his should bring any mortal creature injury. Yet his own wife was prophesying shipwreck for them.

While Carlyle was occupied in Scotland, Jane made ready to end her own visit. Never since her marriage had she been so supremely unhappy. And he also, it was plain from his letters, was suffering intensely. Yet when the Barings summoned him, he had gone.

At Seaforth Jane could find no escape from her tormenting thoughts. Without knowing quite why—with a blind, instinctive seeking for relief—she went to Manchester on Geraldine's invitation. Nothing seemed more unlikely than that good should come from this flight to Geraldine—Geraldine with her volatile temperament and impetuous ways.

Unbelievably, providentially, Geraldine—all her effervescence suppressed—gave her the very treatment which was needed. First she let her rest. Then, as soon as she discovered Jane was ready to take an interest in the things about her— the mills and the great commercial establishments of the industrial city served the purpose admirably—Geraldine arranged an active schedule of visits to factories and the like that kept Jane continually on the go. The two days she had originally intended to remain expanded into several weeks. And Geraldine's regimen at last brought something like color into Jane's cheeks and something like calm into her heart.

But when she returned to Chelsea, she found everything just as it had been before. Year in, year out, her husband's calls at Bath House continued; Lady Harriet's invitations to them both, to Carlyle, or to Jane alone, continued—requests that they come to Addiscombe, to Bay House, or to the Grange. When Bingham Baring, on his father's death, assumed the inheritance and Lady Harriet became Lady Ashburton—it was still the same.

Lady Harriet, Jane could plainly see, was waging a campaign to win her. In fact, as always, she was in reach of victory. Jane could do nothing but succumb—it was wiser to force oneself to make the best of a situation instead of the worst. Amazing, she thought, how Lady Harriet, at the least sign of a reactionary turn—and Jane occasionally tried them—could ply her once again round her little finger. By Heaven, she *was* the cleverest woman that was ever known or heard of! She could reduce to willing thraldom any person she might choose to capture.

"Sit down, my Dear," said caustic old Samuel Rogers at a party given by Dickens, "Sit down, my Dear—I want to ask you; is your husband as much infatuated as ever with Lady Ashburton?"

But during the past years Jane had been studying her part. She would not be a fluttering dove for such a fox as Rogers. "Oh, of course," she replied, with a laugh, "why shouldn't he be?"

Rogers pressed on relentlessly. "Now—do *you* like her," he questioned, "tell me honestly is she kind to *you*—as kind as she is to your husband?"

"Why you know it is impossible for *me* to know *how* kind

she is to my husband; but I *can* say she is extremely kind to *me* and I should be stupid and ungrateful if I did *not* like her."

Rogers could not hide his disappointment. He was not getting at all the response for which he was fishing. "Humph! Well! it is very good of you to like her when she takes away all your husband's company from you—he is always there, isn't he?"

"Oh, good gracious, no!" answered Jane lightly, with a touch of sarcasm, "he writes and reads a great deal in his own study."

"But he spends all his evenings with her I am told?"

"No—not all—for example you see he is *here* this evening."

Rogers was vexed. He had not been able to confuse the wife. He had been irritated all evening by the husband. Carlyle's brilliant, opinionated conversation dominated every gathering and his powerful voice quite drowned out the feeble tones which old age imposed on the Banker-poet.

"I *see* he is here *this* evening," he remarked by way of parting shot, "and *hear* him too—for he has done nothing but talk across the room since he came in."

A very devilish old man, Jane reflected, but he had got no satisfaction out of her!

Only when she was ill, only when she was very tired, only when conditions at home were extremely vexatious, did her emotional nature break through the brittle poise she could assume. At such times she might write in confidence to a friend: "I do think there is much truth in the Young German idea that marriage is a shockingly immoral institution, as well as what we have long known it for—an extremely disagreeable one."

When she visited the Ashburtons themselves, Jane was sure that no one but her husband had any inkling of the state of her secret mind.

Chapter Twenty-Nine

JANE was planning for herself, in that summer of 1849, a unique excursion—she would visit Haddington. Her sensitivity, the emotional upsets she experienced when she let her thoughts wander probingly in the past, had kept her, since her mother's death, from seeking out those places in Scotland most intimately connected with her early life. And Haddington, her birthplace, where her father lay buried, she had shunned for a far longer period. She had not laid eyes on her native town since the days when she and Carlyle, in their first years of marriage, had lived in the city of Edinburgh.

To prepare herself for the adventure, Jane determined to travel northward by easy stages, stopping off to visit various friends on the way. After Haddington, she would join forces with her husband, who by that time would be back from a trip he was planning to Ireland.

Her last pause, before Haddington, was in Yorkshire, where she was the guest of W. E. Forster, who had entertained her husband and herself two years before when they enjoyed the novel experience of being tourists together through the colorful Peak District. On that excursion, Forster, indeed, had been their capable director and had guided them triumphantly through the best sights of Derbyshire. Thomas had been much relieved to find someone ready to assume the responsibilities and leave him free to his own reflections and his pipe. That year there had been no book in the making to harass him, and Jane had kept her own ghosts securely under lock and key.

Mrs. Carlyle, thought Forster at the time, was like a girl in her delight at every new scene and every novel circumstance. She was one of those rare women a man could talk with all day, or listen to all day, with equal pleasure. And the Master, too, had been a first-rate companion. Beneath his misanthropy Forster had quickly discovered a rich mine of genial, hearty kindness. Of course he constantly uttered remarks that shocked one's ideas and principles, sacred or profane. His will was tough as leather, but not a constant influence. With tact, one could get one's way well enough. No use arguing, of course. He took not the slightest notice of argument, nor even of a contradictory fact. But a quiet, simple protest, if absolutely needed, after a Carlylean explosion, saved one's intellectual integrity and gained respect. With all his sternness, amounting at times almost to ferocity, there were such gleams of tenderness, so bright and so warm, that it was impossible not to love him. And his eccentric humor drew laughter out of all manner of everyday, trivial occurrences. Without this merciful safety-valve of humor, thought Forster with a shudder, what a fearful, fiendlike creature he might be in his darker moods when the devil of dyspepsia was in him.

After breakfast, on Tuesday, July 24, Jane took the train from Rawdon. The last stage of her journey had begun. Forster, without any urging, announced that he would accompany her part of the way. He was himself bound for Ireland to share with her husband the concluding days of travel there.

At five in the afternoon the train reached Morpeth, not far from the Scottish border. Jane did not wish to come to her destination worn out by journeying. She would stop at the inn there, the Phoenix, for the night, to be fresh and rested next day. Out of the goodness of his heart, Forster refused to leave her yet. Jane was amused to see how he clung to the masculine theory that a woman, accompanied by two boxes, a writing-case and carpet bag, was ill adapted to travel by herself.

Chops and cherry-tart at the Phoenix made a pleasant dinner. Then Jane and her companion, on her suggestion, sauntered along the banks of the Wansbeck though a drizzling rain obscured the clock and the quaint figures on the ancient tower which were the pride of the little town. She was glad to drink the steaming brandy negus which Forster ordered for her on their return. Had she been alone, she might not have mustered the audacity to command so masculine a potion for herself. Then, before the rousing fire in the parlor, they chatted cosily till twelve.

With her excited anticipations, Jane had not dared to hope

for sleep, yet she never woke till past daybreak. The morning was bright as diamonds.

Her train did not leave till afternoon. Together she and Forster wandered about the town and even ventured into the wooded countryside, with the barrier of the Cheviot Hills, and Scotland's border, lying beyond.

William Edward saw her off at the station. Jane wished to Heaven she were already at her destination. Strange, what tricks one's temperament could play! She was almost ready to change cars at Berwick-upon-Tweed and scurry back to London. Yet no, she would persist. "Me can do what me's bid," she used to say as a little child when any difficult matter lay ahead, and she had bidden herself to rediscover Scotland.

She would enter Haddington as a stranger, she decided; after twenty years' absence no friend remaining there would recognize her. Not even the Donaldsons, her parents' oldest friends, must know who was so near them! After a visit to Edinburgh, she would return to make herself known. Now, she told herself, she could not front the fuss these dear people and other acquaintances would be sure to make.

That was Jane's excuse for thus entering incognito the city of her birth. What she would not recognize, in the middle-aged common sense which she prided herself on possessing, was that deep within her the old romantic spirit urged her on into the novelty of this experiment—she would come to Haddington like a visitor from another sphere to see herself as a girl walking lightly down its familiar streets.

Dunbar was approaching; the next stop would be hers. She recognized Peer Bridge. Once, when she had driven with her father in the gig as he made his medical visits, she had crossed that chasm. He had placed his arm tightly round her while she gazed, awestruck, into the depths.

At Dunbar, an old lady in a widow's dress, and her young daughter, got in. A boy in yeomanry uniform, obviously the girl's lover, was there to bid good-bye. How like her own youth that seemed: the garrison, the brilliant scarlet uniforms, the gay balls, in those years directly after Napoleon's exile at St. Helena and Byron's departure to liberate Greece! How she had grieved to learn of her favorite poet's death! And Byron's verses seemed so childish now.

Jane stole a glance at the old woman. Gracious powers, that shriveled widow was buxom, bright-eyed, rosy Mrs. Frank Sheriff of her girlhood in East Lothian! And this child, who had a lover now, had got herself born in the interval.

To test her anonymous state, Jane asked her traveling companion a question about the journey. The widow replied with that compassionate distinctness and detail which one reserves for foreigners or idiots. No need to worry that any one would penetrate the disguise wrought by the years!

Jane grew every instant more excited. To insure herself against recognition, she had used on her luggage, not tags bearing her own name, but other people's visiting cards. At Longniddry, where she was forced to wait fifteen minutes for the Haddington local, she was amazed, then dismayed, at the sedulous attention of her porter. Even after helping her with her luggage he hovered questioningly about. Surely it was not possible that he had recognized her! At last he made a low bow. "I was not aware that any of the family were in this quarter," he said respectfully. Was her little game up? At the carriage door, after he had taken care of her boxes, he spoke again. "Excuse me, ma'am, but I was in the service of the brother of Mr. Humphrey St. John Mildmay." Of course! She had quite forgot that it was Mrs. Mildmay's card which she had fastened to her luggage!

At Haddington station, brand new since the days of the coach, the *Good Intent*, that used to jounce sedately between the burgh town and Edinburgh, Jane glanced timidly from her railway window, then dismounted, forced out of the past by the immediate problems of luggage and lodgings. No cabs stood in the driveway; only a dusty little omnibus which seemed already full to bursting. Jane, mindful of the strict regulations of London, remarked to herself that obviously there was not place for her. She must have spoken louder than she realized. "Never heed! come in! that makes no difference!" cried the passengers inside at a breath.

She was set down at the George Inn, where Carlyle, twenty-eight years before, had stayed that first evening of their meeting when Edward Irving had brought him down from Edinburgh. A new landlord, and a sleepy-looking waiter, showed Jane to the best chamber—a first floor room, large, old-fashioned, with the usual whiff of must and mildew. Jane sat down by one of the three windows facing the thoroughfare and looked towards her old house across the way. The same street, the same buildings, but smaller, and so very silent. She had seen it often in her dreams at Chelsea. Now, with the actual sight before her eyes, it appeared even more dreamlike. With the coming of the railway, Haddington had lost much of its old activity. It was a small place near a great city; not the proud burgh town of former years. Jane rang the bell and ordered tea.

The afternoon had yet some hours of daylight in it. She summoned the waiter. Could she be shown the old church yonder? she inquired, indicating the tower of the venerable Abbey, the beautiful Lamp of the Lothians, as familiar to her as the interior of her drawing room at Chelsea—though she spoke as if she were seeing the building for the very first time. The keeper of the keys was fetched. Like a stranger, she let herself be conducted along the way, every inch of which she knew by heart. There was the school house, where, triumphing over the boys, she had won the title of *Dux* in studies. There was the play ground; there the bowling green.

Her guide fumbled at the church-gate and flung it open. She begged him to wait; she would not need him for the present. New graves—many of them—crowded the small enclosure. She passed among them and entered the ruined choir, its arches open to the sky, the grass dark green in the twilight. A couple of fresh, smartly got up tombs had intruded on the ancient peace of the enclosure. Beside them, his—her father's—looked old, very old. Round it were nettles growing, and the stone was dark with lichens. Jane bent over the inscription. Moss filled the lettering so one could scarcely read the words. But as she looked more closely, she observed that two lines had quite recently been cleared. Who had been there before her, still caring after twenty-nine years? The graceful arches knew, the old walls knew, but would not tell. Here was eternal silence, sadness too, but rest without end.

Would she not care to walk through the building? inquired the sexton when Jane returned to the gate. She entered the nave of the Abbey, restored as the church. Her family pew, she saw, had not been relined since she and her parents had occupied it. The once green cloth was white with age. In the gathering darkness, Jane fancied she could see shadows. There, in her usual corner, sat her beautiful mother, and beside her, that fresh-looking girl—herself.

It was time to escape from all such phantoms!

She would return in the morning, to clear the moss from the inscription. She asked the sexton where he lived. "Next door to the house that was Dr. Welsh's," he answered, with a sharp glance at her face. Then, after a moment's silence, and in a very gentle voice, he remarked, "Excuse me, me'em, for mentioning that, but the minute I set eyes on ye at the 'George' I jaloused it was her we all looked after whenever she went up or down." Jane could control herself no longer. She burst into tears like a child caught stealing apples.

"You won't tell of me?" she asked. The old man nodded assent.

The River Tyne, as it had done for ages, slipped gently past its verdant banks. Swallows, in the gathering dusk, wheeled and dipped above the tranquil water. Jane walked alone by the margin, to take the customary evening stroll so familiar in her teens. Where were the laughing boys and girls who used once to flock there? All gone now, and few had come to take their place. The town, in very truth, had fallen into silence and desertion. Two little children wandering hand in hand were the only living beings whom she met. Like babes in the woods, they seemed, in a land of unreality. Yet everywhere she looked, the trees, the paths, the grass, had exactly the same appearance of years and years ago when she had left this place to be married. Even the puddles of last night's rain lay in the hollows she used to step across.

Leaving the byways, Jane walked swiftly down the main street. Almost all the names she was once familiar with had disappeared from the shop signs. But that on the cooper's stall was the same. Seized by the whim, she entered. Two little quaighs caught her eye, and these she bought as though she were a tourist after souvenirs. The shopkeeper was a loquacious man and with very little prompting embarked on a long history of the past and present of the town.

"Dr. Welsh's death was the sorest loss that ever came to

the place," he remarked, shaking his head, when the talk turned to the burgh's roster.

"Had he a daughter?" Jane inquired.

"Yes; Miss Welsh! Remember her well! The tastiest young lady in the whole place, but," he added, "she was very—not just to call proud—very reserved in her company."

"And what became of her?"

"Oh, she went away to England, and died there."

More than ever, Jane felt like her own ghost. She left the shop. In front of Sunny Bank, where lived her godmother, Miss Donaldson, she paused a moment. How tranquil it looked! An almost irresistible impulse to rush in and make herself known tugged at her heart, but she overcame it. Perhaps in the morning she would break her resolve, but not tonight, not in her present state of feeling, must she enter that quiet house! She bent over and kissed the gate; then, like a shadow, crept away.

Once more at her inn, she rang for candles, a glass of sherry, and a pitcher of hot water. Her feet were wet from the dew among the graves. She mixed herself a negus and drank it off.

How spend the evening that stretched before her? She opened her letter-case. The scratch of her pen alone broke the silence. The George Inn, the town of Haddington, the very world itself seemed asleep. Only from the Town Hall, a familiar voice spoke at intervals—the tower clock marking the passage of the hours. Eleven, then twelve, it struck, and yet Jane's pen traveled, line after line, across the sheets. "Thomas Carlyle," she wrote, "Galway, Sligo, Ireland." She sealed the letter. Her candle had almost guttered away. A moment later, she snuffed it out.

At half-past five she woke. Another perfect day, bright and beautiful. She picked up her writing of the night before. Her candle, just lighted, was standing on the table. She thrust the letter in the flame. Poor Carlyle! She must not harass him with any such account of her adventures! Too much emotion, by far, had been recorded in those close-packed sheaves. All that pent-up tempest had best be gathered back into the vale of silence.

At six, Jane was standing before her father's house. How

bedraggled it looked now, in need of paint and whitewash! Yes, it had seen far better days. With a shudder, Jane moved on.

The air in the churchyard, in contrast to the oppressiveness she had sensed at her altered home, seemed purer, more easy to breathe. The sexton had agreed to meet her there at eight. The gate was still locked. She was an hour before the time. Jane made a dash at the high wall, clambered over, and tumbled down inside. A lone pedestrian, an oldish man, who chanced to be approaching at the moment, stopped in amazement and rubbed his eyes. What ailed that woman thus to storm the impassable? Strange, something familiar about her too! "That's Jeannie Welsh!" he muttered, "no other woman would climb the wall instead of going in at the gate!" Yet what a silly thought! Jeannie Welsh had married long ago, and gone to London.

When the gate-keeper came at eight, he was amazed to find Mrs. Carlyle already in the yard.

"How in the world did you get in?"

"Over the wall."

"No! surely, you didn't mean that!"

"Why not?"

"Lord's sake then," said the man in real admiration, "there's no end to you!"

When Jane was ready to leave, the sexton turned inquiringly to her. "There is one man in town, me'em, you might like to see, James Robertson, your father's old servant."

Their own old Jamie! What was he doing? A waiter at the Star, she was told. The sexton added he would send him round.

Too early yet for Sunny Bank. She spent a few moments inspecting the old schoolhouse. She had found the door ajar, and a woman busy scrubbing the floor within. The maps and geometric figures of her own day had given place to texts from Scripture and silly half-penny pictures. The building where Edward Irving had once taught had become an Infant School. Jane looked to her old place. Once, she remembered, the master, coming at seven to open school, had found her already seated there, sound asleep after two hours' study, her black locks like a bookmark on the open leaves of the mighty atlas.

Sunny Bank had never looked more lovely, more inviting than when Jane, half an hour later, stood before its hedge of red roses in full bloom, a border that reached from the gate to the very house itself. At Jane's knock, a tidy maid-servant answered. Jane did not give her name. "Are your ladies quite well?" she inquired.

"Miss Jess and Miss Catherine are quite well; Miss Donaldson rather complaining."

"At what hour do your ladies get up?"

"They are up, me'em, and done breakfast."

How should she introduce herself?

"What name shall I say?" inquired the maid, as if in answer to her unspoken question.

"None; I think perhaps my name would startle them more than myself;—tell them someone they will be glad to see."

Jane entered and sat down. The first to come was Miss Catherine. She remained at the door quite speechless, staring at the visitor.

"Oh, Miss Catherine, don't be frightened at me!" exclaimed Jane in dismay.

"Jeannie! Jeannie! Jeannie Welsh! My Jeannie!" How blessed to lock arms about each other!

When she left Sunny Bank, Jane promised she would return many times again. The railway had at last made traveling so easy. Unless unavoidable circumstance prevented, they would see her every summer.

On her way back to the inn, the cooper at whose shop she had paused the night before, spying her from the door, planted himself in her path. Would she not oblige him with her name? he asked; he was sure that he knew her. When she told him, adding that the rumor she was dead contained a certain amount of exaggeration, a pleased grin wreathed his face.

"How many children have you?" he inquired.

"None."

"None?"—in a tone of astonishment. "None at all? Then what on earth have you been doing all this time?"

How should one answer such a question? "Amusing myself," said Jane.

The cooper started, then regained his composure. Would she not accept a little gift for old time's sake; something small and fancylike, to take to London?

At the inn, after breakfast, the chambermaid knocked at the

door. A gentleman to see the lady, she announced. Jamie! She hurried to the parlor. There was Jamie, sure as life! She flung her arms round his neck. The old fellow was crying, he was so glad to see her. He had decked himself in his Sunday clothes for the occasion.

"You knew me, Jamie, at first sight?"

"Toot! we knew ye afore we seed ye!"

"Then you were told it was me?"

"No; they told us just we was to speak to a lady at the 'George,' and I knew it was Mrs. Carlyle."

"But how could you tell, dear Jamie?"

"Hoots! who else could it be?"

Dear, funny old Jamie! she could have hugged him again.

It was nearly eleven, the hour for her train. Her bag was packed. She must hurry on to Edinburgh. But there was one thing more to be done. "Thomas Carlyle, Galway, Sligo, Ireland," she wrote for the second time. She explained the fate of the previous letter and the reasons for its cremation. "I have now only time to write the briefest of notes; but a blessing from here I must send you; to no other mortal would I, or indeed could I, write from this place at this moment; but it comes natural to me to direct a letter to you here, and that is still something, is it not?" And she signed it, "Ever your affectionate,

"Jeannie Welsh."

Chapter Thirty

*T*HE decade or more that began with the year of revolutions, 1848, wrought those changes in the history of
nations and of men so surprising as they happen, so
to-have-been-expected in the sight of posterity.

As crisis after crisis burst over Europe, the radical exiles,
many of them familiar figures at Cheyne Row, poured over
the Channel for their brief hour of triumph. In Paris, men
once befriended by the Carlyles were in the saddle. Mazzini
was on his way to Italy—his dream of republican unity no
longer so incredible; the despotic Austrians who for many
years had ground his country under heel apparently at last on
the run.

Then, in politics, a reaction had set in. Imperialism seemed
once more dominant, and even in France, a president set himself up as Emperor—Napoleon the Third. It was this picture-
book ruler who helped turn Mazzini's dream to nightmare.
In Rome, the Pope, who for his own aggrandizement favored
the Austrian despots, had been driven out and Mazzini elected
chief triumvir of the city. Then the liberty-loving French, of
all people, spurred on by the wish of Napoleon the Little to
gain the support of French Catholics and a foothold on the
peninsula, sent an expeditionary force against the city. Though
ringed about by foreign enemies, Mazzini conducted the affairs
of Rome with unexpected acumen and common sense. In the
vast palace of the Quirinal, his as head of the state, he lived
in a single room with the frugality of the meanest citizen. But
the republic was doomed. For almost a month, against overwhelming odds, Rome held out. Then the assembly, seeing
the hopelessness of further resistance, voted that Mazzini should
surrender. He was ready to die behind the final barricades,
maintaining to the end the right to be republican. Instead, he

went once more into exile, returning to his life of endless plotting.

For many months the Carlyles had received no direct word from him. Then, one afternoon, while Jane and her husband were entertaining company, Mazzini, as if by magic, reappeared. Hearing his voice in the hall, Jane rushed to greet him. Carlyle, forgetting all his scorn of the arch revolutionist's political philosophies, sprang forward too. "How white it has grown!" exclaimed Jane, stroking Mazzini's hair. There were tears in her eyes, and her voice faltered. He had a gray beard now, instead of black mustachios. "You must recollect, my Dear," he said, "that in the old times I needed always to have a barber to shave me—and in the camp with Garibaldi, and flying for my life, I could not of course take everywhere with me a barber! And so my beard had to grow and now and then be cut with a scissor."

England, during the decade, in a fever of excitement, had fought the Crimean war—Carlyle protesting the while at the folly and destruction—and shortly after it was over, people began wondering why the campaign had ever been allowed to start.

In these years of unrest, Carlyle's nerves became more and more inflamed. Though he had lost faith in the ballot, his sympathy for the cause of the forgotten men, the poor workers, was painful in its intensity. If privation, if actual famine continued among them in England, if they were denied the right to labor, there could be no telling the ultimate horrors which might result. At last his pent-up indignation found release in a series of scorching denunciations issued, as they came hot from his pen, as the *Latter-Day Pamphlets*.

What a row they had kicked up among the sons of privilege! Jane was amazed at its violence, and disturbed, too, at the falling away of many of her husband's oldest friends—members of the very class he had wished to warn against the perils of the times. During the period of the pamphlets the majority of the callers at the house was made up of the members of her own congregation. Thomas, like a child who has exploded an extra large firecracker, was shocked and pained at the uproar. But presently the echoes died away.

In the realms of the mind, great philosophies—during the decade—were conceived, pondered, or neglected; great works were written, praised to the skies, damned to hell, or merely ignored while lesser books captured attention. At the end of the period, Charles Darwin's epoch-making *Origin of the Species* had appeared, and the first two volumes (four more were yet to follow) of Carlyle's most ambitious work, *The History of Frederick the Great,* had been published.

By middle life—in 1848, Carlyle was fifty-three, Jane forty-seven—years travel swiftly, though days themselves may seem erratic in their course: some painfully creeping while others run. Life, crowded with emotions and events or stagnant in a mire of dull routine, settles to a pattern.

At the outset of the day of revolutions, Emerson, the American friend, had revisited England and slept in the guest room at Cheyne Row. The spectre of poverty he knew once to have been there had ceased to haunt the house. The Carlyles were even saving money. Jane made three hundred pounds a year serve all demands of living. She was manager, and Carlyle saw to it that she got the due amount. Once only had she been forced to ask for more, when unavoidably rising expenses ate up the funds. Even then her lightness of touch did not desert her. Like a British Chancellor of the Exchequer, she drew up for submission an imposing documentary report—labeled "Budget of a Femme Incomprise." Whereupon her husband, as Prime Minister, increased the appropriation.

Even in their youth, Jane and Thomas had witnessed many deaths. But middle years multiply these partings. Old Mrs. Carlyle, Tom's peasant mother, had gone at the age of eighty-three, her famous son at her bedside. Edward Sterling, too, had died, following not long after John, his brilliant, charming, ill-fated son. Jane unfortunately was not in London to receive the Thunderer's last call. Though almost helpless from a stroke, he was brought by carriage to Chelsea in hopes of a farewell. How often she had made a jest of that old man's affection! Yet possibly, she mused, his was the truest she ever possessed. She would miss him sadly—the kindly, irascible, lovable, provoking old man. Youth, too, had gone from their circle. Charles Buller, genial, delightful, gay, the cleverest of the younger men in Parliament, had most unexpectedly died just when he seemed ready to fulfill Carlyle's prophecies for political success.

But other friends had filled the gap. Always, Thomas and Jane held a fascination for young people. William Allingham and Aubrey De Vere—charming Irishmen and poets—had entered the famous door at Cheyne Row. Arthur Hugh Clough, the best man, in Dr. Arnold's opinion, who ever saw the playing fields of Rugby; Thomas Woolner, the young sculptor; and Holman Hunt, the painter. Jane corresponded with each in reply to their often naïve, confidential letters. That a gap of years lay between her and them seemed never to occur to these men. Anthony Froude, a young scholar and former Fellow of Oxford, came also—full of a somewhat awestruck, fearful admiration of Carlyle; a romantic sympathy for his wife. He was sure that he had never seen a more unusual, appealing woman. What black hair she had, raven black! Her eyes—sad in rare moments of day-dreaming—had a dangerous light in them for all their kindly warmth. The sight of her pale face, at that first meeting, followed him through the years.

Not only young men; young women, too, entered Jane's life and valued her friendship. Mrs. Alexander Gilchrist, who later, after her husband's death, traveled to America to become the intimate of Walt Whitman, settled in Cheyne Row to be Jane's neighbor. Youthful Ellen Dwight Twisleton, wife of Carlyle's admirer the Honorable Edward Twisleton, M.P., became in turn a devoted admirer of Jane.

Women of the highest nobility continued to discover her: Lady Lothian, Lady Amberley, and others. Lady Ashburton's mother, the Dowager Lady Sandwich—more amusing, even, and as clever as her daughter—had been mentioned to her as the most insolent of English Peeresses. But Jane utterly denied the impeachment. She found her precisely the one among these aristocrats with whom it was easiest to talk without the least thought of blood—as though both were women living on a few hundred pounds a year.

And she intimately entertained the youngest generation too. "Will you go with me?" she remarked one day to Jane Lydia, her godchild, at the Macreadys, setting her down from the place of privilege, her lap, as she rose to leave for Chelsea.

"I should like it very much."

"That she would!" said Mrs. Macready, who had overheard the conversation, "and you need not be afraid of her misconducting herself, for she is a good child."

Merciful heavens, they were taking her seriously! To introduce a godchild into her house when her husband was acting as though he himself were the godparent of every nation of prodigal, wayward Europe would surely never do. Yet she decided to risk it. So the little girl was deposited at Cheyne Row for a three days' visit.

Jane ran horses with her, dressed dolls, and executed her every command. How very active a six-year-old could be, even though small and delicate! Really one could scarcely believe it. Her husband had been less appalled than Jane expected, but she could not convince herself that under his calm he did not nourish a homicidal impulse to wring the child's neck. Night would be the test. Heaven forbid that the infant should burst out crying.

What a deal of washing and combing lay hidden in so tiny a girl! Finding Lydia's clothes all sewed together, Jane was in some perplexity just how to get them off. But at last the child was ready. It would never do to put her in the spare room, next to Carlyle. So Jane popped the little thing in her own bed and kissed her good-night. Would she burst out crying? Jane waited anxiously. Instead, the oddest little sound arose—Lydia was singing to herself.

At twelve, Jane retired, but not to rest. All night long her bedfellow's small feet or sharp elbows prodded and pummeled her with restless energy. By morning, though the child had slept well, Jane herself felt quite exhausted. Certainly, there were penalties attached to this function of being a godmother. But when Lydia, waking at seven, threw her arms round her neck and exclaimed "Oh, I am so glad to be here!" Jane melted.

She was no novice with children. Thackeray's daughters, without their mother now (she was in an asylum), often visited Cheyne Row. Through many years, till they were quite grown up, the practice continued.

They had first come on a wintry day—numb with cold and a little frightened. A fire was burning cheerily on the hearth of the downstairs dining room, and before it were two steaming cups of chocolate. "I thought you would be frozen," remarked the hostess, reaching a cup to each girl. No need, after that, to be nervous and on one's guard. The chocolate became an accepted ritual of these visits, and Thackeray's daughters, sitting cosily by the fireside, sipping their drinks and warming their hands on the pretty china, would linger through the afternoon while their hostess superintended the feast, invited the girls' confidences, and talked after her spirited fashion. Their eyes took in the room—the fascinating screen which Mrs. Carlyle had made, covered all over with pictures, drawings, prints, and portraits without end (their father himself had drawn several); the paneled walls; the paintings. But most of all, they watched their hostess. Anne, the elder of the two, thought how much she herself, save for her animation, looked like a painting. She was so slim, so bright, so upright and alive in her place. She resembled one of those grand ladies with the awesome names and titles their father sometimes took them to call on—not at all the sort of person one might expect in such a modest house. Always becomingly dressed, Anne noticed: most queenly in black velvet trimmed with delicate point lace. Anne's father had shown her some portraits by a man named Gainsborough. Gainsborough should be living now, decided Anne; he was just the artist to paint Mrs. Carlyle.

As the girls grew older, their hostess sometimes told them stories about her husband—his droll sayings, his struggles with his books. She seemed very, very proud of him. But Anne remembered one remark: "If you wish for a quiet life, never you marry a dyspeptic man of genius!"

Once she had spoken of self-control. "We have all," she said, "a great deal more power over our minds than it is at all the fashion to allow, and an infinity of resource and ability to use it." She paused, then continued: "There was a time in my own life when I felt that unless I strove against the feeling with all my strength and might, I should be crazed outright. I passed through that time safely; I was able to fight it out, and not to let myself go. People *can* help themselves; that I am convinced of, and that fact is not nearly enough dwelt upon."

These were the events, these some of the people that filled Jane's years. Always, in the background, was the commanding figure of Lady Ashburton. There was no escaping her. But neither was there escape from Jane's new dog, little Nero. In her untired moments, Jane saw each in fair perspective.

Deep mystery surrounded Nero's ancestors. Some authorities declared him to be a Cuban spaniel. Others were insistent he was a Maltese. And a few contended that he was a not very distinguished specimen belonging to the excellent clan of Scotsmen that hailed from the Isle of Skye. But as a dog he was magnificent. So Jane had named him Nero.

He had been presented to her by a Manchester devoté of her husband. This admirer, when he made the gift, had done so without consulting the master of Cheyne Row. Surely her husband would manifest a whim to kick his foot through the animal! Yet when Nero arrived—so perfectly beautiful and queer-looking, exclaimed Jane with rapture—Carlyle not only withheld his toe but looked positively flattered when the beast mustered the hardihood to spring on his knee as he sat puffing tobacco by the fire.

Carlyle had survived an army of Jane's pets—pets of every description from the lower forms of life to the human. There was never any telling what sort of waif she might bring home. Once she had rescued a sparrow from street urchins who were teasing it. Most of these creatures her husband regarded with a tolerant amusement. He was even ready to take care of them during his wife's absence. There had been her leech, for instance. A leech was a most superior pet, Jane insisted. It was like the human soul: could do without visible food during most of its stay on earth. "The leech is very well," Carlyle dutifully reported when Jane was away. "I went and saw it this morning; it has an allowance of fresh water every day, and complains of nothing, lying all glued together at the top of the glass (the little villain), and leading a very quiet life of it."

Canaries were more perishable creatures. There was Chico, who had come with them to Cheyne Row. Chico got a wife and produced two children, but like prodigal sons they flew away into the trees of the garden and vanished towards swift destruction. Then Chico, noticing his careworn, tattered spouse, fell murderously upon her and pecked a hole in her head. But the gods did justice, and cut the thread of his disreputable life.

Jane's cats were a constant menace to her canaries and to household tranquillity as well. She counted it very fortunate that her husband was absent when one of them produced kittens in his bed. After Nero's advent, cats at Cheyne Row tended to grow more and more nomadic, for though he was no bigger than they, he enjoyed teasing them.

Nero turned out to be an almost barkless dog and rarely even whined. At night he slept at the foot of Jane's bed. By day he followed her like a shadow, and enjoyed dozing in her lap, though in his waking hours he was a sprightly, active little dog. How very comforting it was to have something alive and cheery and very fond of one always near in the house!

So virtuous a dog, full of sense and engaging qualities, must surely have some failings. Jane set out to find them. She took Columbine, her handsome white cat, in her lap and started to pet her. Yes, Nero could be jealous! His manifestations of jealousy exceeded her most sanguine expectations. He retired under the sofa, and neither coaxing nor cake could persuade him out. He answered all her blandishments with an angry growl, and would not emerge till Columbine was banished from the room.

Street arabs, as Jane discovered to her sorrow, made a practice of snatching dogs which they returned to their owners only after being paid a suitable ransom. What a horrid feeling to find oneself suddenly minus one's dog! One moment Nero had been trotting at her feet, the next he was gone. Jane presently recognized him in the distance, tucked under the arm of a dog-stealer. Luckily, at the cooper's shop (the tradesmen all knew Jane and adored her) one of the clerks ran out and collared the man. Nero had other adventures with these body thieves, but Jane, with amazing luck, always managed to snatch him from them. Once, when he had been stolen, the postman brought him back. He had been hunting for Nero all the while he should have been delivering letters. A pot of beer, that time, had sufficed for Nero's ransom.

Jane was glad to observe her husband's continued benevolence towards Nero. When he returned from a trip to Paris with the newly married Robert Brownings, he brought, as a birthday gift, a leash and collar, articles purchased by him in the fashionable Rue de la Paix. He even enjoyed going for his evening walks with Nero ranging at his heels.

There was a certain risk involved in letting the two go out together. "Is that vermin come back?" Carlyle demanded, as he let himself in with his latchkey late one night. At Jane's horrified "No!" he banged to the door and vanished. For twenty minutes Jane waited in dismay. At last she heard her husband's returning footsteps. Oh, joy, he was gollaring at something! Jane knew what that bad something was. She could have better spared a better dog!

Yes, Nero was a comfort, but most emphatically he could be a source of fright. One morning, while she was lying in bed, and Elizabeth, Helen's successor, was dusting in the living room, Jane was startled by a scream. Then she heard Elizabeth rush downstairs like a strong wind, and out into the street. A minute later, she could hear her slowly reascending the stairs. The bedroom door opened. There stood the maid, her face pale, Nero's limp body in her arms. He had been watching sparrows from an upper story window—a favorite diversion—and fallen out.

"*Is* he killed?" asked Jane, mustering her selfpossession.

"Not *quite*—I think, all *but!*"

Carlyle came down from his bedroom on the floor above, his chin soapy from shaving. "Has anything happened to Nero?" he inquired.

"Oh, Sir," said Elizabeth, "he *must* have broken *all* his legs, he leapt out at *your* window!"

"God bless me!" said Carlyle, and returned to his shaving.

Nero recovered.

Chapter Thirty=One

WHEN Jane went on visits to the Grange or elsewhere, she generally left Nero behind. Lady Ashburton possessed a parrot (the green chimera, Carlyle
named it) which Nero might fall on and destroy—a fearful
breach of etiquette.

Since inheriting the title, Lord and Lady Ashburton annually gave splendid house parties at the Grange over Christmas
and New Year's for the elect who were their friends. These
occasions provided Lady Ashburton with her court, and the
meeker wives among the guests attended in the rôle of ladies-
in-waiting. The revelers never included members of the aristocracy alone. Lady Ashburton—witty, sharp, and a conversa-
tional tactician—liked to have about her the cleverest men of
letters of the day. Chief among her writers, of course, was
Thomas Carlyle.

"Boreas," she called him for the tempests which he raised.
"My dear old prophet Carlyle," she would exclaim affectionately, "there is nobody like him! Has one any right to more
than one such friend in a life time?" Rumors were bound to
fly concerning so great a lady. She had fallen in love with
Carlyle, according to one story, but he had behaved well in
the matter and had incurred the gratitude of Lord Ashburton,
who, it was noticed, remained always his friend.

"You are the only person in the world who dares put a ring
through his nose!" said William Brookfield to his hostess at
the Grange. When comments like this reached Jane, they gave
her bitter water for the drinking. It was her prerogative to
tone down Carlyle's extravagant remarks; she resented hints
of her abdication. Yet for the most part, because Lady Ashburton was a mistress of social tact, her holiday gatherings were
not marred by any unpleasantnesses.

Certainly she knew how to skim the cream off for her parties; one wondered what she did with the mere relations and duty people who generally overrun a country house. In would pour her rich array of visitors: like flights of tropical birds, like nymphs and satyrs from the wood, like potentates from the East, like top-hatted gentlemen and officers in gold braid attending sacrosanct speech-day at Eton. There would be a cloud of world-known savants; a doctor this and professor that from Cambridge and from Oxford. Even a Prime Minister at times, and no end of the wittier Parliamentarians. Bishops, and if they were brilliant or handsome, representative of the lesser clergy like young William Brookfield. And physiologists and poets, artists and historians, men about town and mere nobility. Lord Gifford, a pleasant, sanguinary being who in his lifetime had killed sixty-five tigers, eleven elephants, and a multitude of bears; Lord Bessborough; Lord Carnarvon; and Lord and Lady Canning. And through the crowd, like a detonating comet, flashed Carlyle.

The horde of incoming guests would quite dominate the train from London. At Andover Road, the nearest approach to the Grange—trains stopped there at Lord Ashburton's command —private carriages would be waiting for the ladies and gentlemen, an omnibus for the valets and maids, and a large dray to move the hill of luggage. On arrival, each unattached visitor was assigned a private chamber, and there were suites for families—Mr. and Mrs. Carlyle, privileged above the rest, had separate bedrooms and other special favors. Within the house, guests furtively gazed at the display of old masters, the interiors by Inigo Jones, the conservatory packed with flowers out of season. Among the orchids and palms one could puff one's pipe or cigar, for Lady Ashburton was a modern hostess, willing to socialize the still-banned practice of mixed smoking. Tennyson liked to retire into a blue haze among the potted orange trees, and Thomas Carlyle would join him. Lady Harriet's husband—quiet, unassuming, kindly—would be a partner in the pleasant sin.

Breakfast at nine forty-five; luncheon at two; dinner at seven-thirty or eight. Everything was arranged for conversation, though where Lady Ashburton presided, neither the talk nor the food was ever heavy or lacking in spice. The most continental epicures were at once aware that a French chef plied his art in the kitchen. Before a formal dinner, Lady Ashburton dined first, in her rooms, alone. Then, at the sumptuous table, she could give all her attention to hospitality.

An ideal hostess, people said, whose skillful management and gracious habits oiled wheels already exquisitely smooth in their action. And though she was the center of attention, she never appeared to intrude, yet she spoke to every guest. She knew how to make herself missed by occasional intervals of non-appearance, so that her enthusiasts would rally about her the more eagerly when she reappeared. With the single exception of Carlyle, she was always the best talker, and without exception the best converser in the room. Her manner of speech, though she could be serious and profound, was generally playful, and often took the form of comic fiction or exaggeration. Nobody, exclaimed her devotés, could tell a story as well as she. Yet this claim of omniscience did not go without challenge from a minority. Mrs. Carlyle—Milnes and others privately whispered—had the same technique and could excel the hostess when she wished. Too bad she so infrequently essayed her arts at the Grange! But of course, how could she twinkle with an equal brightness here in this alien heaven?

Carlyle, as a man, need exercise no such restraint. Not even in his own parlor, when his spirits were good, would he be so communicative, so cheerful, and so entertaining. Though some thought that he spoke with almost wilful unreason, all enjoyed the arresting spectacle of Carlyle at his best. The grotesque force of his stories delighted his listeners. He reveled in tales of his own people, ending each with an infectious, mighty guffaw. Once—he began—some Scottish lairds were celebrating royally, as was their custom in the hearty unregenerate times of a century before. Their drinking bout had been going on for six or seven days when another friend chanced to come to the house. He gazed inquiringly at the bleared faces: one lacked its familiar rubicund hue.

"Disna the Laird of Invercaldy look unco *gash* the day?"

"Aye, he may weel look gash," answered the host, "he's been dead these twa days!"

Of course Carlyle's volcanic eruptions, in this genteel company, were sometimes embarrassing. He would occasionally lash himself into anger as he spoke, trying the nerves and patience of his hearers. But Lady Ashburton's influence over the orator could usually avert the mischief. Once he was expatiating on the paramount duty of silence. Someone touched him lightly on the arm. It was his wife.

"Why do you touch me?" he exclaimed with impatience. Then his face relaxed: "I know very well why you touched me, and you were quite right. I had much better practice silence than preach it!"

Though everybody was interested in Mrs. Carlyle, there were almost as many opinions about her as there were guests in that diverse company, a few of whom were her intimates though many knew her scarcely at all. Very peculiar, some thought her to be. Lady Ashburton, they noticed, gave her far more attention than she usually granted to members of her sex. She had a way of remaining in her own room during the early part of the day. Yet when she did appear, even those who hardly knew her could not be unaware of her presence. A few were rather shocked by her. Who was this woman who unexpectedly said things that rivaled the remarks of their hostess? Before their interrogating gaze, Mrs. Carlyle assumed an attitude of proud defiance. Some, with ears only for her husband, thought of her as an easy, modest person, generally rather quiet and subdued. They were startled by her occasional emergence on the center of the stage, generally when Lady Ashburton herself was not there. If festivities lagged, she could revive them with electrifying results. For the rest to watch a few of the gentlemen at target practice was dull enough. Once, while this was going on, Mrs. Carlyle took command of the proceedings. She begged Lord Ashburton to load his gun with a common tallow candle. It would pierce the wooden target as readily as a bullet, she insisted. The spectators were incredulous. Bang went the gun, and away flew the candle, drilling a large hole through the board. Once she had saved a moribund game of blind-man's-buff. She agreed to walk blindfolded in as direct a line as possible to a fixed point about a hundred yards down the tree-bordered avenue. Statesmen, wives dignified or prim, men of letters—an audience twenty or thirty strong—lined up to watch the fun. At first Jane's progress was straight enough. But not for long. The spectators rocked with undignified merriment as she groped

among the trees. The act, they declared, was as good as a pantomime in a play.

During mornings at the Grange, there was riding on the
downs, and sometimes skating on the lake. And since Lord
Ashburton's coverts were well stocked with birds, the sports-
men could have their shooting—a thousand pheasants bagged in
a single day. This last amusement always provoked the wrath
of Mrs. Carlyle. The sound of firing made her sick. Think of
the bodily and mental state of the surviving birds when the
sport was ended! Men could be very great beasts.

Games and entertainments filled the evenings. When Boreas
himself could be induced by Lady Ashburton to take part in
a charade, it was a spectacle indeed. *Bouts Rimés* were sometimes indulged in, though with professional writers present,
other guests had to be on their mettle. But there were always
diversions which gave an equal chance to all. Two persons
would be banished from the room, then two others, chosen
by vote, would be completely enveloped in sheets, save that
the eyes were left exposed. It was then the duty of the pair
who had been excluded to guess the identity of the swathed
figures. Very embarrassing to gaze deep in the eyes of one's
own wife, then name another woman! The game of Earth,
Air, and Water was another favorite. "I am an Ass!" rumbled
Carlyle, his voice full of self-scorn, scorn of all creation, and a
trace, too, of sympathy for the creature named. Then he would
rapidly count to ten and throw the handkerchief at charming
Mrs. Brookfield to go on with the play.

Lady Ashburton usually had among her guests some famous
musician whom she would cajole into performing—Chopin, for
instance, a delicate tremulous man who played divinely. Or she
would ask Tennyson—now famous and Poet Laureate of England—to read aloud, though Carlyle always escaped from the
throng of worshipful listeners.

Such were the Christmas house parties at the Grange, and
such the doings and amusements. Gentle, thoroughbred Mrs.
Brookfield, though her family was of the best and her husband a rising young clergyman, found herself sometimes almost bewildered by these great affairs. Certainly the first venture into such brilliance left one blinking like an owl in the
sun. She was amazed to notice that Mrs. Carlyle, also, seemed

at times a little ill at ease. She had never fancied that Mrs. Carlyle could be in the slightest degree upset by the mode of life at the Grange. In her own home—Mrs. Brookfield had dined several times at Cheyne Row—she could surely meet with more *esprit* than she was likely to find even at Lady Ashburton's.

With Carlyle regarding these holiday weeks at the Grange as a fixed routine, Christmases at home were an exception. But circumstances occasionally kept the pair at Cheyne Row. When this happened, there were usually visitors to form an impromptu party.

The weather, one holiday at home, awoke in Jane the memory of almost forgotten Scottish winters—a regular blizzard which did not melt as usual into intolerable slush. The clean snow acted on her like strong drink. Reckless of consequences —she was now past fifty—she went out into the swirling whiteness and took running slides along the pavements, her bonnet dangling in the wind on its ribbon down her neck. Like any child, between slides, she scooped up handfuls of the snow to taste it.

Heavens, she was tempting providence! At home, she waited for the blow to fall. Surely her idiocy would bring on the usual attack of influenza. But somehow, it didn't.

That Christmas, young William Brookfield was a caller. He was alone in London, his wife away nursing her ailing father. He had just dropped in, he explained, to extend the season's greetings; he was on his way to Mortlake to call on some friends.

"Are you dining there?"

"Oh, I am going to dine at home."

"Stay and eat with us!" said Jane.

Thomas warmly seconded his wife's request, a genial smile lighting his face. Brookfield had not expected the luck of such an invitation.

During the meal he took careful note so that he could report the details to his wife. Soup; after that an odd-shaped but excellent cut of mutton, with potatoes. Carlyle gazed at the roast in humorous despair, then handed the carving set to his guest.

"It's not the butcher's fault," said Jane with a chuckle, "it was to have been only a leg, but when you agreed to stay the loin was added!"

Every now and then the host, who had resumed the knife and fork as badge of office, would add a choice piece of crackle to the liberal helping on his guest's plate, with a homely, unconscious friendliness that was touching. There was glorious nut brown ale from "The Cricketers," a nearby tavern, and presently Jane added a bottle of excellent Madeira. Then came woodcocks, and finally a plum pudding with brandy sauce.

Nothing epic, nothing grand, but honest fare, honest friendship, and wonderful people!

"What did you do with yourself, yesterday, Brookfield?" asked an acquaintance, the day after Christmas.

"Oh! I dined with a great man who I am always proud to tell of."

"What, Lord Lonsdale?"

"Goodness, no!" exclaimed the Carlyles' guest.

Chapter Thirty=Two

AS ALWAYS, when Carlyle was doing a book, the problem was where to work. With Frederick, every room in No. 5 Cheyne Row had been tested and found wanting. Each year, Chelsea was growing noisier. SILENCE! Silence was what he needed. So Thomas launched into a cherished project—on the very top of the house he would have a sound-proof study built. Jane washed her hands of the enterprise. This chamber was of her husband's devising, his and that of his engineering friend, John Chorley.

Up went a large scaffolding, and a regiment of Irish workmen swarmed over it like monkeys and spread themselves about the roof. They pounded and thumped, they rent and tore at the timbers, they battered down the bricks and plaster till the house was filled with eddying dust clouds and chaos come again. So tremendous a racket in the cause of silence had rarely been raised. Carlyle wandered about in distraction and declaimed against the wretchedness of the materials that modern builders used. These workmen had less knowledge of construction than the horses in the street! They seemed oblivious to the fact that the lath and plaster of the roof did not constitute a floor. Crash! and one of them would come plunging through the ceiling of Carlyle's bedroom to hang suspended by the armpits in a vortex of splinters and lime. They never learned from experience. As Jane, in the upstairs room, was stooping over a drawer, the legs of an Irish hodman plummeted through the roof just missing her head. Had he broken her neck, she declared, it would have been herself, not Carlyle, who would be provided with a silent apartment through all eternity.

When at last the work was done, it proved to have its serious imperfections. In winter, Carlyle froze. In the summer, he was cooked out of his attic study and forced to write under the

awning in the garden. Bit by bit, Jane remedied the abuses.
She banished the complex, useless stove, an invention recommended by the builder, and had a fireplace installed. She
patched other botches. And Carlyle, though he disliked the
room and worked there under protest, pushed onward into the
wars of Frederick.

Well for Jane that she had many acquaintances! Though her
husband discovered it hard to like him, his chief companion
now was Frederick. When he sought diversion, his walks for
health led him often to Bath House.

Men, of course, continued to wait on Jane. Yet now there
were women also, in closer intimacy than she had ever experienced. Miss Jewsbury, who had moved to London, was a frequent caller. She had learned how to manage Jane and quiet
her nerves—the time was past when Geraldine was regarded
as a nuisance or merely as a source of amusement. Younger
women, too, came. Chief among these newest friends was Ellen
Twisleton. Ellen was an American, a member of the Dwight
family in whose veins flowed Boston's most royal blood. Young
Edward Twisleton, British commissioner, had met her there
and fallen in love. Ellen Delight he called her; she had the
buoyancy and the loveliness of the Graces. When he brought
her over as his wife, she conquered aristocratic London. Lord
Saye and Sele, her brother-in-law, declared her a worthy candidate not merely for presentation to the Queen but for the
Court of Venus itself.

The pageantry of England's fashionable season at times
rather oppressed her spirit, though it could not mar her charm
nor dim her happiness. She was like a gentle, soft-winged night
moth strayed among flaming butterflies. London society, for
her, was an Alice-in-wonderland adventure. But though she
could enjoy the well-bred, rich, self-satisfied world that her
husband's rank placed her in, she liked better the circle of
his literary friends. They were less artificial, and more fun.
The elect of England, she decided, tended to lack humanity
and warmth.

Soon after her arrival she had been taken to meet the Carlyles. She was amazed to learn where and how they lived.

Real poverty, she felt, and in the wretchedest neighborhood!
Yet they interested her more than any other persons. There
was something heroic about them. She was at first rather puzzled by their faces. In repose, both had a sad expression, as
if life were a terribly severe experiment and they had fought
against all its storms. But as soon as they began talking she
quite forgot this idea. Carlyle's wife had received her so cordially, and laughed and talked so gaily. How strange it was,
after meeting well-bred, negative people, to be plunged suddenly into this charged atmosphere! Only at Lady Ashburton's did she experience anything like it. She was glad that
neither Mrs. Carlyle nor Lady Ashburton had taken an aversion to her. Mrs. Carlyle she was really fond of; she had a
heart and was not fashionable! Ellen hoped that she would
like her too. What a vivid person she was; certainly the best
woman talker she had thus far met—somewhat caustic but
intensely amusing.

At the Grange, Jane took Ellen under her wing and helped
her through the first awesomeness of the occasion. She took
her, in London, to meet Elizabeth Barrett Browning. What
beautiful, thick brown hair the poet had, and tiny hands! She
noticed the fondness with which Mrs. Browning greeted her
companion. Preferring to hear these women talk, Ellen kept
herself in the background.

As months, then years passed by, Ellen's affections for Mrs.
Carlyle, and her admiration, grew ever stronger. At the Bishop
of London's, a remark was repeated to her that caused her
great pleasure. Mrs. Carlyle had been asked by Anne Thackeray who was her greatest friend. "Mrs. Twisleton," said Jane.

Ellen wished that Carlyle would not be so persistent in his
Jeremiads. Sometimes they made her very weary. And she was
troubled about Jane. In spite of her husband's fame, in spite
of her wide circle, in spite of her independence and spirit, Mrs.
Carlyle seemed a being in need of comradeship. She struck
Ellen as the one person among these selfsufficient British to
whom her affection might really mean something.

"All the best ladies I know are delicate," wrote Thomas
Woolner to a friend in the winter of 1856. "Mrs. Carlyle has

been ill a long time; she scarcely sees any one and cannot get out and she looks dreadfully weak; it grieves me to look at her."

Jane had little use for physicians and still less for medicine. The blue pills taken by her husband, his drafts of castor oil, filled her with dismay. But only an iron-willed woman could stand out against all doctoring. With her sleeplessness, her colds, and her headaches, Jane was a very interesting case; doctors were always trying to ply her with the entire list in the pharmacopœia. Laudanum was a drug still quite frequently employed; it was often included in the medicines prescribed for Jane. To stop an inflammation on her chest, she had been given tartar-emetic and opium. The main result, she noticed, was that it left her weak as water. But since opium brought sleep, it was difficult to resist the use of it. She knew about the beautiful visions it was supposed to give; none ever came to her. The dream she remembered best was not a dream at all, but a waking experience. She was lying, she thought, on a tombstone. She knew it well—a grave in Scotland. Slowly, slowly, she felt herself turning to marble: her hair, her arms, her whole body petrifying and blending horribly with the stone of the grave. One hand yet remained free. In it she held an instrument of sharp steel with which she was engraving words below the old inscription. They were those of her own epitaph.

Jane had taken again to writing in a journal. She mistrusted diaries. A journal of thoughts and feelings was apt to aggravate whatever was factitious and morbid; it could do one little good. But the impulse was insistent. She must, of course, try to keep off feelings and stick to facts.

She was interrupted at her desk by her husband's return from Bath House. That eternal Bath House! How many thousand miles, she wondered, had Carlyle measured in his walks between Chelsea and it? For each span, there was always another milestone between herself and him. When first she had noticed that ponderous yellow house at the corner of Bolton Street, how little had she dreamed that through years and years she should carry every stone's weight of it on her heart.

About feelings already! She had promised herself not to make this journal a *miserere*. She would take a dose of morphia

JANE CARLYLE
IN HER FIFTY-SIXTH YEAR

By permission of E. P. Dutton & Co.

that night to capture the impossible, some sleep. Those weaklings who trembled in fear that immortality was an illusion and had a terror of annihilation did not realize what their yearning would mean. If only they could be put on the infinitesimal quota of sleep she could win for herself, they would soon long for the very oblivion which they dreaded. Unfathomable, everlasting, unconscious sleep was the only conceivable heaven.

Fine weather outside, but indoors it was blowing the devil of a gale. As she did whenever possible, Jane hurried out into the open to get the mold that gathered upon her brushed off by human contact. But sometimes she did not go for calls. She walked instead for the good in walking, with no other objective than to tire herself into a fatigue too deep for thinking. It was October. She remembered just such a day ten years before; the same dreamy, tranquil autumn weather, the same tumult of mind within.

A summons to defend an appeal before the Tax Commissioners at Kensington had been delivered at the house. Her husband must not be allowed to go. He would be sure to run his head against a post in his impatience. Besides, if she went, though she dreaded the ordeal, she could put it behind her once it was finished. Thomas would not get the better of his feelings for weeks.

She took a cab; an unusual extravagance, but she wished to save her breath for talking.

"Tax office"—she read over the door of a dirty old house in Hornton Street. Half a dozen men were already assembled in the waiting room. One or two she recognized: the young apothecary who kept a shop in Cheyne Walk, the old jeweler who cleaned her clocks. The face of each individual bore a worried look, in spite of the banter of a sickly enough sort which all kept up, exactly like yokels talking and laughing very loud as they passed a lonely graveyard at night. Among all these males, Jane longed for a woman to appear. She felt embarrassed and out of place. At last one member of her sex, then another, entered, as men continued to gather by threes and fours.

"First come lady," said the clerk. When Jane reached the inner sanctum she noticed three men at a table spread with papers. Two looked fairly harmless, but the third was a big, insolent brute with a bloodless face: obviously the cock of that particular dung heap. The meekest one, an owl-like creature with ledger and pen, broke the silence.

"Name?"

"Carlyle."

"What is this?" exclaimed the big one. "Why is Mr. Carlyle not come himself? Didn't he get a letter ordering him to appear? Mr. Carlyle wrote some nonsense about being exempted from coming, and I desired an answer to be sent that he must come, must do as other people."

"Then, sir, your desire has been neglected, it would seem, my husband having received no such letter; and I was told by one of your fellow Commissioners that Mr. Carlyle's personal appearance was not indispensable."

"Huffgh! Huffgh! What does Mr. Carlyle mean by saying he has no income from his writings, when he himself fixed it in the beginning at a hundred and fifty?"

"It means, sir, that, in ceasing to write, one ceases to be paid for writing, and Mr. Carlyle has published nothing for several years."

"Huffgh! Huffgh! I understand nothing about that."

"I do"—it was the horned owl who whispered confidingly into Jane's ear—"I can quite understand a literary man does not always make money." He sunk his voice still lower: "I would take it off," he murmured, "but I am only one voice here, and not the most important."

"There," said Jane, flinging Chapman and Hall's account on the table, "that will prove Mr. Carlyle's statement."

"What am I to make of that? Huffgh! we should have Mr. Carlyle here to swear to this before we believe it."

"If a gentleman's word of honor written at the bottom of that paper is not enough, you can put me on my oath."

"You! you, indeed! No, no! we can·do nothing with your oath."

"But, sir, I understand my husband's affairs fully; better than he does himself."

"That I can well believe; but we can make nothing of this." And the bloodless faced commissioner flung the document on the table.

The horned owl picked it up.

"But, sir," he said, "this is a very plain statement."

"Then what has Mr. Carlyle to live upon? You don't mean to tell me he lives on that?" pointing to the account.

"Mr. Carlyle, I believe," murmured the not most important voice, "has landed income."

Jane drew herself up in all her Scottish pride. "Of which," she said, "I have fortunately no account to render in this kingdom and to this board."

"Take off fifty pounds; say a hundred," ordered the chief collector, and the horned owl entered a figure in the record. "If we write Mr. Carlyle down a hundred and fifty he has no reason to complain, I think. There, you may go. Mr. Carlyle has no reason to complain."

When Jane returned to Chelsea, she found her husband preparing to go to Bath House for the evening. She put on her bonnet. She would seek company with Geraldine.

For three months, Jane did not touch her diary. Then she picked it up again. Once more she would try to stick to facts. "Look straight before you, Jane Carlyle, and, if possible, not over the heads of things either, away into the distant vague. Look, above all, at the duty nearest hand, and what's more, do it."

All very well and good, but four weeks of illness had left her incredibly weak. Sickness sometimes got the best of duty. No galloping over London at present, as though she had on seven-league boots. She had tried a single mile that day, and thought it a great accomplishment. This physical weakness was most disheartening; if only she had some person to take hold of and lean on! Yet at times she roused herself to bursts of feverish activity. "Last week I was all for dying; this week all for ball dresses," she wrote on May the first.

"June 21, 1856. The chief interest of to-day expressed in blue marks on my wrists!"

That summer, she one day entered the sitting room where she had chanced to leave her journal. A visitor, who had somehow entered unannounced, held the diary in his hand and was browsing through its pages.

When she was angry, Jane had a tongue like a cat's; it could take the skin off at a touch. Her own husband could vouch for that. More than once he had experienced her anger; it could strike with the force of lightning.

Appalled by her burst of rage, the unhappy visitor slunk away. Her husband himself had never turned even the most harmless of those pages, and now this caller had pried into her most secret thoughts, thoughts she was herself uneasy at thinking. She would write no more in her book.

At a party given by Lady Goodrich, Jane found herself taken in to dinner by Holman Hunt. She had seen and praised his "Hirling Shepherd" at his Chelsea studio, and much to his delight had even brought her husband to look at his pictures. But this evening, he was dismayed to find his partner unexpectedly less cordial. He had been defending his friend Millais, who had run off with Ruskin's wife. She had been miserably unhappy with Ruskin, Hunt contended; there was every justification for the conduct of the lovers. "If because husband and wife are not in accord they should separate, many marriages would be annulled," dryly remarked Mrs. Carlyle.

Jane pondered deeply concerning marriage. It was not the institution itself that caused such misery in life; it was the demoralization, the desecration of which it was susceptible.

In September of that year, while Jane visited friends at Haddington, Scotsbrig, Thornhill and Edinburgh, Carlyle went off for a fortnight's stay with the Ashburtons at Kinloch Luichart in the Highlands. Dismal, rainy, chilling weather, he reported, and himself quite miserable.

In October, when the Carlyles were back in Chelsea, Lord and Lady Ashburton left for a winter on the Riviera. Carlyle was working doggedly at Frederick. In December he gained another helper—despite hazards, volunteers were ever at hand to work for the master. The new assistant was an earnest young man named Henry Larkin. Mrs. Carlyle, seated at her needlework, was alone in the drawing room at his first call. Very gracious, but reserved and with a burdened look—he thought her. Yet the next time he called, all the darkness, seemingly, had cleared away, and her face was lighted with the brightest of welcomes. He was amazed at these changes of mood. Evidently, too, there was within her a teasing playfulness of spirit and a merry way of seeing things.

New Year's, 1857, came, and Jane, as usual, wondered who would be her first caller. Then spring, and the thought of another summer.

In the early months of the new year, reports and rumors had come from France to Chelsea. Lady Ashburton, people said, was ill; more ill than usual. Nonsense! declared Carlyle; with her group of friends about her, she was sure to have the pleasantest of winters! But in April, when Venables, a mutual friend, called, he brought really disturbing news. Even then Carlyle refused to believe. She was coming to London soon; had indeed reached Paris in her journey homeward. "Bath House is vacant," he wrote, "but safe and ready; how ready would it and other objects be for you!" Where could she find a healthier climate than her own Hampshire?—so quiet, so wholesome, so beautiful. He had dreamed a daydream, he reported. In a silent grove of her woods he would have a little brick cottage, two rooms and a kitchen, with a deaf and dumb old woman to take care of him. He would see his benefactress once each evening, when the day's work was over.

Lady Ashburton did grow better. The hopes of Cheyne Row were being justified. Lord Ashburton was in London, making preparations for her immediate return. She would take a house at St. Leonard's for the summer, to win back her health in the sea air.

Then, on May the fifth, Richard Monckton Milnes came in the evening to the Chelsea parlor. Lady Ashburton, he said, was dead.

Jane's first response was a sense of utter shock—shock and confused dispiritment. With Brookfield, Carlyle had gone to the Grange for the funeral. All her men, all her court were in attendance and in tears—Thackeray, Lord Granville, Stanley of Alderley, Lord Bath, and the others.

"She has left me an inheritance of great price," wrote Lord Ashburton to Carlyle, "the love of those who loved her. I claim that of you in her name; and I am sure it will be rendered to me." While Lord Ashburton lived, he had, in sincerest, fullest measure, the friendship of his wife's favorite companion.

How peacefully, how beautifully Lady Ashburton had died,
thought Jane on hearing the story. The sick woman had risen
to dress, when a feeling of weakness overcame her. "What is
this?" she asked the doctor, who had run to support her. "You
are going to faint, it is nothing; you mustn't mind these faint-
nesses." He put his arm round her as support. She clasped her
hands on his other arm and leant her forehead on his shoulder.
She gave a sigh, and was gone.

Jane longed to get away—a reassuring breath of her native
air was what she needed.

At Sunny Bank, Haddington, she had never seen the country
look so lovely. On the threshold of the house, Miss Jess opened
her arms to her. Within was her godmother, nearly blind now,
advancing with hands outstretched, groping the air and calling
out, "Is that my bairn?"

How calm, how quiet Jane felt now, after the earlier fever.
Thomas sensed it too through her letters. Her notes resumed
the old brightness. "Be kind to Nero, and slightly attentive to
the canaries," she admonished. "God keep you! your affectionate J. W. C."

Chapter Thirty-Three

AN UNKNOWN entity by the name of George Eliot had fallen into the habit of sending Jane presentation copies of his novels. In 1858, *Scenes from Clerical Life* had been dropped at the Chelsea house. Jane could not divine what inspired the author with the good thought of giving *her* the book. Not personal regard, surely; there was no Eliot among her acquaintances. An indirect approach, perhaps, to her husband, known to be so busy with his History of Frederick?

Jane began the first of the three tales in the volume, "The Sad Fortunes of the Rev. Amos Barton." Once she had started, she could not stop. All night she read till she had finished.

Few novels could move her, yet this one had. It possessed a quality ever more rare in current fiction, the quality of understanding. A *human* book, she found it, written out of the heart of a live man, not merely out of the brain of an author; a book full of tenderness and pathos yet without a scrap of sentimentality, of sense without dogmatism, earnestness without twaddle. The first tale, that of Amos Barton, appealed to her most. No hero, this commonplace clergyman—dull, tactless, disliked by his flock, and, like most country rectors, enormously underpaid. One disliked him, yet recognized his plight and, more poignantly, that of his overworked, self-sacrificing wife. She died from general wretchedness, though her death won her husband a tardy victory—the compassionate regard, at last, of his parishioners.

Any man or woman who could write with such penetrating knowledge of mankind's problems would make an ideal friend. Who might the author be? Because of the name, Jane, in her conjectures, of course started with the premise that the writer would be masculine. Yet the beautiful feminine touches in the book astonished her. A man of middle age perhaps; not a clergyman—the book was far too revealing for that—but the cousin or brother of a country rector. A man with many children, and a dog—a dog he loved as she did little Nero.

Jane wrote a letter of thanks to the mysterious unknown. Some day, she declared, she hoped to have the honor of shaking his hand.

When *Adam Bede* was published and became the talk of the town, Jane was curious to see if she would get a copy.

"What should George Eliot send it to you for?" remarked Carlyle.

"Why shouldn't he, as he sent me his first book!"

"You are just like all women," exclaimed her husband, "you are always forming unreasonable expectations."

Someone was rapping at the knocker. Little Charlotte, the servant, scampered to the door. When she returned, she bore a brown paper parcel in her hand. Within lay *Adam Bede*.

More than ever, Jane's curiosity was piqued. When she sent an enthusiastic letter of thanks, in care of Blackwoods, the Edinburgh publisher, the answer she received was written, plainly enough, in a masculine hand.

An intriguing mystery! Perhaps if the writer were a woman she used a secretary to attend to her correspondence. Jane's friend Dickens insisted that these books were by a woman, and even looked knowingly at Jane. The authorship of the Brontë novels had been ascribed to her on their anonymous appearance. Her admirers were always seeking to make an author out of her.

George Eliot's own publisher, John Blackwood, to everyone's astonishment, was uninformed, too, concerning the sex of his new phenomenon. When Jane's acquaintance, Lord Stanley, had put the question to him, he replied that he was as much in the dark as all the rest.

John Blackwood was well content with his prize, though he was curious also. An intermediary, George Henry Lewes, had made all arrangements. "For several reasons," George Eliot had written, "I am very anxious to retain my *incognito* for some time to come, and, to an author not already famous, anonymity is the highest *prestige*. Besides, if George Eliot turns out a dull dog and an ineffectual writer—a mere flash in the pan—I, for one, am determined to cut him on the first intimation of that disagreeable fact."

Heaven forbid! *Adam Bede* had sold remarkably well. Its publisher was sure he had uncovered a vein of gold.

When the book's author sent in a list of persons to receive presentation copies, all the names were those of men, save one —Froude, Dickens, Thackeray, Tennyson, Ruskin. The exception—Mrs. Carlyle. Surely a person would not send herself her own novel? Or would she?

As for Jane Carlyle, she continued her guessing and kept her ears open. Some said Bulwer was the hidden author, yet Bulwer would never do. One or two persons whispered that it was Mary Ann Evans, the influential sub-editor of the *Westminster Review*. But most would not credit the rumor. They were far more interested in the amazing scandal that had clouded her good name. When no one dreamed that such a thing could occur, she had suddenly run off with Lewes, though he had a wife and two children. Jane had been rather troubled what to think concerning that escapade. When, years before, she first met Mrs. Lewes, she had found her an attractive little thing. Lewes and she appeared to be a perfect set of love birds cuddled together on a perch. But Jane's quick eye soon noticed that the female was hopping further away and assuming a somewhat critical view of her mate. And then—this amazing elopement! Sanctimonious London glared indignantly at the tarnished woman.

What if Mary Ann should really prove to be the wise moralist of *Amos Barton*? Incredible to believe!

Yet it was so.

Jane was not the only person who was astonished. "Is it really true that *Adam Bede* is the work of Miss Evans?" asked Elizabeth Barrett Browning, "the woman, as I have heard of her, and the author as I read her, do not hold together."

Jane soon had a chance to judge for herself. At a dinner arranged by Frederick Chapman she found herself seated between Lewes and Miss Evans—the pair were living together now in London. Jane had always liked George Lewes. One of the ugliest men she ever knew, pock-marked and faced like an ape, but an amusing, light-hearted little fellow. But Mary Ann —the moralist, the sympathetic philosopher! Was it possible?

There was something almost laughable in her present honors as the city's most talked-of female. So slow, so heavy! Why, she looked propriety personified! Indeed the pair of them were so homely it was impossible to believe any harm could lie behind their faces.

In her moments of banter, Jane would insist that George Eliot had quite mistaken her rôle. Nature had intended her to be the most exemplary of women and she had blundered into the opposite camp. But when Carlyle, as was his wont, pitched into Jane's favorite, George Sand, and what he defined as her erotic novels, Jane bridled at the charge. England had small right to cast the first stone across the Channel when she had a George of her own right there in London. To renounce George Sand as a teacher of morals was fair enough, but was it quite consistent?

Poor little Nero, his sight was failing him; he was getting old and asthmatic. Jane hated to see him so feeble. Nero and she had been such close companions. Some of her friends, knowing how practical-minded she could be, were amazed at the strength of her devotion for a dog.

The material problems of Nero's care and education had never been hard to meet. When circumstances interfered with Nero's being exercised, the postman would take him along while he delivered letters. Washing, too, was easily arranged. For sixpence a week, Nero went out with the laundry, and returned, pure as snow, next day. Only once, when the laundress put too much starch into the water, had the scheme gone wrong and Nero been inconvenienced.

When Carlyle, after a restless night, came morosely to breakfast, the infatuated little beast would dance round him on its hind legs. So, thought Jane with a rueful smile, should she do too but could not. Her husband, for all his pretended indifference, was flattered by such unwonted capers to his honor and glory.

Sometimes, of course, he teased poor Nero. He would snap the fire tongs at him to make him growl. Once, by way of experiment, he tied an empty tin to Nero's tail which sent the poor beast scampering over the house in the greatest terror. Such conduct, the great man's wife emphatically declared, was a form of amusement unfit for a philosopher—low, degrading! But Nero forgave his master.

He was the only creature in the world who could with impunity interrupt Carlyle at his labors. Up he would patter to the garret, scratch at the door, and be let in. Once, when the dog had thus applied, his master, stooping over, was surprised to see a letter dangling from Nero's collar. Inside was a saddler's business card with the picture of a horse on it, and a cheque for fifty pounds drawn to his order by Jane. Of course! His birthday! He had quite forgotten. His wife was making over to him half of a legacy that she had just received so he could buy a horse for exercise. With a lump in his throat, he gazed at Jane's messenger. Then he returned the cheque. He could not let her sacrifice her money to such a purpose.

Friends who accompanied him at night for his eleven o'clock walk noticed how carefully he looked after Nero, whistling to him occasionally—not with his lips, but with a small pocket-whistle—lest the dog stray into mischief or come to grief. Once, when Nero was not along, Carlyle stopped in the middle of the street and stooped over. He had found a piece of bread. He cleared the dirt from it and laid the morsel on the curb-stone. "The sparrows or some hungry dog will be glad of that bit of bread," he remarked.

At first Nero had not taken greatly to the sea. The master's passion for bathing puzzled him sorely. During one vacation, when the family were united on the Firth of Forth, Carlyle had picked the dog up and flung him into the water. Nero scrambled out and shook himself; then, without a look behind, he marched home. For several days he refused to follow Carlyle to the strand. Early one morning, as Thomas struck out from shore—he liked to bathe naked in the ocean—he became gradually aware of a kind of swashing behind him. There was Nero, in voluntary humble partnership, ready to swim with him to Edinburgh or to the ends of the earth.

Ten years of Nero, before destiny overtook him. At last, in Jane's very sight, a recklessly driven butcher cart ran over him. He was returning from market with little Charlotte when the accident happened. Poor Nero, in Charlotte's arms—he looked like a tiny crushed spider, his eyes fixed and protruding from his head. Jane placed him in a warm bath, then dried and wrapped him up carefully to warm the spark of life that flickered within. Next morning, he could swallow the milk she fed him by spoon. And at midday, when she said "Poor dog!

poor little Nero!" he tried to wag his tail. Little by little he began to recover, but henceforth he was a shattered dog. The wheel had crushed his lungs.

"Never dog has given trouble more disproportionate to its use and worth than Nero has to me," remarked Carlyle, some months later, to the Gilchrists who were calling, as Nero lay wheezing by the fire.

"It has been worth it all!" said Jane at once. But Carlyle would not take back his words. The dog's existence was an absurdity. It would be a kindness to kill the beast.

The guests were a little shocked. Then Mrs. Carlyle spoke again. "If he is to be believed," she said, "he shouldn't make affectionate speeches to Nero in the garden when he thought no one heard."

Carlyle looked sheepish, but could make no denial. "Poor little fellow!" he had said, "I declare I am heartily sorry for you! If I *could* make you young again, upon my soul I *would!*"

Nero and Carlyle had tried one final midnight walk together. But it would not do. The dog fell behind, and Tom had to gather him in. Poor little dim-white speck of life, of love, fidelity, and feeling, surrounded by the darkness!

The little dog grew rapidly worse. There was further talk of prussic acid. "My Dear," said Carlyle, "it is an act of Roman Virtue that is demanded of you; and so you surely will not shrink from it."

But she did—a small tragedy, she told herself, very small, and yet, more heart-rending than some grander ones.

Just as Jane was going out, Dr. Barnes, her new physician, chanced to call. The dog was suffering dreadfully, he said, would suffer still worse if he lived. Jane understood. She nodded her consent. She could not herself hand Nero over; Charlotte had to do that. But she kissed his head as he lay in Charlotte's arms. He licked her cheek.

She shut herself in her room. She had not cried so, she believed, since she was a little child.

As for Jane's husband, he was so distressed he could not control the tears in his voice. Impossible, he told himself, that the death of Nero could so move him. Yet there it was! He felt, he declared, quite unexpectedly and distractedly torn to pieces by the misery of the thing. Jane liked him better for those words than for all the philosophy that ever came out of his head.

Next day, so visitors would not notice her swollen eyes and smile at grief "about a dog," Jane took a long carriage ride during the usual hour for calling. People could be so gauche. One woman, trying to be of comfort, had suggested, "Why not have him stuffed?"

"Stuffed?" exclaimed Jane, her eyes flashing with indignation, "would you stuff your baby?"

For years he had been a bulwark against loneliness. Now he was gone. What was become of that beautiful, graceful little life, so full of love, and loyalty, and sense of duty? Was it extinguished, abolished, annihilated in an instant, by three drops of prussic acid, while the brutalized two-legged, so-called human creature who dies in a ditch lives on, forever, even though he has caused nothing but pain and disgust to all concerned and has outraged all duties? She, for one, could not believe *that!*

Jane's husband was an old lion now, but very much king of the London jungle. Venerating strangers arrived from the ends of the earth and treated him as though he were a talking monument or sentient volcano. They would knock at the famous door in Cheyne Row, and demure little Charlotte would usher them into the drawing room where they would find the grim philosopher and his wife. But if Carlyle liked his visitors— though he dreaded interruptions to work—he quickly relaxed. He would sit on the floor by the hearth, his legs stretched out full length before him, charge his long clay pipe, then puff contentedly away, stopping at short intervals to talk on all manner of things in the style of one of his later books. On the sofa would be the great man's wife, with sewing-work before her—stockings or more intimate apparel, to the shock of modest callers schooled in the reticence of the age.

And what talk one heard at Cheyne Row—more vivid, more interlaced with metaphor than any other conversation in greater London! Persons, books, opinions—something memorable on everything under the sun.

Oh, yes, Louis Napoleon, now Emperor of France, he had known him well. Used to see him, in his early exile, in this very neighborhood, with his arms folded over his chest and his

eyes fixed on the ground in a melancholy stare. A poor opera
singer in search of an engagement, that was the sort of creature he resembled. Homer? There had never been such a
person! Homer was the name given to a joint stock company of
ballad-singers. The new doctrine of evolution—Erasmus Darwin was a frequent caller at the house, sight-seeing visitors
whispered, and Charles came sometimes, too—the book, *Origin
of the Species*, filled one with contempt! From Darwin's point
of view, Adam was no other than a fortunate orangutan who
had succeeded in rising in the world.

Sometimes, to the admiring gaze of these strangers, one of
Carlyle's famous contemporaries would stroll into the room—
Alfred Tennyson with the face of a prophet of old, or John
Ruskin. It was amusing to see how Ruskin managed his friend.
Carlyle, flying in the face of all of the great art-critic's cherished opinions, would say the most outrageous things, whereupon Ruskin would treat him as though he were a naughty
child. "Now, this is too bad!" he would murmur gently, laying his arm across the declaimer's shoulder.

Ruskin was telling a story about a man he had known who
in a fit of bad temper had shot at his own father. Fortunately
he had missed. "Only accident," declared the narrator, "prevented him from being a murderer!"

"No, no!" interposed Carlyle, "he *was* a murderer; and"—
with far greater disgust—"a very bad shot!"

Habitués of the Cheyne Row parlor, in these years, had
grown thoroughly accustomed to the course of things there.
The master certainly could talk much exasperating and eloquent nonsense. Yet what of that, if the show were good?

"Why, when Mazzini was here the other night, you took
the side of the argument that Mr. Pelly did this evening!"
remonstrated Jane.

Her husband paused long enough in his demolishment of
Mr. Pelly's opinion to reply, "And what's the use of a man
if he cannot take two sides of an argument?"

Carlyle, thought some who knew him well, was an anachronism in what they fondly considered a logical age. He
renounced discussion and reasoning and trusted to vision and
insight. He would attack this man and that for not being able
to take any clear and coherent view of the nature of things,

"AN INTERIOR AT CHELSEA," BY ROBERT S. TAIT
By courtesy of Lord Northampton and The National Trust

and then be quite as confused himself. Was he vexed and harassed by the very lack he complained of in others? Yet perhaps this intuitive power was the key to his fame and source of his eloquence.

The scope of his hates and sympathies was tremendous. He would pass in a moment from talk of Frederick or Napoleon to some little account of the misfortunes of an old peasant woman, a story told with such feeling as to bring moisture to the listener's eyes. The world's greatness, as he understood it, lay chiefly in the past. A new race of men was needed—God-fearing, honest, sincere (his favorite qualifications), if the earth was to avoid the terrible calamities which he saw impending—the bloodshed and destruction.

But Carlyle's vehemence in discussing public affairs, an apologist decided, rose from the torture he suffered in seeing the errors and agonies of mankind—civil war in the United States, and bloody insurrection in Europe. Wars he always condemned.

Yet Carlyle, though he spoke often with such bitterness, had, like his wife, the magic gift of consolation. If sorrow beset any among his acquaintances, if they lost their hopes, if work failed, or their children died, they could seek him out and be sure of understanding help.

At other times, when the atrabilious prophet swore at the follies of the age, it took a brave man to stand against him. Jane needed all her skill to prevent his outbursts from cracking the very walls of her little parlor. Quietly she would renew his cup of tea—five cups, at least, in an evening—then, with a deft word at the right moment, she would direct him into a safer channel. If a young caller, with reckless temerity, seemed ready to challenge a statement, Jane, from her post to the side of the orator, would quietly hold up a warning finger and shake her head.

When he argued with his peers, to keep the peace was not so easy. Sometimes, as though the room were the House of Commons, she would cry "Divide! Divide!"—the parliamentary signal for the end of debate. Sometimes, when the battle raged, she would interject some little remark so irresistibly droll that, in spite of her husband's grim visage, she could make him laugh—and the spell would be broken. But not always was the cause of peace thus readily served. Henry James, Ralph

Waldo Emerson's presentee, was there one day when she was having her difficulties. Two others beside himself were in the room, one a great burly fellow determined to defend O'Connell, the Irish politician, though it was plain to see that this particular topic was exciting Carlyle into a veritable frenzy.

Henry James—Mrs. Carlyle had dexterously warned him to prepare for storms—watched the gathering clouds with interest. Up rose the din of politics in a fierce and merciless mêlée. All through tea the debate continued. On the American's right, as they sat at table, was his hostess. Very gentle and estimable, he thought her. On his left raged the belligerent and bellowing guest. Presently James felt Mrs. Carlyle's foot reach gropingly over his. She wished to nudge the shoe of his infuriated neighbor to implore a truce. Success crowned her efforts, but not quite in the way expected. No sooner did her husband's opponent feel the pressure of her foot than he turned savagely on his hostess.

"Why don't you," he fiercely screamed, "why don't you, Mrs. Carlyle, touch your husband's toe? I am sure he is greatly more to blame than I am!"

A moment of utter silence. Then the whole company broke forth in a burst of uncontrollable mirth.

Even casual visitors, who had been told of Mrs. Carlyle's brilliant and delightful talk, could not help regretting the extinction of her voice when her husband was in the midst of his declamations. They would see her upper lip quiver ever so slightly, as it did before she uttered some droll remark, then what she said would be lost in the hubbub, or appreciated only by her nearest neighbor, as was plain from his delighted grin.

Not always, however, did she thus consent to play second fiddle. At times, when the company in the little house at Chelsea was miscellaneous, the claims of the hostess to be heard conflicted with those of the host, and the result would be a cross-fire of conversation between herself and another guest which, plain to see, rather irritated Carlyle.

At one of Samuel Rogers' breakfast-parties, when Carlyle's thunder was immediately followed by his wife's sparkle, the sardonic host, as though in soliloquy, was heard to remark: "As soon as that man's tongue stops, that woman's begins!"

Jane and Alexander Gilchrist were cosily chatting in the parlor: the talk about the Duke of Malakoff and his brutal frankness. She had been present at a party where Lady Jersey, once Byron's admiration, rather foolishly boasted that she had no regrets for the past.

"Ce n'est pas vrai, madame," said the Duke, "you regret your youth, and you regret the fading beauty of your daughter!"

Had he been told, Jane inquired of Gilchrist, about the Duke and Skittles, the courtesan?

Yes, he had heard of her, but was eager for a further account.

"A very pretty and very wicked lady," began Jane, "who rides about the park . . ."

At that moment, Carlyle entered the room.

Gilchrist had to go without the story.

Chapter Thirty=Four

*T*EN years in the valley of the shadow of Frederick. By no deceits of the imagination could Jane count them good ones. Their beginnings had been clouded by miasmas from the Grange; their never endings by the worries of her husband's intense preoccupation. The latter state of affairs, of course, she had come to regard as a necessary fact of existence. She could make a life of her own within it, and this she had done. Yet the heavy salvos of Frederick's siege of Chelsea could not be ignored. *The French Revolution, Cromwell,* her husband's other work, had been trivial in comparison. Carlyle, always vocal when distressed, was very ready to admit the difficulties of the task. "In my young time," he exclaimed, "I had no work that was not a mere flea bite to this which lies appointed for my old days!"

Jane's conscience, when she took occasional vacations, always troubled her. Poor Carlyle!—he was sure to overwork himself. "Go and see my unfortunate husband," she begged Thomas Woolner, "and go often, if you please, till I come back!" The proofs of the first two volumes had reached her while she was away at Edinburgh. "Oh, my dear," she wrote, "what a magnificent book this is going to be! the best of all your books!"

Carlyle, toiling at Chelsea, told her that her words had given him the one bit of pure sunshine that had visited his gloom. Try as he would, he was having a hard time working up admiration for his subject. Old Fritz, perversely, simply would not shape up into the hero suggested by earlier study. What the devil had he to do with this German Frederick? No satisfaction writing such a book—labor and sorrow only! Yet once in, there could be no turning back.

As for Jane, she soon began actively to dislike the hard-bitten old despot. To what purpose, she asked herself, was Carlyle trying to turn a boar's ear into a silk purse? Better for

Frederick's own times, as well as hers and Carlyle's, had he died as a babe.

Lately this unlaid and unlayable ghost of Frederick had broken all bounds. Jane compared his evil deeds to a fire-and-brimstone Presbyterian clergyman's description of the devil: "With the trumpet of Discord in his mouth, and the Torch of dissension in his hand, he goeth about as a roaring Lion seeking whom he may devour. And when he hath set Son against Father and Husband against Wife, he returns to his Den with a *horrible grin on his countenance,* rejoicing in the mischief he has wrought!"

Not only Frederick, but dyspepsia, was raising havoc with Jane's husband. Every morning little Charlotte—she adored the master, for all his somewhat frightening ways—trotted up to his room with a steaming hot cup of coffee mixed with castor oil. This horrid potion he would down with a shake of his head and a grimace, exclaiming ruefully "Ay, ay—it's gey wersh!" Little time for exercising now. A hurried walk or ride after dark was all he got. Up to the roots of his hair in work, he sat snowed under his drifts of paper, the various bundles held together—his own invention—by the wooden pins used by washerwomen to fasten laundry on a line. Even in their short chats at dinner, when Jane told her husband her news of the day, his mind was apt to wander to his book and he would give her, for the hundredth time, full details of the battle of Mollwitz.

When proof sheets came, though the day was Christmas, he toiled grimly on. Sundays, except for the fact that there was moderate quiet in the streets—no barrel organs then, or rumbling of carts—were like other days to him. He always agonized over proofs. Sometimes Jane offered her advice. Here was a digression, she suggested; might it not be omitted? Idiotic!— her husband generally exclaimed. But a day or so later he would remark, "I think I shall strike out so and so," and Jane would have her quiet triumph. She hated to find fault with his work; what he needed was encouragement.

Not only did Carlyle drive himself, he also drove his volunteers—amiable Joseph Neuberg, plodding, efficient Henry Larkin, and the rest. Dispatch! dispatch was necessary with those maps, the master would exclaim—though in the next breath he would add there was no terrific hurry. Whereupon Larkin quoted Goethe's words gleaned from Carlyle's early *Wilhelm Meister*—"like a Star, unhasting and unresting."

"Ah," interposed Jane, "Carlyle is always hasting and *never* resting!"

For all her teasing of him, Larkin was very fond of Jane Carlyle. Nothing pleased him more than when he could be of service to her. As he watched the extraordinary couple, misgivings deepened in his stolid, none-too-clever mind. Mrs. Carlyle laughed and joked; yet surely, with her husband's moody absorption, she must at times feel utterly lonely and miserable. Certainly she was ill. She confided to him that she had been troubled recently by pain in her right arm—neuralgia, Dr. Barnes had called it.

Young Thomas Woolner was plotting with Tennyson's wife —Alfred had lately married—to bring the Carlyles for a rest to the poet's house in beautiful Farringford, on the Isle of Wight. But the scheme fell through. "I wrote your message to her," Woolner informed Mrs. Tennyson; "the enclosed will explain the rest: when you write to me, please send it back for I never like to destroy her letters—unless, of course, you wish to keep it. You will see the mighty man of genius is not so easily managed as a pet bird. I think if he could see his wife's weak state so keenly as he can spiritual truths, he would not let his plans interfere with her little projects for health-seeking. The last two years have made sad havoc in her constitution."

There were times—though, dimly, he saw the end of work in sight—when Carlyle feared he might die before the book would be finished. Frightful to him, he declared, was this last portion of his task, with Larkin and everybody falling away, and his own poor strength on the edge of doing the like. Another autumn was approaching, and 1863 would be over. A while before, he had been encouraged by the hope that this year would bring release. Yet here he was, the most tired of captive mortals, still tugging at the galley-oar.

One imperative need burned in his consciousness: *to get*

through with the book. For the saving of himself, and Jane too, *that* was obligatory. Nothing must interfere.

Carlyle was returning from a horseback ride—the streets muddy from rain, his spirits dreary and oppressed. It was Tuesday, the twenty-second of September. Frederick again, that night, then again next morning. For how many more days thereafter? One little flicker lighted his glooming spirits. For twenty minutes before setting to work he could chat with Jeannie. Rarely did she fail to have something bright and pleasant to tell him. Wonderful how she could sift from her quiet day those stories for his entertainment! Already he could visualize the drawing room—a cheerful fire burning, the place in mellow chiaroscuro from the flame. There would be his pipe and tobacco, and a spoonful of brandy in hot water, and Jeannie, the presiding deity over these things.

"Mrs. Carlyle has not returned," announced the upstairs maid—within the year, Jane had set up a two-servant establishment when lessening strength compelled her to ignore economy in that particular. "She has gone to see her cousin in the city," the girl added. Oh, yes, he remembered: that young widow, Mrs. Godby—poor relation of her mother—whom Jeannie was being kind to.

Alone, he ate his dinner, then rested on the sofa. He tried not to be impatient. She would be there soon.

A sound of wheels; the clip-clop of a horse in the street. The noises stopped—near the house, apparently. Was she returning, not by omnibus, but by cab because of the lateness? Why the delay in coming up? He grew dimly uneasy. Why were the maids stirring about so? He called, but received the vaguest answer. He hurried down the steps.

Jeannie sat almost fainting in a chair, her white face drawn in pain. A mishap in the street, he gathered from Larkin. Together they carried her upstairs to bed. Soon Dr. Barnes arrived. No bones broken, he declared, after examination. Rest and quiet should heal what damage had been done.

Carlyle felt somewhat relieved. No fractures at least—that was some comfort. But the hurt Jane had suffered, he feared, was a bad enough matter. A sorry business, any way one looked at it. With things as they were—Frederick so troublesome and all—there was no call for destiny to impose additional burdens.

After her visit to Mrs. Godby, he learned, Jane had walked to Cheapside to catch her bus. As the Chelsea omnibus approached, she had stepped to the street. A cab driving rapidly up swerved unexpectedly toward her, forced over by excavations. Jane had leapt for the curbstone, but struck her foot against the edge and plunged to the pavement. Even as she was falling, she had remembered her neuralgic arm. In a desperate effort to save it, she twisted so violently about that the motion tore the ligaments in her side. Next instant, she had found herself lying helpless in the street, a crowd surrounding her.

Never could Jane forget her drive home by the cab into which a policeman had lifted her. Yet even in her pain, her thoughts had turned to Carlyle. He must not be worried by this accident; she would appeal to Larkin, who lived next door in the Gilchrists' old house, to smuggle her to her room. Her purpose had failed in part. But she was able to persuade Dr. Barnes not to let her husband know the extent of her injuries.

Three days and nights of nearly sleepless torment, then Jane's injured leg hurt only when she moved. But her arm, stiff and sore before from neuralgia—or whatever it was—still caused her a good deal of suffering. Within a week, however, she felt well enough to design various rope contrivances that enabled her not only to ring her bell but to shift herself about on her bed. Her room was always ready to welcome callers, and Jane's friends soon began dropping in. Everyone was so kind, the very thought of it almost made her cry.

Three times a day, from his solitary vigil with Frederick, Carlyle would pop in for a visit. He was much amused by her gadgets. To strengthen her, Dr. Barnes had prescribed frequent sips of champagne. Jane gaily demonstrated the automatic cork that the apothecary had furnished. A turn of a screw, and up spurted the champagne, to be instantly captured again when the spoon was full by another twist of the handle.

Yes, all was coming right again, Carlyle told himself. They would have a good winter; he would get his misery of a book *done*, or at least almost done, before spring.

Late one evening, in the third week after the accident, as

Carlyle was studying in the upstairs drawing room—Jane supposedly asleep—his wife's bedroom doors suddenly opened. There in the double portal, leaning on his knobbly staff of hazel wood, a look of childlike joy and triumph on her face, she stood. In her Indian dressing-gown she looked like a little girl; not a woman of sixty-two, though unconquered by weakness and years. As Carlyle gazed at her, she seemed like a radiant spirit come to brighten his lonely night.

After another three weeks, Jane made up her mind life was very dull if it had to be spent in the same sofa corner. Why not venture out? Really, she was doing so much better than could have been hoped! Little Carina Barnes, Dr. Barnes's daughter, now married and become Mrs. Simmonds, was going to have a baby. Jane was worried about the child who was about to have a child herself. Directly after the baby's arrival, Jane sent the husband a little note and a message for his wife: "Give her my love and compliments on her cleverness—and *It* a kiss for me and congratulations for having got duly born! I suppose it is very *red?*"

When she was strong enough to write, Carina indignantly denied the redness. She had a favor to ask: would Mrs. Carlyle be her daughter's sponsor and let her bear her name? Carina wished her at the christening. Could she manage that, Jane wondered? She refused to promise, but she would try. Though hardly as strong as the baby, she had already ventured, once, to see it. But that reckless expedition, attempted after eight weeks of seclusion, had nearly wrecked her.

November fourth was the day. Mustering her courage, she struggled to the waiting cab. She missed the christening itself— a proxy had been appointed—but came in time for the reception. A little silver bowl, engraved with the baby's name, was her gift.

Jane felt suddenly very ill. Excitement had kept her going, to be followed by complete exhaustion and chills that tripled the throbbing ache of her injured arm and side. Hopefully she waited for the attack to pass. Instead, it grew rapidly worse. Her cousin, Maggie Welsh, was summoned to Chelsea to keep house and manage doctors, nurses, and visitors.

The sufferer was plunged into a veritable sea of agony in which she struggled drowning month after month. Other physicians had been summoned to consult with Dr. Barnes. Did these touted specialists help or hinder his wife's recovery? her distressed husband wondered as he watched the horrid after-effects of the opiates they administered. Jeannie tried to hide her pain from him; tried to spare his nerves for Frederick. Already the book's end was delayed, and Carlyle was fearful that the history would bulge into a sixth volume.

Sometimes, in the midst of his work, when he came to the sickroom for brief visits—longer were not permitted—she could persuade him she was better. Sometimes she was unable to conceal her agony. A hideous pain, she said: common, honest pain, were it cutting of her flesh or sawing of her bones, would be luxury in comparison.

For his life, he could not fathom what might be the extent of the danger. Was there exaggeration; a tendency toward morbid despondency? Yet the illness seemed positive enough— a physical, throbbing, burning torment day and night, dreadful to witness.

Now and then, in the long winter mornings as he labored at the history, the thought struck him with a cold shudder of conviction that here lay death; that his world would smash to pieces in the abyss, and "victory," up there in his garret, be it never so complete, could not save her nor be possible without her.

Her intellect was clear as starlight, but in her pain she feared she would lose her sanity. "Dear," she said, "*promise* me that you will not put me into a mad-house, however this go? Do you *promise* me, now?" The look in her eye at that instant was like to break his heart. With a rush of compassion, he vowed it would never be.

"Not if I do quite lose my wits?"

"Never, my Darling; oh, compose thy poor terrified heart!"

She was to be buried, she directed, at Haddington, in her father's grave. Her possessions were to be distributed among her truest friends and those whom her charities long had aided.

None who saw her in her illness believed she could live.

Through the early spring, she lingered, and into the approach of summer. The doctors, losing hope, were ready for desperate measures. She must go to St. Leonards, to try the influences of the sea.

A cold, damp, blowy day—March second—the day of her leaving. A newfangled invalid carriage, so built that it could be put in the train itself, had been hired to take her to the station. In his strong arms, Larkin carried her downstairs and laid her on the couch. "I don't think you'll find me very heavy," she whispered.

Attendants bore her to the ambulance. It had a small rear door through which a patient had to be slid feet first. More like a hearse than a carriage—black, low, hideous—thought Larkin. Obviously Mrs. Carlyle shared his idea. As he helped to lift her in he heard the stifled shriek she involuntarily uttered. This miserable assistance, he believed, would be the last poor service he should ever render her.

At St. Leonards, two rooms in the house of a Dr. Blakiston were prepared for Jane and her cousin, Maggie Welsh. The sea was hoarsely moaning close at hand; the skies sunk in darkness overhead. Carlyle had to reach home that night. He caught the last train back.

Two or three times, that spring, he came up from his work in London to visit his wife. Dr. Blakiston, on these occasions, always spoke with a swaggering tone of hope. "We must try St. Leonards further," her husband said to Jane, "I shall be able to shift down to you in May!"

She looked gratefully at him.

Carlyle rented a house beside the shore. He settled his book affairs as best he could, then moved his work to St. Leonards, putting his writing desk in a shoddy little room on the ground floor. The weather had grown milder. On pleasant days, Jane was lifted into a carriage for a drive. Soon she was taking morning and afternoon excursions. "One of your drives is with *me*," said her husband.

For several weeks there was a hint of improvement. Carlyle stuck doggedly at his work, though successful writing was difficult under the circumstances. By the middle of June, his wife began again to lose ground. The roar of the sea, lashed by freshening summer winds, became unbearable. After nine days and nights of almost total sleeplessness, she suddenly determined to move. Her husband could stay in the house, if he chose, to finish his book.

Jane's purpose burned with clear intenseness. She would

fly to the North, to Scotland, to old companions and quiet scenes. John Carlyle accompanied her on her way. Very imprudent, said John, grumbling at her folly, but her determination could not be shaken.

Mary Austin's simple house, the Gill, on the Solway between Dumfries and Annan, was her destination—Mary, Carlyle's sister, who had often visited at Craigenputtock. Jane had always been fond of Mary and respected her prudent, thrifty ways. Years ago, Mary had married a carter. By industry the pair had done well in farming, and now lived in Annandale as honest, moderately prosperous country folk.

The first letter Carlyle received from the Gill told of a miraculous nine hours' sleep. But Jane realized that she needed medical advice as well as quiet; risky to be without it. Thornhill, where her friends the Russells lived, was near at hand. Jane's faith in Dr. Russell was great; he never gave heavy dosages of pills or drafts of vile concoctions. His practical measures seemed always effective. So after a week at the Gill, Jane moved to Mrs. Russell's.

She continued to improve. Drives with her friends, fresh milk, and wholesome air—these were the doctor's medicines. Every day she sent off a letter to her anxious husband. As each arrived he could perceive a lift in his wife's spirits. To little Charlotte, no longer in her employ, but still a friend and correspondent, she wrote an announcement: "*Now*—for the first time since I fell ill, I begin to believe that I shall *really recover!* to, at least, a bearable state of health! and that I shall be thankful for all my sufferings; for they have taught me much that I was needing to be taught."

Jane's triumph was not merely a conquest of physical illness; it was spiritual as well. Never in all her existence had she felt so serene, so free of doubts and uncertainties, so ready to believe in those forgotten, discredited faiths—joy and peace.

When she returned to Chelsea, she was wearing the brooch which she had bequeathed to Mrs. Russell—that bitter winter in Cheyne Row—when she knew she was going to die. Now, with life again before her, she accepted both back.

At Chelsea, all was in readiness—her room fresh-papered, new paint where there was need, and a shining cleanness everywhere. A momentary shadow of dread had crossed her consciousness at thought of re-entering that house where she had suffered physical torment. But it vanished, never to return, before the enthusiasm of her welcome. Her husband came rushing down from his workroom—John had brought her from the station—her maids rejoiced to have her back, and even Columbine the cat threw off her feline aloofness in the general excitement. Columbine was very old now, but Jane had not the heart to dispose of her. Nero and Columbine had always been good friends, and to put her away would have seemed like a breach of faith. True, she was a nuisance: Carlyle insisted on feeding her at table, with resultant spots in the rug. But Jane, with a glint in her eye, felt sure she could check the abuse.

October 1, 1864, was the day of Jane's return. Fragile indeed, yet with a marvelous brightness and spirit. Her hands were so thin that had she held them to the light the sun would have glowed right through them. A wisp of a woman now, made visible chiefly because of her voluminous clothing. She looked frail enough for an autumn wind to blow away.

Yet, Carlyle noticed, she kept wonderfully hearty, though he trembled each day lest he find all altered. As he passed her bedroom in the morning—Dr. Russell insisted on rest— he was amazed anew at the sparkle of mirth in her greeting. Her friends at once began to call as of old. Thomas Woolner was delighted to see how well she looked. Verily, he said, it was like a resurrection from the dead.

Fresh milk had been prescribed, difficult to get in London. But the problem was solved through the thoughtfulness of Gerald Blunt, the Chelsea rector, who arranged that a warm tumbler be brought daily to No. 5, Cheyne Row direct from the clerical cow who munched the daisies on the lawn of the Rectory garden.

Driving had long been Jane's favorite recreation. When Carlyle, before the accident, suggested she use a hired carriage, she at first refused because of the cost. "More difficulty in persuading you to go into expense," exclaimed her husband, "than other men have to persuade wives to keep out of it!" But she had finally agreed to take two drives a week. In the back of Carlyle's mind, as he saw the benefits she won, lay the thought

that he must buy a horse and carriage. He could readily afford
it now. But business of that sort took on mountainous proportions and quite upset him. With Frederick so exacting, how
could he find time to arrange the purchase? So the impulse
rested.

It had grown more insistent now. He appealed to the ever
useful Joseph Neuberg: "Help me if you can!" he wrote,
specifying the needs. So the carriage was bought and a little
mare, Bellona, to draw it.

Jane was radiant over her husband's gift. "What gives me
the most joy," she said to Larkin, "is that he did it *entirely
himself;* I never suggested it; on the contrary, I had always
discouraged the idea."

A homely enough brougham, but it served. With Sylvester,
reliable old coachman, at the reins, she could renew many
friendships in London which her helpless state would otherwise have compelled her to neglect. She greatly enjoyed taking
boon companions for drives—Anne Thackeray, now a young
woman of twenty-eight; Mrs. Oliphant, the novelist; and others. Along they would jog, in the old fly, and Jane's talk would
make her fellow passenger quite forget the passing sights.

All through the winter her husband struggled to throw off
that incubus, Frederick. Almost thirteen years the despot had
been sitting on his shoulders: triple the time which Thomas
had expected.

On January 15, 1865, the last pages of his manuscript were
taken to press. On February fourth, the final batch of proofs
came in, and by the sixth, had gone back to the printers.

The siege was over.

"Were I once out of this," said Carlyle while in the dust
heaps, "it is my fixed purpose to rest for the remainder of my
life." He would attempt no further books. His task in the
world would be finished. He was even seriously minded, he
declared, to quit the city—this horror of a Babel—for a place
of rural peace and contentment. Jane was no longer hostile to
the thought. A country place of their own, at least for summers,
might do very well.

There were bonfires and huzzas in all the reviews for the
History of Frederick II of Prussia. A new generation of critics
had arisen, and in place of the lack of understanding and vi-

tuperation of former years, there was fulsome praise and the title of grand patriarch of letters for the author. How the old hero-maker could fashion an appealing character out of such materials quite bewildered some of his friends. Of course, he created the very gods he worshiped. To convert that brute Frederick into a thing to be admired—aye, and to get men to fall down before it, declared one acquaintance, was a greater miracle than to build a world out of nothing.

All this praise, said the author, meant naught to him; he cared nothing for it. Frederick, he insisted, was in itself a baddish book, though he had done his best with it. The main cause for rejoicing was that the weight had been cast off. Heaven be blest, he now had sanction to be done with all such business throughout eternity.

In March, he and Jane left on a four weeks' visit to friends in Devonshire. Carlyle's wife was wonderfully happy in the retreat they had come to, with its lovely hills and valleys, its pleasant old villages nestled in the hollows. What purity of earth and sky, what fresh new green of leaves, after the soot and mud of early spring in London! Carlyle seemed to be getting real good of the place. He had the loan of a galloping pony, named Rubbish, who tore with him through the dales in a most salutary and gratifying manner. This insistence on hard riding was alarming, but one could do nothing but hand Thomas over to his friends the Destinies—beings so constantly referred to in his books.

Jane in her drives with her hostess had discovered a house for sale, cheap. A Devonshire Craigenputtock, she thought it— fields and woods without the bleakness.

"There's the place—buy that!" she urged.

"I fear you would die of the solitude in six months," replied her husband.

"Oh, no!" said Jane. She would see to it that she should not lack for company.

Carlyle was not sure about the project, but took it under advisement.

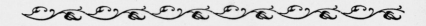

Chapter Thirty=Five

*A*FTER a visit to Annandale, Carlyle returned in mid-
September to Cheyne Row. Jane was already there, having got back earlier that very day. She had spent part
of her summer at home, part away on visits. Her last stop had
been at Folkestone for a two weeks' stay with a spinster friend,
Miss Davenport Bromley, who kept pug dogs for pets but was
otherwise an admirable person. Why not get a pug herself,
the hostess had suggested? But Jane made excuses on the plea
of loyalty to Nero.

Carlyle was tired from his journey—"a vile day of railway-
ing, like Jonah in the whale's belly!" But as soon as he entered
the parlor, there was Jane to cheer him up.

Now that his task was over, people came in greater numbers
to the house. John Forster, Erasmus Darwin, and Tennyson,
as always, and many more besides. Tyndall and Huxley, men
of science, called, and so did artists—Holman Hunt and Ford
Madox Brown. Froude, now a rising historian, was becoming a
frequent visitor with whom Jane's husband enjoyed going for
walks. The Marchioness of Lothian, the Countess of Airlie, and
other noble friends arrived to drink tea with Jane. And the
Blunts, of Chelsea Rectory, were often in and out.

Jane had her own calls to make. She frequently lunched at
the rectory, and on very special occasions entered its flagstoned,
ample kitchen to ply her skill in the making of marmalade.
She went sometimes to see Mrs. Oliphant. Their friendship
had ripened during the latter's work on a *Life* of Edward Irving. A tragic person, Mrs. Oliphant, though a brave one. Her
husband, a painter, had died at Rome of consumption, leaving
his widow penniless and with three young children to bring
up. These she was able to support by her writing, though because of frequent illness they were a heavy drain on her purse.
Once when Jane stopped at the house, there was Mrs. Oli-

372

phant, horribly frightened, with Cecco, her youngest son, in a convulsion. Jane did what she could to help. And that very evening, as Mrs. Oliphant waited fearfully for a possible recurrence of the seizure, she received a note from her late visitor. Mr. Carlyle, wrote Jane, when he heard of the trouble, had bidden her immediately to convey the message that a sister of his had suffered just such an attack, which was never repeated.

"God bless them!" thought Cecco's mother, putting away the letter.

Nothing cheered her more than calls from Mrs. Carlyle. The great man's wife could make the oddest, most startling remarks. She had been discussing with her the domestic relations of some of the age's famous people. Mr. Carlyle seemed the only virtuous one among the lot.

"My dear," answered Jane, "if Mr. Carlyle's digestion had been stronger, there is no saying what he might have been!"

It flattered and amused Jane to inspect the work of the several artists who insisted on saving Carlyle's likeness for posterity. Ford Madox Brown had put her husband in a picture which Jane gazed at proudly in the Annual Exhibition, and Woolner, with her advice and help, had completed a bust. Carlyle's likeness, remarked the sculptor, was as difficult to catch as the flash of a thunderbolt.

But the great event of the winter for Jane was her husband's election to be Rector of Edinburgh University—an unexpected recognition from the very nation and town where he had waged such a long and uphill fight for emergence at a time when to the eyes of most of his acquaintances he was merely the uncouth son of an Annandale farmer. The rectorship was an honorary office—a principal or chancellor carried on the actual duties of administration—with a three-year term of service. An inaugural address was the sole requirement involved, though the University hoped also to gain the benefit of its current Rector's advice. Gladstone had served the latest term and was now about to retire.

In October Carlyle was told of his nomination, in November he was elected. The rival candidate was Disraeli, whom some people spoke of as a coming prime minister of England.

In the election for the rectorship, Carlyle had polled double the vote of his opponent.

The new Rector pretended to think lightly of the distinction. But his wife could see that he was pleased; this accolade from Scotland, so long delayed, was a wholesome tonic to him. Jane harbored no silly illusions concerning such awards—as honors they meant little to her. But anything that proved to the world what she had always been sure of—her husband's essential greatness—was her delight.

When he first accepted the nomination, Carlyle had done so under the proviso that no inaugural speech would be required of him. Twenty-five years had passed since his last platform appearance, and he shrank from the thought of having to stand again before a crowd of people. But Jane privately assured her friends that there would be an address. She was proud of the Lord Rectorship and meant to insist that Carlyle fulfill his obligations.

As soon as the election was announced, an avalanche of congratulatory messages descended on Chelsea. An inane, amusing hurly-burly of empty praises—thus Carlyle described the hullabaloo. But in spite of his denials, those from friends gratified his heart.

"It is a real pleasure," wrote William Brookfield, "to see mankind touching its hat to its heroes when it *does* find them out; tenfold greater when the hero has never accelerated the process by enlisting drum and trumpet in his service."

"Would you like to know what Mr. Carlyle said on reading your letter?" Jane asked the sender. "What he said is this: 'Well! Upwards of a bushel of letters,—I should say a bushel and a half, have come within the last week to "congratulate" me on this most deplorable event, and the only really pretty one of them all is Brookfield's; as really friendly, graceful letter as a man could wish to receive.' "

Monday, April 2, 1866, was the date fixed for the inauguration. As the time approached, various plans were considered. An invitation from Monckton Milnes, now enjoying the title of Lord Houghton, had come from Fryston, bidding the Rector and his wife break their journey by stopping at his house for a night or so. Jane pondered the question. Should she accompany him or not? A sharp pain in her back—so intense

Thomas Carlyle

Photograph by Elliott & Fry, Ltd.
By permission of E. P. Dutton & Co.

it seemed almost to stop her heart—assailed her in moments of agitation. What if in her excitement it should incapacitate her on the journey itself, to the distraction of her poor husband? Reluctantly she decided not to go. When she wrote her refusal to Lord Houghton, she added the suggestion that perhaps, in the coming summer, she could visit him under more normal circumstances.

As April drew near, Jane was sure that she had made the wiser choice. Carlyle's anticipatory dread and her own nervousness were hard enough to cope with.

On the morning of March twenty-ninth, John Tyndall, who was to be her husband's companion on the way, drove up to the door. Carlyle was ready and waiting. But before he left the house, Jane hurried from the drawing room to the back parlor, where a bottle of old brown brandy stood on a little table. She poured a moderate quantity into a tumbler, then reached for the siphon in the wickerwork container. Her husband drank the mixture off. Then she gave him a little flask of the fine, well-aged cordial. He was to take a wee drop just before the address, she whispered.

They kissed each other twice, then Carlyle turned to leave. At the door, Jane suddenly motioned to Tyndall.

"For God's sake send me one line by telegraph when all is over!"

He promised to do so.

Tyndall and Edinburgh's next Rector were enthusiastically greeted at Fryston. Dinner was fashionably tardy that night, and quite an affair of state. And after it, Carlyle, to Tyndall's dismay, plunged with full vigor into a lively discussion. What would the elaborate meal and this after-excitement do to his friend's nervous system?

Railways had multiplied since Carlyle's last visit to Fryston. They now clasped it in a ring, and their whistles were active through the night. When Tyndall came to Carlyle's bedroom in the morning, he found him distracted. He had not slept one wink! He could never face that crowd at Edinburgh!

Deftly Tyndall explained the situation to the host, and the pair plotted together. For breakfast, instead of the household's customary fare, a very simple repast of tea, with milk and an

egg beaten up in it, was given to Carlyle. Then he and Tyndall,
through the latter's arranging, each mounted one of their host's
mettlesome horses. Carlyle's was a large bony gray, with a
villainous tough mouth. But the rider, though his hand was
no longer as strong as it used to be, presently mastered the
beast. Through lanes, over fields, along the high-roads, they
sped. After five hours of riding, the friends returned. Their
horses looked like cavalry chargers after a day of battle—
mud on their fetlocks and white foam over their manes.

A wholesome dinner was waiting. After finishing it, Lord
Houghton's distinguished guest, just as he would have done
at home, donned his gray dressing gown and lighted his long
churchwarden. The flunkies passing silently to and fro were
almost jolted out of their studied impersonality by the sight
of the visitor stretched at full length on the carpet near the
hearth, blowing the smoke from his pipe over the coals and up
the chimney.

Other guests were present that evening, and discussion soon
raged. Tyndall saw his ward ready to dash impetuously into
the fray. He laid his hand on Carlyle's shoulder. "We must
have no more of this!" he warned. Carlyle arched his brows
good-humoredly.

Tyndall had with him a flask of choice pale brandy. He
mixed some with soda-water, and gave Carlyle a good stiff
tumbler. The men prepared to retire for the night.

"I have no hope of sleep," remarked Carlyle, "I will come
to your room at seven in the morning."

Tyndall's Irish face expanded in a smile. "I think you *will*
sleep, and if so, I will come to your room instead of your coming to mine."

At seven next morning, Tyndall stood before the door. Not
a sound within. At eight, he was met with equal silence. Not
till nine, when he listened again, did he hear a stirring in the
room. He peered in. Carlyle's face, when he hailed his companion, was positively seraphic. Never before had Tyndall seen
it glow with such good-humor. What an amazing change! How
quickly the man, with his enormous, sensitive range, could slip
from the demoniac to the godlike!

"My dear friend," remarked Carlyle, "I am a totally new
man; I have slept nine hours without once awaking."

Edinburgh, at the time, had no University Hall. Accordingly, for the Rector's inauguration, the largest public room in the city was chartered by the University authorities—Music Hall, in George Street.

The address was to begin at three o'clock. But long before that hour, at the city railway station, and at stations in other towns in Scotland, there was unusual stir and bustle. The gathering throng contained many distinguished faces, and in its rising murmur one could hear the frequent recurrence of the name—Carlyle. What did he look like? What was he going to say?

By one o'clock there was a huge gathering before the main entrance to the Hall. It took a person almost half an hour to get inside. All available tickets had long since been disposed of, but with such a throng there could be little control over admissions as the torrents of humanity kept boiling in through every avenue and rolling along the back of the crowd into each vacant nook and corner.

The dignitaries had assembled in an anteroom near the platform: Carlyle himself; the venerable Sir David Brewster, now chancellor of the University, one of the very few men, in Carlyle's youth, who had recognized his genius and helped him along the way; Huxley; Andrew Ramsay, the geologist; Thomas Erskine, liberal expounder of the Gospel; Tyndall—each to receive an honorary degree. Carlyle himself had politely refused one.

"How do you feel?" asked Tyndall, looking into his friend's face. The Rector smiled faintly, but shook his head and said no word.

"Now you have to practice what you have been preaching all your life," encouraged Tyndall, "and prove yourself a hero." Again, Carlyle said nothing. His lips were dry; his throat felt as parched as on that London lecture platform twenty-six years ago. A pitcher and some water stood on a table. He poured a few drops of brandy into the glass—from Jane's flask—and drank it off. The academic procession was forming to march to the platform.

Carlyle had no prepared address. Several times he had tried to write one, but the results were never to his satisfaction. "You are to speak extempore," Jane had admonished him.

The men went forward in their gold-laced robes, as the audience, keyed to a high pitch of expectation, stood up to cheer—waving hats, handkerchiefs, and the programs giving the order of events. The conferring of honorary degrees was to come first, then the Rector's address.

Carlyle sat quiet during the preliminaries, scanning the faces before him, among which several carried his memory back through time to his early boyhood. And the vast sea of faces stared up at him. It saw a striking figure with deep-set eyes beneath overshadowing brows. A rugged man, honest-looking, sad when his features were in repose—his shaggy hair still dark, his rough beard iron gray. Like a piece of unhewn granite, he looked, full of its natural strength and cragginess of outline— unchipped and never polished to any standard design.

A tall, handsome young student rose to announce the University's choice: the rectorship had been awarded to Thomas Carlyle, the foremost of living Scotchmen.

Carlyle stood waiting for the cheers to end. With a twist of his shoulder, all unconsciously, the new Lord Rector threw off his ornate robe. Old Brewster, the principal, could not repress an amused, appreciative smile at the typical action.

He began to speak: "They tell me," he said, using the Annandale accent which half a lifetime's residence in London had scarcely changed, "they tell me that I ought to have written this address, and out of deference to the counsel I tried to do so; once, twice, thrice. But what I wrote was only fit for the fire, and to the fire it was compendiously committed. You must therefore listen to and accept what I say to you as coming straight from the heart."

After the address, when Tyndall, hastening to send his telegram, left the hall, the roar of acclamation was still ringing in his ears. "A perfect triumph!" he wired.

There was to be a birthday party, that night, at John Forster's. Maggie Welsh, staying at No. 5 Cheyne Row with her cousin, and Mrs. Warren, Jane's new housekeeper, were helping her to dress. But Jane could not get her mind on the task. At that very moment, Carlyle was passing through his ordeal. Had he been going to be hanged, she whimsically declared, she could not have taken the matter more to heart. Surely there would be a message soon.

A double rap at the street door.

"There it is!" Jane exclaimed.

"I am afraid, Cousin," said Maggie, "it is only the postman." But Jane could never mistake his knock.

Jessie, the housemaid, came running up the stairs, a telegram in her hands—Tyndall's. Jane read it herself, first, then repeated it aloud to the gaping women.

"Eh, Mrs. Carlyle! Eh! hear to that!" exclaimed Jessie.

"I told you, ma'am, I told you how it would be!" cried Mrs. Warren, while Maggie twittered like an agitated wren. They clapped their hands in excitement and executed a sort of leap frog round Mrs. Carlyle.

Suddenly Maggie noticed a deadly pallor sweep over Jane's face. "Get her some brandy!" she exclaimed in alarm.

Soon Jane had recovered herself. She felt ashamed of her momentary collapse, but the nervous tension of these last few days, coming to such a climax, had been rather too much to bear.

With the telegram still in her hand, she left for the party. Dickens was there, and Wilkie Collins, as well as Forster, the birthday child, and Forster's wife. Jane entered the room exultant, waving Tyndall's message in the air. The group broke into cheers; with boundless glee they drank the Rector's health. And Forster, in his joy over Carlyle, sent down a glass of punch to Sylvester, waiting outside in the carriage. Good Sylvester! When she had told him the news, his lips had trembled in his effort to express his gladness over the master's triumph. Little things like that, among the large, thought Jane, made the whole affair positively delightful.

The choicest part of the general rejoicing over her husband's success, she felt, was the enthusiasm and personal affection shown by his friends. Not since her girlhood, she declared, had she been so fond of everybody round her; so charmed with the world. At Forster's she was in her keenest mood. Jokingly, to Dickens—he was always after her to write—she outlined the plot of a novel. None of the writing women came near her, thought Dickens. He knew the lot—George Eliot, the Brontës, and so forth. None excelled her. Very good, excellent! he exclaimed. Jane did not quite complete the résumé of the action. Next time they met, she promised, she would finish it.

Her husband, according to plan, was not to return at once to Chelsea. There were dinners in Edinburgh and elsewhere which he could not avoid and after these were over he would spend a day or so in Annandale and Dumfries, to cool down after the heat of the effort.

Surely he would come back rested—no books, henceforth, demanding to be written, no upsetting tasks to be done.

During his absence, Jane received many congratulations at Cheyne Row. Mrs. George Welsh, her aunt, was among the visitors. Jane had never quite forgot the disapproval of her family when she had taken Carlyle in marriage. "Now all my own people will know," she said to her aunt, "now everybody will know, what a great man my husband is!"

From Tyndall, Jane presently got the full details. As he shook hands on leaving, he was amazed at the pressure of her lithe fingers. The warmth of welcome had ever been his, but that almost convulsive grip astonished him. Next the address itself arrived, inscribed in her husband's writing: "To my Jane: earliest copy (Scotsbrig, 17 Apr.)."

Carlyle's visit was intended to be brief, but a sprained ankle had delayed him. It was better now, he wrote; he could even get a shoe on the injured foot.

Jane, somewhat unwell after the excitement, had gone to Mrs. Oliphant's at Windsor to recover sleep. She was feeling better now, and greatly rested. Saturday, the twenty-first of April. Her husband was coming back to her Monday. On Saturday morning she wrote a final letter to him. Perhaps he would not receive it in time, yet it was worth the effort. That noon she was to dine with the Forsters, and in the evening Mrs. Oliphant and several friends were coming for tea to meet newly married Mr. and Mrs. Anthony Froude.

Sylvester was waiting at the door. Jane now had the responsibility of a brand new dog to take with her in the carriage. She had not really wanted the little beast, but the circumstances of its arrival permitted no refusal. It had belonged to pretty young Mrs. Chapman, the publisher's wife. She had died, two weeks before, after losing her baby. She had asked that the dog be cared for by Mrs. Carlyle.

At Palace Gate—the Forsters'—Jane was full of glee. "Carlyle coming home the day after to-morrow!" she announced. Towards three she drove away, to air Tiny, Mrs. Chapman's bequest, in Kensington Gardens.

Near Queens Gate, in the Park, she bade Sylvester halt the brougham. She stepped from the carriage to give the little dog a run by the margins of the Serpentine. His exercise over, she lifted him once more into the seat beside her. Had he enjoyed a sufficiently active scamper? As they neared Victoria Gate, Jane decided to put him down once more.

A carriage—she had not seen it—drove rapidly up. Jane's heart missed a beat as she saw the dog make directly for the path of the vehicle. Tiny gave a thin cry as a wheel ran over his paw. She leapt down and lifted him in her arms. He was not much hurt; merely frightened. She laid him on a cushion in the brougham.

Sylvester drove on. He followed the Big Drive, then up by the Serpentine again, then down past Victoria Gate. When no orders came from his mistress, he repeated the circuit. From his driver's perch he could just catch a glimpse of Mrs. Carlyle's hands folded in her lap. But why no request that he drive her home? She rarely lingered on the way. He stopped the horse. No word from Mrs. Carlyle. A pedestrian was passing. Thoroughly alarmed, Sylvester did not wait to scramble from his seat. He asked the passer-by to look within the carriage.

Mrs. Carlyle was dead.

That night, as the guests arrived at No. 5 Cheyne Row, they found, not their brilliant hostess, but Mrs. Oliphant waiting to meet them at the door. They could hardly believe what she told them. Mrs. Carlyle had seemed in unusual health and spirits. No one had dreamed of danger.

She lay upstairs on her bed. The light of two wax candles gleamed in the room; shone on her face—dignified, beautiful, calm as in easy sleep. These tapers were the very ones meant to cast their rays on the animation of Jane's first London party. Now, they shed their light on her in death.

During a previous illness, when she thought she might die, though she had kept her suspicions from her husband, she had given certain instructions to Mrs. Warren. These candles, put away unlit and carefully preserved ever since the day she had chided her mother for too extravagant expenditures for the party, were to serve her as directed.

Chapter Thirty=Six

*L*ATE Saturday evening a telegram was delivered to Carlyle. So many congratulations! He was weary of them all. He tossed the message, unopened, to his sister. She slit the envelope and glanced at the sheet. Her face went bloodless. She handed the telegram back to her brother.

Without a word, he got up and climbed the stairs to his bedroom. They could hear the door close behind him. For hours there was the murmur of his voice as if in prayer.

Next morning, as was needful—he was so dazed and shaken —they led him to wander in the green Sabbath fields, the spring fields with the everlasting skies above them. It was difficult for him to think at all; to grasp the meaning of this infinite sorrow which had peeled his life all bare and in a moment shattered his world to universal ruin. Alas, the inexorable years, that cut away the souls one loves, who love as deeply in return!

Carlyle was now in his seventieth year; he did not think to survive her long—yet he had sixteen more years to live. Jane had died at sixty-four. His memory could not picture her in age. He saw her always, in his visions of her, not as a suffering woman, but as the bright and sunny girl of his days of courting.

He reached Haddington on the morning before the funeral, and stayed at the house of William Dods, old schoolmate of his wife. They had taken Jane upstairs. Carlyle went out to the garden at the rear, and walked, by himself, up and down, for a long time. When at last he came in, he wished to see his wife. With a wild look he demanded to know where they had put her. Dods spoke to him, and presently he grew quiet and did not again ask to see her face.

He left the house, as the day was ending, to walk the streets. The sun was almost gone. No matter; let it set.

How suddenly had she been snatched away from him, and the light of his life as if gone out! Always she had wrapped him round like a cloak, to keep the bitter cold from him.

Late, very late now; he must go back. But he dreaded the very thought of attempted sleep. Horrible one's first awakening in the morning, reality once more exposed beneath the sinking puddle of confused and ghastly dreams.

He must build anew what life he had left; he must work. That was what she would wish. Yet how difficult the task, with her no more beside him!

Dr. Welsh's house, with its peaceful garden. It lay in the desolate moonlight, in the quiet of the hours. He glanced at the windows of the room where first he had seen her. Yes, Irving had brought him, he recalled; they had tramped on foot from the city. In the twilight, from those very windows, that bright pair of eyes had been fixed inquiringly on him— she the loveliest young creature he ever beheld, so sparkling with grace and talent! Through the blackness he felt her again above him; the vision clear as it once had been, forty-five years ago, in the warm summer dusk.

Bibliographical Note

I HAVE sought to write this biography of Jane Welsh Carlyle on the testimony of the contemporary evidence and in the idiom of the Carlyles and of those who knew them. By far the largest body of material is to be found in the twenty published volumes of the correspondence of the Carlyles and in Thomas Carlyle's *Reminiscences* and other writings. If space permitted, I might cite all references to these materials; but to do so would swell this bibliographical note out of proportion. Unless there is a special reason, I shall therefore make no further mention of them. If not otherwise identified, direct quotations come from this source. Many letters have also been drawn on which have thus far been printed only in periodicals. For the most part, these are indicated in connection with chapters where they were of greatest service. In addition, I have used manuscripts in such repositories as the National Library, Edinburgh, Scotland, the John Forster collection in the Victoria and Albert Museum, and the collection in the Carlyle House, Chelsea, London.

The works of two of Carlyle's biographers have been of great service: that of James Anthony Froude, his literary executor, and the six-volume biography by David Alec Wilson.

What follows is a condensed presentation of the more important sources, other than the published volumes of correspondence and the *Reminiscences*.

CHAPTER I

In *Wotton Reinfred*, an attempt at autobiographical fiction, and in *Sartor Resartus*, Carlyle gives information about his courtship which, when studied in conjunction with his correspondence, is of great assistance in piecing out the details of his first call on Jane Welsh. The manuscript of *Wotton Reinfred*, never completed, is now in the possession of the John Pierpont Morgan Library, New York City. It was first printed in the *New Review*, VI, 1–30, 141–165, 285–313 (1892). I have drawn to some extent on *Sartor Resartus* in several other chapters as well. Mrs. M. O. W. Oliphant's standard life of Edward Irving (London, 1862) has been useful in this chapter and in others where Irving plays a part. *Last Leaves*, by Alexander Smith, Edinburgh, 1868 (third edition), also gives first-hand information on Irving's character, appearance, and early career. Some previously unpublished letters by Carlyle in *Scribner's Magazine*, XIII, 416–425 (April, 1893), shed light on Carlyle's friendship with Irving. In his *Edinburgh Sketches and Memories* (London and Edinburgh, 1892), Carlyle's friend David Masson discusses Carlyle's University days and early career in Edinburgh. *Reminiscences of Haddington*, by J. Martine, Edinburgh, 1883, gives an account of the town's history and social life, while in his *Autobiography* (London, 1905), Samuel Smiles, a native son of Haddington and contemporary of Jane Welsh, furnishes some useful reminiscences. Another native son, David Davidson, who was an acquaintance of Jane Welsh in youth and later became a friend, in *Memories of a Long Life* (Edinburgh, 1890) adds details and contributes information on Irving in Haddington.

Chapters II and III

Some of the sources just mentioned have contributed to Chapters II and III as well. In addition, information has been obtained from "Eight New Love Letters of Jane Welsh," *Nineteenth Century Magazine*, LXXV, 86–113 (January, 1914), and "More New Letters of Jane Welsh Carlyle," *Nineteenth Century Magazine*, LXXVI, 317–349 (August, 1914). M. D. Conway, in his *Thomas Carlyle*, New York, 1881, supplies some details on the Carlyles (early life in Edinburgh as described by Carlyle himself) and publishes for the first time certain letters relative to this period.

Chapter IV

Lord Cockburn's *Life of Lord Jeffrey*, London and Edinburgh, 1852, has been drawn on in this chapter and in others. Francis Lockhart's anonymously published *Peter's Letters to his Kinfolk*, Edinburgh, 1819, is rich in intimate details on Jeffrey and other persons of Edinburgh. While several other journals and memoirs have supplied particulars, I should make special mention of Harriet Martineau's three-volume *Autobiography*, published in London in 1877, which furnishes illuminating side lights on Jeffrey's personality. The chief source, however, on the relation of Jeffrey and Mrs. Carlyle has been the collection of forty-nine manuscript letters from Jeffrey to the Carlyles which I have been able to draw on through the courtesy of the National Library of Scotland.

CHAPTER V

Information on De Quincey used in this chapter, and in a short section of Chapter VIII, has come in the main from the following: *Thomas De Quincey*, by H. A. Page, London, 1877; "Nights and Days with De Quincey," by James Hogg, *Harper's New Monthly Magazine*, January, 1890, and *De Quincey and His Friends* by the same writer, London, 1895; *Personal Recollections of De Quincey*, by John R. Findlay, Edinburgh, 1886; *Thomas De Quincey*, by David Masson, New York, 1882. The last-named author's *Edinburgh Sketches* has likewise been useful, as has M. D. Conway's *Autobiography*, London, 1904.

CHAPTER VI

Among the published volumes of Carlyle's correspondence is *The Correspondence Between Goethe and Carlyle*, edited by C. E. Norton, London and New York, 1887. This volume, of course, is the chief source on Goethe.

CHAPTER VII

Memoirs of Old Friends, by Caroline Fox, London, 1882, furnishes the anecdote told on p. 62, about the tastes for literature developed by Mrs. Carlyle's maids.

CHAPTERS VIII AND IX

The letter inviting De Quincey to Craigenputtock, referred to on pp. 65–66, is given by H. A. Page in his *Thomas De Quincey*, II, 278–281. Some details concerning Irving's visit to Craigenputtock are taken from Carlyle's account of it as reported by M. D. Conway in his *Thomas Carlyle*. When the idea of *Sartor Resartus* was first conceived, the work was christened after the name of its hero, which was first spelled Teufelsdreck. For the sake of uniformity I have followed the later spelling, Teufelsdröckh.

CHAPTER X

David Hogg, in his *Life of Allan Cunningham*, Dumfries and London, 1875, gives part of Carlyle's speech at the dinner described early in this chapter and supplies other information. Fuller details on Jane's thoughts and activities during Carlyle's absence in

London are supplied in "More New Letters of Jane Welsh Carlyle," *Nineteenth Century Magazine*, LXXVI, 317–349 (August, 1914). Most of the direct quotations in this chapter are taken from that source.

CHAPTER XI

Much information on the London years not directly supplied by published writings of the Carlyles or contained in the manuscript letters at Edinburgh comes from Francis Espinasse's *Literary Recollections and Sketches*, London, 1893. Details on London itself have been taken to considerable extent from Peter Cunningham's voluminous handbooks of London, the first of which appeared in 1849. Jane's share in the preparation of the memorial for Goethe, mentioned toward the close of this chapter, is described by Anne Thackeray Ritchie in her *Chapters from Some Memoirs*, London, 1894.

CHAPTER XII

In *English Traits*, Boston, 1856, and in his manuscript diary, Emerson has described the visit to Craigenputtock. Carlyle's remark on the provincialism of literature (p. 129) was made to Francis Espinasse and recorded in the *Literary Recollections*. Among other places in the correspondence, Carlyle refers to forebodings over the move to London in a letter to Eckermann dated 6 May, 1834, and first published in the *Yale Review* for July, 1926. Hunt's remark on his joy at the prospect of having Carlyle as neighbor comes from his *Correspondence*, edited by his eldest son (London, 1862).

CHAPTER XIII

Descriptions of Chelsea and the Carlyle House, and of the Carlyles' early residence there, have been drawn from many sources. The most useful are: *Memoirs of Gerald Blunt of Chelsea*, London, 1911; *Memorials of Old Chelsea*, by Alfred Beaver, London, 1892; and Leigh Hunt's *Autobiography*, London, 1860. A series of Mrs. Carlyle's letters printed for the first time in Volume XLIX of the *Strand Magazine* (1915) supplemented the chief sources. M. D. Conway's *Autobiography* also supplies several details. Carlyle's remark quoted on p. 137 is from the last-named source. An undated letter from Mrs. Carlyle to Leigh Hunt in the British Museum, and other manuscript data dealing with Hunt's opinion of Mrs. Carlyle, have been drawn on in this chapter. The sentence quoted on p. 152 comes from the just mentioned letter.

Chapter XIV

Materials concerning Irving cited as used in Chapter I have been supported in Chapter XIV by the following: *An Autobiographical Fragment*, by B. W. Procter, London, 1877, and Carlyle's obituary notice on Irving printed in *Fraser's Magazine*, XI, 101–103 (January, 1835).

Chapter XV

Memoirs of the Life and Writings of Thomas Carlyle, with Personal Reminiscences, by R. H. Shepherd, London, 1881, gives Carlyle's account of the destruction of the first volume of *The French Revolution* and of its rewriting. Most of the direct quotations bearing on these episodes are derived from this record. But other sources have been drawn on also, the following being the most important: *Conversations with Carlyle*, by Gavan Duffy, New York, 1892; Conway's *Autobiography;* and *The Letters of John Stuart Mill*, London, 1910. Mrs. Carlyle's suspicions of Mrs. Taylor's part in the misfortune were told to Mrs. Gilchrist as reported in *Anne Gilchrist, Her Life and Writings*, by H. H. Gilchrist, London, 1887.

Chapter XVI

Information on the Sterling family and their relations with Carlyle is derived chiefly from the following books: *The Life of John Sterling*, by Thomas Carlyle, London, 1851; *A Correspondence Between Sterling and Emerson*, Boston and New York, 1897; *Thomas Carlyle, A Study*, by John Heywood, Manchester, 1881; and *Memories of a Hostess* (Mrs. J. T. Fields), edited by M. A. DeWolfe Howe, Boston, 1922. In the dialogue about the kippered herring (p. 180), Jane assigns to a visitor some of the questions which elicit Helen's responses. To simplify the passage, I have given all these questions to Mrs. Carlyle.

Chapters XVII and XVIII

Since Chapter XVII is derived almost wholly from the sources described at the beginning of this bibliographical note, no others are recorded here. In Chapter XVIII, Miss Kemble's admiration for Carlyle is mentioned in her *Records of a Girlhood*, New York, 1879, and *Further Records*, New York, 1891. Additional information on Miss Kemble is offered by letters from R. M. Milnes, published in his life by T. Wemyss Reid, London, 1890. Miss Martineau's *Autobiography* has contributed largely to this chapter as well as to later ones. Among other sources the following give information on the reception of Carlyle's *French Revolution:* R. H. Shepherd's *Carlyle,* which repeats Landor's opinion; *Tennyson, Ruskin, and Browning,* by Anne Thackeray Ritchie, London, 1892, which gives Hallam's response; and the *Journals and Correspondence of Lady Eastlake,* London, 1895, where Jeffrey's comment is recorded.

CHAPTER XIX

In addition to the writings of the Carlyles, the material on Mazzini is drawn largely from these sources: *Life and Writings of Mazzini,* London, 1864–1870 (4 vols.); *Maria Mazzini e il suo ultimo Carteggio,* Genoa, 1927; Mazzini letters in the *Nineteenth Century Magazine,* vol. XXXVII (May, 1895); Mazzini's *Letters to an English Family,* edited by E. F. Richards, London, 1920–22; *Memories of London in the Forties,* by David Masson, Edinburgh and London, 1908; G. J. Holyoake's *Bygones Worth Remembering,* London, 1905, and *Sixty Years of an Agitator's Life,* London, 1892; *The Letters of Elizabeth Barrett Browning,* edited by F. G. Kenyon, New York, 1897. Also from these previously mentioned sources: Duffy's *Conversations with Carlyle,* Espinasse's *Literary Recollections,* and H. Martineau's *Autobiography.*

CHAPTER XX

Spedding's letter to Milnes at the beginning of this chapter is quoted from *The Cambridge "Apostles,"* by Frances M. Brookfield, New York, 1906, a book which has supplied several other details. Buller's remark about Milnes comes from this source. Reid's biography of R. M. Milnes not only quotes letters from Milnes relating to his friendship with the Carlyles but contains several from the Carlyles as well, used in this chapter and elsewhere throughout the present book. Information on Milnes has also been obtained from Espinasse's *Literary Recollections,* and Emerson's *Journals,* Boston, 1909–1913. Carlyle's remark about Milnes as president of the Heaven and Hell Amalgamated Society comes from the *Letters of the Hon. Mrs. Edward Twisleton,* London, 1928. She was an intimate friend of Mrs. Carlyle. The reception of the lectures is amply recorded. Details are chiefly from Harriet Martineau's *Autobiography* and Caroline Fox's *Memories;* the *Correspondence of Henry Taylor,* edited by Edward Dowden, London, 1888;

"Thomas Carlyle," by M. D. Conway, in *Harper's Magazine*, LXII, 888–912 (May, 1881); and *Memoir and Letters of Charles Sumner*, Boston, 1877. Further descriptions of D'Orsay, to supplement the Carlyles', come from *Old Acquaintances*, by J. T. Fields, Boston, 1876; *Leaves from the Note-books of Lady Dorothy Nevill*, London, 1907; and *Correspondence of Abraham Hayward*, edited by H. E. Carlisle, London, 1886.

CHAPTER XXI

In this and later chapters, material from Mrs. Carlyle's letters has been augmented by *Selections from the Letters of Geraldine Endsor Jewsbury*, London, 1892. The Forster collection of manuscripts in the Victoria and Albert Museum, London, has been drawn on for information concerning John Forster and the Carlyles. Additional light on Forster's personality comes in the main from Emerson's *Journals* (published and in manuscript); Percy Fitzgerald's *Recreations of a Literary Man*, London, 1882; Espinasse's *Literary Recollections;* and Forster's own *Life of Charles Dickens*, London, 1872.

CHAPTERS XXII AND XXIII

Chapter XXII is derived almost wholly from the Carlyles' writings. Some sources on Fitzgerald used in Chapter XXIII are *The Life of Edward Fitzgerald*, by Thomas Wright, London, 1904; and *Letters and Literary Remains of Edward Fitzgerald*, London and New York, 1889. Responses to Jane as seen in society may be found in the following materials: "Some Letters and Conversations of Carlyle," by Edward Strachey, *Atlantic Monthly*, LXXIII, 821–834 (June, 1894); Espinasse; Duffy; *Some Personal Reminiscences of Carlyle*, by A. J. Symington, Paisley, 1886; *The Life and Letters of Charles Darwin*, by Francis Darwin, London, 1887; and *A Century of Family Letters*, edited by Emma Darwin, London, 1915. The two last-named supply information on Erasmus and Charles Darwin to add to comments by the Carlyles. In his biography of Carlyle, David Alec Wilson quotes for the first time several letters which passed between Carlyle and Lady Ashburton. The letter given at the end of Chapter XVIII is from this work.

CHAPTERS XXIV AND XXV

Chapter XXIV comes almost wholly from the Carlyles' letters. In Chapter XXV, Masson's first impressions of Mrs. Carlyle are

given on pp. 35–38 of his *Memories of London in the Forties*. Miss
Jewsbury's protest, quoted on p. 282, occurs on p. 75 of her *Letters
to Jane Welsh Carlyle*.

Chapter XXVI

Materials used in Chapter XIX have also been drawn on in
Chapter XXVI. Mazzini's letter to his mother, quoted on p. 286,
may be found in the original Italian in *Scritti*, XIX, *Epistolario*
(Edizione nazionale, Emola, 1906–   ), IX, 304–305. It is dated
8 Oct., 1840. Carlyle's letter to the *Times* appeared in the issue of
19 June, 1844. Margaret Fuller, among others, in her *Memoirs*
(II, 187), Boston, 1852, speaks of Carlyle's arguments with Mazzini, and so does Emma Darwin in *A Century of Family Letters*.
In a letter quoted in Reid's life of Milnes (I, 332–33), Milnes speaks
of Mrs. Carlyle's exasperation at having her correspondence read by
the Foreign Office. Both Gavan Duffy and David Masson *(Memories of London* and *Conversations with Carlyle)* speak of Mazzini's
stronger position in London after the letters episode and its attendant
publicity.

Chapter XXVII

Helen Mitchell's remark at the beginning of this chapter was
reported to Espinasse and given in his *Literary Recollections*. It was
his opinion that with *Cromwell*, Carlyle reached his zenith. The details of Fitzgerald's terpsichorean escape from Cheyne Row and his
responses to *Cromwell* came from *Some New Letters of Edward
Fitzgerald*, London, 1923. Robert Browning (*Letters*, London,
1899, I, 151) vouches for Thomas Carlyle's competence in pouring tea for guests during Jane's absence. A large number of first-
hand descriptions of Tennyson exist. To supplement those by the
Carlyles, Ellen Twisleton's in her *Letters* and Henry Taylor's in
his *Correspondence* are useful. Jane's remarks about *Sordello* are
quoted by Conway in his *Autobiography*, II, 23. The catastrophe of
the teakettle is told by Thackeray's daughter Mrs. Ritchie, pp.
198–99 of her *Tennyson, Ruskin and Browning*, as are Carlyle's
uncomplimentary remarks on Tennyson's poems on Greek subjects.
The conversation on Tennyson's pension comes from Reid's biography of Milnes, I, 295–96. The account of Jane's playing of "Macpherson's Lament" is given by Carlyle in a letter of 26 October,
1844, written to Fitzgerald and quoted in Fitzgerald's *Letters and
Literary Remains*. I have taken the liberty of turning one sentence
from indirect to direct discourse.

Chapters XXVIII and XXIX

Most of the material comes from the Carlyles' writings and correspondence. The letters from Mazzini may be found in Froude's *Carlyle's Life in London*, London, 1884, I, 381–82, 384–85. A few details of Mrs. Carlyle's trip to Haddington are supplied from T. W. Reid's *Life of the Right Honourable Edward Forster*, London, 1888 (fourth edition).

Chapter XXX

A useful account of Mazzini at Rome, and afterwards, is that in Margaret Fuller's *Memoirs*. Froude's impressions of Mrs. Carlyle are found in his biography of Carlyle and other writings. Anne Thackeray Ritchie, in her *Chapters from Some Memories*, reports Mrs. Carlyle's conversations on the occasion of the calls by the Thackeray children.

Chapter XXXI

Aside from reports by the Carlyles, detailed accounts of Grange house parties are found in the Brookfields' correspondence published in *Mrs. Brookfield and Her Circle*, London, 1906. Several quotations from this work are made in the present chapter. Ellen Twisleton's *Letters* and H. Taylor's *Autobiography*, London, 1885, should be mentioned among the funds of information on entertainments at the Grange. An interesting characterization of Lady Harriet is that by R. M. Milnes in his *Monographs, Personal and Social*, London, 1873. Mrs. Elizabeth Bancroft's *Letters from England*, London, 1904, is also useful. While these sources give a picture of Mrs. Carlyle at the Grange, the following add important details: *Reminiscences*, by Goldwin Smith, New York, 1910, and "Some Reminiscences of Jane Welsh Carlyle," *Temple Bar*, LXIX, 227–233 (1883). The conversation recorded on p. 335 is given by G. S. Venables in "Carlyle in Society and at Home," *Fortnightly Review*, XXXIII, 622–642 (May, 1883). Brookfield's account of the Christmas dinner at the Carlyles' is from *Mrs. Brookfield and Her Circle*. I have turned some of the reported conversation from indirect to direct discourse.

Chapter XXXII

Mrs. Twisleton's *Letters* supply information on her friendship with Mrs. Carlyle given at the opening of this chapter. Jane's comment on this friendship is reported in Anne Thackeray Ritchie's *Letters*, London, 1924. Woolner's remark on Mrs. Carlyle's ill-health is in a letter dated 17 December, 1856, in *Thomas Woolner, His Life in Letters*, by Amy Woolner, London, 1917. The details of Mrs. Carlyle's dream as described on p. 342 were told to Caroline Fox and reported in her *Memories*. Mrs. Carlyle's diary for the years 1855–56 was printed by Froude, with certain omissions, in *The Letters and Memorials of Jane Welsh Carlyle*, London, 1883. The entry for June 21, 1856, was not given, and the original, I believe, no longer exists. The record survives in a copy of the diary made by Carlyle's niece Mary Aitken. The entry in question was printed by Herbert Paul in his *Life of Froude*, New York, 1905. A photographic reproduction of Mary Aitken's manuscript copy of the entry may be seen facing p. 93 of Waldo H. Dunn's *A Study of the Froude-Carlyle Controversy*, London and New York, 1930. In addition to Carlyle's report in the *Reminiscences* of Mrs. Carlyle's coming on a visitor in the act of reading her diary, John Tyndall mentions the incident, as told to him by Mrs. Carlyle, in his *New Fragments*, London, 1892. I have somewhat condensed the quotations given from the diary. Mrs. Carlyle's remarks at Lady Goodrich's party are reported by Holman Hunt in his *Pre-Raphaelism and the Pre-Raphaelite Brotherhood*, New York, 1905. In addition to sources already mentioned for Lady Ashburton, Reid's biography of R. M. Milnes supplies details on her illness and death.

CHAPTER XXXIII

George Eliot's Life, by J. W. Cross, gives details to supplement Mrs. Carlyle's comments on the author of *Adam Bede*. A collection of Mrs. Carlyle's letters edited by Reginald Blunt and published in *The Forum*, LXVI–LXVII (1921–22), supplies additional information on her last years. This is among the sources drawn on in Chapter XXXIII and the concluding chapters of the present biography. The anecdote about Nero's being sent to the laundry (p. 352) comes from "Some Reminiscences of Jane Welsh Carlyle," *Temple Bar*, LXIX, 227–233. The conversation with the Gilchrists concerning Nero is reported in the life of Anne Gilchrist. Many first-hand accounts of talk at Cheyne Row exist. Among the more useful are: William Allingham's *Diary*, London, 1907; *Fifty Years*, by Henry Parkes, London and New York, 1892; and *A Memoir of William Lecky*, by his wife, London, 1909. Carlyle's remark about Homer was reported in Conway's *Autobiography*. The dialogue with Ruskin comes from *The Correspondence of George Richmond*,

R.A., and His Son, London (n.d.). While these sources mention Jane's part at Cheyne Row, Henry James's *Literary Remains,* Boston, 1885, is especially valuable for reporting the occasion of Carlyle's tirade against O'Connell and Jane's efforts to restore peace. George W. Smalley's *London Letters,* London, 1890, mentions Mrs. Carlyle's use of the word "divide!" on such occasions. Charlotte Cushman's *Letters and Memories,* Boston, 1879; Mrs. Oliphant's "Recollections of Carlyle," *Appleton's Journal,* XXV, 510–21 (1881); and Espinasse also supply details. The conversation given at the end of the chapter appears on p. 73 of *Anne Gilchrist, Her Life and Writings.*

CHAPTER XXXIV

Larkin's observations of the Carlyles, and his quotations of conversations, are found in his "Carlyle and Mrs. Carlyle; a Ten Years' Reminiscence," *British Quarterly Review,* LXXIV, 28–84 (July, 1881). Woolner's letter on p. 362 is quoted from his biography. Mrs. Carlyle's letters published in *The Strand Magazine,* XLIX (1915), and in *The Forum,* LXVI–LXVII (1921–22), are especially filled with details concerning her accident and subsequent illness. An interesting account of the visit to Devonshire as described at the end of the chapter is in "Carlyle and John Forster: An Unpublished Correspondence," *Quarterly Review,* vol. CCLXVIII (1937).

CHAPTERS XXXV AND XXXVI

In Chapter XXXV, Mrs. Oliphant's *Autobiography and Letters,* New York, 1922, has supplied details and conversations, as has Reginald Blunt's *Memoirs of Gerald Blunt of Chelsea.* Most of the immediate details of Carlyle's Address at Edinburgh have been drawn from contemporary accounts in the daily press. Some other useful sources are: M. D. Conway's *Autobiography* and his *Carlyle* (Conway was present at the installation); *Writings by the Way,* by J. C. Smith, Edinburgh, 1885; *Last Leaves,* by Alexander Smith; and G. W. Smalley's *London Letters.* Brookfield's letter quoted on p. 374 is from *The Cambridge "Apostles,"* by Frances Brookfield. Tyndall's account of the trip to Edinburgh and his description of subsequent events are from his *New Fragments.* The details of the birthday party at John Forster's and Dickens' remarks on Mrs. Carlyle come from Forster's *Life of Dickens.* Jane's comment to her aunt (p. 380) is quoted from "A Sheaf of Letters from Jane

Welsh Carlyle," *Cornhill Magazine,* LXI, 493–510, 622–638 (1926). To supplement Carlyle's accounts of his wife's death in his *Reminiscences* and previously cited materials, the following source has been drawn on: *Letters of Robert Browning to Miss Isa Blagden,* Waco, 1923 (letters of March 19 and April 19, 1866). The description of the party Mrs. Carlyle was planning, interrupted by her death, is given in Reginald Blunt's "Mrs. Carlyle and Her Housemaid," *Cornhill Magazine,* XI, 456–67 (October, 1901), which also supplies details concerning her death. The sources of the last chapter are obituary notices in the contemporary press and Carlyle's own writings.

Index

Abbotsford, 31

Aberdeen, 277

Adam Bede, by George Eliot, 350-351

Addiscombe Farm, 249-250, 263, 302-303, 306, 307, 308, 309, 311

Adelaide, Queen, 183-184

Airlie, Lady, 372

Allingham, William, 326

Amberley, Lady, 326

America, 123, 124, 160, 181, 198, 203, 204, 206, 265, 284, 326, 358

Amos Barton, by George Eliot, 349-350

Ampton Street, London, 105, 107, 108, 109, 112, 113, 118, 131, 136, 162

Anderson, James, 55-56

Annan, 1, 2, 70, 76, 154, 155, 156, 184, 193, 234, 368

Annandale, 1, 5, 19, 70, 71, 112, 120, 132, 155, 205, 310, 368, 372, 380

Antoni, Countess Clementina degli, 175-176, 184

Apocalypse, The, 115

Apsley House, London, 106

Arnold, Dr. Thomas, 326

Ashburton, (the first) Lord, 228, 303, 311

Athenaeum, The, 117, 230

Athenaeum, Boston, Massachusetts, 124

Austin, Mrs., 105, 131, 169

Austria, 289, 323-324

Austrian Embassy, London, 290

Autobiography, Benvenuto Cellini, 63

Baillie, Matthew, 8

Balzac, Honoré de, 233

Barbier de Séville, by Pierre Beaumarchais, 188

Baring, Lady Harriet (afterwards Lady Ashburton), 228-229, 249-250, 252, 262-264, 302-312, 326, 329, 332-337, 341, 346, 347-348

Baring, William Bingham (afterwards Lord Ashburton), 228, 264, 310, 311, 332, 333, 335, 346, 347

Barnes, Carina, 365

Barnes, Dr., 354, 362, 363, 364, 366

Barnet, Bessy, 137, 138, 140, 176

Barry Cornwall, See W. B. Procter

Bastille, Paris, 127

Bath, Lord, 347

Bath House, London, 228, 303 ff., 311, 340, 342, 345, 347

Battersea Bridge, London, 145, 287

Bay House, Alverstoke, Hampshire, 304, 311

Beethoven, Ludwig Van, 21

Beggar's Opera, by John Gay, 152

Belgrave Square, London, 138

Bellona, Mrs. Carlyle's mare, 370

Bentham, Jeremy, 99

Berwick-upon-Tweed, 315

Bessborough, Lord, 333

Betty, Craigenputtock servant, 93, 100-101, 102

Bible, The, 115

Birmingham, 34

Blackwood, John, 350-351

Blackwood's Edinburgh Magazine, 26, 34, 38, 91

Blakiston, Dr., 367

Blunt, Gerald, 369, 372
Bordeaux, France, 174
Boston, Massachusetts, 181
Brewster, Sir David, 377, 378
British Government, 290
British Museum, London, 183, 282
Bromley, Miss Davenport, 372
Brontë sisters, 350, 379
Brookfield, Rev. William Henry, 222, 332, 333, 337-338, 347, 374
Brookfield, Mrs. W. H., 336-337
Brown, Ford Madox, 372, 373
Brown, James, 3
Browning, Elizabeth Barrett, 330, 341, 351
Browning, Robert, 293, 294-295, 330
Bryden, Dr., 68, 70
Buccleuch Place, Edinburgh, 25
Buchan, Earl of, 25
Buller, Charles, 45, 60, 111-112, 132, 160, 163, 201, 222, 223, 247, 249-251, 263, 326
Buller, Edward, 243-252
Buller, Mrs. Edward, 98, 243-252, 263
Buller, Reginald, 243-252
Bunsen, Baron, 228
Burns, Major, 284-285
Burns, Robert, 61, 91
Burns, by T. Carlyle, 52, 54-55, 57, 88
Bury St. Edmunds, 243, 250, 251
Butler, Mrs. Pierce, See Fanny Kemble
Byron, George Gordon, 10, 13, 113, 149, 151, 229, 315, 359

Caledonian Chapel, London, 14, 114
Calthorpe, Lord, 249
Cambridge University, 111, 171, 222, 333
Canning, Lord and Lady, 333
Caplegill, 121
Carlton Club, London, 271
Carlyle, Alexander, 40, 43, 49-50, 51, 60, 61, 67, 77, 82-83, 92, 102, 119, 194
Carlyle, James, 1, 19, 58, 60, 119-120, 168, 170

Carlyle, Mrs. James, 19, 20, 39, 62, 84, 103, 120, 199, 310, 325
Carlyle, Jane and Thomas (this listing is a chronology; look under separate headings for further information), first meeting (1821), 1-11; courtship (1821-1826), 12-15; residence in Edinburgh (1826-1828), 16-48; move to Craigenputtock (1828-1831), 49-102; winter's residence in London (1831-1832), 103-121; final period at Craigenputtock (1832-1834), 122-135; move to London (1834), 136-153; residence in London through publication of *French Revolution* (1834-1837), 154-209; residence in London, middle period (1837-1849), 210-312; Jane's excursion to Haddington (1849), 313-322; till death of Lady Ashburton (1849-1857), 323-348; till publication of *Frederick the Great* (1857-1865), 349-371; final London years (1865-1866), 371-384
Carlyle, Janet, See Mrs. Robert Hanning
Carlyle, Jean, Alexander Carlyle's wife, 102, 119
Carlyle, Jean, Thomas Carlyle's sister, 58, 79, 155
Carlyle, Dr. John, 64, 71, 72, 73, 87, 89, 104, 121, 123, 175, 189, 190-191, 295, 368, 369
Carlyle, Margaret, 72, 73, 168
Carlyle, Mary, afterwards Mrs. Austin, 49, 239, 368, 383
Carnarvon, Lord, 333
Catholic Apostolic Church, 155-157
Cavaignac, Godefroi, 187-188, 194, 213-214, 256
Cavaliers, the, 152, 253
Cellini, Benvenuto, 63
Chalmers, Dr. Thomas, 4, 114
Chapman & Hall, publishers, 237, 344
Chapman, Frederick, 351

Chapman, Mrs. Frederick, 380, 381
"Characteristics," by T. Carlyle, 117, 118, 124
Cheapside, London, 197, 364
Chelsea, London, 131, 134 ff., 140, 143-146, 152, 157, 162, 174, 176, 183, 187, 195, 196, 204, 207, 208, 212, 216, 228, 242, 243, 252, 259, 265, 269, 288, 290, 293, 294, 304, 311, 317, 325, 327, 339, 342, 345 ff., 358, 360, 365, 368-369, 374, 380
Chelsea Hospital, London, 144, 183
Chelsea Rectory, London, 369, 372
Cheviot Hills, 315
Cheyne Row, London, 135, 138, 142, 144, 148, 157, 159, 162, 164, 166, 184, 186, 200, 203, 204, 209, 214, 216, 217, 229, 239, 243, 251, 254, 255, 258, 263, 265, 267, 273, 288, 292, 297, 299, 300, 302, 323 ff., 327, 329, 330, 337, 340, 347, 355, 368, 369, 372, 378, 381
Cheyne Walk, London, 144, 145, 343
Chico, Jane's canary, 136, 138, 141, 329-330
Chopin, Frédéric François, 336
Chorley, Henry, 230
Chorley, John, 339
Church of Scotland, 2, 6, 47, 68, 69, 154
Clare, Countess of, 121
Clifton, 208
Clough, Arthur Hugh, 326
Cock Tavern, London, 297
Coleridge, S. T., 31, 171
Collins, Wilkie, 379
Columbine, Mrs. Carlyle's cat, 330, 369
Comely Bank, Edinburgh, 18, 20, 23, 24, 29 ff., 35, 36, 40, 44, 46 ff., 51, 53, 76, 79, 87, 103, 104, 113, 130, 139, 142
Concord, Massachusetts, 181
Confessions of an English Opium Eater, by Thomas De Quincey, 34 ff.

Cook, Anne, 178-179, 191, 193-194, 196, 197-198, 199, 202, 255
Corday, Charlotte, 127
Corstorphine Hill, Edinburgh, 31
Craigcrook, Edinburgh, 31, 74, 76, 77
Craigenputtock, 16, 39, 40 ff., 46, 48 ff., 53, 57 ff., 64 ff., 70, 72, 73, 75 ff., 81, 83, 84, 91, 92, 99, 102 ff., 114, 117, 119 ff., 126, 129, 130, 133, 135, 140 ff., 146, 154, 159, 161, 165, 166, 171, 181, 241-242, 256, 368, 371
Craik, George, 295
Crawford, Scotland, 244
Crawford, Madame, 231
Cremorne, London, 144
Crimean War, 324
Cromwell, Oliver, 152, 235, 244, 252, 253, 258, 273, 281, 283, 292-293
Cromwell's Letters and Speeches, by T. Carlyle, 283, 292-293, 306, 360
Cumberland Hills, 65, 236
Cunningham, Allan, 91, 112, 271

Daniel, Book of, 115
Dante Alighieri, 175, 219, 277, 288
Darwin, Charles, 257, 356
Darwin, Erasmus, 257-258, 261, 267, 269, 275, 277, 287, 356, 372
D'Eichthal, Gustave, 109-110
Democracy, 186, 219
De Quincey, Thomas, 34-38, 65-66, 76
Derbyshire, 313
de Staël, Madame, 9, 126, 148
De Vere, Aubrey, 326
Devonshire, 371
Diamond Necklace, The, by T. Carlyle, 127, 198
Dickens, Charles, 206, 237, 254-255, 276, 277, 284, 293-294, 311, 350, 351, 379-380
Diogenes, 87, 88
Disraeli, Benjamin, 373

Divinity School, Edinburgh University, 2
Dods, William, 383
Don Quixote, by Cervantes, 58
Don Saltero's Coffee House, London, 144
Donaldson, the Misses, 315, 319, 321, 348
D'Orsay, Count, 229-231
Dublin, 208
Dumfries, 39, 48, 50, 58, 60, 61, 64, 65, 70, 72, 75, 79, 83, 84, 91, 100, 109, 121, 122, 145, 193, 207, 234, 235, 239, 368, 380
Dumfries Courier, 101, 119
Dumfriesshire, 39, 41, 46, 73, 76, 108, 136, 143, 178, 193, 196
Dunbar, 315
Dunscore, 68, 70, 83, 165

East Lothian, 7, 316
Ecclefechan, 90, 119, 155, 170
Eccleston Street, London, 203
Edinburgh, 1, 4, 6, 7, 16, 18, 20, 21, 23, 27, 29, 31, 32, 34 ff., 39 ff., 46, 47, 49, 50, 52, 57 ff., 62, 64 ff., 68, 71, 76 ff., 81, 82, 86, 91, 104, 113, 121, 125, 126, 156, 160, 171, 205, 255, 313, 315, 316, 322, 346, 353, 360, 375, 377, 380
Edinburgh Review, 24-27, 28, 29, 40, 43, 44, 52, 54, 57, 74, 75, 76, 81, 86, 109, 117, 118, 133
Edinburgh University, 2, 3, 18, 21, 34, 50, 133, 373, 377-378
Eliot, George, See Mary Ann Evans
Elizabeth, Mrs. Carlyle's maid, 331
Ely, 252
Emerson, Ralph Waldo, 123-124, 125, 126, 160, 181, 198, 204, 206, 222, 255, 265, 325, 358
England, 47, 75, 84, 103, 106, 154, 158, 172, 174, 187, 188, 205, 206, 214 ff., 222, 247, 252, 258, 265, 270, 282, 319, 324, 340, 352, 373
Erskine, Thomas, 377
Eton, 333
Europe, 186, 323, 327, 357

Euston Square Station, London, 240
Evans, Mary Ann, 349-352, 379
Every Man in His Humor, by Ben Jonson, 294
Examiner, The, 118, 163
Ezekiel, 69

Farringford, Isle of Wight, 362
Fenwick, Isabella, 211
Fernicarry, Scotland, 115
Fitzgerald, Edward, 253-254, 292-293
Fleet Street, London, 105, 197
Folkestone, 372
Fonblanque, Albany, 163
Foreign Office, British, 290-291
Foreign Quarterly, 81, 86
Foreign Review, 44, 59, 237
Forster, John, 237-238, 256, 257, 276, 284-285, 294, 372, 378-379, 380, 381
Forster, Mrs. John, 378-379, 380, 381
Forster, W. E., 256, 313-315
Forth, Firth of, 1, 2, 7, 19, 353
France, 84, 110, 184, 188, 323, 347
Frankfurt-am-Main, 73
Fraser, James, 124, 131, 160, 169, 198, 227
Fraser's Magazine, 117, 133, 160, 181, 198, 201
Frederick the Great, 340, 357, 360-361
Frederick the Great, by T. Carlyle, 325, 339-340, 346, 349, 360-363, 364, 366-367, 370-371
French Revolution, 125, 126-127, 161, 162, 176, 186-187, 189, 230, 231, 235
French Revolution, The: A History, by T. Carlyle, 127, 160-162, 164-170, 176, 180-182, 184, 185-186, 188-189, 194, 198, 199-201, 205, 206-207, 211, 212, 215, 217, 222, 224, 231, 235, 253, 283, 360
French Revolution of 1830, 187
Frere, Hatley, 115
Froude, J. A., 326, 351, 372, 380

Froude, Mrs. J. A., 380
Fryston, 233, 234, 374-376

Gainsborough, Thomas, 328
Galway, Ireland, 319, 322
Gambardella, Spiridione, 265-269
Garibaldi, Giuseppe, 324
George Inn, Haddington, 11, 316-317, 318, 319, 321-322
German Literature, Historical View of, by T. Carlyle, 79, 81, 87
German Romance, translated by T. Carlyle, 18, 28
Germany, 43, 64, 71
Gifford, Lord, 333
Gilchrist, Alexander, 354, 358-359
Gilchrist, Mrs. Alexander, 326, 354
Gill, the, Dumfriesshire, 368
Giovane Italia, See Young Italy Association
Gladstone, William Ewart, 373
Glasgow, 4, 5, 6, 51, 71, 157
Glencaple, 92, 104
Godby, Mrs. 363, 364
Goethe, Johann Wolfgang von, 10, 13, 18, 36, 43-44, 45, 72-74, 87, 94, 109-110, 121, 122, 124, 125, 362
Goethe, Ottilie von, 44, 60
Goodrich, Lady, 346
Gordon, John, 36
Graham, Sir James, 290-291
Grange, the, Winchester, 303, 311, 332-337, 341, 347, 360
Grange's, London, 269
Granville, Lord, 347
Grasmere, 35
Great Britain, 44, 175, 191
Greave, Alison, 19
Greece, 315
Green Park, London, 106, 138
Gunter's, London, 277

Haddington, 1, 3, 5, 6, 7, 12, 14, 16, 47, 71, 94, 142, 313, 315-322, 346, 348, 366, 383-384
Hallam, Henry, 206
Hamilton, William, 23, 34, 206
Hampshire, 304, 347
Hampstead, London, 152

Hanning, Robert, 190
Hanning, Mrs. Robert, 190-191
Harry, Mrs. Carlyle's horse, 50, 122
Harvard University, 181
Havre, France, 250
Headingley, 234
Helvellyn, 236
Heroes and Hero Worship, by T. Carlyle, 225-227, 234
Hiddlestone, Jessie, 379
Hiddlestone, Margaret, 279
Highlands, the, 2, 346
Hoddam Hill, Dumfriesshire, 39
Hoffmann, E. T. A., 195
Holborn (street in London), 105, 123, 189
Holland, Lady, 228
Holland House, London, 228
Homer, 356
Hornton Street, London, 343
House of Lords, 108
Hunt, Holman, 326, 346, 372
Hunt, Leigh, 118-119, 120, 123, 131, 135, 147-153
Hunt, Mrs. Leigh, 148-149, 150-151
Hunt, Percy, 150
Huntingdon, 252
Huxley, T. H., 372, 377
Hyde Park, London, 106, 107, 120

India, 245
India House, London, 162
Inglis, Henry, 61, 66
Ireland, 313, 314
Irving, Edward, 1-11, 12, 13, 14, 45, 47, 68-72, 104, 105, 114-117, 120, 130, 132, 154-158, 316, 321, 384; Life of, by Mrs. Oliphant, 372
Irving, Mrs. Edward, 114, 116, 154, 157
Irving, George, 96, 104
Isaiah, 69
Italy, 13, 123, 149, 157, 214-216, 218, 220, 265, 286, 288, 289, 291, 323

James, Henry, 357-358
Jeffrey, Charlotte, 53-57, 108
Jeffrey, Francis, 23, 25-33, 34, 43, 45-46, 52-58, 59, 64, 74-77, 78, 81-82, 83-86, 87, 88, 94-95, 96, 97, 98, 99, 103, 108, 109, 112-113, 118, 132-134, 143, 149, 160, 205, 206, 255-256
Jeffrey, Mrs. Francis, 27, 31, 53-57, 76, 77, 108
Jeffrey, John, 31
Jeffrey family, 60, 68, 74-76, 83-86
Jersey, Lady, 359
Jerusalem Delivered, by Tasso, 237
Jewsbury, Geraldine Endsor, 232-233, 234, 259-262, 263, 282, 305, 308, 310-311, 340, 345
"Johnson," by T. Carlyle, 117
Jones, Inigo, 333
Julie, Heroine of *La Nouvelle Héloïse*, 13

Katrine, Loch, 3
Keats, John, 149, 152
Kemble, Fanny, 201-203
Kemble, John, 201
Kennedy, Nell, 85
Kensington, London, 152, 154, 162, 163, 343, 381
Kensington Gardens, London, 107, 132
King's Road, London, 138
Kingston-on-Thames, 164
Kinloch-Luichart, 346
Kirkcaldy, 1, 2, 4, 6, 7, 14
Kirkpatrick, Kitty, 98
Knox, John, 8

Lake District, 65, 211
Lammermuir Hills, 7
Lancashire, 232, 234
Landor, Walter Savage, 206
Lansdowne, Lord, 229
Larkin, Henry, 346-347, 361, 362, 363, 364, 367, 370
Latrade, M., 213
Latter-Day Pamphlets, by T. Carlyle, 324
Lectures by T. Carlyle, 222-227, 230

Leeds, 234, 256
Leslie, Professor, 133
Lewes, George Henry, 350-351
Lincoln's Inn Fields, London, 237
Little Charlotte, Mrs. Carlyle's servant, 350, 351, 354, 355, 361, 368
Liverpool, 92, 103, 104, 191-193, 196, 234, 240, 241, 244, 302, 304, 306
Lockhart, J. G., 44
London, 27, 39, 44, 45, 47, 71, 76, 91, 92, 96, 99 ff., 103 ff., 113, 114, 118, 120 ff., 128 ff., 135 ff., 140, 143, 144, 146, 154, 155, 157, 159 ff., 168, 171, 172, 175, 177, 178, 183, 186, 189, 191, 194, 198, 202, 203, 205 ff., 209 ff., 214, 215, 223, 228, 230, 232, 234, 236, 239, 240 ff., 278, 286 ff., 305, 310, 315, 316, 320, 321, 325, 333, 337, 340, 341, 345, 347, 351, 352, 355, 367, 369 ff., 378
London and Westminster Review, 174, 198, 206, 277, 351
London University, 45, 69
Longniddry, 316
Lonsdale, Lord, 338
Lothian, Lady, 326, 372
Louis XVI, 187
Louis Philippe, 187, 188, 213
Lytton, Edward Bulwer- 166, 351

Macdonald, Grace, 51, 61, 62
Macready, Jane Lydia, 326-327
Macready, Miss, 213, 302
Macready, Nina, 284
Macready, William, 213, 237, 284, 294
Macready, Mrs. William, 213-214, 284, 294, 302, 327
McKnight, Craigenputtock servant, 100
MacTurk, Isabella, 94
Mahomet, 226
Malakoff, Duke of, 359
Malthus, T. R., 26
Malvern, 207

Manchester, 190, 193, 282, 304, 308, 310
Manchester-Liverpool Railway, 191-192, 193
Marat, Jean Paul, 127
Marie Antoinette, 127, 231
Marie Antoinette, vie Privée de, by Madame Campan, 126
Marshall, James, 234
Martin, Isabella (See also Mrs. Edward Irving), 6
Martineau, Harriet, 203-205, 222, 236
Maryland Street, Liverpool, 121, 241
Masson, David, 277, 293
Mathew, Father, 278-279
Maxwelltown, 84
Mazzini, Giuseppe, 213, 214-221, 256, 258, 261, 262, 275, 276, 280, 285-291, 286, 307, 323-324, 356
Mazzini, Maria, 220-221
Michael Place, London, 268
Mildmay, Mr. and Mrs. Humphrey St. John, 316
Mile End, London, 278
Miles, Eliza, 105, 112, 114, 116-117, 136, 147
Miles, Mrs., 105, 112, 136
Mill, James, 99
Mill, John Stuart, 99, 110-111, 123, 124, 125, 160, 162-164, 166-169, 187, 206, 226, 263
Millais, J. E., 346
Milnes, Richard Monckton, afterwards Lord Houghton, 222-223, 233-234, 259, 297, 334, 347, 374-376
Milton, Dumfriesshire, 83
Milton, John, 78, 105, 187, 277
"Mirabeau," by T. Carlyle, 198
Mitchell, Helen, 179-180, 229, 230, 231, 274, 280-281, 292, 293, 331
Moffat, 48
Moir, George, 73
Mollwitz, battle of, 361
Montagu, Mrs. Basil, 27, 96
Monteagle, Lady, 306
Moore, Thomas, 26

Morgan, Lady, 266
Morpeth, 314
Moxon, Edward, 295
Mozart, W. A., 21
Munich, 89
Murray, John, 96, 97, 98, 99, 100
Muzzi, Muzio, 289

Nancy, maid at Craigenputtock, 62, 80-81
Napier, MacVey, 74, 109, 118
Napoleon Bonaparte, 4, 25, 212, 230, 248, 315, 357
Napoleon III, 323, 355-356
Naseby battlefield, 253, 258, 293
Nero, Mrs. Carlyle's dog, 329-331, 332, 348, 350, 352-355, 369, 372
Neuberg, Joseph, 361, 370
New England, 181, 204
New York, 61
Newby, 235-236
Newton, Isaac, 167
Nith River, 16, 51, 84, 95
Nithsdale, 16, 71, 130
"Noctes Ambrosianae," by Christopher North, 34, 35
Nooly, the Craigenputtock cow, 122
North, Christopher, See Wilson, John
Nouvelle Héloïse, La, by Rousseau, 13, 15

O'Connell, Daniel, 358
Odes, by Thomas Moore, 26
Old Curiosity Shop, by Dickens, 254
Oliphant, Mrs. Margaret, 370, 372-373, 380, 381
Oliver Twist, by Dickens, 254
Omar Khayyam, 293
Origin of the Species, by Charles Darwin, 325, 356
Oxford University, 326, 333

Palace Gate, London, 381
Panizzi, Anthony, 282
Paradise Lost, by Milton, 78
Paris, 138, 187, 323, 330-331, 347

Parliament, 96, 106, 249, 252, 259, 291, 326

Parliament, Houses of, 145

Past and Present, by T. Carlyle, 258-259, 262, 273, 279, 292

Paulet, Mr., 234, 302, 307

Paulet, Mrs., 234, 302, 307

Peak District, 313

Peebles, 48

Pelly, Lewis, 356

Pepoli, Count, 175, 184

Perth, 1, 70

Piccadilly, London, 106, 138

Pickwick Papers, by Dickens, 206, 254, 255

Piedmont, Italy, 214

Pius IX, 323

Princes Street, Edinburgh, 20, 35, 50

Procter, W. B., 27, 45, 121

Puritans, the, 253, 292

Quarterly Review, 26

Queen Anne Street, London, 257, 258

Ramsay, Andrew, 377

Rawdon, 256, 314

Regent's Square, London, 114

Rennie, George, 13

Revelation, Book of, 70, 115

Richardson, Mrs. Caroline, 76

Rio, Alexis François, 212-214

Riviera, the, 346

Robertson, James, 320, 321

Robertson, John, 277

Rogers, Samuel, 113, 311-312, 358

Roland, Mémoires de Madame, 126

Rome, 114, 305, 323, 372

Rousseau, J. J., 14, 15

Rubaiyat of Omar Khayyam, 293

Rugby, 326

Ruskin, John, 346, 351, 356

Ruskin, Mrs. John, 346

Russell, Dr., 240, 368, 369

Russell, Mrs., 368

Rydal Mount, 65

Rydal Water, 65

St. Andrews University, 45-46

St. Antoine, Faubourg de, 127

St. Helena, 7, 315

St. Ives, 252

St. Leonards, 347, 366-367

St. Paul's Cathedral, London, 142, 287-288

St. Preux, character in *La Nouvelle Héloïse*, 13-14

St. Simonians, 109-110

Sampson, the executioner, 127

Sand, George, 233, 259, 352

Sandwich, Earl of, 264

Sandwich, Lady, 326

Sanquhar, 51

Sartor Resartus, by T. Carlyle, 88-90, 91-92, 94, 95, 96-100, 104, 124, 129, 131, 133, 160, 161, 181, 189, 198, 201, 204-205, 232, 235, 262, 274

Saye and Sele, Lord, 340

Scenes from Clerical Life, by George Eliot, 349-350

Schiller, J. C. F. von, 10, 13, 18

Schiller, by T. Carlyle, 13, 28, 73

Scotland, 1, 47, 48, 54, 69, 71, 74, 75, 83, 109, 113, 114, 120, 121, 131, 133, 140, 147, 157, 183, 189, 198, 205, 206, 224, 234, 239, 241, 242, 273, 294, 310, 313, 315, 342, 368, 374, 377

Scotsbrig, Dumfriesshire, 58, 79, 83, 102, 103, 119, 121, 190, 199, 206, 310, 346

Scott, Walter, 23, 28, 31, 34, 44, 121

Seaforth, 234, 302, 307, 309, 310

Serpentine, the, London, 107, 132, 381

Shankland, Robert, 194

Shelley, Percy Bysshe, 149, 152, 230

Sheriff, Mrs. Frank, 316

Sibbald, Augusta, 11

Sibbald, Rev., 11

Siddons, Mrs. Sarah, 201

"Signs of the Times," by T. Carlyle, 75

Singleton, Archdeacon, 208

Sismondi, J. C. L., 287

Skiddaw, 236

Solway Firth, 57, 84, 235, 239, 368
Sordello, by Robert Browning, 294
Southey, Robert, 121, 206, 211
Spain, 25, 248
Spedding, James, 222, 294
Speke Hall, Lancashire, 309
Stanley of Alderley, Lord, 347, 350
"State of German Literature," by T. Carlyle, 44
Steele, Richard, 144
Sterling, Anthony, 173, 271, 299-301
Sterling, Mrs. Anthony, 299-301, 303
Sterling, Edward, 171, 172-173, 207-208, 243, 268-272, 273, 275, 325-326
Sterling, Mrs. Edward, 171, 172, 173, 207-208, 243, 270-272
Sterling, John, 171-172, 173-175, 201, 270, 300, 326
Stockbridge, Edinburgh, 19
Stodart, Bess, 60, 64, 125
Strand, London, 105, 117, 123, 143
Sue, Eugène, 233
Suffolk, 243, 252
Sunny Bank, Haddington, 319, 320-321, 348
Swift, Jonathan, 144
Sylvester, Mrs. Carlyle's coachman, 370, 379, 380, 381

Tale of Two Cities, by Dickens, 206
Tatler, The, 144
Tavistock Square, London, 95, 104, 105
Taylor, John, 163, 164, 167-168
Taylor, Mrs. John, 162-164, 169, 263
Templand, Dumfriesshire, 16, 50, 66-68, 80, 83, 95, 103, 109, 121, 189, 193-196, 207, 211, 234, 239, 241, 243
Tennyson, Alfred, 222-223, 258, 293, 294-298, 333, 336, 351, 356, 372
Tennyson, Mrs. Alfred, 362

Thackeray, Anne, 327-328, 341, 362, 370
Thackeray, Harriet Marian, 327-328
Thackeray, William Makepeace, 206, 222, 255, 284-285, 328, 347, 351
Thames River, 106, 135, 138, 144-145
Thornhill, 194, 279, 346, 368
Times, The, London, 172, 206, 266, 291, 294
Tintern Abbey, 207
Tiny, Mrs. Carlyle's dog, 380, 381
Torryburn, 1
Tottenham Court Road, London, 215
Troston Rectory, 243-252, 258, 273
Twisleton, Edward, 326, 340
Twisleton, Mrs. Edward, 326, 340-341
Tyndall, John, 372, 375-378, 379, 380
Tyne River, 318
Tynemouth, 236

"Ulysses," by Tennyson, 296
Urr Water, Dumfriesshire, 57, 78

Venables, G. S., 347
Vendée, France, 212
Victoria, Queen, 184, 226, 231, 340
Voltaire, 68, 277
"Voltaire," by T. Carlyle, 68

Wales, 273
Wallace, Sir William, 8
Warren, Mrs., Jane's housekeeper, 378, 382
Weimar, 44, 60, 73, 94, 121
Wellington, Duke of, 106, 162
Welsh, Elizabeth, 95
Welsh, Mrs. George, 380
Welsh, Helen, 192-193, 241
Welsh, Jeannie, of Liverpool, 192-193, 241, 244, 246, 251, 260, 296

Welsh, Dr. John, 3, 4, 6, 7, 12, 16, 142, 313, 317, 318-319
Welsh, Mrs. John, 5, 12, 14, 16, 17, 20, 40, 41, 47, 50, 66-67, 79-80, 83, 94, 119, 183-185, 193-195, 211-212, 224, 234, 239-241, 243, 313, 318
Welsh, John, of Liverpool, 121, 191-193, 302
Welsh, Maggie, 365, 367, 378-379
Welsh, Robert, 53
Welsh, Walter, 16
Westminster, London, 145
Westminster Abbey, London, 143
Whitman, Walt, 326
Wight, Isle of, 208, 271, 273, 362
Wilhelm Meister, by Goethe, translated by T. Carlyle, 13, 28, 34, 43, 62, 362
William IV, King of England, 162, 183

Wilson, Jane, 203, 222
Wilson, John, 23, 34, 35, 45, 76, 91, 121
Wilson, Thomas, 203, 222
Windermere, Lake, 65
Windsor, 243, 380
Woolner, Thomas, 326, 341-342, 360, 362, 369, 373
Worcester, 208
Wordsworth, William, 25, 35, 65, 121, 211
Wotton Reinfred, by T. Carlyle, 18, 40, 87-88
Wye, Valley of the, 207

Yorkshire, 233, 313
Young Italy Association, 218, 219, 286, 289

Zoe, by Geraldine Jewsbury, 259-260, 262